*Religious Melancholy
and Protestant Experience
in America*

RELIGION IN AMERICA SERIES

Harry S. Stout, *General Editor*

Religious Melancholy and Protestant Experience in America

JULIUS H. RUBIN

New York   Oxford
OXFORD UNIVERSITY PRESS
1994

Oxford University Press

Oxford   New York   Toronto
Delhi   Bombay   Calcutta   Madras   Karachi
Kuala Lumpur   Singapore   Hong Kong   Tokyo
Nairobi   Dar es Salaam   Cape Town
Melbourne   Auckland   Madrid

and associated companies in
Berlin   Ibadan

Published by Oxford University Press, Inc.,
200 Madison Avenue, New York, New York 10016

Oxford is a registered trademark of Oxford University Press, Inc.

Library of Congress Cataloging-in-Publication Data
Rubin, Julius H.
Religious melancholy and Protestant experience in America / Julius
H. Rubin.
p.   cm. — (Religion in America series)
Includes bibliographical references and index.
ISBN 0-19-508301-6
1. Depression, Mental—Religious aspects—Christianity—History of
doctrines.   2. Anorexia nervosa—Religious aspects—Christianity—
History of doctrines.   3. Protestant churches—United States—
History.   4. Depression, Mental—United States—Epidemiology.   6. United States—
Church history.   I. Title.   II. Series: Religion in America series
(Oxford University Press)
BT732.4.R83   1994   280'.4'0973—dc20   93-23964

2 4 6 8 9 7 5 3 1

Printed in the United States of America
on acid-free paper

In Memoriam
Lena Rosemoff Rubin
1911–1981
May God's peace be upon her

Preface

This book is about religious melancholy in American Protestant experience from colonial settlement to the present evangelical awakening. Melancholy here refers to an affect, a distinctive stance toward life, a grieving over the loss of God's love, and an obsession and psychopathology associated with the spiritual itinerary of conversion. The religious melancholiac desired, above all else, to foster, through godly living and the practice of piety, an inward devotional life marked by a warm, personal relationship with God. Yet, those who would know God in moments of rapture and contemplation so frequently found themselves forsaken by God.

I first encountered cases of religious melancholy during my doctoral research in sociology. I began reading the medical records and correspondence of mental patients admitted to the Hartford Retreat during the 1820s through the 1840s. This period coincided with a religious revival called the Second Great Awakening in America. Asylum records frequently included letters from referring physicians, ministers, family, and friends that introduced the patient to the asylum staff. Here, captured in the exquisite handwriting of the Retreat's scribners, were the accounts of hundreds of cases of persons who felt forsaken by God, immobilized by spiritual crisis, trapped in a slough of despond— religious melancholia. The modern asylum sequestered and concentrated cases of religious melancholia, collecting within one institution Millerites in despair when prophecy failed, disconsolate ministers and missionaries, those convinced they had committed the unpardonable sin (blasphemy against the Holy Spirit), others who felt that they had grieved away the Spirit during protracted meetings or New Measure revivalism, and self-accused sinners who attempted to fast unto death. These examples provide only a partial anatomy of religious melancholiacs in nineteenth-century asylums.

I have long wanted to investigate and understand the origins and "career" of religious melancholy, a disease and concept that was once commonplace among Americans but by the early twentieth century had become relegated to the status of a delusion associated with an underlying mental disease. This book is research in the spirit of Michel Foucault, to uncover from the multi-layered stratigraphy of our historical archeology of knowledge the spiritual sickness once known as religious melancholy. We shall look to Martin Luther, John Calvin, and the seventeenth-century English pietistic Puritans for the doctrinal origins of religious melancholy, first identified by Robert Burton in 1621. Religious melancholy made the transit to America in the seventeenth century, and has been revitalized in the four eras of national religious revivals— the great awakenings. Thus, religious melancholy has remained a distinctive aspect of the American conversion experience from Michael Wigglesworth to Billy Graham.

This work is a dialogue with many authors who have cleared a path for me to follow, including Max Weber, William James, and contemporary social historians Philip Greven, John Owen King, Stanley Jackson, Charles Lloyd Cohen, Charles Hambrick-Stowe, and Richard Rabinowitz. These authors have enriched and sustained me by investigating questions that traverse disciplinary boundaries.

Several faculty at Saint Joseph College in West Hartford, Connecticut, have contributed to this work. I am grateful to Barbara Lacey for sharing her study of Hannah Heaton. Judith Perkins assisted by translating a Latin text on religious melancholy. Dennis Barone has shown generosity of spirit in sending me an unending series of articles, reprints, and citations that pertain to my work, including the insight to research the "slight hectic" of William Tennent, Jr. Catherine Posteraro has provided heroic assistance in database searches and interlibrary loan acquisitions.

I have benefited from a sabbatical during the spring of 1989, reductions in teaching load, and Saint Joseph College summer mini-grants that have facilitated my research, travel to collections, and writing. I could never have completed this project without the use of numerous research libraries, special collections, and historical society materials. I was fortunate to enjoy privileges at Yale University's many libraries, especially the Manuscripts and Archives holdings of Sterling Memorial Library, Beinecke, and the special collections of the Yale Divinity School Library. I wish to acknowledge the Ruth B. P. Burlingame Library of the Institute of Living, Hartford, Connecticut; the American Antiquarian Society in Worcester, Massachusetts; the Watkinson Library, Trinity College, Hartford, Connecticut; the Day-Stowe Foundation Library and Archives, Hartford, Connecticut; the Houghton Library, Harvard University; the Bodleian Library, Oxford University; the British Library, London, England; the Connecticut Historical Society Library, Hartford, Connecticut; the New Canaan Historical Society, New Canaan, Connecticut; the Newport Historical Society, Newport, Rhode Island; and the New Haven Colony Historical Society, New Haven, Connecticut.

At Oxford University Press, from the beginning, Cynthia A. Read saw promise in my imperfect manuscript and guided the project through the review process. Peter Ohlin provided much appreciated words of support and encouragement during the manuscript revisions. I owe the greatest debt to the anonymous reader whose detailed suggestions helped me produce a better integrated and focused essay.

Writing is an act of faith, the mustering of an "inner assurance" and conviction that we indeed have something of value to contribute to anonymous publics from across many disciplines. I wish to thank my wife, Loretta, for her unflagging support and for the moments of gentle reassurance.

New Haven, Connecticut   J. H. R.
September 1992

Contents

*Religious Melancholy
and Protestant Experience
in America*

1

The Protestant Ethic and the Melancholy Spirit

Doris Lessing has produced a contemporary version of Bernard de Mandeville's *Fable of the Bees* in a series of five radio addresses reprinted under the compelling title, *Prisons We Choose to Live Inside*. Lessing uncovers a fundamental irony, a coda of modern sociology: when viewed from the perspective of studied detachment of the outside observer, the actions of individuals and groups who pursue rational ends appear irrational in their consequences. The political ideologies that mobilized masses in incessant warfare in this century—socialism, fascism, imperialism, anti-imperialism, nationalism—contain this irony. So it is with cultural revolutions, countercultures, movements toward modernization, and anti-modern protests; and with religious awakenings, reformations, and revitalizations in Islam, Christianity, and other faiths.

> There is no epoch in history that seems to us as it must have to the people who have lived through it. What we live through, in any age, is the effect on us of mass emotions and of social conditions from which it is impossible to detach ourselves. Often the mass emotions are those which seem the noblest, best and most beautiful. And yet, inside a year, five years, a decade, five decades, people will be asking, "How *could* they have believed that?"[1]

The Protestant Reformation built one such prison in which believers chose to live. John Bunyan declared in *Pilgrim's Progress* that Christian, the model for every believer's spiritual pilgrimage in this world, languished in an iron cage, a prison of spiritual desolation. The promises of God's assurance of election and salvation remained ever outside of his grasp. Today, we marvel at how men and women could be so consumed with a conviction of sin, voluntarily embracing a spiritual regimen and internal discipline of an inner, psychological prison known as religious melancholy. How is it they as believers could succumb to the experience of being forsaken by God, in terror before the withdrawal of divine love?

Religious melancholia is a culturally and historically specific form of depressive disorder, a special variety of melancholy. Stanley W. Jackson's *Melancholia and Depression* provides an indispensable guide for anyone inter-

3

ested in the medical history of affective disorders in Western civilization, particularly religious melancholia. The idea of melancholia has been associated with a variety of dejected states conceptualized as: (1) a disease or cluster of ideational and physical symptoms with a distinctive pathophysiology, (2) a mood, disposition, emotional tone or temperament.[2] Peoples everywhere and in all times have suffered ill-fortune, loss, bereavement, and injustice, and have responded with what we today term reactive depression. However, melancholia as a disease assumes pathological dimensions only as a severe, immobilizing, and protracted syndrome that exceeds culturally prescribed forms of mourning for personal or collective loss.

Melancholia as a clinical psychopathology was first identified by the Hippocratic writers in the fifth century B.C. as a disease of humoral imbalance, an excess of black bile—the melancholy humor produced by the spleen. Afflicted persons experienced a fear added to sadness, aversion to food, despondency, and sleeplessness. Galen, in the second century A.D., systematized humoral medicine, creating the clinical standard through which melancholia would be perceived for the next two thousand years. Melancholia represented a chronic, nonfebrile form of madness marked by fear, sadness, world-weariness, and suicidal inclinations.[3]

The Elizabethan world embraced melancholy as a fashionable affectation, an ethos or way of life distinct from the classical disease.[4] This English malady affected the Renaissance style of the fifteenth-century Florentine philosopher Marsilio Ficino. As Juliana Schiesari argues in *The Gendering of Melancholia*,

> Depression became translated into a virtue for the atrabilious man of letters. And it is significant that melancholia—at least this form of it—became an elite "illness" that afflicted *men* precisely as the *sign* of their exceptionality, as the inscription of genius within them. The fluctuations between "exultation and despair" became a hallmark whereby the *homo melancholicus* defined his difference from the common crowd or *vulgus*. . . . Depression for "qualified" men thus became a sign of spiritual greatness. . . .[5]

Schiesari provides a feminist critique of the discourse of the melancholy artistic temperament that legitimated the genius of men while relegating women to the gender-specific and mundane tasks of mourning loss. However, as a style of life and ethos that promoted a melancholic temperament in the cause of ultimate aesthetic values demanding genius, inward heroism, and a spiritual aristocracy that separated the gifted from the commoner, artistic melancholy represents a secular equivalent to religious melancholy. The Protestant saint considered melancholy a special chastisement from God to encourage spiritual maturation. The twice-born saint afflicted with a morbid-mindedness needed to act, as William James has argued, as a religious genius. The propensity for inner suffering on a heroic scale distinguished the regenerate saint from the mass of unconverted humanity. Religious melancholy differed from artistic affectation by providing ample opportunity for women's participation in religious genius, redemptive suffering, and the experience of feeling forsaken by God.

During the late sixteenth century religious melancholy added another variation to this disease of humoral imbalance or temperament. Religious melancholy was an obsessional psychopathology derived from a "stance," "style of life," or "life order" founded upon the realization of ultimate religious values. Timothie Bright's (1550?–1615) *Treatise of Melancholie* identifies a type of melancholia without an apparent cause that is associated with the salvation panic of the pietistic Puritans, whose consciences oppress them with an overwhelming sense of sin. Sufferers live in fear of God's wrath, of eternal damnation, obsessed with their sinfulness.

Religious melancholy was prevalent from the seventeenth through the nineteenth centuries among Protestant groups, particularly evangelical Pietists, who forged a distinctive religiously grounded personality founded upon the personal relationship of the individual to God. They sought ascetic mastery of self and contemplative union with Christ. Evangelical Pietists organized their lives according to a systematic practice of piety and sought the inward psychological assurance of their status as children of God. Believers who embraced this life of spiritual pilgrimage not infrequently found themselves descending into the "slough of despond," the enduring symbol of religious melancholy in Bunyan's *Pilgrim's Progress*. Religious melancholy, first identified by Robert Burton in *The Anatomy of Melancholy* in 1621, comprised three interrelated conditions: (1) the ontological status of humanity stained by innate depravity and sin engaged in the futility of worldly follies; (2) the crises of spiritual passage and conversion in which each penitent felt forsaken by God's love—the awakening and terror before God's law, the danger of damnation and the utter helplessness of each soul to engineer their own salvation through human agency; and (3) a distinctive psychopathology characteristic of evangelical Protestants. As a form of madness, religious melancholy entailed extreme guilt about sin—obsession with having committed unpardonable sins through blasphemy against the Holy Spirit. With clear and terrifying evidence of their damnation, of having grieved the Holy Spirit and sinned away the day of grace, the mad could find no solace in this world and only the haunting specter of eternal punishment in the next.

Religious melancholy constituted one of a number of depressive illnesses associated with spiritual defects. Medieval monastics and laity suffered from a religious complex of symptoms, sorrow-dejection-despair, known as the sin of *acedia*, or sloth in regard to spiritual duties. Jackson relates that "the spiritual authors of the twelfth century and the Scholastics of the thirteenth century had tended to emphasize the state of mind in acedia (weariness, disgust, lack of fervor, sorrow), but, influenced by the increased activity of confessors and preachers, the common man's image of acedia came to center on spiritual idleness or neglect in the performance of spiritual duties."[6] The spiritual lassitude and deadness of acedia differed markedly from the Protestant experience of religious melancholy. For the religious melancholiac, no amount of obsessively pursued practical devotions could remit the stain of sin and the terror attendant to the conviction of desertion by God.

Burton's work will receive a more detailed consideration in the conclud-

ing section of this chapter. At this point it suffices to point out that he created a new diagnostic category of melancholia: a new psychopathology that
marked the conversion narratives of evangelical and pietistic Protestants, who,
from his perspective as a moderate Anglican, appeared in the throes of religious enthusiasm, trapped in a web of doctrinal error and irrational excess.
"True religion," and "authentic Christianity" promoted the universal health,
well-being, and salvation of humanity. Religious enthusiasm, excess, and error
brought human misery, including a subspecies of love-melancholy—the "religious melancholy" of those who felt forsaken of God's love.

Jackson surveys the medical literature informed by Burtonian categories
from the seventeenth century until the late nineteenth century and discovers
one enduring motif.

> The trend that had been crystallized by Burton in his introduction of reli-
> gious melancholy continued to serve the concerns about and attacks on
> those given to enthusiasm and related atypical experiences. Whether cler-
> gyman, physician,or layman, those who reacted against religious enthusi-
> asm and other challenges to the established religious order explained many
> of these phenomena as aspects of mental disorders, particularly melan-
> cholia.[7]

Jackson fails to note that religious melancholia was not "atypical" in the
experiences of many diverse Protestant sectarians. Burton had established a
standard for "true" and "authentic" religion that was synonymous with what
Philip Greven has characterized as moderate or genteel Protestant temperament.[8] Enthusiasm and error referred to evangelical and revivalistic forms of
Pietism or world-rejecting sects. Jackson does not understand that Burton and
those who adopted his diagnostic ideas refused to "perceive" the pathogenic
aspects of "true" or "authentic" religious practice. In their estimation, religious melancholia could only result from the enthusiasm of a deviant or heterodox group, or the erroneous application of true principles of piety. The
diagnostic category of religious melancholy provided a politically charged
instrument to discredit heterodoxy while simultaneously shielding Protestant
Pietism from any allegation of involvement in the depressive illness that so
plagued its adherents. In this way, the medical and pastoral category of religious melancholy served as an apologetic—or defense of the faith—for true
believers from both evangelical and anti-evangelical groups; each used this
concept to defend their faith and discredit the other. Thus, James Robe would
present conversion narratives from the Scottish Awakening in 1742 that rival
Jonathan Edwards's clinical depictions of religious melancholy in New
England's Great Awakening in his *A Faithful Narrative of the Surprising Work
of God* (1734).

Both Edwards's work and James Robe's *Narrative of the Extraordinary
Work of the Spirit of God at Cambusland, Kilsyth* defend the evangelical
morphology of conversion as "true religion" and the work of God's Spirit,
not as religious melancholy. Both present lengthy case studies of believers in
their pilgrimage toward salvation and godly living. Robe denies that evan-

gelical religion, as the intercession of the Spirit of God in human history, could ever cause religious melancholy. Yet, he recounts case after case of evangelical humiliation, terror of conscience, despair, suicidal inclinations, self-accusations of blasphemy and the unpardonable sin, and fear of having sinned away the day of grace—the panoply of symptoms associated with religious melancholy. Robe makes this assertion because the spiritual pilgrimages that he presents offered evidence of successful conversion experiences—the joyous repose in Christ.[9]

Robert Blakeway's *An Essay Towards the Cure of Religious Melancholy in a Letter to a Gentlewoman Afflicted with It* (1717) provides another variation on Burton's theme of true religion versus enthusiasm. He argues, "it is absolutely false that the Christian Religion interdicts the Gratification of any of our Faculties in earthly Pleasures and Enjoyments. . . ." Rather, moderate religious exercises and the soul's repose in God ". . . improves and advances the Perception of Pleasure to its highest Pitch, and yields an inexhausted Treasure of incomparably more solid Joys."[10] Indeed, the spiritual quest results in a "Union & communion with the Lord," as the ravishing godly affections excite the soul to fervor.[11]

However, as Blakeway explains, many Protestants succumbed to erroneous ideas concerning God and religious duties. They fell prey to melancholy while assiduously devoting themselves to the practice of devotional piety, seeking psychological union with God. Blakeway remains unaware of the connection between the pursuit of ravishing godly affections and the "dark night of the soul," when God withdraws his countenance from the saint. The idea of religious melancholy produced by the humoral imbalance of black bile and the bodily predispositions to mental alienation made the pathogenic elements of Pietism appear epiphenomenal to somatic disease.

Souls weakened by bodily ill health frequently fell into the error of perfectionism—the quest to live immune from sin and alienation from God's love. The perfectionist's endeavor foundered upon the "desire to be more holy than you can be in this mortal state," leading to obsession with sin and blasphemy, and self-accusations of infidelity and unpardonable sin.[12] Blakeway consoles Evangelicals first awakened to their sin and despair as they confront the "terrors of conscience." "Oh! What shall I do? Whither shall I fly?" when God withdraws his grace and Spirit.[13] He hopes to assuage their doubts, advising the melancholiacs that the experience of feeling forsaken by God augurs spiritual growth. God's desertions are partial and temporary: "The greater your Sorrow for Sin is at present, the more acceptable to God, and the less shall it be here after. . . ."[14]

Eighteenth-century English clergymen adopted Burton's category of religious melancholy and Richard Baxter's *Practical Works* as aids to diagnose and treat the conversion crises they encountered in the course of their pastoral duties. Benjamin Fawcett's *Observations on the Nature, Causes and Cure of Melancholy* (1780) provided detailed clinical presentations of religious melancholy. Fawcett encountered many persons of "serious piety" who lapsed into a protracted spiritual desolation. These men and women felt forsaken by

God, past all hope of salvation, obsessed with blasphemous thoughts, and beset with self-accusations of having committed the unpardonable sin against the Holy Ghost.[15] The afflicted would exclaim, "I am the vilest of sinners. There is no hope for me. I am lost. I am undone. I shall never obtain mercy."[16]

In addition to medical and religious treatises that elaborated on Burton's discussion of religious melancholy, two popular eighteenth-century spiritual biographies helped acquaint ever-widening publics in Europe and America with this spiritual sickness. Timothy Rogers's *A Discourse Concerning Trouble of Mind, and the Disease of Melancholy* (1691), and William Cowper's *Memoir of the Early Life of William Cowper, Esq.* (1816) apply religious melancholy as a diagnostic category to the lives of two exemplary Christians.

Rogers portrays religious melancholy as the experience of being forsaken by God. As Jackson explains:

> Themes of anguish, terror, guilt, bitterness, sadness, desolation, and suffering are interwoven throughout. . . . At first he prayed and had poured out his troubles to God, but eventually he became so discouraged that he could no longer pray. A recurrent theme in this and subsequent chapters . . . is a sense of loss expressed in terms of a soul "that is under desertion" with the implication that God had withdrawn or departed from the deserted soul, which was then alone, sorrowing, and desolate.[17]

William Cowper suffered five distinct episodes of religious melancholy and was admitted repeatedly to a private asylum over a forty-five-year period; truly this was a sickness unto death. Like Rogers, he suffered from times of feeling forsaken by God. At other times, he enjoyed evanescent moments of rapture—of joyous communion with God. Each season of forsakenness brought battles with Satan, suicide attempts, and infinite despair. Toward the close of his life in 1792, after twenty years of unbroken religious melancholy, Cowper writes, in a letter to a confidant, that "I have had a terrible night— such a one as I believe I may say God knows no man ever had. . . . Rose overwhelmed with infinite despair, and came down into the study execrating the day when I was born with inexpressible bitterness. And while I write this, I repeat those execrations, in my very soul persuaded that I shall perish miserably and as no man ever did."[18]

The Burtonian idea that religious melancholy was produced by error and enthusiasm persisted until the nineteenth century. The English physician George Burrows, in a 1828 treatise, *Communication on the Causes, Forms, Symptoms and Treatment of Insanity*, blamed religious enthusiasm as "the great predisposing cause of what is designated religious madness."[19] In 1843 John Cheyne wrote that evangelism and revivals invariably created epidemics of religious insanity. "So prevalent is the notion that religion leads to derangement of mind, that when an individual first betrays symptoms of insanity, the question is often asked—'Is he a Saint?'"[20]

By the closing decades of the nineteenth century, as Jackson concludes: "Religious melancholia as a distinct disease, or even as a subtype of melancholia, had essentially disappeared. It was still occasionally acknowledged as

a theme from the past. But all that was really left from this 'disease' of earlier times was the recognition that some clinically depressed persons suffered
from religious delusions."[21]

Religious melancholy left its stamp upon the conversion narratives of
pietistic Protestants for three hundred years, only to pass from the scene,
supplanted by new psychiatric nosologies that relegated religious ideas and
anxieties to the status of the epiphenomenal delusional "contents" of somatic
mental disease.

In the spirit of Michel Foucault's archeology of knowledge, we must
uncover the medical and religious commentaries concerning religious melancholy and attempt to reconstruct the *mentalities* of those who in past times
felt forsaken by God. In the spirit of ethnopsychiatry, we must recover the
culturally specific and historically unique aspects of religious melancholy.

Ethnopsychiatry and the emerging discipline of cultural psychology deny
that there exists a single, invariant "human nature," a universal form of the
organization of self and personality, or one uniform psychiatric nosology such
as the *Diagnostic and Statistical Manual III-R*. Western psychiatry is seen as
reductionistic, interpreting symptoms without reference to cultural contexts,
and reifying "a Western cultural and psychological form, according it the status
of universal disease."[22]

In *Culture and Depression* Arthur Kleinman and Byron Good call for a
renewed emphasis upon clinical descriptive research on the phenomenology
of depressive disorders by focusing upon the broadest issues of the individual
in the life-world analogous to Hallowell's notion of the self in the "culturally
constituted behavioral environment."[23] They maintain that a phenomenology
of depression must proceed from a reconstruction of the individual in the life-
world—"the culturally organized patterns of perceiving time, space, body, and
person, the symbolic organization of experience, the nature of 'realities' in
the social and psychological life, and the forms of discourse and social interaction through which such realities are constructed."[24]

Ethnopsychiatry presupposes that cultural life-worlds and their mediation
to individuals form the central theoretical concern in the study of depression
in culturally and historically diverse milieu. For example, Gananath
Obeyesekere's essay "Depression, Buddhism and the Work of Culture in Sri
Lanka" examines the life-world of Buddhist laymen or "householders." The
householder, unlike the monk, lives within the world, taking a spouse and
mundane calling and embracing the burdens of providing for family and
dependents, cheerfully resigned to the five precepts of Buddhism. However,
the laity recognize the eschatological significance of this world as temporary,
illusory, and filled with suffering. During holy days of *sil*, or after loss and
bereavement, the householder temporarily abandons secular life and engages
in meditation (*bhavana*) on the ontological nature of despair in the Buddhist
vision of existence. Meditation evokes images of the putrescence of the body
as an object of revulsion, filled with feces. In this manner all personal suffering engendered by illness, death, misfortune, betrayal, and injustice reflects
the meaning of human existence within the Buddhist tradition and achieves

expression through a decidedly religious vocabulary. Obeyesekere defines this process as the "work of culture." As in Freudian "dream work" or "grief work," individuals employ the symbolic resources available to them to transform aggressive, libidinal, and painful motives into culturally desired meanings.[25]

The propensity of evangelical Protestants, historically or contemporarily, to undergo religious melancholy constitutes, according to the ethnopsychiatric perspective, a "culture-bound syndrome"[26] inextricably tied to religious conversion and the meaning of the believer's relationship to God. Culture-bound syndromes are modalities of illness and suffering peculiar to specific culture milieus and are constituted of the specific meanings, tensions, and ambiguities conveyed to persons by symbolic cues and articulated through the work of culture.

The concept of religious melancholy as a culture-bound syndrome allows us to reconstruct the mentalities, or life-worlds, of evangelical Protestants in past times, and to reconsider how the patterning of the soul's pilgrimage toward salvation, the *ordo salutis*, created a new form of obsessional pathology. In Protestant culture areas we shall encounter new forms of "personality," distinctive patterns of life-organization, and a unique emotional economy. Unlike Burton, who maintained that true religion, freed from error, could only promote the happiness and well-being of humanity, we will discover that a system of theology and practice of piety led to distinctly pathological consequences for believers who struggled to forge a life in precise conformity with these ultimate religious values.

Any study of religious melancholy in America must necessarily reevaluate themes introduced by John Owen King in his important work, *The Iron of Melancholy, Structures of Spiritual Conversion in America from the Puritan Conscience to Victorian Neurosis*. King examines an enduring myth that has helped shape the American character and experience, which each generation has embraced and elaborated as a cultural legacy for succeeding generations. In this case myth refers to the chartering ideas and abiding metaphors that create the foundation of an American character and collective identity.

From the first settlements in New England until the late nineteenth century, King explores the vicissitudes of the myth of spiritual pilgrimage, which is fraught with psychological anguish, trauma, and desolation. The genre of American spiritual autobiography, built on the seventeenth-century English tradition of Bunyan, Baxter, Burton, and other theologians of practical divinity, created a myth of the representative Christian life that was branded by the iron of religious melancholy, replete with obsessional symptomatology. The English texts provided *exemplars*—narratives of successful conversions for New England's visible saints to appropriate. They in turn embraced the iron of melancholy, seeking rebirth in the red-hot travail that was considered the distinguishing mark of Godly affliction visited upon his elect. In so doing, Cotton Mather, Michael Wigglesworth, Samuel Sewall, and others created the myth of religious America. The texts of spiritual autobiography contained the blueprints for forging a Christian life. And these plans organized and shaped the experiences of Americans sojourning in this vast, howling spiritual wilderness:

> Within the earlier lives, whether oral or written, Puritan authors described symptoms of melancholy that they read as signs of salvation—the hellish or blasphemous temptation, for example, which when carefully observed reflected for the Puritan not the depravity but the grace of one so tempted. By the end of the nineteenth century the meaning attached to such obsessional ideation had precisely reversed: a horrid thought indicated that one might become morally insane. The Puritans' case of conscience had been transformed itself into the Victorians' neurological "case."[27]

King devotes chapters to the elder Henry James, William James, Josiah Royce, James Jackson Putnam, and Max Weber. Each author was an heir to the cultural legacy of religious melancholy. Each "religious genius" interpreted this myth of American character and sought to recast the meaning of obsessional neurosis in light of the issues of his day. And each took his own personal materials of spiritual crisis and attempted to universalize hard-won insights and achievements to guide others in the pilgrimage toward salvation.

This study is indebted to the arguments advanced in *The Iron of Melancholy*, but retraces the history of an American obsessional pathology not solely as the unfolding of a cultural myth shaped by a religious or intellectual elite, but as one guided by the questions of historical sociology. We shall investigate religious melancholy among Protestant New Englanders, founders of the "New England Way," and participants in the First and Second Great Awakenings in period from 1740 to 1850. The case studies of religious melancholy are derived from published and unpublished diaries and spiritual narratives of this period, and from case histories of patients admitted to an asylum for the insane, the Hartford Retreat, during its first twenty years of operation, from 1823 to 1843.

Like Burton, we shall seek to understand the anatomy of religious melancholy, discovering the heretofore unnoticed syndrome of evangelical anorexia nervosa in the First and Second Great Awakenings: sinners who would fast unto death and starving perfectionists among Oberlin New School Presbyterians. We shall reconstruct case histories of religious suicide among evangelicals who became convinced of their unpardonable sin and hypocrisy. The anatomy of religious melancholy extends into the fourth religious awakening of the post–World War II era—the New Evangelicalism. Even after the diagnostic category of religious melancholy passed out of usage, evangelical Protestants continued to succumb to depressive illness and obsessional pathology that marked, for example, the conversion narratives of participants in the Billy Graham crusades, and among neo-Pentecostals and neo-Fundamentalists.

Ideas have long histories. In the spirit of King's *Iron of Melancholy*, we shall review the transformative breakthroughs to modernity associated with the sixteenth-century Reformation by examining the special elective affinities between the ideas of self and salvation and the propensity of the faithful to embrace, voluntarily, a psychological pilgrimage of incessant warfare against the self *(psychomachia)* that resulted in melancholy and frequently in mental alienation.

We next consider Max Weber's pioneering study, *The Protestant Ethic and the Spirit of Capitalism* and William James's *The Varieties of Religious Experience.* Weber's thesis endures as a penetrating, multidimensional account of the relationship between religion and economic rationalism. We can identify the important interconnections between the Protestant Ethic and mental illness; specifically, this research identifies one expression of the Protestant Ethic, evangelical pietism, and its relationship to one form of mental illness, religious melancholy.

Melancholia's Heirs: Max Weber and William James

Max Weber identified the Protestant Reformation as one among a number of critical cultural and institutional transformations that gave rise to modern Western rationalism. The sixteenth- and seventeenth-century Reformation in Germany, Switzerland, and England transformed the concept of self; of religious identity; of conscience; congregation; and the relationships of the faithful to God, to church group, and to fellow believers.[28] The Reformation gave powerful impetus to the quest for spiritual perfection, a religious virtuosity no longer limited to the monastic or sacerdotal elite of medieval Catholicism. This mass religious virtuosity invariably structured experiences that resulted in scrupulosity and melancholy for many. Weber's theory offers powerful clues to the historical origins and cultural logics of these religious experiences, and the emergence of the exacting ethos that patterned and reformed Protestant selves.

According to Weber, following the Protestant Reformation, in the Occident, and particularly within Calvinist and Puritan sects, the concept of personality emerged. The self was organized around a central core of ultimate values, driven to achieve an inner consistency of motive and action and, as an instrument of these transcendent purposes, embracing the concept of the ascetic warrior, the Christian soldier who battles in *auto-machia* against the natural self and rejects the world in order to remake it according to God's will. Furthermore, Weber maintained that this Occidental personality possessed an "ethic of inwardness" (*Gesinnungsethik*) distinguishing each person as a unique individual who actively fashioned his character and identity as a potter shapes the raw material of clay on the wheel.[29]

Harvey Goldman summarizes Weber's concept of the Occidental personality, identifying four critical elements:

> First, unification and systematization of life on the basis of an ultimate and sacred value, usually provided by prophecy; second, ascetic conduct, built on the subjugation of the natural self that faith in the value makes necessary but only strength of character makes possible; third, an orientation toward the realization or service of the value in practical action and

the making over of the world, embodied in fighting as a soldier of God on the battlefields of self and world; and fourth, a channeling of human energies and purposes through the discipline of the calling.[30]

Personality represents the practical rationalization of a life, the inner obligation to achieve a unified, consistent plan of rational conduct constituted by distinct values. Weber viewed religious virtuosi who embraced lives of this-worldly or other-worldly mysticism or asceticism as distinctive types of personalities representative of the great salvation religions in the East and West, and rationalized according to divergent value positions. Yet nowhere in the world religions, in Buddhism, Hinduism, Confucianism, Taoism, Islam, and ancient and medieval Judaism and Christianity did the breakthrough to the practical rationalization of life occur. Only where the concept of an ordered universe created by a single transcendental deity, as systematized by ethical prophecy, has required that believers find salvation through religiously motivated mastery of self and world has the practical rationalization of a life and personality occurred. Only when believers were denied recourse to institutionalized means of grace or sacramental-magical practices to remove the stain of sin and the inner burdens of guilt and despair did they feel compelled to seek assurance and comfort through the constant motives of a life fashioned according to religious values.

The Protestant Reformation, which developed along Calvinist lines, demanded for the first time that all believers achieve a personality informed by the religious virtuosity of inner-worldly asceticism. Weber declared these burdens heroic, "hero ethics," and saw this quest as an existential condition of modernity, whether one chose a vocation as religious virtuoso, or a vocation in science or politics.[31]

Weber showed little interest in neurosis or pathological forms of personality. However, he understood the immense psychological burdens of suppressing emotions and drives that every "personality" felt duty-bound and called to bear. E. B. Portis explains that "Weber was well aware that suppression could lead to 'repression' which, in turn, could lead to hysteria, compulsions, phobia or other neurotic symptoms. Regardless of the dangers, however, emotional suppression is a requirement of personal identity."[32] Herein lies the clue to Weber's understanding of personality and mental illness. In a letter to his co-editor of the *Archiv für Sozialwissenschaft und Sozialpolitik*, Edgar Jaffer, rejecting the publication of an article by a Freudian, Weber explains just how exacting the demands of personality can be and how Freudian therapy, like the auricular confession of Catholicism, while relieving guilt, cannot assist in the hero's ethical quest.

> There is the "heroic" ethic, which imposes on men demands of principle to which they are generally not able to do justice, except at the high points of their lives, but which serve as signposts pointing the way for man's endless striving. Or there is the "ethic of the mean," which is content to accept man's everyday "nature" as setting a maximum for the demands which can be made. . . . The father confessor and the pastor of the old type had

no other task in this direction than this (ethic of the mean) and Freudian
therapy is simply a revival of confession. . . .[33]

The heroic ethic demanded sacrifices without consideration of costs and
consequences, without compromise to consistency and purpose, and without
recourse to forms of therapy–religious or secular—that could relieve the overpowering sense of guilt during periods of self-doubt or lapses in conduct.
Weber understood the pursuit of personality as a Faustian ceaseless striving
that was antithetical to the rest cures and stress avoidance therapy advocated
by the mental hygiene movement of the late nineteenth century. He ridiculed
mental hygiene as the "cheapest kind of 'cost accounting'" of the burdens
and sacrifices of ethical conduct. He rejected out-of-hand the "ideal" of the
"normal health snob." Weber linked personality and ethical heroism with the
psychic costs of ceaseless striving to make a life devoted to ultimate values
and ethical responsibility. Individuals imbued with personality would suffer
unrelieved guilt at failures and inconsistencies, tension with the orders of the
world, and for some, mental disorders and suicide. These represent the "costs"
of heroic ethics and personality. Weber seems to have made the concept of
personality synonymous with obsessive-compulsion or the suppression of
emotion characteristic of hysteria. To have a personality, Weber appears to
argue, means to live life immersed in the suffering and conflict of neurosis.

In 1904–1905 Weber published *The Protestant Ethic and the Spirit of
Capitalism* as a series of five related essays in the *Archiv für Sozialwissenschaft
und Sozial Politik*. The third of these essays, "The Religious Foundations of
Worldly Asceticism" identifies the doctrinal elements of Protestantism that
gave rise to a distinctive form of practical rationalism, life-order, and personality.

He begins his essay by identifying several Protestant sects—Calvinists,
Pietists, Anabaptists, Methodists, and Puritans—that produced a wholly new
type of religious rationalism during the sixteenth and seventeenth centuries
in Switzerland, Germany, England, and the Netherlands. In these early writings, Weber does not focus upon the intellectual-theoretical dimensions of
ethics, dogma, or systematic theology: "we are interested rather in something
entirely different: the influence of those psychological sanctions which, origi-
nating in religious belief and the practice of religion, gave a direction to practical conduct and held the individual to it."[34]

Weber is interested in religious ideas that form the foundation for coher-
ent world views and result in the rationalization of practical conduct. He
introduces dogmas only to demonstrate their contribution to practical rationalism and the formation of a life-order and corresponding type of personality. Weber investigates ". . . practical-psychological motives by which a particular religion induces actual ethical conduct."[35]

Weber reiterates this point in his fifth essay, "The Protestant Sects and
the Spirit of Capitalism":

> . . . it is not the ethical *doctrine* of a religion, but the form of ethical con-
> duct upon which *premiums* are placed that matters. Such premiums oper-

ate through the form and the condition of the respective goods of salvation. And such conduct constitutes "one's specific ethos" in the sociological sense of the word.[36]

Excerpts from the Westminster Confession of 1647 and Calvin's *Institutes* illustrate the Protestant worldview. In Reformation theology, God had become an utterly transcendental deity who created the world according to a preordained plan that predestined some to suffer everlasting death and damnation while others enjoyed everlasting life and salvation as God's elect. Because the natural man born into sin was a finite and corrupt creature and disabled from performing good works to earn salvation or change God's purpose, the Calvinist could do nothing to win grace or salvation or ultimately know God's inscrutable purpose. Humanity simply existed as God's instrument, caught in a nexus of ethical commands and ordered to obey God's will and glorify Him in all things.

> In its extreme inhumanity this doctrine must above all have had one consequence for the life of a generation which surrendered to its magnificent consistency. That was a feeling of unprecedented inner loneliness of the single individual.[37]

Such lonely souls invariably confronted the ultimate question of *certitudo salutis*—the certitude of their eternal fate. They could not expect help from others in their quest for assurance. This form of Protestantism ended magical and sacramental avenues of grace. No priest could interpret God's word or offer absolution of sin in the confessional. No church proffered sacramental grace, no savior interceded to redeem an individual in the light of God's immutable degrees.

> To the Catholic the absolution of his Church was a compensation for his own imperfection. The priest was a magician who performed the miracle of transubstantiation, and who held the key to eternal life in his hand. One could turn to him in grief and penitence. He dispensed atonement, hope of grace, certainty of forgiveness, and thereby granted release from that tremendous tension to which the Calvinist was doomed by an inexorable fate, admitting of no mitigation. . . . There was no place for the very human Catholic cycle of sin, repentance, atonement, release, followed by renewed sin. Nor was there any balance of merit for a life as a whole which could be adjusted by temporal punishments or the Churches' means of grace.[38]

The Protestant Ethic, that ethos of practical rationalism and life regulation whereby the isolated believer struggled to achieve an inner, psychological assurance of God's election and grace, emerged from the wholly irrational concern for salvation. Pastoral writings instructed the Calvinist to work ceaselessly, methodically, in a mundane calling to fulfill the God-willed demand that brotherly love find expression in service to the commonweal. Each individual was bound to consider himself or herself chosen and to combat all doubts, to create the inner, psychological conviction of election. Work became the technical means of dispelling doubt, of actively constructing a life as God's tool, doing his will, increasing his glory and seeking the highest good, *certitudo salutis,* the certainty of salvation.[39]

During a 1910 colloquium sponsored by the German Sociological Society at Frankfurt, Weber clarified the question of the certitude of salvation in an exchange with Ernst Troeltsch, Ferdinand Toennies, and Georg Simmel.

> This certitude can be won in various ways. First of all it is not a sociological certitude, but a purely psychological question that is therewith touched upon, but one which has sociologically interesting consequences. The most extreme contrasting poles which exist are, on the one hand, the forms of world-rejecting religiosities (which we also experience in modern times) . . . characteristic of certain parts of primitive Christianity: a kind of "acosmic" love of man, that is the one possibility. On the other hand, there is its most extreme counter pole: the Calvinistic religiosity which finds the certitude of being God's child in the to-be-attained "proving of oneself" *(Bewahrung) ad amjorem dei glorium* within the given and ordered world. . . . that the individual feels himself placed within the social community for the purpose of realizing "God's glory" and therewith the salvation of the soul.[40]

Weber understood that the existential "need for salvation" could never find definitive resolution in any empirical or objective evidence of election. The closest approximation to certainty of salvation came from the lifelong cultivation of an inner, psychological attitude, an obsessive and continual quest for the distinguishing marks of election. The believers who undertook this quest, themselves embedded in the life-order of Reformation dogma, developed a distinct character or personality *(Gesamthabitus)* guided by the practical rationalism and imperatives of the Protestant Ethic. They championed the religious virtuosity of the inner-worldly ascetic.

Weber emphasized the irony that an irrational quest for the psychological certitude of salvation leads to the most decisive rationalization of practical conduct—inner-worldly asceticism. Asceticism had escaped from the monastery and required that every believer live as a saint in the world.[41] Now all believers needed to organize their lives as unitary, integrated personalities, directed by inner principles and ceaseless striving toward the realization of a "heroic" ethic of conviction that imposed a tyranny of demands on everyday living.

The Protestant ethos of religious virtuosity directed ascetic practices toward the mastery of life in this world. The saint as twice-born, whose regeneration followed God's preordained plan, fashioned life according to the principle of sanctification of all conduct as the fulfillment of God-willed ethical commands, directed toward increasing and magnifying the glory of God. As such, the inner-worldly ascetic refused to surrender to the sensuous pleasures of the flesh and the corrupt world, remaining ever sober and alert, never eating or drinking to dullness or intoxication. Not celibacy, but avoidance of any sexual and erotic pleasure, guided the Protestant who married and reared children in accordance with the command "to be fruitful and multiply," bringing new souls into God's dominion and thereby increasing his glory. The inner-worldly ascetic rejected all sportive play, gambling, or artistic diversions as dangerous; these practices wasted precious time, although physical exercise to maintain health was deemed acceptable. Although poverty was not required of the believer, luxuries, conspicuous consumption of wealth, and any form of feudal ostentation were rejected as wasteful idolatries of the flesh. Above all else, ceaseless labor in a mundane calling received new ethical validation as a God-pleasing activity for the soul's continual quest for *certitudo salutis*.

Weber understood that the saint adopted this ethos and ordered personality in a continual, lifelong quest for the psychological assurance and reassurance of religious certitude. The regenerate souls who appropriated this tyrannical ethos and whose actions served to sanctify and glorify God expected to grow in grace and wisdom in the course of a lifetime. Yet they never gained immunity from temptations or from the possibility of growing spiritually cold through backsliding and religious declension. To combat these evils, religious virtuosi practiced routine and continual exercises in piety, delved deeply into their lives through self-examination, and submitted to fraternal correction and supervision by co-religionists in their sectarian congregations, where membership remained limited to the religiously qualified of God's elect.

The Protestant virtuosi knew no respite and enjoyed no refuge from the arduous struggle to remake their selves, to find and continually to recover the inner peace that marked the assurance of God's love and grace. By relentlessly employing the ascetic method, in warfare with the "natural man," believers chronicled their spiritual progress in diaries, aware that God could see through empty actions and know the true intention in their hearts.

> . . . vigilant self-control of the Puritan had as its positive aim a definitely qualified conduct and, beyond this, it had as an inward aim the systematic control of one's own nature which was regarded as wicked and sinful. The consistent Pietist, would take inventory, a sort of bookkeeping practiced daily even by such an *Epigonus* as Benjamin Franklin, for the supramundane, omniscient God—saw the central internal attitude.[42]

Weber developed a structural phenomenology of religious experience depicting how religious rationalism created life orders that fostered a unique organization of personality or character.[43] He demonstrated the unintended special elective affinity between a religious ethos that validated work in a mundane calling as one cultural legitimation for emerging modern capitalism.[44]

Weber considered the Protestant Ethic to be one of the decisive turning points in the developmental history of the West and the breakthrough to a modern world.[45] He constructed the historical ideal type of the Protestant Ethic with certain broad questions in mind. This construct, like all ideal types, offered a simplified, somewhat exaggerated reconstruction of historical cases presented as a logical utopia, in their most rationally consistent and precise form.[46] Weber was well aware that his ideal typical formulations of Protestantism tended to exaggerate aspects of active asceticism by simplifying the historical and empirical complexities of the diffusion of Protestantism in

England, North America, and Europe. He acknowledges, "we can of course only proceed by presenting these religious ideas in the artificial simplicity of ideal types, as they could at best be seldom found in history."[47]

For Weber, the activist, ascetical believer who worked heroically in a mundane calling and created the inner, psychological assurance of grace was the successful resolution to the Protestant's existential dilemma. The sober, rational saint who organized life according to ascetic principles in order to free time and energy for the service of God eschewed emotionalism. Yet at the core of Protestant life-order and personality stood a "mighty enthusiasm,"[48] the emotional and irrational quest for salvation. Weber noted passing instances when saints were struck down by religious melancholy, unable to secure these desired inward experiences of God's abiding love. Especially among evangelical Pietists, Weber noted

> . . . the emotion was capable of such intensity, that religion took on a positively hysterical character, resulting in the alternation which is familiar *from examples without number and neuropathologically understandable, of half-conscious states of religious ecstasy with periods of nervous exhaustion, which were felt as abandonment by God.*(emphasis added)[49]

Nevertheless, the propensity of inner-worldly ascetics to suffer from religious melancholy escaped Weber's notice, and the special affinity between the Protestant Ethic and the melancholy spirit was relegated to a residual category in Weber's sociology of religion, unnoticed by contemporary sociologists.

William James, a contemporary of Max Weber, also produced a pioneering study of Protestant conversion and religious experience. In *The Variety of Religious Experience*, he focused upon the very questions that Weber placed on the margin. Writing in 1902, James undertook an investigation of the inner experiences of religionists, focusing upon "religious geniuses" who heroically attempted to shape their lives to be consistent with religious values and motives. For James every religion articulated theologies that provided a distinct conception of the universe and demanded ethical obligations of believers by their creator. Although ostensibly a general work on religion, James's essays actually explored Protestantism, in particular, the forms of religious experience found within early nineteenth-century New England spiritual biographies. He defined Protestantism as a religion of morbid-mindedness, which saw the natural orders of the world as depraved and the human body as evil and required a saint's effort to remake the world in God's image and find rebirth (the religion of the twice-born) through a protracted and painful conversion experience. A religion of morbid-mindedness viewed the unconverted individual as a vile creature living in sinful alienation from God and warring against the self. James argued that the existential condition of the unconverted in a religion demanding rebirth necessarily engendered a religious melancholy among the faithful. Here James defines religious melancholy, noting "the congruity of Protestant theology with the structure of the mind as shown in such experiences."[50]

> If the individual be of tender conscience and religiously quickened, the
> unhappiness will take the form of moral remorse and compunction, of feel-
> ing inwardly vile and wrong, and of standing in false relations to the author
> of one's being and appointer of one's spiritual fate. This is the religious
> melancholy and "conviction of sin" that have played so large a part in the
> history of Protestant Christianity.[51]

James even included, as an anonymous case history, the story of his own
father's psychopathology. Excerpted from the diary of Henry James the elder,
it depicts a prolonged melancholy and religiously motivated, suicidal anorexia.
James's work neglected the complexities, vicissitudes, and diversities of Protestant groups from the Reformation to the nineteenth century, and he collapsed his argument into an ahistorical formalism. He does alert us, however,
to the critical relationship of religious melancholy to the inner experiences
and existential conditions of believers committed to the worldview and life-
regulation of evangelical Protestantism.[52]

William James's commitment to reconstructing the inner experiences and
ascetic organization of conduct of saints who shaped their lives according to
Protestant structures allowed him access to the pathological dimensions of
Protestant character and personality that Weber neglected. James's essay reads
like a confessional biography, as he comes to terms with his own morbid
conscience and sick soul, and as an act of filial piety to the religious melancholy of his father. John Owen King argues that

> The *Varieties* works as a composite biography, a course of lectures in which
> James, by piecing together bits of autobiography from a broad range of
> history, moves an ideal "religious genius" through a transformation,
> refashioning the landscape of the pilgrim's journey in the terms of the new
> psychology. The *Varieties*, a book of spiritual biography, reads like a
> synecodoche of James's entire life. James takes his allegorical figure from
> carnal security—"the religion of healthy mindedness" (liberal, ameliora-
> tive, and quick to be shattered)—through panic fear and crisis, to ultimate
> glimpses of glorification.[53]

William suffered from a protracted religious melancholy that began with a
panic attack in 1869–1870, replicating the mental breakdown of Henry James,
Sr. William languished in despondency, succumbing to the mental alienations
of his era—agoraphobia, hypochondria, and neurasthenia. He suffered debilitating back pain, nervous exhaustion, dyspepsia, eye troubles, and insomnia.
As a victim of chronic fatigue, pain, and invalidism, he looked to a variety of
healing cults for treatments that included galvanic shock, hydrotherapy, and
mind cure. King explains that "James' greatest works, his *Psychology* and
Varieties of Religious Experience, reflect the productions of his own self-
defined melancholy mind. They are flowerings that were preceded by horrid
depressions (the *Varieties* itself was written in bed in James' neurasthenic
chamber)."[54]

In 1900, before he delivered the Gifford Lectures, published as *Varieties*,
writing from the baths of Bad-Nauheim where he received treatment for his

chronic melancholia, James instructs his young daughter, Margaret, about the obsessional core of the experience of the inner life. James tells her to expect melancholia as the necessary suffering requisite to enlightenment,

> Among other things there will be waves of terrible sadness, which sometimes lasts for days; and dissatisfactions with one's self, and irritation at others, and anger at circumstances and stoney insensibility, etc., etc., which taken together form a melancholy. Now, painful as it is, this is sent to us for an enlightenment.[55]

William James and Max Weber met during Weber's trip to America in 1904, and Weber was profoundly influenced by *Varieties*, citing James in his Protestant Ethic essays.[56] They shared an ill-veiled disdain for the mental hygiene movement, or the religion of healthy mindedness. Both grappled with the existential questions of modern life—the struggle to wrest from the materials of culture an inwardly meaningful stance toward life and work, to embrace the demon that held together the fibers of their lives.[57] Each in turn valorized the heroic, ascetic struggle of a vocational ethos and the idea of personality as a life given to the realization of ultimate values. And both were heirs to religious melancholy as men who had experienced mental breakdowns early in their careers, and whose lives were marked by nervous exhaustion and debility.

Weber's developmental sociology of Western rationalism viewed the Protestant Ethic as key to understanding the process of economic rationalization in modern society. He recounts the consequences of this ethos in the famous "poet's lament."[58] The modern world had become an iron cage and Weber indicts the compulsive, obsessional nature of vocational asceticism.

> In the field of its highest development, in the United States, the pursuit of wealth, stripped of its religious and ethical meaning, tends to become associated with purely mundane passions, which often actually give it the character of sport.
>
> No one knows who will live in this cage in the future . . . (this) mechanized petrifaction, embellished with a sort of convulsive self-importance. For of the last stage of this cultural development, it might well be truly said: "Specialists without spirit, sensualists without heart; this nullity imagines that it has attained a level of civilization never before achieved."[59]

James explored the emotional and psychological dimensions of religious melancholia for persons trapped within this "iron cage," and within the life-order of evangelical Pietism. Had Weber chosen to pursue the logical consequences of his structural phenomenology of religious experience, he would have written a sixth essay on the Protestant Ethic. This work, like James's *Varieties*, would have investigated "the Protestant Ethic and the Melancholy Spirit."[60] Succeeding generations of sociologists would then have pursued the relationship between religiously grounded personality and religious melancholy, self-assured that they continued in the spirit of Weber's pioneering research agenda. However, this was not to be. The challenge is to explore the roads not taken by Weber, to redirect and shift the focus of the historical ideal type, "the Protestant Ethic," to examine the relationship of a religiously grounded life-order and personality to distinct forms of melancholy and mental disorders. The analysis proceeds in the spirit of Weber along avenues he did not emphasize: first, by considering the origins of the Protestant dilemma in the lives and dogma of Martin Luther and John Calvin, next, by exploring the vicissitudes of Protestant personality in English and American Puritanism.

Martin Luther's Anfechtung

Martin Luther forged the prototypical notion of Protestant selfhood and identity in his prophetic resolution of deeply personal, lifelong spiritual crises, through a transformation of the relationship of man and God and through the subsequent reformation of the Catholic church. Erik Erickson's enduring insights from *Young Man Luther* underscore the magnificent creative synthesis produced by a young man in the throes of episodic inner turmoil.[61] Luther's creative solutions to personal crises transcended a private spiritual journey, and became the foundation for a new integration of personality and spiritual identity, and the impetus for a collective religious movement that shattered Christendom. Erickson, quoting Kierkegaard, describes Luther as a "patient"— an archetypal religious attitude—leading a life of "imposed suffering, of an intense need for cure, and . . . a 'passion for expressing and describing one's suffering.'"[62]

The psychohistorical and intrapsychic origins of Luther's crises remain obscure and mired in controversy since the publication of Erickson's work more than a generation ago. Fortunately, the immense enterprise of "Luther scholarship," particularly in Germany, has illuminated Luther's "solutions" to these crises and their significance to to the dilemma of Protestant personality and identity. We may never know the origins of Luther's depressions, but we understand the historical significance of Luther's struggle to heal his troubled conscience. Writing in 1545, a year before his death, he offers an autobiographical account of his suffering as a sinner who could not find forgiveness in the sight of an angry and righteous God.

> Although I lived an irreproachable life as a monk, I felt that I was a sinner with an uneasy conscience before God; nor was I able to believe that I had pleased him with my satisfaction. I did not love—in fact, I hated—that righteous God who punished sinners, if not with silent blasphemy, then certainly with great murmuring. I was angry with God, saying "As if it were not enough that miserable sinners should be eternally damned through original sin, with all kinds of misfortunes laid upon them by the Old Testament law, and yet God adds sorrow upon sorrow through the gospel, and even brings his wrath and righteousness to bear through it!" Thus I drove myself mad, with a desperate disturbed conscience. . . .[63]

Luther's reflections capture the crisis that led to his theological and personal breakthrough in the period from 1514 through 1519. Born in 1483, educated at the University of Erfurt, earning a master's degree in 1505 at the age of twenty-one, Luther suffered his first crisis during a thunderstorm, when he vowed to enter a monastery and devote his life to God if he was spared. From the first crisis until the breakthrough he experienced while lecturing on the Psalms as a doctor of theology in Wittenberg, Luther ruminated on the alienation of man from God. The icon of Christ holding a sword in one hand representing the wrath and judgment of God oscillated with the image of the lily of God's love and mercy emerging from Christ's ear.[64] During the celebration of his first mass, having taken the final vows as a monastic, Luther describes being stricken by "Holy terror," relating "I am dust and ashes and full of sin."[65] How could a "pygmy" pretend to offer the sacraments and stand before the majestic God?

In utter conformity with the late-medieval church, Luther searched for relief from this inner terror. Scrupulosity—obsessive concern with sinfulness and failure to find forgiveness and God's mercy—together with the other extreme, acedia—or spiritual lassitude and deadness—afflicted many individuals throughout the long history of monasticism.[66] The cure of souls combined personal spiritual guidance and casuistic interpretation of canon law by a personal spiritual advisor with the techniques of confession, penance, and absolution to guide and comfort the troubled conscience.[67] Luther tortured himself with confession, at times spending as long as six hours in an attempt to recall and list every sin in his life from childhood to his young adulthood. Still he felt uneasy, had he remembered them all? What could he do about the sins that remained outside of his awareness? The confessional compounded his malaise. If the exemplary life of the monastic as a religious virtuoso paved the way to heaven, then Luther would pursue the most exacting other-worldly asceticism possible in search of an elusive self-perfection. A monk could seek perfection in austerities and fasting, vigils, and mortifications of the flesh. Yet, in the midst of these heroic efforts, Luther never realized the promised inner tranquility and release from sin. Instead, he posed the question, "Have you fasted enough?" A pilgrimage to Rome, indulgences, and the intercession of saints failed to satisfy him. In 1511 Luther was transferred to Wittenberg and placed under the spiritual guidance of Johann von Staupitz. Staupitz advised him to pursue a doctorate at the University of Wittenberg and devote himself to theological study. In the context of his advanced studies, and subsequent preaching and work in the Psalter, Luther crystallized his solution to the vexing problem of his scrupulosity.

Luther's interpretation of *iustitia*, or the righteousness of God, asked how God could justify sinful man if righteousness meant that God would render good for good and evil for evil. God would offer simple equity, rendering to each man his due according to the precept *virtus reddens unicuique quod suum est.*[68] Sinful actions would invariably result in the deserved wrath of God and divine punishment. The sacramental grace of the church, in the form of indulgences (excess merit accumulated by saints offered for sale to sinners), the cycle of confession, penance, and absolution, pilgrimages and austerities, and mystic flight could not undo the awful righteousness of God in Luther's eyes.

Tormented by Paul's Epistle to the Romans and the idea of "the justice of God," Luther felt overwhelmed by sin that knew no forgiveness. He captured this experience in the opening stanza of a hymn.

> In devil's dungeon chained I lay
> 　The pangs of death swept o'er me.
> My sin devoured me night and day
> 　In which my mother bore me.
> My anguish ever grew more rife,
> I took no pleasure in my life
> 　And sin had made me crazy.[69]

Only through a reformulation of the conception of God's righteousness could Luther explain the extension of God's mercy and forgiveness to man. The "righteousness of faith," or *iustitia fidei*, was a concept that portrayed righteousness as an unmerited gift of grace through the intercession of the Savior, Christ.[70] God's love, as manifested in Christ's suffering on the cross to redeem mankind, overcame the alienation of the unworthy sinner from his creator. In his own words, Luther speaks of this breakthrough:

> Night and day I pondered until I saw the connection between the justice of God and the statement that "the just shall live by His faith." Then I grasped that the justice of God is that righteousness by which through grace and sheer mercy God justifies us through faith. Thereupon I felt myself to be reborn and to have gone through open doors into paradise. The whole of Scripture took on a new meaning, and whereas before the "justice of God" had filled me with hate, now it became to me inexpressibly sweet in greater love.[71]

How could Luther arrive at the position of the righteousness of faith and the assurance of God's free gift of grace for unworthy man? In the midst of his spiritual crises of 1514, Luther experienced something akin to the "death of the self," of despair, which he would identify as *anfechtung*. He used the materials of his particular crisis to shape the crux of Protestant theology— *anfechtung* and the Theology of the Cross.

Luther languished in the fundamental alienation of man from God. However, this alienation would spark a crisis that served as the preparatory work to bring the believer closer to God. Alister McGrath summarizes Luther's understanding of the spiritual centrality of *anfechtung*.

> Through the experience of the *opus alienum Dei*, the sinner finds himself driven to despair, his confidence in himself totally shaken; finding himself under the wrath of God, he counts himself as damned. Yet through this experience of the strange work of God, the sinner is enabled to appropriate the proper work of God: by experiencing the "delicious despair" of *anfechtung*, the sinner learns to trust only in God as known in the cross of Christ, and thus comes to be justified.[72]

In the depth of angst and dread, Luther asked if he alone suffered fear and trembling and such holy terror as to commit the unpardonable sin— despair of God's mercy. The image of the crucified Jesus who cried out in pain asking why God had forsaken him proved to be the key for Luther. God, through the intercession of Christ, would offer saving grace freely to true Christians. Plunging the sinner to depths of desolation, God raises the sufferer with faith and grace. The believer, renewed and humbled and bonded to God in a special personal relationship, is assured of the promise of salvation. *Anfechtung* suffered by Christ on the cross on man's behalf redeemed Luther and all believers, who could receive this grace by faith alone.

Paul Tillich views Luther's notion of *anfechtung* as the "transmoral conscience" that demanded that the believer go beyond simple obedience to the ethical demands of moral law and participate "in a reality which transcends the sphere of moral commands."[73] By linking the individual in crisis directly to God and requiring a form of inner illumination of God's spirit to assuage the doubts of *anfechtungen*, Luther places the conscience beyond the confines of conventional ethical authority. Now each conscience looks inward for illumination of God's purpose to ascertain right action and conformity to his will. Tillich asserts that the transmoral conscience does not deny conventional morality but is "driven beyond it by the unbearable tensions of the sphere of law."[74]

> In psychological terms this means: in so far as we look at ourselves, we must get a desperate conscience; in so far as we look at the power of a new creation beyond ourselves we can reach a joyful conscience. Not because of our moral perfection but in spite of our moral imperfection we are fighting and triumphing on the side of God, as in the famous picture of Duerer, "Knight, Death, Devil," the knight goes through the narrows in the attitude of a victorious defiance of dread and temptation.[75]

Luther understood that the crisis of *anfechtung,* when resolved by faith, marked the beginnings of a lifelong spiritual itinerary. Repeatedly through the course of life, the believer would lapse into despair. Through prayer, humility, devotion to Scripture, and direct combat with Satan, Luther confronted his depressions. As Bainton notes, "Luther felt that his depressions were necessary. At the same time they were dreadful and by all means and in every way to be avoided and overcome. His whole life was a struggle against them, a fight for faith."[76]

Luther's remedy became the standard for all who would know God by faith and seek the promise of salvation. Now all Protestants would encounter periodic *anfechtung* in their quest for the certitude of salvation. As Paul Hacker notes, "since it is impossible to retain this certitude permanently, Lutheran faith is inevitably accompanied by *anfechtung*."[77] McGrath understands depression and religious despair as a perennial and authentic part of spiritual existence. He writes: "In order for the Christian to progress in his spiritual life, he must continually be forced back to the foot of the cross, to begin it all over again (*semper a novo incipere*)—and this takes place through the continued experience of *Anfechtung*.[78]

How clearly Kierkegaard understood Luther as a patient—the capacity for self-imposed suffering and profound need for cure. The frequent onset of depression or *anfechtung* was viewed as an occasion for the reapprehension of faith and opportunity for spiritual growth. Believers, following the path of Luther, appropriated this model of the spiritual life. Depression in the quest for *certitudo salutis,* defined as the "delicious despair" of *anfechtung,* constituted an essential and recurrent feature in the Lutheran origins of Protestant personality. By assertive faith, one could overcome despair and find consolation in God's free gift of grace and mercy.

Gerhard Ritter captures this dynamic tension of religious life-order and personality, as set in motion by Luther.

> His religion is the religion of the heroic *Willenmensch* who bears about in his own breast the contradictions of good and evil which rend the world asunder. . . . Its unresolved internal contrarieties have filled the spiritual life of Germany with ever new tensions.[79]

John Calvin's Anxiety and Solicitude

Like Martin Luther, John Calvin (1509–1564) suffered from religious anxiety throughout his life. Both shaped their doctrines out of the material of their inner spiritual crises.[80] Calvin's last will and testament evidences this persistent anxiety at the end of his life, despite his many accomplishments as a pastor, theologian, and reformer.

> Alas . . . the will I have had, and the zeal, if it can be called that, have been so cold and sluggish that I feel deficient in everything and everywhere. . . . Truly, even the grace of forgiveness he has given me only renders me all the more guilty, so that my only recourse can be this, that being the father of mercy, he will show himself the father of so miserable a sinner.[81]

In *John Calvin, A Sixteenth Century Portrait,* William J. Bouwsma writes of Calvin, "although his career was filled with accomplishments, his inner life showed few signs of the progress which he associated with godliness; he was still wrestling at the end of his life with self-doubt, confusion, and contradictory impulses that had been with him at the beginning."[82] A life of episodic self-doubt, resting on the foundations of spiritual anxiety and terrible fears of personal insufficiency, remains part of the theological legacy bequeathed by Calvin's doctrines and unsuccessful resolutions of his own spiritual malaise.

In 1535, Calvin published the first edition of the *Institutes of the Christian Religion,* which combined an exacting rational argument with a passionate pleading that captured the existential nature of his angst, which he attributed to every person. God had created Adam in *imago Dei* and given to man a rational mind and ordered heart as the seat of emotions; Adam's sin shattered this perfection. Banished from paradise, ridden by physical ills, excessive and disorderly emotions, and a now-corrupt nature, man existed in sin and alienation from the Creator.[83] Succeeding generations bear the legacy of Adam's original sin as beings corrupted by self-pride, ridden by disorder and excess, whose mind, will, and heart remain trapped in total depravity:

> For our nature is not only destitute of all good, but it is so fertile in all evils that it cannot remain inactive. . . . that everything in man—the understanding and will, the soul and body—is polluted and engrossed by this concupiscence, or, to express it more briefly, that man is of himself nothing else but concupiscence.[84]

Only a radical break, like Paul's conversion on the road to Damascus or the conversion experience of Augustine, could effectively turn the natural man away from his sinful proclivities and toward a life of self-control and order sanctified according to God's commands. The new man who experienced regeneration could look with new eyes, feel with a renewed heart, and will with an unblemished ethical purpose. Calvin's interrelated doctrines of faith and repentance account for the possibility of the recovery of the *imago Dei* and the other-worldly salvation of *meditatio futurae vitae.*

The doctrine of justification by faith alone is the keystone of Calvin's thinking. Faith is the inner assurance that God's love abides,[85] a "saving transaction" between man and God.[86] Through the operation of faith, each individual possesses a sense of religious personhood or personality and engages in direct, personal communication with God without the mediation of church, sacrament, or priest. In the spiritual exercises of prayer, self-examination, and diary keeping, among other pieties, the believer reflects upon and relates inner experience and outer conduct to God's Word and his commands.[87] In the conduct of this practical piety, the believer's mind, heart, and will, through the agency of the conscience, open to direction from and communication with God.

Faith proceeded, according to Calvin, by a special operation of *unio mystica.* God acquitted the elect believer from the guilt of sin, offering this wholly gratuitous remission of sin by the righteousness imputed to man by Christ. Stuerman explains Calvin's special understanding of the believer's "possession" of Christ the Redeemer: "Christ's righteousness is reckoned to us by God's mercy, not because *we* have been renewed, but simply because *Christ lives in us.* Calvin's idea seems to be that Christ lives in us by faith without our possessing him.[88]

In the *Institutes,* Calvin writes that the believer experiences the dwelling of Christ within as a key to *certitudo,* or the intensely personal assurance of God's mercy.[89] "Christ the Redeemer appears, by whose hand our heavenly father, out of his infinite goodness and mercy, has been pleased to succor us, if we with true faith embrace this mercy, and with firm hope rest in it."[90] Faith produced *illuminatio,* the mind's enlightenment, and *obsignatio,* the sealing of the heart with religious and pious affections.[91] This multifaceted operation of faith within the believer turned the once-alienated creature toward God, and began the lifelong spiritual journey and pilgrimage of the believer in warfare against remnants of the natural man and the powers of Satan, in search of elusive perfection and the restoration of the original *imago Dei.*

The action of faith produced repentance—the inner transformation and conversion, or turning one's life to God. Calvin outlined the spiritual itinerary or "morphology of conversion" of the stages of repentance as *timor Dei,* mortification, and vivification. Initially, the faithful suffer deeply through the recognition of their sinfulness and confront the awful fear of God, or *timor Dei*, in fear and trembling before the divine tribunal. Calvin called this "bearing the cross" of adversity in their public lives and special, humbling adversity in their inner, ceaseless warfare against sin, Satan, and the temptations of their still-carnal natures. Calvin warned the faithful, "Those whom the Lord has chosen and honored with his intercourse must prepare for a hard, laborious, and troubled life, a life full of many and various kinds of evils. . . ."[92]

Bearing the cross meant accepting Christ's life and passion as a model of self-denial that led to mortification of "creatureliness" and concupiscence, and the dying of the natural self. Vivification of the new self saw the believer restored to the harmonious integration of mind, will, heart, and sensation, confirmed again in the image of God.[93] In sobriety, moderation, and methodical self-control, the regenerate made a life in obedience to God's will and for his greater glory. Calvin directed all believers to feel and experience emotions profoundly and deeply. But the elect should not express these passions in outward emotional display, zeal, or enthusiasm. "A Christian feels, though he does not indulge in grief and sorrow."[94]

Calvin knew that grace was not universally available to all, and this formed the basis of unrelenting religious anxiety. God predestined only a few to enjoy election, and none could know with certainty their status, given God's transcendental and fundamentally inscrutable will. The particularism of grace and the inability to resolve doubts regarding one's *certitudo salutis* made conversion as much a cultural artifact as an individual experience. The elect alternated between a conscience "secured in peaceful rest and calm tranquility,"[95] and "anxiety. . . as to our future state."[96] The faithful never escaped the lifelong alternation of peace or serene joy with renewed fear and trembling, religious anxiety in which they asked, "Do I enjoy true faith or self-deceit?" Calvin describes the inner struggles of the elect to recover, periodically, the *certitudo* of faith. "For they are harassed by miserable anxiety while they doubt whether God will be merciful to them. . . . Thus their knowledge stopping short leaves them only midway, not so much confirming and tranquillising (*sic*) the mind as harassing it with doubt and disquietude."[97]

Calvin compounded religious anxiety by depicting conversion as the first step in a pilgrim's continuous, progressive, slowly evolving spiritual itinerary.

> . . . let us everyone proceed according to our small ability and prosecute the journey we have begun. . . . Therefore let us not cease to strive, that we may be incessantly advancing in the way of the Lord; nor let us despair on account of the smallness of our success; for however our success may not correspond to our wishes, yet our labor is not lost when this day surpasses the proceeding one; provided that, with sincere simplicity, we keep our end in view, and press forward to the goal. . . .[98]

The pilgrim never realized self-perfection and could only hope that the first seeds of faith planted during repentance and regeneration would be nurtured by a ceaseless struggle to overcome sins of the flesh and the bitterness of still-unredeemed parts of the believer's soul. Calvin admonished the faithful:

> Those are grossly mistaken who conceive that the pardon of sin is necessary only to the beginning of righteousness. As believers are everyday involved in many faults, it will profit them nothing that they have once entered the way of righteousness, unless the same grace which brought them into it accompany them to the last steps of their life.[99]

Calvin wrote of the alternation of assurance and doubt, security and anxiety in the Christian life.

> When we say that faith must be certain and secure, we certainly speak not of an assurance which is never affected by doubt, nor a security which anxiety never assails. We rather maintain that believers have a perpetual struggle with their own distrust, and thus far from thinking that their consciences possess a placid quiet, uninterrupted by perturbation.[100]

Calvin offered pastoral advice to the perplexed, counseling perseverance in their journeys, and prayer, careful examination of the Word, and diligent work in their calling. These remedies would sustain the faithful and aid them in their combat against despair and unbelief. Yet, anxiety would remain a permanent feature of the Christian life as fashioned by Calvin's doctrine.

Bouwsma devotes a central chapter to Calvin's concept of anxiety and attributes to him the "terrible triad of attritional subjectivity"—anxiety about the fear of death, the torment of the guilty conscience, and the fear of divine judgment.[101] Thus, the elements of predestination, the lack of certitude, and the requirement of self-examination to ascertain a lifelong journey of progressive spiritual growth fuse together intentionally in Calvin's theology to engender religious anxiety. Anxiety proved useful for bringing sinners to repentance. He writes that "God succors us when he sees us oppressed by anxious thoughts."[102] Calvin depicts the anxiety of the guilt-stricken Everyman, standing before the bar of justice in a divine tribunal:

> Whenever I descended into myself, or raised my mind to thee, extreme terror seized me—terror which no expiations nor satisfactions could cure. And the more closely I examine myself, the sharper the stings with which my conscience was pricked, so that the only solace which remained to me was to delude myself by obliviousness.[103]

Calvin, as a physician of souls, argued that each believer must suffer vexations. Fear stimulated men to action, as the spiritually drowsy half-dead must be awakened to their predicament.[104] Methodical self-examination, according to Calvin, would invariably disclose our failures to fulfill God's will and bring self-conscious recognition as repentant sinners. "The only way to please God is to be severe in censuring ourselves."[105]

For Bouwsma, Calvin's concept of anxiety comprised two sensations. First was vertigo and disorientation; the sinner, struck down by pangs of a guilty conscience, simultaneously experiences a loss of identity, of inner direction.

Second was the experience of reality pressing down on one's chest, "crushing out his life and breath."[106] Indeed, anxiety could take control of the sinner beyond the desired point of inducing repentance. The terrors of vertigo, disorientation, and suffocation immobilized the sinner. Calvin depicts a religious anxiety that fills the sinner "with anguish of conscience and torment of deceit. For everyone is distressed by his own deceit, and his terror grows; everyone is driven to madness by his own wickedness."[107] For Calvin, such extremes of spiritual anxiety evoked images of the abyss and the labyrinth where sinners suffered a disintegration of the self, powerless to overcome their alienation from God.[108] Ultimately, believers who lapsed into spiritual extremes experienced "solicitude" or anxiety arising from a distrust of God's power to help. Akin to Luther's *anfechtung,* when the sinner lapsed into despair over alienation from God, solicitude represented the soul who knew no exit from the abyss of anxiety, from the labyrinth of hopelessness.[109] To doubt God's love manifested a lack of faith, and without full assurance, or *certitudo,* the believer could not find justification and the remission of sins that augured regeneration and other-worldly salvation. Solicitude marked the soul in extremis, a spiritual desolation and despair that fed on itself. For doubt and despair over lack of faith were themselves indictments of the absence of faith.

The Pattern Established—Evangelical Pietism

The doctrines of Luther, Calvin, and other Reformation theologians introduced a type of religiosity that spread from the Reformation on the Continent into Puritan England, and found its most consistent expression in the nonconformist sectarians who settled in New England. Known as evangelical Pietism, this variant of Protestant belief emphasized: (1) experiential oneness with God; (2) the quest for spiritual perfection through the *ordo salutis* of conversion; (3) reliance upon the objective authority of the biblical Word as interpreted by the prepared heart of the new man, himself transformed by the "ingrafting" of a dynamic, organic relationship between the believer and Christ; and (4) the opposition to and endeavor to refashion, by evangelical means, the sinful orders of the natural man and the world.[110] C. C. Goen defines these essential aspects of evangelical Pietism.

> . . . all pietists agreed that true Christianity has its main locus in a meaningful relationship of the individual to God. For this reason they stressed personal repentance and faith, warm devotion, and assurance that they were in truth the children of God. Always strongly biblical and intensely missionary, pietism encouraged lively preaching to persuade unbelievers and complacent church members to commit themselves cordially to the obedience of faith. In short, the character of pietism required it to be aggressively conversionist.[111]

Evangelical Pietism fused together disparate elements, including mysticism-illuminism, narcissism, inner-worldly asceticism, evangelical fervor to convert the masses and transform the world in God's image, and a particu-

larism of grace founded upon the doctrine of predestination. Wherever these
five elements coalesced, most notably in the dissenting groups that came from
England, Holland, and Germany to America,[112] one found the propensity of
souls to suffer protracted religious melancholy.

Luther and Calvin introduced a mystical-illuminist dimension to Protestant identity by requiring all believers to cultivate a continual personal relationship with God; to know God through the unfolding of the "transmoral
conscience" by the souls' inner light and through the experience of *anfechtung*,
or solicitude. The inner light of the soul formed a vessel to receive the spirit
of God through the Holy Spirit. In this manner God healed a troubled conscience, and the soul found spiritual guidance in the form of assurance of right
action in conformity with God's will.

Geoffrey Nuttall's *The Holy Spirit in Puritan Faith and Experience*
examines the role of the inner light in Puritan thought. Believers sought illumination by the spirit of God as an intensely personal movement of individual
conscience, which, informed by the Word of God, gave them purpose and
orientation.[113] Puritans practiced "discerning the Spirit" to rid themselves of
self-deceit and hypocrisy, to direct their lives "God-ward" as humble children of God in the spirit of those adopted by Christ.

This practice of discerning the spirit was marked by oscillating cycles of
joy and desolation, reflecting the intense emotional catharsis associated with
the assurance of faith and salvation followed by dark nights when coldness
and spiritual lethargy brought renewed episodes of desolation. This pattern
of conscience and character influenced many succeeding Protestant sects. As
Benjamin Nelson notes, "the important link between late medieval mysticism
and Protestant illuminism was the concept of the spark or witness of God in
the soul (*scintilla animae, syneidesis*)."[114]

The transmoral conscience of the solitary Protestant individual fostered a
unique form of narcissism. The practice of systematic and lifelong self-examination repeatedly focused the believer's concern upon the state of his or her
soul, the progress towards grace, and the intensity of religious affections.
Repeatedly, the believer envisioned him- or herself as standing alone before
the bar of justice of the divine tribunal. Like the romantic lover caught in the
throes of passion and misery, pining and longing for the lost or unattainable
love object, so the narcissism of the transmoral conscience evokes a litany of
self-absorbed, self-reflective emotions, experiences, joys and agonies, alone on
the stage in the cosmic drama with God. Lewis Bayly's *Practice of Pietie*,
second only to Bunyan's work in its popularity, depicts the pilgrim as meditating upon the severity of God's law for sinners. The law will smite the pilgrim like a hammer; the law provides a mirror to reveal the sinner's imper-
fections.[115] John Bunyan's spiritual autobiography, *Grace Abounding to the
Chief of Sinners,* portrays God's love and mercy to one so cast down as to
consider himself the greatest of sinners.

Although mystical-illuminist and narcissistic, Protestant character and
identity did not promote quietism or contemplative flight and rejection of the
world. Rather, the believer sought assurance in effective, successful conduct

in a mundane calling, and by ascetic mastery of self and world. Despite the intensity of spiritual affections and emotions, notwithstanding the narcissistic self-involvement, Protestant self and character were fashioned out of the materials of methodical self-control, the ruthless suppression of outward emotional display, zeal, or fanaticism. Calvin particularly demanded that the godly and reprobate alike submit to the complete round of external discipline and regulation in the ordered and hierarchial spheres of family, church, and state. Whatever the inward turmoil, the Protestant endeavored to conduct life as a sober, rational, moderate discourse.

The elements of continental evangelical piety found fertile soil for transplantation to England in the middle of the sixteenth century. English Puritanism was simultaneously a political movement, a century-long controversy regarding church polity, and a system of devotional Pietism that attempted to bring the masses to Christ by plain preaching and evangelical methods. It is this last topic that proves central to our discussion.

English Puritanism forged a *praxis pietatis* by reinterpreting the covenant of grace and rationalizing the spiritual itinerary of the *ordo salutis*. After the translation and publication of Calvin's *Institutes* in English in 1561, English Puritan divines appropriated Calvinistic devotional piety, but reinterpreted key elements.[116] Most notably, orthodox Reformed theology pictured conversion as the sinner taken by storm, violently wrenched from the depravity of concupiscence, and in a moment turned toward God. Conversion as viewed by William Perkins (1558–1602), Richard Rogers (1550–1618), and Richard Greenham (1535–1594), however, proceeded as a slowly progressing and prolonged journey of the Christian life characterized by pilgrimage and struggle, "wayfaring and warfarin [sic]."[117]

Puritans developed accounts of their own regeneration to serve as guideposts for the conversion of the masses. The work of the Holy Spirit imparted grace to the unconverted, gradually and by incremental degrees. The natural man, although utterly depraved, could, with the assistance of the Spirit, read God's Word and Law with new illumination, and enlighten his heart. Thus, the man who would find grace had a duty not to "grieve the Spirit" but to prepare to enter God's covenant of grace. Norman Pettit defines this new doctrine of preparation as it emerged in Puritan thought after 1570. The natural man would respond to Law and Scripture in a gradual way through

> . . . a period of prolonged introspective meditation and self-analysis in the light of God's revealed Word. In this process, man first examined the evil of his sins, repented those sins, and then turned to God for salvation. From a conviction of conscience, the soul moved through a series of interior stages, always centered on self-examination, which in turn were intended to arouse a longing desire for grace.[118]

A prepared heart, open to receive the experiential infusion of the Spirit and saving grace, did not guarantee salvation or soften the rigors of predestination and the particularism of grace. "The lost soul could be left in utter confusion, between preparation and conversion, in 'horror of heart, anguish and perplexity of spirit'. . . ."[119] The doctrine of preparation did, however, structure and systematize the *ordo salutis* and rationalize the process of conversion.

Puritans prepared their hearts to enter the covenant of grace—God's absolute pledge to redeem the fallen man through the freely proffered remission of sins made possible by Christ the Redeemer. The believer did not play a passive role in the face of divine sovereignty in this two-party covenant between man and God. Puritan Pietism recast this relationship by affirming the active, volitional character of each believer's choice to "own the covenant" by fulfilling the conditions and performances of this agreement and embracing the stages of conversion—humiliation, justification, sanctification, and glorification. The covenant of grace provided the absolute assurance of God conditioned by the performances of the believer. This relationship between sinner and God escaped the Arminian position that, in Puritan belief, distorted man's capacity to win salvation by good works. The covenant of grace eschewed the other extreme of antinomianism, which viewed salvation by faith alone, passively, as revelation in one's heart directed by God.[120] Reflecting the antimony of divine sovereignty and human freedom, the covenant of grace affirmed the necessity of the believer's actively shaping a life founded upon ethical maxims, informed by divine purpose.

Although inscrutable and ultimately unknowable, the God of the covenant revealed Himself and entered into a intimate, secure compact with each Christian. John Von Rohr states that "there is a deep personalism in the covenant relationship, and God who has drawn near within it lays claim to a personal response. It is in free acceptance that this covenanting God becomes truly one's own God."[121]

Richard Rogers's Seven Treatises (1592) was the first systematic exposition of the *ordo salutis* in Puritan thought. Rogers depicted conversion as a gradual and variable process that differed among individuals. The stages of conversion are guideposts by which believers could understand and interpret their own pilgrim's progress. For Rogers, conversion proceeds according to the "work of the Spirit." First Work required the sinner's heart to be pricked by godly terror occasioned by the preaching of the Law. Second Work cast down the siner into an agonizing certainty of sin. Third Work required self-humiliation, and Fourth Work was the agency of God, through his Spirit, placing the believer within the covenant of grace. The work of the spirit prepared the believer to experience the moment of grace.[122] The four works of the Spirit prepared the believer for a call that was a summons to a new life. The *ordo salutis* proceeded next with the stage of justification and remission of sins through imputation of the righteousness of Christ. The regenerate Christian then devoted his or her life to sanctification or ethical conduct in fulfillment of God's will, to magnify God's glory.[123] However, the pilgrim girded him- or herself for ceaseless struggle against the continuance of sin in this life. Finally, the saint entered the last stage of earthly life, what Baxter saw as glorification in the personal assurance of the blessing of heaven. ". . . It is the perfect endless enjoyment of God by the perfected saints, according to the measure of their capacity to which their souls arrive at death. . . ."[124]

Richard Baxter's *Treatise of Conversion* represents the culmination of two generations of Puritan inquiry in the "sober reason" of the believer's quest for salvation, from the first step of a special effectual calling or vocation through repentance, regeneration, sanctification, and glorification. With detailed precision, he delineates the turning of the worldly, carnal, and depraved man toward God. The heart prepared, in repentance of past sins, forsakes the vain glories of this world, and embraces the child-like humility and humiliation of "godly sorrow." Baxter understands conversion as the turning point that prepares the pilgrim for a continual journey of devotional piety marked by inner struggle. He writes: "But when converting grace hath changed their hearts, O how the case is altered with them! Then godly sorrow is even as it were natural to them; and they that could not endure it, as now even cherish and indulge it. It is a voluntary sorrow. . . ."[125]

The daily practice of prayer, meditation, and diary keeping convinced the saint that "whosoever is justified of God, and freed from condemnation, is a judge and condemner of himself."[126] Baxter argues that the hearts of the converted become extremely sensitive to the remnants of sin in their still-carnal natures. The practice of self-examination will repeatedly uncover these offenses and produce renewals of godly sorrow and humilation. ". . . The remnant of their mortified sins is heavier on their soul, than the mountain of unmortified sin was to them before (conversion); they send out more groans and cries to God, because of their daily failings and infirmities than they did before. . . ."[127] Yet, the anger turned against themselves, when before they felt anger toward God, produces a self-loathing that augurs the promise of this-worldly peace and heavenly salvation. Baxter captures how the humilation and self-loathing of godly sorrow produce the opposite result, peace and hope, for the wayfaring and warfaring pilgrim. "The very humility of the saints hath a high design: when they be in the dust, in self-abhorrence and self-condemnation, they are aspiring thence as high as heaven: their humble confession, and tears, and groans, have a tendency to that glory, which is above the sun."[128]

Baxter's discussion of conversion reflected his considerable knowledge of Puritan thought, his own personal journey outlined in *Reliquiae Baxteriane*, and his therapeutic expertise as a "physician of souls" in the pastoral care of over two hundred cases of conscience. Baxter was convinced that the pilgrim would grow in grace and assurance in the course of a lifetime of piety and self-examination:

> When thou hast discovered thy true state, pass sentence on thyself accordingly; either that thou art a true Christian, or that thou art not. Pass not this sentence rashly, nor with self flattery, nor with melancholy terrors; but deliberately, truly, according to thy conscience, convinced by Scripture and reason.[129]

Pilgrims who adopted the method of humilation and godly sorrow did not always achieve the moderating, sober, and rational outcome, but lapsed into scruples and melancholy terrors.

With Baxter, Puritan Pietism shifted emphasis away from the outward ethical "preciseness" or the godliness of earlier generations, who strived to fashion their lives in conformity with God's law. Now the godliness of ascetic ethical conduct was informed by an inner "holiness,"[130] made public in formal testimonies and baptism when joining a church, or published in confessional diaries, spiritual autobiographies, and funeral sermons.[131] Indeed, the private confessional diary that recorded the fruits of daily self-examination provided the material for the new genre of published spiritual autobiography that recorded the inner pilgrimages of saints, offering experiential proofs of truths of Christianity and exemplary models to guide fellow travelers.

In *The Puritan Experience*, Owen Watkins relates that the evangelical work of pastors in preaching, writing, counseling, and exhorting was intended to assist persons from all classes "to find the way of salvation and work out the application of the Gospel to every part of their lives."[132] Spiritual autobiographies allowed the believer to externalize the inward journey and present the testimony of a life before publics deeply exercised over their own spiritual pilgrimage. Watkins argues: "Puritan autobiographies were the product of a Puritan conviction that the highest art a man could practise was the art of living, that the only masterpiece worthy of the name was to be achieved in the most complex and difficult of all forms of creative endeavour: a human life."[133]

These early Puritan autobiographies, like Baxter's account of the humiliation and godly sorrow of the converted saint, recorded the making of lives forged in the crucible of incessant spiritual warfare against the self. George Goodman terms this struggle *auto-machia* and offers a poetic lament for the continual struggle of all believers who seek heaven.

> I sing my SELF; my *civil-warss* within,
> The *Victories* I Howerely lose and win;
> The dayly *Duel*, the continuall strife,
> The *Warr* that ends not, till I end my life.
> And yet, not Mine, not onely Mine,
> But every-One's that under th'honor'd Signn
> Of Christ his Standard, shal his Name enrole,
> With holy Vowes of Body and Soule.[134]

John Bunyan's allegorical tale, *The Pilgrim's Progress*, and his spiritual autobiography, *Grace Abounding to the Chief of Sinners*, the most widely read works of this genre, exemplify the theme of the self in *auto-machia*, oscillating between times of comfort and despair. Bunyan does battle with Satan over his persistent obsessions with rejecting Christ and having committed the unpardonable sin of blasphemy against the Holy Spirit. Bunyan writes of his despair without solace after more than a decade of warfare against his self.

And now I was both a burden and a terror to myself. I was weary of life and afraid to die. How gladly I would have been anyone but myself, anything but a man, and in any condition but my own! It came to me frequently that it was impossible for me to be forgiven and to be saved from the wrath to come.[135]

Some fifteen years after beginning this journey, Bunyan finally felt secure in his conversion. He writes, "It was as though I had awakened out of a nightmare."[136] Bunyan's life, like Baxter's considered treatises, provided accounts of the way of salvation to guide every believer through life's pilgrimage. These Puritan divines had elaborated an experimental structure of voluntarily imposed suffering and spiritual warfare against the self. *Auto-machia* promised that only by descending into the depths of despair could the believer hope to ascend into the heights of assurance of salvation. Yet, how could the promised results of *auto-machia* be realized in the face of the fundamental doubt about one's status of election raised by predestinarian dogma?

Puritan dogma understood that God had unconditionally predestined some believers to election and others to eternal damnation. Divines urged 2 Peter 1:10 upon their flock, "which spoke of the need to 'make one's calling and election sure.'"[137] With methodical self-examination, believers searched their hearts, wills, and conduct for evidence of renewal and devotion to God's will. Saints needed continually to recover the evidence of assurance, to combat doubt and despair in life's pilgrimage. Rohr explains:

> The need here is to search out still more fully the "experimental knowledge" which can reveal the presence and power of God's working. It is to enter into the depths of personal experience, to probe the hidden recesses of the spirit, and to read carefully the signs of inner attitude, feeling, and life. It is to be sensitive to both the shoutings and the whispers of grace, as God works with varying intensities and the soul receives with varying degrees of responsiveness.[138]

During times of meditation, devotion, and humilation, *auto-machia* brought the saint low in self-reproach and godly sorrow. Then, as in the case of Thomas Bolton, the voice of God, the Holy Spirit, ravished his heart and assured him, "thou art the childe of God."[139]

However, saints could never ultimately know God's plan and their preordained status of election. Doubt, despair, times of spiritual dryness, and "dark nights of the soul" assailed believers with troubled convictions that God had abandoned them; God's grace remained hidden from their hearts. A considerable body of pastoral theology emerged to guide ministers as physicians of the soul and to heal the troubled consciences of the faithful. Most notably, Richard Baxter's *The Right Method For A Settled Peace of Conscience and Spiritual Comfort,* and William Perkins, in *A Discourse of Conscience,* established the principal methods of pastoral care.

Baxter's calm, reasoned treatise reassured the perplexed that all godly individuals suffered doubt, troubles, and spiritual afflictions sent by divine providence as tests and as opportunities for spiritual growth. Such afflictions were "normal" or natural for the godly and augered ultimate success. Through a sequence of thirty-two directions, Baxter guided the believer in a method for recovering peace and assurance. Baxter directed the troubled faithful toward reappropriation of faith by reiterating the familiar ground of Puritan belief. The treatise reaffirmed the stages of the *ordo salutis,* the nature of faith, the imputation of Christ the Redeemer who remits sin, and the abundant, tender mercies and love of God in the covenant of grace. Baxter did not dwell upon predestination, the particularism of grace, and the fundamental inability of the saint to find *certitudo salutis*. In response to the vexing question of assurance and doubt, Baxter replied, in direction XIX ". . . That those few who do attain assurance, have it not either perfectly or constantly (for the most part) but mixed with imperfection, and oft clouded and interrupted."[140] Baxter counseled believers to accept doubt or limited assurances, and not to expect sustained infusions of mystical or illuminist joy. In direction XXI he exhorted: "Be thankful if you can but reach to a settled peace, and composure of your mind, and lay not too much on the high raptures and feelings of comfort which some do possess: and if ever you enjoy such feeling joys, expect not that they should be either long or often."[141]

Direction XXIX lists and answers twenty ordinary doubts, including spiritual deadness, backsliding, unbelief, want of piety in prayer, doubt of grace, feelings of sinfulness and commission of the unpardonable sin against the Holy Spirit, failure to grow in grace, blasphemous thoughts, and fear of death. Baxter assuaged these doubts with an appeal to Puritan devotional piety and the duty of living the Christian life. "Remember that it is not your vexation or despair, but your obedience and peace that God desireth."[142]

Baxter called upon the believer to undergo an inner pilgrimage, an *ordo persuasionis*, according to Rohr:

> . . . when afflictions came and doubt assailed, much of the counsel given was itself related to this internal form of evidencing: absence of evidence has been the experience of saints; God sometimes hides clear evidences; God uses the lack of such evidences for positive purpose; the growth of evidence is by degrees.[143]

Baxter recognized that many desperate Christians labored under a mistaken sense of duty, seeking out prolonged bouts of humiliation and godly sorrow in order to find the inner assurance that Christ had indeed adopted them as one of God's children. The Christian life "seems a thraldom and torment" "and the very business of a Christian's life and God's service, is rather taken to be scrupling. . . ."[144] He argued that these excessive scruples, obsessions with sin, and prolonged self-punishment reflected an erroneous understanding of the duties required of saints in this world. Indeed, in all his writings Baxter pleads for moderation and sober reason in the search for evidence of election. Excessive and protracted religious affections produce melancholy terrors or "sad distempers," the antithesis of the desired comfort and assurance. He explained:

> Misapprehending the state of duty, and the very nature of a Christian life, must needs make sad distempers in men's hearts and conversations. Many Christians look upon broken heartedness, and much grieving, and weeping for sin, as if it were the great thing that God delighteth in, and requireth of them; and therefore they bend their endeavours this way; and are still striving with their hearts to break them more, and wringing their consciences to squeeze out some tear; and they think no sermon, no prayer,

no meditation, speeds so well with them, as that which can help to grieve or weep.[145]

In these quotations from direction XXXII, at the conclusion of Baxter's treatise, he argued that the incentives and directives of self-examination, humiliation, and adoption that constitute the marrow of Puritan devotional piety urged many troubled souls toward prolonged and excessive religious exercises, leading to mental alienation and melancholy. Baxter reported these findings from his own pastoral work with cases of conscience. However, he noted that true faith and the correct practice of Christian duty *must* promote comfort and assurance, not scrupulosity and melancholia. As a divine profoundly concerned with the evangelical winning of souls and the healing of doctrinal and political controversies, he could never admit a causal relationship between evangelical piety and mental alienation. How did he reconcile the many cases of religious melancholy that came to his attention with the doctrinal necessity that true religion promote only the health and spiritual welfare of believers?

Baxter adopted the conventional medical understanding of the cause of melancholia—a humoral imbalance—a physically determined disease resulting in prolonged sadness without cause, distempered emotions, and deranged reason. When such weakened and diseased individuals were exposed to religious doctrines, they lapsed into a melancholy characterized by religious themes. Only those individuals so predisposed by an existing physical disease, a humoral imbalance, became ill. Baxter wrote:

> But I have often known weak-headed people, (that be not able to order their thoughts,) and many melancholy people guilty of . . . thinking too much and too seriously and intensely on good and holy things, whereby they have overthrown their reason, and been distracted. . . . I would therefore advise those melancholy persons whose minds are so troubled, and heads weakened, that they are in danger of overthrowing their understandings, (which usually begins in multitudes of scruples, and restlessness of mind, and continual fears, and blasphemous temptations, where it begins with these, distraction of mind is at hand, if not prevented) that they forbear meditation, as being no duty to them. . . .[146]

William Perkins's *Discourse of Conscience* (1596) also distinguishes between "normal" religious affections of the pious and melancholic distemper. In his discussion of the causes and treatment of sadness or sorrow, Perkins argues:

> Sorrow, that comes by melancholy, ariseth onely of that humour annoying the bodie: but this other sorrow ariseth of a man's sinnes, for which his conscience accuseth him. Melancholie may be cured by physicke: this sorrow cannot be cured by anything but by the blood of Christ.[147]

Perkins understood the chief case of conscience as that sorrow attended by despair, doubt, and the absence of assurance of election. In his extensive pastoral practice, he recognized that this greatest distress of mind—despair—brought self-condemnation, and "comes at length to desperation, if it be not cured."[148] The despair afflicting the troubled conscience required a practical divinity that, like Baxter's work, urged the perplexed to reaffirm the *ordo salutis*, regain their faith, and accept the promise of God's covenanted love, remission of sin, and salvation. Perkins, like Baxter, counseled many religious melancholiacs who came for pastoral care. In his view, these anguished souls suffered from a mental disease of somatic origin He rejected any connection between the structure and experience of evangelical piety and the propensity for saints to break down under the crushing burden of making a life consistent with this variant of Protestant life-order and personality.

Robert Burton published *The Anatomy of Melancholy* in 1621 under the pseudonym "Democritus Junior." Writing in the spirit of the classical Democritus, Burton produced an anatomy of melancholy by dissecting the nature of humanity as both a solitary being and a social animal, promising to reveal a "new science"not from direct empiricism or clinical observation, but by distilling the many truths mined from over one thousand works of classical and medieval learning. In the preface to the reader, Burton, under the guise of Democritus, reveals that he remains an alienated observer of the world, closeted as a divine in the academy, himself a sufferer of melancholy. From this vantage point of the detached intellectual, living in the world but remaining aloof and not of the world, Burton writes a learned, excoriating indictment of the chaos, folly, and madness of people and social institutions.

Nothing escapes Democritus' notice and penetrating sarcasm. Politics, statecraft, religion, knowledge and scholarship, law and justice, love, marriage and the family, economy and professions, and the ubiquity of warfare, injustice, and irrationality in social relations; all these provoked Burton's laughter. Melancholy, so "universal a malady," "an epidemical disease,"[149] disordered all human thought, action, and emotion, and marred societal institutions through chaos, corruption, and injustice. Burton, through the voice of Democritus, exposes this folly, and demonstrates the causes, symptoms, and cure of melancholy. His "anatomy" places the very core of evangelical Pietist doctrine on the table for dissection. Not surprisingly, Burton concludes his tome with a discussion of religious melancholy.

Melancholy here represents a fundamental imbalance of the somatic humors—black bile—consistent with the classical medicine of Galen. However, Burton the Anglican divine rejects somatic determinism and maintains that body and mind operate in dynamic interrelation, that something more fundamental causes melancholy as an ontological attribute at the core of the human condition. Man's innate depravity, founded on the legacy of Adam's original sin, destroys the perfection and order of a creation fashioned in God's image. Now man is a diseased creature in a disordered world, alienated from what he once was—God's perfect creature in an ordered universe.[150] Burton maintains that "We are thus bad by nature, bad by kind, but far worse by art, every man the greatest enemy unto himself. We study many times to undo ourselves, abusing those good things which God hath bestowed upon us, health, wealth, strength, wit, learning, art, memory, to our own destruction. . . ."[151]

Flawed by innate depravity, human reason falls prey to incessant misunderstandings, error, and perturbations of the mind. The faculties of the will and the heart are also perverted by sin. Like Calvin in the *Institutes*, Burton sees chaos, disorder, excesses, and concupiscence in all things. Only in so far as people adopt the ascetical ethical code of work in a calling, and charity (brotherly relations between people as required by God), can they remake their lives and societies in conformity with God's will. "Be not solitary; be not idle." Burton's aphorism offers the cure for melancholy through the transformation of human nature and social organization. If individuals forge personalities of methodical self-control and reason, and recast society in conformity with the Word, then melancholy can be overcome.

> . . . so we, as long as we are ruled by reason, correct our inordinate appe-
> tite, and conform ourselves to God's word, are as so many living saints:
> but if we give reins to lust, anger, ambition, pride, and follow our own
> ways, we degenerate into beasts, transform ourselves, overthrow our con-
> stitutions, provoke God to anger, and heap upon us this *Melancholy*, and
> all kinds of incurable diseases, as a just and deserved punishment of our
> sins.[152]

Burton's presentation of the proximate causes of melancholy details how individuals lapse into mind sicknesses when they fall prey to all-too-human passions. Self-love, covetousness, gaming and worldliness, depraved appetites of pride and ambition, anger, and desire for revenge plunge the disordered heart into melancholy. The stings of fortune and adversity—death, loss, and accident—produce melancholy. Only the regenerate, twice-born soul can escape it. However, Burton also discovers, paradoxically, the existence of religious melancholy for believers who suffer profound despair in their very quest to overcome the existential melancholy of the human condition of de-pravity.

Identifying it as a distinct form of love-melancholy caused by a defect in man's relation to God, Burton writes, "I have no pattern to follow, as in some of the rest, no man to imitate. No Physician hath as yet distinctly written of it."[153] He had uncovered the irony that believers seeking to transcend melan-choly, through a conversion marked by the infusion of God's love, experi-ence the most intense religious melancholy. Before he analyzes this paradox of Protestantism, he examines the myriad forms of unbelief and non-Chris-tian religion. Burton reviles the errors of "Papist" or Catholic belief and prac-tice, and underscores the deleterious effects of all forms of paganism, idola-try, religious wars, atheism, and superstition. He informs the reader that these departures from true religion are not founded upon the love of God and thus lead to melancholy. His principal discussion of religious melancholy, how-ever, involves his English and European Protestant contemporaries.

Evangelical Pietists who committed doctrinal error, by which Satan pol-luted individuals' hearts with temptations and sinful obsessions, remained alien-ated from God's love, and suffered the terrors of conscience, despair, and hopelessness. Only the infusion of faith—the assurance that God's love abides in the soul of the believer—could justify the sinner, and turn the depraved one toward God by renewing his or her mind, will, and heart. The absence of God's love trapped the believer in the ontological melancholy of the human condition, as defined by Burton. As Ruth Fox argues, melancholy is cured by Christ: ". . . all of the abominable unnatural deeds of which a conscience-stricken man can accuse himself, for all of the fearful misconceptions of Scripture he can devise, Burton gives back one answer, that to be a man in a universe of love is to be capable of receiving the love of God."[154]

Burton recounts the problems of devotional piety: weakness of faith, misunderstood Scripture, the scrupulous conscience, excessive meditations, doubt and despair over one's status of election. He retraces the familiar ground covered by Perkins and accepts the explanation that humoral imbalances predispose believers to melancholy. "The body works upon the mind, by obfuscating the spirits and corrupted instruments, which Perkins illustrates by the simile of an Artificer, that hath a bad tool, his skill is good, ability correspondent, by reason of ill tools his work must needs be lame and unperfect."[155]

Burton's description of the symptoms "Despair, Fear, Sorrow, Suspicion, Anxiety, Horror of conscience, fearful dreams and visions,"[156] derived from the work of Felix Plater, reveals the seriousness of religious melancholy as mental alienation.

> Never was any living creature in such torment before, in such a miserable estate, in such distress of mind, no hope, no faith, past cure, reprobate, continually tempted to make away themselves: Something talks with them, they spit fire and brimstone, they cannot but blaspheme, they cannot repent, believe, or think a good thought, so far carried . . . that they are compelled against their will to harbour impious thoughts, to blaspheme against God, to the committing of many horrible deeds, to laying violent hands upon themselves, & c. . . .[157]

Untreated, religious melancholy frequently resulted in suicide or confirmed madness. With proper physic—diet, air, exercise—and comforting pastoral care, religious melancholy could be cured. Burton's pastoral advice reflected the prevailing techniques of his time: reminding the scrupulous that the infinite mercy of God would remit sin, calming doubts over election and predestination:

> . . . all are invited, but only the elect apprehended: the rest that are unbelieving, impenitent, whom God in his just judgment leaves to be punished for their sins, are in a reprobate sense; yet we must not determine who are such, condemn ourselves, or others, because we have an universal invitation; all are commanded to believe, and we know not how soon or late before our end we may be received.[158]

Burton directed the perplexed toward a life of religious moderation, calm reason, and measured fellowship and work.[159] Although he explained religious melancholy as the result of predisposing physical imbalances of the humors compounded by religious error and the temptations of Satan, Burton's concluding statement indicates ambivalence.[160] Here, he believes that excessive piety causes melancholy.

> Last of all: if the party affected shall certainly know this malady to have proceeded from too much fasting, meditation, precise life, contemplation of God's judgments (for the Devil deceives many by such means) . . . let him ease the soul by all honest recreations, refresh and recreate his distressed soul; let him direct his thoughts, by himself and other of his friends. Let him read no more such tracts or subjects, hear no more such fearful tones, avoid such companies . . . .[161]

How ironic that believers who wished above all else to escape melancholy through the *ordo salutis*, by shaping a life of active ascetic self-mastery, work, and *caritas* (charity), suffered religious melancholy that frequently ended in suicide. How striking that Burton, who disclosed, through the voice of Democritus, his own melancholy struggles, appears to have ended his life by suicide. He composed his epitaph as "Known to few, unknown to fewer, here lies Democritus Junior, to whom melancholy gave both life and death."[162] Burton's thesis, like the structure of evangelical Pietism, hinged on faith in the reception of God's love. In its absence, the believer fell into the "dark night of the soul" that for many offered no exit save through madness or suicide.

Burton identified a new form of spiritual desolation among Puritans evidenced in the charges made against them by Catholics and Anglicans during the troubled history of sectarianism and controversy in England in the late sixteenth and early seventeenth centuries. "Robert Burton invented a new name for pathological doubt about one's spiritual state, religious melancholy, and he charged that the Puritans were tearing and wounding people's consciences, so that they were almost mad with fear and sorrow."[163] Burton, an Anglican don, entered the fray by discovering religious melancholy as endemic among nonconformist and separatist believers.

Religious melancholy reportedly prevailed among Cambridge Puritans in the period from 1580 to 1600.[164] Richard Napier, an Anglican minister and astrological physician who practiced in the English Midlands from 1597 to 1634, treated nearly three hundred religious melancholiacs, Puritans who suffered from what Napier regarded as "Puritanical consciences," "salvation panic," and obsessions with sinfulness.[165] Michael MacDonald and Terrance Murphy, in *Sleepless Souls, Suicide in Early Modern England*, uncover the same sectarianism and contentiousness—charges by Anglicans and Catholics alike—of religious melancholy and suicide among Puritans.[166]

The true incidence of religious melancholy is unknowable. However, by the late 1500s Puritan practical divinity had incorporated suicidal crisis as an integral and expected part of the morphology of conversion. Pastoral works defined suicidal despair as the work of Satan tempting the godly into doubt or blasphemy.[167] Richard Sibbes, Greenham, Perkins, Baxter, and Bunyan urged all pilgrims to resist the fiery darts that Satan sent into their hearts, to wage a cosmic battle against evil. All believers now could expect to confront the challenge met by Christian and Hopeful, tempted by Giant Despair to kill themselves in Doubting Castle.

2

Evangelical Pietism in America

The New England Way

English Puritans suffered religious intolerance in the 1620s at the hands of William Laud and King Charles I. Laud delivered a sermon to Parliament in 1626 impugning Puritanism as an affront to church and state. He redoubled the persecution of nonconformist groups after his appointment as Archbishop of Canterbury in 1633. Many fled England, and after a brief sojourn in Holland, migrated to America, founding Massachusetts Bay and other New England settlements. As God's faithful on a divinely appointed mission—an "errand into the wilderness"[1]—they came to American shores freed from Old World restrictions and contamination. Here, evangelical Pietism could be instituted in full measure. John Winthrop's sermon, "A Modell of Christian Charity," preached aboard the flagship *Arabella*, proclaimed that New England would be like a city on a hill, a model for all the world to see; a new Jerusalem forged in a national covenant with God, a church covenant uniting the regenerate to one another, and a covenant of grace between God and each believer.

The errand into the wilderness begs to be interpreted in the light of Robert Burton's *Anatomy of Melancholy* and his discourse on the human condition. These people in a new land would leave behind the folly of the Old World and institute a "holy commonwealth," eradicating the causes of melancholy and implementing Burton's cultural therapeutic. Here regenerate believers called to God's service would actively build a social order founded upon the true religion, and foster bonds of Christian charity and fraternity among believers. How ironic that the endeavor to remake the world and humankind by instituting a new social order peopled by "new," regenerate men and women who might escape the melancholy bound inextricably with the human condition of depravity, instead resulted in a collective American identity stamped by what John Owen King terms "the iron of melancholy."[2] Burton's cultural therapeutic, when applied in full measure in the American experiment, led to a collective identity and individual temperament marked by melancholy.

The New England Way crystallized the various elements of evangelical Pietism into a theocracy built from God's blueprint and founded upon a congregational church polity that restricted full church membership to the regenerate "visible saints" who had undergone public scrutiny and probation, and had made an open testimony of the workings of God's spirit in their hearts. Conversion proved the key to the covenants with God and the promise that America would become a holy commonwealth set apart as an example for emulation. Through individual acts of conversion, believers entered into the covenant of grace, joining churches as visible saints and thereby enjoying full social and political rights in this theocracy. Bound together in a church covenant, collective discipline, and *caritas*, churches kept their members free from sin and devoted to executing God's will. Church discipline, together with the strict patriarchal discipline of family government and the civil government, promoted orderly relations for saints and the unregenerate alike. In this manner, America could fulfill her destiny as God's chosen land with God's chosen people, in preparation for the millennium.[3]

An alternative interpretation of the motives and meanings of the founding generation likens them to immigrants undergoing the ordeal of uprooting, rejecting the possessive individualism of the nascent capitalist market economy to create a more traditional, family-based communitarian social order. Fleeing the emotional numbness and spiritual malaise of the English Puritan movement in the 1620s, which was deadened by the encroaching utilitarianism of the counting house, New Englanders tried to maintain the fervor of a persecuted minority movement in the absence of a resistant majority.[4]

In *The Puritan Ordeal*, Andrew Delbanco argues that New England's founding immigrants brought distinctly English ideas of covenant, millennialism, and preparationism to American shores and anguished about whether they had deserted England in her time of need. Given the considerable costs of passage and the considerable economic resources of the immigrants, it is obvious that the Puritans did not abandon England because of poverty or for economic opportunity, but for a distinctly religious motivation.[5] Alternating between hope and doubt, they faced the questions of collective identification and announced to themselves and the world that they were truly God's elect, bound together and to the divine by covenant as the new Israelites and builders of the "New Jerusalem." In this cause the obligations of devotional piety would infuse daily life, the demands of preparationism and the necessity for the soul's conversion would lay the foundation for building these Puritan communities.[6]

With so much at stake, conversion involved individual, community, and collective destiny. New Englanders adapted Puritan devotional piety by rationalizing the *ordo salutis* and giving the process of turning one's life to God a distinctly American stamp. Charles Lloyd Cohen's *God's Caress, The Psychology of Puritan Religious Experience,* examines the progressive rationalization of the New England morphology of conversion as it built upon the work of William Perkins and other English divines. In his "emotional ethnography" or "psychological history," Cohen finds that for the first generation, the essence of the New England Way, was an evangelical piety centered on the inner experience of the emotional confrontation with grace offered by the Holy Spirit. In the familiar *ordo salutis* delineated by William Perkins and others, the believer, aided by a prepared heart and the covenant of grace, traveled the spiritual itinerary: first, recognition of original debility and innate depravity, conviction of sin before God's law, terror in the face of divine anger, godly sorrow and humiliation leading to a state of holy desperation and the collapse of self-will and pride. Second, upon acknowledging one's helplessness before God and submitting wholly to Him, the sinner received adoption as a child of God through the intercession of Christ's mercy. Conversion required the turning toward God—the believer experienced rebirth as a restored and renewed person endowed with powers of agency to will, see, reason, and feel as God's servant and tool; sanctified to do God's will. Evangelical piety paradoxically fostered self-reliance in the guise of dependence on God, and self-confidence and agency knowable only through total submission to divine sovereignty.

New England Puritans routinized lifelong self-examination and *automachia*, defending against spiritual deadness and complacency and requiring that saints repeatedly repent, to regain the sense of faith and emotion that characterized their first conversion. Cohen argues that evangelical Pietism promoted a "modal personality"; the believer lived in continual, paradoxical tension between humiliation and confidence, sin and perfection, impotence and power, and despair as the object of God's wrath and joy as the vessel for Christ's mercy and *agape,* or love. He writes:

> . . . as Saints pass through contrition and humiliation to peace, joy and love, they experience coming to power for the first time. Once incorporated and mastered, the repertoire of affections becomes available when the sense of power disappears. In such situations, spiritual deadness or loss of assurance signals that faith is weakening and instigates repentance: Saints review their lives, take note of their sins, and humbly cast themselves upon the Lord. Reaffirming one's weakness solicits recovery of strength, and sense of power returns, its concomitant affections reappear, and godly work resumes.[7]

Through these self-regulating cycles saints grew in grace, strengthened their skills in personal devotion, exercised their agency in God-willed work, and enjoyed the indwelling and infusion of *agape* that washed them in a "peace which passeth all natural understanding."[8]

Charles Hambrick-Stowe argues that these cycles formed the essence of practical piety and were motivated by the anxiety over the state of one's soul. This anxiety informed the daily meditations, prayers, diary keeping, Scripture reading, and periodic fasts and mortifications. Such spiritual exercises required self-emptying to prepare for the renewed experience of infusion by God's grace. For the saint in pilgrimage in this world, daily self-examination invariably revealed sin, declension, and coldness that triggered anxiety. The cycle ended with the feeling of catharsis and the joyful reception of God's love. The writings of Roger Clap, Reverend Thomas Shepard, Samuel Sewall, and Anne Bradstreet speak of an "ecstatic resolution and release of the tension that attended the onset of their devotions. Surprisingly, the words all spontaneously used to express outwardly the fire that burned within came from the poetry of the Song of Songs and the associated bridegroom imagery used by Jesus."[9]

Hambrick-Stowe argues that the mystic aspect of Puritan devotional piety, expressed in images of ravished lovers uniting with Christ, culminated in the seventeenth century in a spirituality pervasive among both divine and laity. Termed "the Puritan contemplative," this religiously organized personality repeatedly went beyond rational asceticism and the search for the assurance of grace to experience the forgiveness of sin in an emotional catharsis: the flood of tears, joy, and comfort attending the immediacy of *agape* in their souls. This contemplative, mystical *unio* and infusion complemented the public, active ascetic who labored diligently in a calling, justified by God's grace, and dedicated to God-willed action and God's glory. Cotton Mather, exemplifies the contemplative as "distinguished from the common practicing believer by the regularity, protractedness, and continuing intensity of the exercises."[10]

After a lifetime alternating between assurance and anxiety, after methodically employing the *auto-machia* of self-examination in his pilgrimage, following habitual daily devotions, public prayer, and a life of active ascetic service as God's instrument, Mather found comfort in mystic-contemplative rapture and ecstasy. The quest for assurance marked the beginning, not the ultimate goal, of spiritual life. For Mather and others who practiced a common piety, "Puritan theology translated into devotional disciplines of repentance for sin and meditation on the glory of heaven, which, over months and years of continual practice, intensified into a higher contemplation of the Divine."[11]

The Puritan contemplative that Hambrick-Stowe encounters successfully balanced the quest for rational assurance with the nonrational infusion of love and mystic *unio*, prevailing through the continual cycles of doubt and consolation. The contemplative never lapsed into a spiritually crippling melancholy or protracted mental alienation. Although the successful contemplative confronted the antinomies of evangelical piety and grew in grace, for others the unrelenting cycles brought on by *auto-machia* produced devastating results.

Sacvan Bercovitch identifies this issue in *The Puritan Origins of the American Self*. The inner journey of the soul in this world was a pilgrimage guided by exemplary models of the faithful, *exemplum fidei*. The burdens of *auto-machia* and the soteriological promises of owning the covenant of grace, the church covenant and the national covenant, overwhelmed many believers:

> The struggle entailed a relentless psychic strain; and in New England, where the theocracy insisted upon it with unusual vigor—where anxiety about election was not only normal but mandatory—hysteria, breakdowns, and suicides were not uncommon. Nonetheless, the Puritans continued with increased energy to regiment selfhood by recourse to the *exemplum fidei*.[12]

American spiritual autobiographies, a new genre of religious and literary expression, emerged in the period from 1630 to 1650. Visible sainthood required a public narrative of the believer's spiritual journey before the assembled congregation, who ascertained the depth and genuineness of the related experience. This was a prerequisite for full admission to church membership.[13] Saints looked to the narratives of others, including the genre of "captivity narratives": stories of believers captured by Indians during the colonial wars, as an *exemplum fidei*.[14]

The written accounts from Thomas Shepard's Cambridge Church (1637–1645) and the published morphologies of conversion of John Cotton, Increase Mather, Edward Taylor, and John Winthrop, among others, reveal a uniquely American pattern.[15] The theme of migration to America, fraught with danger and uncertainty and filled with soteriological significance for individual salvation and national destiny, distinguishes American spiritual narratives from their English counterparts. Where English Pietist accounts are redolent with open, poetic emotion and evangelical fervor, New England conversion, as Patricia Caldwell discovers, was characterized by a prevailing sense of disappointment, inward sadness, bewilderment, spiritual paralysis, and deadness of the heart.[16] Migration and the burdens of their errand into the wilderness filled the first generation with a dreadful sense of their own insufficiency and sin. Caldwell writes that "What is notable in a majority of New England conversion stories is the sense of strain, the meagerness of genuine, fulfilling relief, the contrast between the long, painful tales of struggle and fear, and their endings, so often perfunctory or desperately capped with limp, bland, or hasty resolutions."[17]

These first-generation New Englanders confronted the challenge of expressing their malaise in narrative forms that would communicate the significance of their abiding piety and fervor, their self-conscious awareness of personal insufficiency and sin, and their trepidation at the world-historical significance of their own conversion and the American experiment as God's elect laboring in God's chosen land as the new Israelites. American narratives resolved this problem by means of biblical allegories; believers were called upon personally to interpret their lives and fates as contemporary versions of the Exodus from Egypt going forth into the wilderness to build the New Jerusalem.[18]

The *exemplum fidei* of a distinctively American spiritual autobiography infused each saint's spiritual journey with the broadest biblical and soteriological import. The New England Way reformulated the *ordo salutis* of English Puritanism by making the goal of the pilgrim's progressive spiritual growth, produced in the crucible of self-regulating cycles of *auto-machia*, the formation of the contemplative modal personality. Because of the exacting standards of visible sainthood formalized in the Cambridge Platform of 1648, many migrants failed to measure up and enter the covenants.[19] Many remained trapped in despair, responding to the spiritual example of the soul's anguish in legal terror and godly sorrow, yet unable to proceed in conversion.

By the 1630s, the relentless sermons and appeals by ministers to awaken the slumbering sinners, the call by preparationist doctrine to prepare the heart, had reduced some people to dread, transforming the "broken sinner into a terrified seeker."[20] As Delbanco notes: "New Englanders, it was turning out, were less afflicted by complacence than by anxiety; they were a people locked in fear, which on the one hand was deepened rather than relieved by the preparationists' relentless demand for hewing and hammering the corrupt self, and which, on the other, created conditions for spiritist hysteria."[21]

The "spiritual hysteria" of the Antinomian Crisis of 1637 marked an attempt by prosperous merchants in John Cotton's Boston congregation, led by Anne Hutchinson, to change the protracted and terrible ordeal of conversion. By proclaiming grace flooding the soul in sudden illumination, without the sequential progress of preparationism, antinomians resolved their doubts in an instant by being "ravished" by the Holy Spirit. Now the inner light and the spirit of discernment of the believer supplanted the external authority of the ministry in matters of conversion. God acted and, in a passive state, the believer received the influx of grace. Although the Synod of 1637 convicted Hutchinson of sedition, excommunicated her, and expelled her from the colony and restored the orthodoxy of the New England Way, the crisis demonstrates the extreme psychic burdens of preparationism.

Indeed, many immigrants, disillusioned, returned to England in the 1650s. "The casualties of zeal in New England were not temples of the Antichrist but vulnerable seekers after assurance, people whose expectation of a blinding transformation of the self left every stirring of grace too small. In New England's preparationism—which grew ever more stringent after the defeat of Anne Hutchinson—there was high human cost, and some of the most articulate of those who returned to England said so."[22]

John Owen King terms these psychological burdens, "psychomachia." Here the rationalization of Protestant personality involved, in part, the absolute necessity for the faithful to undergo melancholy and self-alienation. "Melancholy served to demonstrate what no other psychopathological form could: that no person could resist or turn away the evil that God presented at the very edge of conversion."[23]

The Puritan contemplative who found a mature grace in the mystical rapture of *agape* represented the cultural ideal of the healthy Puritan personality. The Puritan melancholic, whose obsessive-compulsive relation with sin led to mental breakdown and suicide, manifested the pathogenic dimension of Puritan personality. Both dimensions, the contemplative and the melancholic, intertwined to form the strands of American evangelical Pietist character and temperament. The melancholy of legal terror and *auto-machia* in warfare against the self were required of every believer who sought to overcome sickness of the soul and find rebirth and rapture as a bride of Christ. Without the preparatory melancholy, the faithful could never know the consolation and joy of the contemplative. Prolonged and excessive melancholy trapped the soul in despair and proved pathogenic, as evidenced by mental breakdowns and suicides.

Philip Greven's *The Protestant Temperament* provides a thorough consideration of the evangelical self in the seventeenth through early nineteenth centuries. In it, he notes a persistent evangelical piety that emerged as a dominant theme and pattern of the American religious experience.[24] Greven locates the formation of evangelical temperament in the religiously informed child-rearing and socialization practices of nuclear, patriarchal households. By methodically breaking the will of toddlers, crushing their sense of self and autonomy and bringing them into habitual obedience and submission to paternal authority and family government, evangelical parents initiated their children into a life of submission and self-denial.

Evangelical parents regarded infants with ambivalence. The child was simultaneously an object of love and of fear—a helpless babe to nurture and a depraved creature or infant fiend. Through the meticulous application of will-breaking and external discipline, evangelical parents campaigned to instill in their children the habits of mind and action of the true Christian: self-denial and humility reflected in simplicity of dress; unthinking, reflexive obedience to parental authority; and self-control in the regimen of a sparing diet and sanctified, godly demeanor and conduct. The internalization of these external regimes of discipline in the continuously active conscience, reflecting and censuring thought, emotions, and conduct, completed the evangelical's early childhood socialization.[25]

Evangelicals were purposely prevented from attaining the developmental goals of basic trust and autonomy and, "for the rest of their lives, they would never be entirely freed from the pangs of guilt and the embarrassments of shame implanted within them during their earliest years."[26] These conflicts reasserted themselves when evangelicals entered youth and early adulthood. At this time in their lives they experienced a growing separation from their parents and parental households, opportunities for self-direction and autonomy, even disobedience towards their parents. The possibility of becoming separate, autonomous adults filled them with feelings of unhappiness and anxiety as they accused themselves of the venalities of pride, self-love, and self-will.[27] Only by conversion and rebirth could they become children again—children of God. To accomplish rebirth, they needed to undergo the requisite warfare against the self, surrendering unconditionally to the absolute sovereignty of God. "Being reborn meant being able, with the help of Divine grace, to have no self-will, and to fulfill the will of God, whatever the consequences for the self or the body."[28]

The discipline of self-denial for the evangelical involved ruthless mortification of the body to conquer the inescapable and sinful flesh, the seat of endless temptations. Greven recounts the excessive fasting, to the point of starvation, practiced by Susanna Anthony during the Great Awakening in 1741. After hearing the revivalist Gilbert Tennent preach, she was filled with self-loathing, leading to mortification.

> It is impossible for the tongue or pen of mortals to describe the agony of my soul; the amazing load that pressed on me. It seemed as though I should

have twisted every bone out of its place . . . though I took only enough to preserve life, yet every mouthful seemed to seal up my condemnation. And therefore I seemed ready to give up, and wholly abstain, rather than endure the distress of mind that every morsel I took filled me with.[29]

In addition to abusive mortifications involving anoretic fasts, evangelicals experienced the "quest for nothingness" of the melancholic persona. Obsessed with suicidal thoughts and inclinations resulting from daily warfare directed against the self, they paid an extreme emotional price for the anger they turned inward.[30] Indeed, the evangelical personality was created out of a deliberate trauma—the parental declaration of war against the willful toddler. Evangelicals spent their lives in a futile attempt to prove themselves worthy of parental love through acts of total submission and obedience. At adulthood, submission to God replaced filial obedience and the need to recover God's love became paramount.

The mystic-contemplative persona directed evangelicals to seek selfless surrender and fusion as brides of Christ and to channel their fulminating anger outward as soldiers of Christ in warfare against the unregenerate. As God's children, soldiers, and brides they found great inner resources to refashion their lives and the world according to divine will, seeking purity and perfection.

Evangelical selves continually alternated between melancholic and contemplative personae, never achieving integration and autonomy; they were always at war with the self and unable to secure a lasting spiritual comfort in divine contemplation. Greven concludes:

> . . . the intensity of their quest for the precise fulfillment of God's law and word, and their unending efforts to repress the self and self-will as thoroughly as possible, made it impossible for evangelicals ever to be truly comfortable with a sense of individual autonomy. Their personalities were too rigid, too defensive, too systematically repressive to enable them to tolerate much liberty for themselves. By leading lives of rigorous purity and precision, they provided themselves with the assurance, stemming from strict compliance to rules set by someone other than themselves, that they were fulfilling the expectations and commands set forth for them by God. Only then could they feel truly free.[31]

The melancholic persona of the evangelical self travelling toward conversion frequently trapped the believer in a pathological condition marked by despair at having committed the unpardonable sin, of sinning beyond the pale of divine mercy, and mortification of the sinful flesh through self-inflicted physical torture, fasting, and anorexia, because the sinner often believed eating compounded one's sin. In the midst of this hopelessness, the sinner, obsessed with suicidal inclinations, at times attempting suicide, longed for death. Here, the protracted despair of religious melancholy crossed the line into religious insanity.

The most striking examples of the psychological consequences of the evangelical Protestant personality's lack of integration, absence of agency and autonomy, and incessant warfare against the self are revealed in Michael

Kenny's study, *The Passion of Ansel Bourne, Multiple Personality in American Culture.* From published reports, diaries, and clinical case histories, Kenny assembles several nineteenth-century cases of multiple personality. These patients were reared in evangelical households, and after lonely and imaginative childhoods, their entry into adulthood foundered in a spiritual crisis of conversion. They could not crush out and smother their worldly, prideful self. They refused to relinquish the nascent powers of agency defined as self-will, evil, and sin. In the white heat of these crucibles of conversion, the self underwent dissociation, splitting into an evangelical personality and a wicked, creaturely personality devoted to worldly concerns. Kenny explains:

> The Protestant soul has considerable schismatic potential—one rich in the symbolism of mental disorder. The self, the theologians reasoned, is to be denied because (it is) tainted by old Adam's sin. Conversion—an essential requirement of the Puritan pietistic tradition—entailed recognition of one's utter worthlessness; again, the autobiographers consistently write of how they were granted a vision of God only in the moment of greatest despair and self-surrender. Paradoxically, the self had to be lost so that it could be found—but some, I think, lost it permanently. . . .[32]

The case best documented with letters, clinical notes, and published, firsthand accounts is that of Mary Reynolds (1784–1854). She was born into an evangelical Baptist family in Birmingham, England. The Reynolds family fled in 1791 as a result of the anti-Jacobin riots and the association of Mary's father, William Reynolds, with these religious controversies. Reynolds and her brother were reunited with their family in 1795 in Lansingburg, New York, where William failed as a grocer. The family removed to the western Pennsylvania frontier and eked out a livelihood in a rude log cabin as a farming household. Her father served as an itinerant lay preacher, and Mary Reynolds grew to young womanhood as the model Christian daughter and woman—imbued with the ethic of female self-sacrifice and devotion. The ordeals of religious persecution, business failure, and the reduced conditions of life in the foothills of the Allegheny Mountains left their mark upon the young woman. Her temperament matched the desolation of her wilderness surroundings.

> Mary's natural disposition tended to be melancholy. Her spirits were low. She never gave herself to mirth, but was uniformly sedate and thoughtful. Was reserved, had no need of company, but on the contrary avoided it— was very fond of reading; and her favorite book was the Bible, to read and meditate on which she was very fond of retiring to some secluded place, where she would not be exposed to interruption. She was much engaged in prayer and devotional exercises and was to all human appearances, deadly pious.[33]

In 1811, at the age of twenty-one, Reynolds suffered the first of a recurring series of "fits," where she fell into an unconscious state resembling the "falling down" seizures that marked the western New Light revivals of this time. After several hours in this state, she awoke to a state of hysterical blindness and deafness. These fits were interludes in the torturous difficulties she experienced during conversion. She condemned herself as the greatest of sinners, deserving of terrible sufferings. The second self that emerged from this *automachia* was the worldly mirror-image of her previous evangelical persona— "a pagan daughter of nature," a free spirit, writing lyrical and romantic poetry filled with sentimentalism about nature.

> In her natural state, she was quite destitute of the imaginative faculty; in her abnormal state, or second state, her imagination was remarkably active & discovered itself, among other ways, in a disposition to write poetry, in writing which, though her poetical effusions were not of a high order, she was very ready. . . . In her natural state she was quiet, sedate, sober minded tending to melancholy; in her abnormal she was cheerful, even immoderately gay and frolicsome in spirit, fond of fun & practical jokes, ardent in her friendships, strong in her dislikes, extravagantly fond of society.[34]

The new Reynolds rejected all parental, medical, and religious discipline. Kenny did not identify the causes of Mary Reynold's multiple personalities or those of Ansel Bourne and the other cases that he reviewed. He did, however, uncover a pathological disorder of dissociated, multiple personality directly linked with one possible resolution to the agonistic existential crises and struggles of the evangelical temperament. Religious melancholy in America was inextricably tied to the *ordo salutis* of first conversion and later spiritual growth that could result in pathological outcomes for each believer. But the works of Kenny, King, Bercovitch, and others suggest that religious melancholy was central to an emerging American national identity and character. Religious melancholy would leave its stamp on our collective identity in the great religious awakenings of New England in the eighteenth and nineteenth centuries. ·

Cotton Mather

Cotton Mather published *Magnalia Christi Americana* in 1700 as the first distinctly "American" historical narrative of New England delineating the special providences that God manifested toward the New England colonies bound in covenant to their deity. Mather provided a bridge across two centuries, relating the aspirations for a holy commonwealth of the Puritan movement in sixteenth-century England to the elaboration of the seventeenth-century "New England Way" of theocracy, congregationalism, and the "visible sainthood" of God's elect. He mastered the rhetoric of the jeremiad, excoriating the populace for their perceived decline of vital piety as measured against the accomplishments of New England's founders, and introduced an evangelical Pietist theology that would support the work of Jonathan Edwards and the innovations of the First and Second Great Awakenings.[35] These innovations introduced collective seasons of spiritual renewal, the cultural transformation of the "American Zion" through the agency of voluntarism and voluntary societies, ecumenical unity among denominational diversity, and the sublime ideal of the conversion of humanity and the world.[36]

Mather's observations on the nature and treatment of melancholy synthesized the extensive body of English pastoral theology and the work of
Burton's *Anatomy of Melancholy*. Yet, Mather applied these sources to a distinctly American milieu and endeavored to understand the surprising and vexatious prevalence of religious melancholy among the first generation of New
Englanders he extolled for their experiential religion. Paradoxically, those who
achieved the highest aspirations of piety and religious vocation succumbed to
the depths of despair. In recording the biographies and recounting the leadership of the founding divines of the first generation in the first volume of
Magnalia, Mather discovered that with perplexing frequency these distinguished pastors languished in religious melancholy. Notables such as Nathaniel
Rogers, Richard Mather, Nathaniel Mather, John Warham, and William
Thompson suffered prolonged despair, many of them going to their death-
beds without the assurance of grace.[37] These exemplaries among the pious
had undergone the arduous task of many years of repentance and humiliation in preparation for conversion. Their outward conduct had passed the careful scrutiny of fellow religionists, and their inner experiences were thoroughly
sifted and analyzed to discover the growth of faith and grace. They made
public testimony of their conversion as visible saints prior to admission to
the church covenant as one of God's elect; they then proceeded through a
time of probation before ordination in the ministry. How strange that churched
and godly men, devoted in their calling and hearts as instruments of the divine
will, found themselves bereft of spiritual comfort, the assurance of grace. How
strange that melancholy struck men who outwardly led exemplary lives and
apparently had little cause to doubt their adoption as children of God. How
troubling that the spiritual leaders and champions of the New England Way,
who assumed the burdens of teaching, guiding, and reassuring the faithful and
assisting them in the difficult pilgrimage towards conversion, were immobilized by spiritual desolation. Mather writes about Reverend Nathaniel Rogers
that "Whence even after he had been a *preacher* of some standing, he had
sometimes very sore despondencies and objections in his own soul, about the
evidences of his own *regeneration*; he would conclude that no *grace* of God
had ever been wrought in him."[38]

Mather considered religious melancholy as a prevailing, endemic affliction among New Englanders. Both divine and laity felt the all-too-common
travail of despair.

> *New-England,* a country where *splenic* maladies are prevailing and perni-
> cious, perhaps above any other, hath afforded numberless instances of even
> *pious people,* who have contracted those *melancholy indispositions,* which
> have unhinged them from all service or comfort; yet not a few persons
> have been hurried thereby to lay violent hands upon themselves at the last.[39]

Mather was not alone in this belief. Church records and diarists noted
cases of melancholy. In his diary, John Winthrop recorded acquaintances
suffering religious melancholy who attempted suicide. Many knew of the self-

inflicted death of Abraham Warner of Hartford. As David Hall suggests, the laity remained fascinated with publicized accounts of despair. "The circulation of these stories may also mean that despair was not something distant, something no one could imagine as occurring to himself. . . . faith was never safe from doubt."[40]

What was religious melancholy? What caused this spiritual sickness unto death? What pastoral and medical care could prevent or alleviate this malady? Mather first addressed these concerns in "The Case of a Troubled Mind," a sermon published in 1717.[41] He defined religious melancholy by two distinguishing complaints: first, God withdrew his countenance, leaving the afflicted bereft of the subjective comfort of God' quickening influence, the infusion of the Holy Spirit, and the assurance of the pardon of sin. Mather termed this complaint the "darkness of a troubled soul." When plunged in this darkness, acts of devotional piety became empty formalities. The sufferer stood immobilized by the terrible prospect of damnation and eternal judgment. Second, the carnal, natural man manifested enmity and rebellion against God and experienced terror before the prospect of God as an enemy.

Like Burton, Mather defined religious melancholy as the existential condition of mankind after the fall and expulsion from Eden. Most people slumbered in this state of sin and depravity by immersing themselves in the vanity fair of worldliness. Blind to their true condition of depravity and unconcerned about the prospect of eternal judgment, individuals devoted their lives to the pursuit of folly in search of pride, honor, material gain, secular knowledge, and/or hedonistic pleasures. When slumbering sinners awakened and felt the darkness of mind and terror as the enemy of God, they perceived their lives and plight as melancholy: hopeless, unloved, vile, and unworthy. Although humoral imbalances of black bile or "splenic" problems might contribute to melancholy, as might temporal troubles and vexations, Mather viewed religious melancholy as a distinctly spiritual sickness caused by sin and inextricably bound to the conditions of humanity in a fallen world. Conversion remained the only cure for this spiritual sickness.

Mather directed melancholiacs to reconcile themselves to God, ask for the assistance of Christ, and proceed again and again through the spiritual itinerary of conversion, repeating these exercises until spiritual consolation stayed. Mather's chapter, *"De Trisibus,"* from *The Angel of Bethesda,* written ten years later as a pastoral and medical guide (but not published until the twentieth century), outlines this itinerary:

> . . . All Possible and Exquisite Care must now be taken, to carry the *Troubled Sinner* through a *Process of Repentance;* And after a due Confession of his Guilt, and Impotency and Unworthiness, *Lead him to the Rock*: Show him a Glorious CHRIST, *Able to Save unto the Uttermost,* and *Willing to Cast out none that Come to Him.* . . . *Comfort him, comfort him, speak thou comfortably to him. Tell him* what the *very great and precious Promises* in the *Covenant of Grace* do now assure him of; inculcate upon him, the *Consolations of God.*[42]

Mather understood that Satan often had a hand in the melancholy of the faithful. The devil possessed and controlled the souls of melancholiacs, tempting them to reject God, tormenting them with obsessional and blasphemous thoughts, and leading them to suicide. Of diabolical possession in melancholy Mather writes:

> The *Diabolical Impression* appears very Sensible, Either when Thoughts full of *Atheism* or *Blasphemy* are shott like *Fiery Darts* into their Minds, and so seriously infest them, that they are even *Weary of their Lives*; or, when their Minds are violently impelled and hurried on to Self-Murder, by *starving,* or *Strangling,* or *Stabbing* and the like.[43]

The omnipresence of evil within the hearts of believers and the world reflected Mather's near obsession with the workings of the "invisible world"— a hidden domain populated by devils, spirit forces, witches, and angels, containing wondrous events as portents of God's providence and including personal angels that appeared to Mather as a seal of the "special providence" of God that his private prayers would be answered. Mather attempted to discover the laws of the invisible world in order to arm believers in their Christian warfare with Satan. He urged those afflicted with satanic temptations to resist with fasting and prayer and to remain steadfast in their battle: "During this *time,* the Devil may grow more furious upon us, the more we do *resist* him. We must *resist* until the *time* which is *prefixt* by God, but *unknown* to us, is expired. . . ."[44] Only then would the devil retreat in temporary defeat.

Reverend Benjamin Colman shared Mather's concern with satanic temptations and vexations that afflicted God's elect. In May of 1711 Colman delivered a sermon called "The Case of Satan's Fiery Darts in Blasphemous Suggestions and Hellish Annoyances," which was published three decades later in 1743 during the First Great Awakening. Likening the religious melancholiac to Job, Colman argues that God's chosen frequently are tempted by Satan to curse God for their sufferings, blaspheme, and renounce their faith. In the explanation of the diabolical causes of religious melancholy, Colman adopts the archaic psychology of Satan shooting fiery darts into the minds of saints, seeking to turn them against the Holy Ghost. "*Satan* sees the natural Profaneness, *Atheism,* and Infidelity of our evil Heart; that there are the *Seeds* of all Impurity, Blasphemy and Melancholy in us, he makes his Advantage of this *natural* Propensity in us, and while he watches to *inflame* the Soul from within itself. . . ."[45] God permits this battle within the souls of believers as a trial of faith, as a purifying experience. This battle pleases God when the afflicted emulate Job's fortitude, resist temptations, refuse to curse God, and persevere until the victory over Satan has been won. Colman offers the following pastoral guidance: read the word of God, hear God's word preached, engage in prayer, both private petitionary and public ejaculatory, beware of solitude and idleness, seek the consolation of friends and a minister, ignore molesting thoughts, and in daily devotional piety reaffirm your humiliation to God. Above all else, avoid despair. "Let such *troubled souls* consider, that these Annoyances from the *Enemy* and the *Avenger* are much rather the hopeful *Symptoms of Grace ruing* in them, than a *graceless State* or the Rule of Sin. . . ."[46]

The only cure or defense against religious melancholy and demonic influence was the assurance of grace, the status of election or adoption as a child of God (*certitudo salutis*), and the ascetical sanctification of a life devoted to God's purposes. Yet, paradoxically, the structure of Puritan and Pietist theology made conversion a lengthy, difficult, and uncertain task available only to a minority, a religious aristocracy. Less than half of New England's people ever came forward to testify as visible saints in the seventeenth century, and this led in 1648 to the innovation of the Half-Way Covenant, which permitted church affiliation for unregenerate believers.[47] Even the converted and pious, as we have seen in Mather's writings, suffered renewed religious melancholy, or troubled minds. God's elect could never achieve the position of perfectionism in the final victory over sin. Through faith and grace their hearts were renewed, but they remained ever trapped in a body prone to sins of the flesh, as symbolized by the image of the carnal mind. God's elect lived in a world redolent with sin and thus needed to remain ever alert as Christian soldiers, in tension with the secular orders of experience to fulfill their vocation as instruments of divine will. With the ubiquity of sin and temptations in their lives, and called upon to practice self-examination to uncover fresh evidence of their sinfulness, the faithful periodically came to doubt their assurance of salvation. They stood self-indicted before God as deceitful hypocrites in the agony of spiritual desolation.

Richard Lovelace examines the theology that induced this spiritual illness of religious melancholy. Known as *tenatio praedestinationis*, this condition caused the faithful to despair of their own salvation. It was reminiscent of the transcendental God of Calvinism who predestined the salvation of some and the damnation of others. God need not accept repentant souls. Mather adopted a Christocentric theology, urging the intercession of Christ's mercy for the humbled sinner. However, this distinctly Lutheran concept proved insufficient for the awful logic of strict Calvinism.[48] The central questions remained: "How could I know if God did indeed accept my repentance? What evidence of assurance could I accept? How could I find certainty of my status of election?"

Seventeenth-century New Englanders relied upon the prodigious literature of Anglo-Puritan pastoral theology as normative guides to chart their *ordo salutis*. The work of William Ames, Perkins, Baxter, Shepard, and Cotton, to mention a few divines, carefully charted the stages of a soul's passage, or "morphology of conversion," to visible sainthood. (These issues will receive more extensive treatment in the next chapter.) The believers who shaped life as a spiritual pilgrimage, seeking the inner psychological and subjective grounds of assurance, used these pastoral guides as road maps to assist them in their journey. Nevertheless, the theology of faith trapped each pilgrim on the horns of a dilemma. On the one hand, the faithful could not receive assurance through the direct and sudden spiritual illumination in the receipt of God's *pneuma*. The antinomian resolution championed by John Cotton and Anne

Hutchinson provided for the sudden, rapturous illumination of the soul by the Spirit, offering direct assurance of election. The "faire and easie way to Heaven," or easy grace of *syllogismus mysticus,* did not survive the Antinomian Crisis of 1637 and remained suspect in Puritan and Pietist doctrine. On the other hand, the Arminian resolution (*syllogismus practicus)* of seeking the indirect assurance of grace through the good works and deeds of the faithful was not permitted.[49] Salvation, by faith alone provided the only avenue of conversion. The perplexing question of how to ascertain certain evidence of the work of faith in one's heart and life had no elegant solution.

The New England Way to assurance prevented both a one-sided reliance upon the direct and sudden infusion of grace of antinomianism and a one-sided reliance upon the Arminian indirect imputation of grace through a progression of good works. Somehow, each candidate for conversion needed to mediate between these two positions, searching for the subjective grounds of faith and assurance. Mather urged the continued, repetitive cycle of the prepared heart, which undergoes repentance, humiliation, and confession of guilt; admission of human inability to save oneself in the face of absolute divine sovereignty; and abandons oneself to a merciful Christ and mightily attempts to believe, in secure faith, the promises of the covenant of grace. Only following years of preparation, laboring through these cycles again and again, did the seeker experience the "confirming 'seal' of the Holy Spirit's operation in assurance."[50] This quest for the inner psychological grounds for assurance placed enormous anxiety upon each candidate that pastoral theology, covenant theology, and casuistry did little to alleviate. For salvation could occur by faith alone and only the solitary individual could plumb the recesses of the soul to discover the purely subjective grounds for the evidence of faith in his or her heart. As Lovelace concludes, this theology of conversion demanded that the process where

> . . . we should examine ourselves to determine whether we are in faith had somehow overshot the mark and wandered into a dangerous climate where spiritual sickness was inevitable, where the majority of those in the congregation were numbed and fearful bystanders while a few of a more volatile temperament were able to achieve a fitful stability of assurance.[51]

Mather's own conversion experience exemplifies these issues. Beginning at age fourteen with his undergraduate studies at Harvard College, and lasting through his probation and ordination as a minister in his mid-twenties, he made the painful and uncertain passage to conversion. At the onset of his spiritual crisis, Mather imposed a regime of severe fasts, prayer vigils, and seasons of self-mortification as he reflected upon his sin. He adopted private obsessional rituals of fasting and prayer as techniques to alleviate feelings of guilt and purified himself to receive the ravishing irradiations of the Holy Spirit and assurance of divine love.

Mather's self-analysis provides an example par excellence of Freud's concept of the "neurotic ceremonial." In his 1907 "Obsessive Actions and Religious Practices," Freud observed the elaborate, repetitive actions of personal rituals that protected the individual from feelings of sin, defilement, or guilt, and aided in the repression of sexual or aggressive instinctual impulses.[52] Unlike Freud's neurotic patients, who found themselves imprisoned in obsessive-compulsive rituals, consumed by guilt yet unconscious of the psychoanalytic sources of their torment, Mather directly connected his guilt with the incomplete repression of the carnal mind and sinful nature. Acts of devotional piety in fasting, meditation, and humiliation helped purify the sinner and prepare the heart for the work of God's grace in the remission of sin and guilt. Calvinist and Protestant Pietism fit Freud's apt description of "religion as a universal obsessional neurosis" that demanded neurotic ceremonials of believers and defined them in a religious vocabulary of the *ordo salutis.*

Mather's neurotic ceremonials, like those of many other religionists, assumed extreme proportions. He fasted until near death. He suffered the symptoms of a "hectic" or extreme emaciation. In the seventeenth century, the term *hectic* referred to a bodily condition or habit symptomatic of consumption or other wasting febrile diseases.[53] However, he did not starve himself to death but continued his course of self-examination, criticism, and abasement. He determined to pursue a life of usefulness and sanctified purpose. Mather suffered repeated episodes of melancholy when God withdrew his countenance, and the crushing awareness of sin filled him with self-loathing. Yet, to Mather these cycles signified the authenticity of his progression towards conversion. As we have noted, the cycles that Mather repeated in this ten-year quest for conversion began with the melancholy trouble of mind marked by the sinner who had grieved the Spirit. Next, the troubled pilgrim imposed private rituals of humiliation and repentance—fasting, prayer, meditation—reflecting upon the utter inability of man and the sovereignty of God. Thus, the pilgrim perceived melancholy as invaluable in the protracted preparatory process leading to conversion. Pastoral theology valued and "induced" these cycles of melancholy by conceptualizing melancholy as central to the culturally approved and desired spiritual itinerary of conversion. The psychodynamics of this experience meant that each believer willingly embraced or induced feelings of dependence, powerlessness, helplessness, worthlessness, and hopelessness.[54]

Even after the initial conversion, melancholy played an important role in the continued, lifelong spiritual growth demanded of the saint. The conversion experience planted a seed of faith that required vigilant nurture, protection from sin, and sanctified purpose. In this manner, the quest for assurance and the evidence of maturing faith and grace only began at conversion and continued in the art of shaping a life as an instrument of God's will, dedicated to his glory. The Puritan saint was not equivalent to the forgiven Catholic sinner, pardoned but expected to sin again. The saint was a "spiritual athlete," a religious virtuoso, a religious hero called to personality in Weber's sense.[55] Recurring episodes of religiously induced melancholy formed a central part of this religiously grounded personality.

Ideally, each cycle of religious melancholy should culminate in the unutterable, evanescent rapture as God's Spirit possessed one's heart. The joyful receipt of God's love, of "God's caress,"[56] was the inner-worldly, mystical "emotional payoff" that offered assurance of the remission of sin, of faith, and the possession of grace. During his early twenties, following his initial conversion experience, Mather recorded in his diary numerous cycles of melancholy and rapture. And with each cycle, his faith matured.

Writing on September 3, 1681, Mather relates the ecstasy of God's caress.

> *Oh! I feel! I feel! I love the Lord Jesus Christ; I love Him dearly, I love Him greatly, yea I love Him above all. And what? Will God love mee, and will my Lord come to dwell with mee? Oh! Joy unspeakable and full of glory!*[57]

Without the seasons of melancholy, the moments of God's caress were not possible. Inescapably, the religiously grounded personality of Puritans valued, expected, and induced repeated episodes of melancholy throughout the life span. This constituted the "work" of Puritan culture in shaping, structuring, and engendering modalities of experience and expression for believers. In this symbolic work, the vocabulary of faith and melancholy informed each person's experience of sickness, ill-fortune and adversity, and grieving. Melancholy transmuted the faithful's feelings of anxiety, anger, and sadness into a self-directed indictment of God's special providence and chastisement for the sins of each saint. Because of the believer's continued sinfulness, God brought adversity and suffering as a warning to the believer to repent and begin anew the itinerary of melancholy to rapture. In this manner, melancholy was the prescribed spiritual exercise needed to assist the saint's maturation of faith. Each season of religious melancholy brought anew feelings of depression—hopelessness, worthlessness, and powerlessness. Each religious melancholy required rituals of humiliation and purification—private fasting, prayer, and meditation. And each religious melancholy brought the danger that the culturally desired outcome of the return of God's love and the strengthening of faith would not eventuate. It was equally possible that the saint could fast until inanition and starvation in a self-destructive evangelical anorexia nervosa. Religious melancholiacs could reject the comforting covenant of grace and remain trapped in hopelessness, convinced that they had committed the unpardonable sin and had grieved the Holy Spirit. Religious melancholy could result in despair and suicide.

Although we have focused upon the example of Cotton Mather as a model of seventeenth-century religious personhood and commitment, a diversity in the depth of religious commitment of Puritans and Protestants existed in Mather's time. In seventeenth-century New England only a minority approached Cotton Mather's fervor as "an apotheosis of Puritan practical theology."[58] Most of the laity limited their commitment to piety as "horse-shed-Christians" who used times of intermission in Sabbath worship to conduct secular business while attending their horses.[59]

Protestant doctrines of conversion also reflect a broad diversity across times and places. As Lovelace argues, the introduction of covenant theology and liberalized antinomian and Arminian tenets during the evangelicalism of eighteenth- and nineteenth-century America lessened the terrifying consequences of a "hyper-Calvinistic" *tenatio praedestinationis*. However, even this lessening of terror did not significantly curb the psychopathological consequences of evangelical temperament. Wherever evangelicals instituted forms of evangelical nurture allied with the ideals of achieving a religiously grounded personality and the inner-worldly experience of the Puritan contemplative, religious melancholy would brand the faithful as they descended into the slough of despair, bereft of God's love.

Evangelical Nurture

At great personal cost, evangelical Pietists achieved the realization of a religiously-grounded personality forged in the lifelong crucible of *auto-machia*. Each believer embraced methodical self-examination and evangelical humiliation in the quest for transcendence of the self—the vile, prideful, worldly, sinful natural creature that was responsible for the separation from God and prevented the infusion of divine love. Evangelicals remained haunted by their alienation from God, never able to find a permanent and abiding assurance of adoption as a child of God. The pathological consequences for adults included poorly integrated personalities, extremes of intrapsychic conflict, melancholy at the loss of the divine love object, and in extreme form, multiple or dissociative personalities. How did evangelical child-rearing elaborate a system of beliefs, traditions, and practices that were inherently abusive to children? In the cause of the highest good—the salvation of a child's soul—evangelicals methodically injured their children's psyches.

Evangelical Pietists' character was the product of religiously informed techniques of child-rearing.[60] Parents felt duty-bound to shape their children's character in godly directions. From the sixteenth through early nineteenth centuries, evangelicals reared children according to consistent guidelines. Infants and toddlers up to the age of two were to receive tender love and solicitude from their mothers, servants, or wet nurses. However, on two-year-olds, parents imposed rigid rules and discipline purposely designed to crush their wills and emerging autonomies. Through corporal punishment and, equally important, the withdrawal of parental love, the child experienced ontological shame. Parents taught the child that failure to conform to the rules of appropriate behavior in the household violated God's commandment of honor and obedience to one's parents. "The earthly parent assumed the cloak of the heavenly Father; an imagined transgression against the parent was transformed into a sin against God. The message the child received was that God and parents were indistinguishable, to be approached with the same fear and trembling . . ."[61]

Autonomy—the power of agency of the self capable of independent and purposeful conduct and the exercise of the will—was impaired by the pervasive authoritarian discipline of the earthly and heavenly fathers. The result was a propensity for *auto-machia* and *anfechtung* among evangelicals who felt guilty, sinful, and vile when they acted with autonomy. One who engaged in autonomous conduct risked the loss of parental and godly love.

Paradoxically, God afflicted his children with special punishments as admonishments to repent. Parents also equated punishment with love. The evangelical personality never developed the capacity for self-assertion and autonomous action but lived a repetitive cycle of *auto-machia* haunted by ontological guilt and shame, and by obsessive rituals designed to purify sin and regain the love of God. As Seymour Byman argues in "Child Raising and Melancholia in Tudor England," the melancholic

> blames himself if affection is not forthcoming. He is guilty. He has not lived up to expectations. Because he equates punishment with love, he actively seeks chastisement, thus developing strong masochistic tendencies. Sadistic impulses are suppressed which in turn promotes feelings of guilt, unworthiness, and a strong need for expiation. The stronger his rebellious feelings, the more the need for atonement. The life of the melancholic sufferer is characterized by a search for a dominant figure who will grant the love and redemption denied by depriving parents. In a religiously oriented society, the figure frequently assumes otherworldly forms.[62]

From the earliest childhood, the will was equated with sin and disobedience. The will must be broken so the child could obey parents and God without opposition. Adult evangelicals were immobilized when confronting the burden of choice or casuistry—the application of an ethical principle to a concrete situation. Which course of action did God will? Was their conduct selfish, carnal, and sinful? What then must they do? The evangelical Pietist's character produced a haunted, guilt-ridden person capable of only limited semi-autonomy. In the blink of an eye, the saint could misstep or lapse in a moment of rebellion. Panic at the loss of God's love ensued, prompting an episode of religious melancholia. Only the repetitive use of rituals of humiliation and mortification to deny the self and seek divine direction and love could protect believers from these panic experiences or heal the melancholic, scrupulous conscience.

The theology of assurance that enjoined the evangelical Pietist to embrace a life-order of inner-worldly asceticism, combined with the contemplative-mystical quest for the rapture of God's love, were congruent with the religiously grounded personality of the evangelical. Evangelical child-rearing intentionally produced persons forever beset by the loss of a primordial love object. Such tormented souls identified with the harsh parent who had inflicted physical and psychic regimens upon them as young children. During early childhood, they had introjected the imago of a parental (and later a) divine monitor and carried into adulthood a punitive internal censor, an intrapsychic compulsion to inflict repeated humiliations.

In *Spare the Child*, Philip Greven has argued that religious melancholy has long been associated with Calvinist and evangelical Protestant religious tradition.

Melancholy and depression have been persistent themes in the family history, religious experience, and emotional lives of Puritans, evangelicals, fundamentalists and Pentecostals for centuries. Assaults on the self and on self-will are the central obsession of vast numbers of men and women from the early seventeenth century to the present.[63]

Contemporary social science would charge that in past times evangelicals were guilty of orchestrating the "soul murder" of their children. Leonard Shengold defines soul murder as a complex, multifaceted process, at times involving one or more form of injury, including sexual abuse, emotional deprivation, corporal punishment, and physical and mental punishments. Soul murder is "the deliberate attempt to eradicate or compromise the separate identity of another person."[64]

Without intending to injure children, acting in the interests of the most elevated spiritual ideals of discipline, and guided by long tradition and religious mandate, parents have attempted to thwart the emergence of autonomous identity by crushing the child's will. When parents systematically impede what we view today as the natural development of a child's ego and autonomous personality, making the child an object designated for the fulfillment of parental needs or purposes, they commit soul murder. Evangelical parents wanted to crush the emerging wills and identities of their children and replace the "natural" creature with a religiously grounded persona organized according to principles of abject obedience to parental and divine mandate and self-loathing defined as "humility." With strict, unyielding regimes of discipline, physical punishment, whippings, beatings, confinements in dark closets, and interrogations, parents went about their task. Children identified parental cruelty as the expression of love, introjecting the pain, humiliation, and suffering imposed upon them as the means to win the unattainable—the inner assurance of "unconditional" parental love and later, "love to God," or the holy affections so cherished by evangelicals.

As adults, evangelical personalities would undergo repetition compulsions, obsessively re-enacting the lessons internalized from foundational cruelty episodes: seek the recovery of God's love, the inward assurance as a child of God. Find God's love through self-initiated humiliation where one despises the prideful, worldly, sinful self. Abhor oneself, and in self-examination rediscover self-loathing as the way to repose in Jesus. Yet, for the heroes of evangelical divinity, the Puritan contemplatives of seventeenth-century New England such as Cotton Mather, Michael Wigglesworth, and Samuel Sewall, religious melancholy, not rapture, colored their lives.

Evangelical child-rearing relied upon what Alice Miller has defined as a toxic pedagogy, or religious belief regarding the concupiscence and wickedness of children. Poisonous beliefs defined the child by nature as a willful tyrant, a small criminal driven by angry, hostile, aggressive inclinations, and a sinful being. Only with proper discipline, methodically administered to eradicate the natural child, could parents suppress the emerging identity and replace it with one more pleasing to God.[65] Children learned to repress their innermost feelings and to achieve self-alienation. Miller presents the case history of the German artist Käthe Kollwitz, born to evangelical parents in Königsberg in 1867 and reared under the sectarian discipline of the Free Religious Congregation. Haunted by guilt, lifelong melancholy, and an obsession with death, Kollwitz was "forbidden to express her true feelings, observations, and thoughts because only good, kind thoughts that are pleasing to God are permitted, then everything that has no place in this 'good' world is relegated to the realm of death."[66]

How could parents impose physical punishment and harsh regimens of discipline upon their children, self-assured of the correctness and ethicality of their conduct? Greven explores the biblical and theological rationales that justified the eradication of a child's autonomy and the suppression of a child's needs and feelings. Protestants borrowed from the long Christian tradition of justifying the physical beatings, whippings, and other disciplining of children by reference to the Old Testament prescriptions in Proverbs, 1 and 2 Samuel, and Deuteronomy. The injunction from Proverbs, "He that spareth his rod hateth his son; But he that loveth him chasteneth him betimes" (13:24) [67] captures the spirit of the aphorism of cruelty: "Spare the rod, spoil the child." In their concern for the salvation their children, parents labored to instill in them the fear of God and dread of divine punishment. The cultural logic of practical piety, soteriology, and Protestant personality coalesced in the understanding that obedience to God was motivated by a love born of fear and the conscious and unconscious memory of pain and cruelty inflicted on children at the hands of their concerned parents.[68]

Philip Greven's most recent writings have investigated the dolorous legacy of evangelical child-rearing and corporal punishment from the Reformation through twentieth-century New Evangelicalism, Pentecostalism, and fundamentalism in America. The leitmotif of the childhood experience of physical cruelty, both unconscious memories of infant abuse and conscious memories of later childhood punishment, characterize evangelical Protestants over the course of four centuries. Guided by scriptural, theological, and traditional rationales, evangelical parents handed down, from generation to generation, a seemingly unbroken chain of regimens for children that continues unabated in contemporary America. Most telling is Greven's discussion of the adult consequences of this system of Christian nurture. A partial catalog would include religious melancholy, dissociative disorders, sadomasochism, obsessive-compulsive syndromes, anxiety disorders, authoritarianism, and domestic violence.

Greven provides a detailed case history in his interpretation of the life and work of Michael Wigglesworth (1632–1704), demonstrating how his apocalyptic poetry was inextricably tied to childhood cruelty.

> What emerges most clearly from an examination of his life and writings is his obsession with affliction, pain, suffering, and punishment. No one knows for certain whether or not Michael Wigglesworth was ever struck physically and suffered the pains of corporal punishment as a child. . . . Pain and punishment and afflictions, which are always experienced as forms of chastisement, are the central themes of Michael Wigglesworth's poetry and

life. Corporal punishment is the experiential core of his entire theology, fundamental to an understanding of his character and thought.[69]

In 1662 Wigglesworth published two poems, written in the voice of the prophet of doom, depicting God's apocalyptic judgment brought forth against the people of New England. *Day of Doom* and *God's Controversy With New-England* sold well and made Wigglesworth renowned among New Englanders, who demonstrated their receptivity to the warnings of the jeremiad. At the time of these writings, Wigglesworth suffered chronic melancholy and invalidism, and proved unable to preach and attend to his ministerial duties in his parish in Malden, Massachusetts. Living in self-imposed captivity and spiritual desolation, he produced striking depictions of the "necessary" sufferings of God's children at the hands of a chastising Father. In Greven's interpretation, "Suffering, for Michael Wigglesworth, is an inescapable part of being a true child of God."[70] This suffering might include the special providences that God visits upon the saints, but also the necessity of using the rod of physical discipline to turn sinful children toward God. In *Day of Doom*, saints at the judgment day discover that they are:

> all Christ's afflicted ones;
> Who being chastised, neither despised
> nor sank amidst their groans:
> Who by the Rod were turn'd to God,
> and loved him the more,
> Not murmuring nor quarreling
> When they were chast'ned sore.[71]

Greven explains that meditation 9, "The Carriage of a Child of God Under his Father's Smarting Rod," from *Meat Out of the Eater*, needs to be seen as an ode to flagellation told from the alternating voice of the punishing adult and the hurting child.[72] This meditation reaffirms the majesty of God and the promises of salvation for the believer smitten by afflictions and chastisements. Stanza 3 defines the outward punishing blows of an adult whipping a child as the means of gaining true repentance.

> If greater be the Blow
> It doth not him dismay:
> Because he knows a Father's hand
> Such stripes may on him lay.
> But he prepares himself
> Betimes to meet the Lord
> By true Repentance, as he hath
> Commanded in his word.[73]

The meditation continues by reaffirming the way of salvation through faith, by repentance of sin, and by the cleansing blood of Christ that shall "cure a guilty-sick Soul, / When 'tis improv'ed by Faith."[74] Stanzas 7–10 introduce the themes of the exercise of evangelical humiliation, as an *inward* source of punishment that proffers true repentance and the recovery of God's love. To be a child of God requires the repetition of internalized self-abnegation, self-loathing, and self-imposed psychic and physical austerities. The image of the invalid, melancholy, isolated widower, confined to his parsonage in Malden, provides a telling depiction of the enormous personal costs paid by one such child of God. In stanza 9, Wigglesworth writes:

> Himself he humbleth under
> The mighty hand of God:
> And for the sake of that sweet hand
> Doth kiss the sharpest Rod.
> He taketh up his Cross,
> Denieth his own will,
> Advanceth God's above his own
> And yielded to him still.[75]

Michael Wigglesworth's diary (1653–1657) records an earlier period in his life, just before the massively disabling breakdown in Malden. He had finished his education at Harvard, stayed on as a tutor at the college, and begun his first preaching as a minister. In these diaries, Wigglesworth confronts the issues of sexual desire, marriage, entry into his ministerial vocation, and the passage to adult autonomy. Not surprisingly, he collapsed in the course of making adult transitions. Evangelical temperament trapped the believer in a psychological conflict—a stasis of semi-autonomy.

Wigglesworth's spiritual diaries record an unending seige, an *auto-machia* against the self. The daily exercise of practical devotion—self-examination, Scripture reading, private prayer and meditation—invariably revealed a catalog of sins to this anxious young man. He found pride, mirth, sloth and backsliding, carnal desires, and the pollutions of nocturnal emission and erotic dreams. He condemned his heart for "whorish" outgoings of spirit after worldly things. And his heart grew cold, languishing in the hypocrisy of outwardly holy acts but inwardly vile motives. Again and again he exclaimed, "I loath my self," "I condemn myself" in the litany of evangelical humiliation and self-abnegation that augured future spiritual quickening according to Puritan practical theology.[76] He wonders if there is no balm of Gilead for this soul sickness.

> Behold I am vile, when thou showest me my face I abhor my self. who can bring a clean thing out of filthiness, I was conceived bred brought up in sin. O redeem from these devouring Lyons the hopeless shiftless soul that thou has purchased.! I deserv to be the stepping-stone of thy wrath why behold I lay my self at the foot of mercy as low as thou wouldst have me, confessing my self the cheeif of sinners. Lord what wouldst thou haue me doe? shew me thy wil, and bow my heart to obey it, and I haue what I do desire.[77]

The spiritual exercises of evangelical humiliation intermittently brought brief interludes of assurance of God's love. He infrequently enjoyed the evanescent Puritan contemplative ideal of a comforting repose in Christ. In the course of seemingly unending accounts of sin, guilt, shame, repentance, and inward agony, Wigglesworth would punctuate his journal with a momentary respite, such as the entry in March 1653:

> On thursday morning the Lord was pleas'd to give me somewhat a heart-breaking meditation of him. so that I thought and will the Lord now again return and embrace me in the arms of his dearest love? wil he fall upon my neck and kiss me? for he was pleased to giue me some secret and silent evidence of his love.[78]

But in the very next paragraph we find him plunged headlong into evangelical humiliation and desolation. "But ah wretched backsliding heart! . . . I abhor myself before the Lord for my shameless pride . . . ."

The practice of devotional piety was pursued by Wigglesworth with special rigor in preparation for the Sabbath worship and preaching. He engaged in private fasts as rituals of purification, intended to restore the fervency of prayer. He wrestled with the Lord, seeking assurance of His love. He writes, "On Sabbath my desire was that my soul might rest in the bosom of God; though I could attain little of it."[79]

Like so many other Puritan contemplatives, Wigglesworth had internalized and systematized the process of evangelical humiliation. He believed that only by waging a constant warfare against the self could he grow in grace and recover the rapturous assurance of divine love as a child of God. The theology of assurance mixed ascetic and mystical elements and structured the spiritual itinerary to recover God's love. In this quest, Wigglesworth adopted extreme manifestations of humiliation that bore special affinities to the early childhood traumas of evangelical nurture. Near the end of the diary he notes, "Remember thou art my father though I be a rebellious child: Oh put a childlike spirit into me . . . ."[80]

Evangelical nurture resonates in the lives of religious melancholiacs—beset by feelings of sinfulness, ontological guilt, and shame. They fall into the "dark night of the soul" without assurance of God's love, abandoned as children of God. The evangelical Pietist theology of assurance and practical divinity supported a religious ethos, worldview, and system of child-rearing, and a religiously grounded personality that was pathogenic. Evidence has not survived to document actual episodes of childhood cruelty, but the adult syndromes of melancholy make retrospective explanations plausible. Evangelical nurture stands in the background, as systematic abuse legitimated evangelical Protestantism and the intrapsychic foundation of the evangelical temperament—a religiously grounded personality. Evangelical nurture helps explain the propensity for obsessive-compulsive rituals of purification of sin through private fasting that we shall encounter in the accounts of evangelical anorexia nervosa during the First and Second Awakenings. Finally, Cotton Mather's life and work synthesized the elements of evangelical nurture, as he suffered both religious melancholy and evangelical anorexia nervosa. Revealed in a

diary and writings, Mather's experience, like that of Wigglesworth, offers critical evidence of how the legacy of childhood cruelty helped fashion adult evangelical personality, and bore a special affinity with religious melancholy as
an American Protestant experience.

Tears of Repentance

In the "conquest of cultures" that occurred when immigrant European set-
tlers encountered indigenous Algonquian tribes of the New England wood-
lands, religion served as a weapon.[81] When tribes had suffered the ravages of
European diseases, defeat in war, land dispossession, and the loss of political
sovereignty, they more easily succumbed to missionary outreach and the appeal of conversion. The pervasive religious melancholy of seventeenth-century
Indian converts, and the carefully recorded spiritual narratives of their "tears
of repentance," recast the trauma of cultural conquest and devitalization at
the hands of Europeans in the terms of a new Protestant vocabulary. However, these native Christians had learned the techniques of evangelical humiliation, and suffered the predictable spiritual desolation of religious melancholy.

Seventeenth-century New Englanders steadfastly held to the manifest
superiority of their European culture, adopting for the seal of the Massachusetts Bay Colony the symbol of the Indian beckoning Puritans to "Come over
and help us."[82] Although depicted in the rhetoric of benevolence and implemented by ministers interested solely in the winning of souls for Christ, from
their inception Puritan missions became an instrument in the colonization and
conquest of native peoples. Interestingly, missionary activity did not begin until
after the attempted extermination of the Pequot tribe in 1637, the depopulation of the Northeastern tribes due to epidemics, and the undermining of native
political authority of sachems and the sacramental-magical authority of sha-
mans. By 1646, following the decade of the Great Migration from England,
50,000 colonists confronted the Massachusetts tribe, which was decimated
by smallpox and reduced from 20,000 souls to a surviving 750 people.[83] During
the 1640s, and until 1690, missions to the Wampanoag, Narragansett, Massachusetts, and other Algonquian tribes achieved considerable success. As Neal
Salisbury argues, "The Algonquians who converted were those whose communal integrity had been compromised step-by-step—from the plague of 1616
to the treaties of political submission—and whose sources of collective identity and individual social stature had been destroyed."[84]

By 1675, the eve of King Philip's War, 2,500 Native Americans, or 20
percent of the native population in southern New England, had converted to
Christianity. These successes resulted largely from the work of Reverend John
Eliot of Roxbury and Thomas Mayhew of Martha's Vineyard. Eliot formulated a written grammar, vocabulary, and translation of catechism in the
Algonquian language. Through Eliot's influence, fourteen "praying towns"
were built as reserves intended to separate de-tribalized Indians from the
influence of white settlement and from other tribes. Each praying town was
a carefully planned community that Eliot thought to be a utopian Christian

commonwealth structured by the revealed truths of God's blueprints in the Bible. Each town would impose a pattern of civilized customs and manners upon savages, "reducing" them from barbarism to civility, forcing them to renounce native ways as a prerequisite to conversion. Native Americans lived settled lives in permanent single-family dwellings and pursued disciplined vocations as farmers, mechanics, and craftsmen. They entered into a solemn town covenant and pledged to obey the ubiquitous laws prohibiting idleness, drunkenness, long hair, naked breasts, body greasing, and fornication. The forces of order—law, religion, and vocational asceticism—would effect a total and uncompromising annihilation of Indian culture, bringing these once undomesticated peoples under the yoke of civility, making them amenable to religious education and salvation.[85]

The praying towns provided devitalized native bands—who had suffered devastating depopulation, economic and social dislocations, and political subjugation to the English colonists—the means to revitalize and preserve their cultures, although altered by Christian and European borrowings.[86] Natives appropriated Christianity and its form of civilization to preserve their ethnic identity on traditional pieces of land in the midst of the deluge of colonial settlement and the ever-present threat of annihilation. As Axtell notes, English racism helped ensure the perpetuation of Indian identity in the midst of large-scale cultural changes.

> Ironically, the acute English sense of cultural superiority—which was colored by racism before the eighteenth century—helped the Indians to maintain the crucial ethnic core at the heart of their newly acquired Christian personae. In colonial eyes, they were still Indians and would always be, no matter how "civilized" or "Christian" they became.[87]

The missionary goal championed the creation of native congregations of "Indian Puritans," shepherded by native ministers. Newly formed soteriological communities of the ingathered faithful bound together in church covenants would replace native solidarities. To this end Eliot translated the pastoral works of Perkins and Baxter and tirelessly worked with the Indians of Natick, instructing, preaching, and guiding individual cases of conscience in anticipation of a harvest of souls.

The spiritual narratives of these conversions, published by Eliot and Mayhew as *Tears of Repentance* (1653), seven years after the beginnings of the praying towns, related the protracted and emotionally torturous *ordo salutis* of Native American Puritans. Each narrative made as a public profession of faith and testimony of a visible saint before the assembled congregation reflected years of instruction, probation, and fraternal watchfulness signifying the authenticity of the renewed heart as made manifest in godly, sanctified conduct.[88]

Eliot emphasized that converts made first confessions and subsequent second and even third confessions over the space of several years until the ministers and congregation gained full confidence in the intellectual rigor of the candidates' command of the articles of faith, the authenticity of the work of grace in renovating their hearts, and the clear evidence that they daily walked with God in the practice of piety.

These narratives depicted a fundamental transformation of converts' orientation toward self, community, and nature as they embraced a Christian cosmology depicting the world and the natural man as vile, sinful, and corrupted. Indian converts all related the melancholy realization of their pervasive sinfulness, of their individuated ethical responsibilities before a creator. William of Sudbury, born Nataous, speaks of this realization and of the evangelical humiliation that the knowledge of God effected on his soul. "I was angry with my self, and loathed my self, and thought God will not forgive me my sins."[89] Eliot reiterated this motif in his literary account of these spiritual exercises, *Indian Dialogues*. In a moment of spiritual desolation a penitent sachem confesses:

> Oh what mountains of sin have I heaped up in my wretched life! I had forgot my sins, and I thought God had forgot them too. . . . I now find my sins are numberless. My own personal sins are many, great and vile. My heart doth loath myself to remember them. They make me abhorring to God.[90]

Eliot also notes the sorrowful, morose, melancholy, and tearful qualities of Indian prayer; the humiliation and infusion of God's *pneuma* in their hearts as the distinguishing marks of authenticity in considering the evidence of native conversions. He observes praying Indians "with such grave and sober countenance, with such comely reverence in gesture, and their whole carriage and with such plenty of tears trickling down the cheeks of some of them, as did argue to us that they speak with much good affection and holy fear of God. . . ."[91] Native Americans were instructed that a gracious God favored his saints and punished his enemies. Thus, the calamitous effects of European diseases upon native communities, the failure of powwows and shamanistic magic to protect and cure the afflicted, the political humiliation of sachems, reinforced by the evident superiority of English technology in warfare, signified God's chastisement for heathen sin and savagery. As Axtell notes, "natives torn from their cultural roots understandably were emotionally fragile when they were confronted by the depressing tenets of Christian sin."[92] These indigenous peoples came to interpret their early lives before the English invasion as a thoroughly sinful existence of heathen savagery in alliance with Satan. Their collective and individual suffering and adversity reflected the harsh rod of God in chastisement for this depravity. Through the meticulous ministry of Eliot, Mayhew, Daniel Gookin, and others, praying Indians received pastoral instruction and catechizement in a Protestant cosmology that systematically answered the questions of theodicy, biblical history and the creation of man and nature, death, and salvation. Not surprisingly, many of the 283 Indians on Martha's Vineyard who entered a church covenant as visible saints in 1753 came to know a personal God who slew the rebellion in their hearts. They suffered religious melancholy.

"Red Puritans," like their seventeenth-century English counterparts who embraced the protracted, difficult, and uncertain journey of the *ordo salutis* in a coldly indifferent logic of predestination, viewed initial religious melancholy as evangelical humiliation before God's law and as part of the religiously valued morphology of conversion. Devitalized Indians espoused Protestant conversion as an emotionally and intellectually satisfying solution to the ruin of their native culture, and as a means to revitalize and preserve some vestiges of their former life.[93] Paradoxically, these "revitalizing" Protestant forms of religious identity also encouraged the practice of piety through self-examination that engendered in many converts lifelong repetitions of religious desolation and melancholy followed by times of assurance and consolation.

Reverend Experience Mayhew's ministry to eighteenth-century Native Americans brought him into daily contact with praying Indians who sought pastoral care in times of sickness or dying, or the cure of souls for troubled consciences. Mayhew reconstructed the lives, spiritual biographies, and laudatory deathbed scenes in his work, *Indian Converts*. Frequently, he came upon praying Indians in sickness or near death, overwhelmed by religious melancholy. Called to the bedside of Sarah Peag, he describes the last hours of this young woman.

> I found her in a grievous Agony, confessing and bewailing the Sins of her Heart and Life. She with many Tears cry'd out against herself as a most vile and wicked Creature, unworthy of the least of God's Mercies, but worthy to be eternally rejected of Him, and to be cast into Hell forever.[94]

Mayhew relates the end of Elizabeth Uhquat, who died in 1723 following years of suffering from a scrupulous conscience. "She now owned herself to be a most vile and sinful Creature, and said God had made her deeply sensible that she was so; have felt all her Sins in order before her Eyes, and made them exceedingly bitter to her Soul . . . . [95]

Experience Mayhew reassures his readers that both Peag and Uhquat enjoyed a spiritual peace and reconciliation with God before death. However, these postscripts of gracious dying only underscore the years of intermittent religious melancholy for Native American Puritans. Indian conversion did indeed offer emotionally and intellectually satisfying answers to adversity resulting from European invasion. Yet, the appropriation of the Protestant conversion experience, religiously grounded personality, and life-order also brought with it religious melancholy as integral to first conversion and, for many, a sickness unto death. Religious melancholy represented a unique form of culturally induced illness, unknown in native society, but so prevalent among converts who toiled in an arduous pilgrimage, seeking the hard-won seals of assurance of their individual salvation and tribal survival.

The Pattern Completed—Religious Awakenings and Revivals

The Half-Way Covenant marked the passing of the visible sainthood of the pioneering generation by instituting opportunities for church membership for persons who lived outwardly respectable lives. Without the experience of regeneration, they remained in protracted preparation, admitted to church fellowship in a "Puritan tribalism" by virtue of their parents' piety, yet barred from receiving communion or voting.[96] These partial measures were devised for the succeeding generations, who turned away from millennialism and devotional piety, whose compromise with worldliness led them to pursue economic gain in land speculation, farming, fishing, and trade. In Connecticut, most half-way members failed to attain full communicant status. Less than one person in five experienced regeneration. This was remarkable, given the decidedly evangelical thrust of most churches. Paul Lucas discovers a pervasive scrupulosity, a religious melancholy among these half-way members. He writes that "Ministerial writings at the end of the seventeenth century and the beginning of the eighteenth century referred often to the overly scrupulous in the congregation, persons who avoided the Lord's Supper and the full membership it entailed because they felt spiritually unworthy and feared damnation."[97]

How to explain this scrupulosity and tension? William McLoughlin argues that this generation of New Englanders came of age during a period of social transformation—the passing of traditional New England society built upon the hierarchial dyads of minister-laity, ruler-ruled, parent-child, and husband-wife. The idealized model of a Puritan village depicted a theocratic communal order, with participants fervently committed to a cohesive single belief system and organically bound to one another through the institutions of the patriarchal family, church, and civil government. Puritan communities were bent on establishing pervasive and interlocking structures to maintain public order and exert continual surveillance and social control over their inhabitants. The powerful institutional controls of town covenants, church covenants, "the brotherly watch" over neighbors, and the court system and legal code enforced strict public moralities. Everywhere citizens were called upon to exercise self-control and discipline, godliness, Sabbatarianism, a work ethic, and the ascetic control of human lusts and appetites. Recent social histories of colonial Massachusetts have revealed how far individuals and communities fell short of this normative ideal.

Roger Thompson's study of popular culture in Middlesex County, Massachusetts, in the later half of the seventeenth century focuses upon family life and sexual misconduct. From civil and ecclesiastical court records he discovered that adolescent girls sent out from their families as servants in neighboring households proved most vulnerable to seduction. Despite strong community sanctions that limited sexuality to the marriage bed, Puritan definitions of premarital sex as a sin of uncleanness and defilement that placed the sinner in jeopardy of salvation, and in the face of parental and community controls, adolescents rebelled, engaging in sex during courtship. Thompson argues that alcohol helped lower inhibitions, and ardent male suitors made declarations of love and promises of marriage. Couples viewed their premarital trysts at expressive sexuality as "making love."

Unlike the statistics from early modern England during the rise of the modern family (circa 1700), where one in five brides went to the altar pregnant, less that 1 percent, or sixty-six cases, of bridal pregnancy were listed in court records. The seventeenth-century sexual double standard punished "deflowered" women most severely for the discovery of their sexual indiscretions. The few who made successful marriages had to choose from a field of eligible widowers, or men of tarnished reputation or of a lower class, resulting in hypogamous marriages and a decline in social standing in their community. Unlike early modern England, where adolescent women engaged in premarital intercourse consistent with a "betrothal license" but could not compel their suitor to marry them, colonial adolescent women could force "shotgun weddings" upon their suitors. In this manner, the influence and power of patriarchs was asserted only *after* the children had asserted themselves in sexual activity and a decision to marry. It remained for parents to clean up the mess made by their children, to salvage family honor, and persuade young men to do the right thing by their lovers.

Thompson reports that two-thirds of the cases of bridal pregnancy involved young women from well-established, pious, and church-going families. He discounts the notion that a "bastardy-prone" lower-class group contributed to the lowering of community standards or a socio-economic determination for premarital fornication and bastardy.[98] In the eighteenth century, communities no longer prosecuted premarital fornication by imposing penalties, ended community surveillance, and abandoned any claim to enforce this moral code. Puritan communities needed to compromise in areas other than the enforcement of sexual morality and the prerogatives of fathers in patriarchal households.

Indeed, the closing decades of the seventeenth century witnessed the transformation from "Puritan" to "Yankee" and are linked to the rising modern commercial middle-class culture in America. Towns divided between prosperous freeholders and propertyless "outlivers," between those committed to town covenants as status-bound communities and those who created new towns of absentee freeholders motivated by land hunger, speculation, and profit-making. An increasingly scattered, religiously diverse populace and a differentiated division of labor marked by new traders and occupations meant an end to the homogeneous, close-knit, and controlled communities under the surveillance of church, family, and town "governments." Gone were the effective external regulations of personal behavior concerning economic ambition, Sabbath-keeping, tippling, gaming, sexual misconduct, and other worldly actions.[99]

Richard L. Bushman summarizes these tensions and controversies that divided believers, embroiled them in litigation and conflict, and diverted them from the pursuit of piety:

> After 1690, in their ambition to prosper, people disregarded the demands of social order. Nonproprietors contested the control of town lands with proprietors, and outlivers struggled with the leaders in the town center to obtain an independent parish. In civil government settlers fought for a clear title to their lands and new traders for currency. Church members resisted the enlargement of the minister's power or demanded greater piety in his

preaching. All these controversies pitted common men against rulers and the laws.[100]

In response to fundamental changes in the New England Way, preachers created a ritual of self-abasement—the "American Jeremiad"—based upon biblical prophets of doom, urging the faithful to revitalize and redirect their efforts in the midst of these social transformations. Sermons recounted the declension, backsliding, and apostasy of the saints and warned that divine providence, ever active in New England's history, had brought many adversities to chastise the wayward nation. King Philip's War, crime, Satan, and witchcraft were manifestations of God's anger and served as "corrective afflictions" to awaken God's chosen, put them on probation, and urge their spiritual renewal.[101]

Although the jeremiad was limited to a ritualized sermon given to the faithful during fast days, election sermons, and other sacred days, a religious awakening in the 1730s struck communities like a "psychological earthquake"[102] akin to a revitalization movement. As William G. McLoughlin argues, "Awakenings begin in periods of cultural distortion and grave personal stress, when we lose faith in the legitimacy of our norms, the viability of our institutions, and the authority of our leaders in church and state. They eventuate in basic restructurings of our institutions and redefinitions of our social goals."[103]

The economic, demographic, political, and religious changes in New England formed the mise-en-scène to the First Great Awakening of the 1730s that swept throughout communities in the Connecticut River valley and effectively restructured American religion throughout the colonies from 1740 to 1760. This awakening was a "pietistic radicalism," which stood in opposition to traditional ministerial, political, familial, and collective authority.[104] This event institutionalized religious diversity and conflict with the creation of Old and New Light divisions, and the spread of heterodox Separatist and Baptist sects.[105] The revival was a leveling, democraticizing process. McLoughlin states:

> It is significant that the new-light revivalists throughout the awakening found that their liberating theology had a profound effect upon the powerless and the poor of society—upon black slaves, upon women, upon Indians, upon children. These suffered more tensions and suppressed rage than most in society and felt the release of conversion . . . more deeply. They could not, however, actualize the new freedom and power they felt except in religious activity—in preaching, saving souls, becoming missionaries (or missionaries wives).[106]

Of the many sociologically significant contributions of the awakening, the emergence of evangelical Pietism as a curative for religious melancholy and scrupulosity proves most important for our discussion. The awakening challenged the Arminianism of the Half-Way Covenant, rejected partial church affiliation for the descendants of saints, predicated upon their righteous conduct, and ended the idea of protracted preparationism that left so many in permanent half-way status. The awakening rejected the compromise of Reverend Solomon Stoddard, who allowed believers full communicant status if they would "own the covenant" as a rational act of will, without undergoing the experience of regeneration. Above all, the Great Awakening revitalized the idea of a sudden, rapturous regeneration of the heart—a total renovation of the believer through the operation of the covenant of grace. The masses were called to submit to an evangelical Calvinist doctrine of the sinner in selfless surrender to the mercy tendered by an absolute, sovereign deity.

An estimated twenty- to forty-thousand persons awoke from the slumber of sin and the spiritual lethargy of lives committed more to the countinghouse than the meetinghouse. Ashamed and guilt-ridden at inattention to devotional piety, the political and economic controversies that divided them, and the pronounced spirit of litigiousness that divided neighbor against neighbor, they turned away from mundane concerns and entered into sacred time. Proponents of the awakening interpreted these "signs of the times" as a manifestation of *kairos*, "the invasion of the temporal by the eternal," the work of the Holy Spirit in converting the masses.[107]

This revival began in 1735 in Jonathan Edwards's Northampton congregation in response to the epidemics of religious melancholy that prevailed among them.[108] The surprising and wondrous visitation of the Holy Spirit showered the anxious with grace. Conversions transpired without undue formalism and unmediated ecclesiastical supervision, by the direct personal communion between the penitent and God. The revival became a social movement, institutionalized throughout the colonies via the campaigns of George Whitefield and Gilbert Tennent in 1740–1743. These revivalists, together with other itinerant preachers, including Edwards, Samuel Davies, Eleazar Wheelock, Samuel Finley, James Davenport, Jonathan Parsons, Andrew Croswell, Samuel Buell, and many others, spread the message of the awakening. Unschooled lay exhorters also received the call to win souls.[109]

The revival sermon delivered in extemporaneous fashion, addressing each of the assembled with a personal invitation to repent, adopted a rhetoric designed to stir their hearts, awaken religious affections, and humble sinners before God. Jonathan Edwards intended to evoke terror in "Sinners in the Hands of an Angry God," their lives hanging by a thread above the abyss of Hell and eternal judgment.

> The God that holds you over the pit of hell, much as one holds a spider, or some other loathsome insect over the fire, abhors you, and is dreadfully provoked: his wrath towards you burns like fire; he looks upon you as worthy of nothing else, but to be cast into the fire. . . . And there is no other reason to be given why you have not dropped into hell since you arose in the morning, but that God's hand has held you up.[110]

Participants in revivals found themselves suspended in a liminal space as they left behind their mundane lives and, with eager voluntarism, submitted to the exhortations of fire-and-brimstone sermons and unceasing prayer meetings where family and friends prayed for their conversion. In this manner, as never before, masses were brought into the *ordo salutis* and embraced a revitalized morphology of conversion. McLoughlin argues that what appeared wondrous to these persons was the fact that God would indeed forgive their sins and offer them the opportunity for salvation. Their declension and worldliness, their moves away from parental control of marriage and careers and the institutional restraints of the traditional order, left them unsettled, disoriented, and guilt-ridden over these sins against their fathers. McLoughlin writes that, "by 1720 the old ideological framework had lost its cultural legitimacy and the people needed new light from God by which to guide their behavior, measure their goals, and establish new sources of communal authority in church and state."[111] The awakening would then legitimate the transition to a modern possessive individualism as each regenerate heart was bound to the commonweal through acts of disinterested benevolence, and to new church communities of the converted.[112]

From detractors of the revival like Charles Chauncey came the charge of religious enthusiasm and excesses that would render the awakening deleterious to the cause of true religion and produce counterfeit conversions. Indeed, the sermon crafted to awaken the terrors of the law for slumbering sinners and convince them of their total dependence upon the sovereignty of God did overwhelm the assembled masses.

> In many places, people would cry out, in the time of public worship, under a sense of their overbearing guilt and misery, and the all-consuming wrath of God, due to them for their iniquities; others would faint and swoon under the affecting views they had of GOD and CHRIST; some would weep and sob, and there would sometimes be so much noise among the people, in particular places, that it was with difficulty that the preacher could be heard . . . .[113]

The awakening that was to resolve the scrupulosity and religious melancholy of so many disquieted souls spawned its own enthusiasm, as participants fell in seizures when smitten with the Holy Spirit or lapsed into religious melancholy and suicide in the context of their conversion crises. Jonathan Edwards's uncle, Joseph Hawley, committed suicide in May 1735, an event that proved the most telling and publicized instance of religious melancholy. Edwards ascribes this tragedy to the recession of the Holy Spirit and the active work of Satan in afflicting a pious Christian gentleman predisposed by a family history and propensity toward melancholy. "The Devil took advantage, and drove him into despairing thoughts. He was kept awake anights, mediating terror; so that he had scare any sleep at all, for a long time together. And it was observed at last, that he was scarcely well capable of managing his ordinary business, and was judged delirious by the coroner's inquest."[114]

Religious enthusiasm characterized the second round of awakenings in Edwards's Northampton congregation in 1741–1742. As Patricia Tracy indicates, "Children left their evening meetings of 'social religion' to go home 'crying aloud through the streets.' By midsummer, 'it was a very frequent thing to see a house full of outcries, faintings, convulsions and such like, both with distress, and also with admiration and joy.'"[115]

The charges of religious enthusiasm made against the awakening prompted Edwards to write a series of works that defended awakenings as the work of God, recasting "enthusiasm" as a holy religious affection—the heart renewed by the love of God. The first work that served to defend and explain the awakening, *A Faithful Narrative of the Surprising Work of God in the Conversion of Many Hundred Souls*, published in 1741, offers clinical accounts of the soul's journey to conversion, derived from Edwards's familiarity with three hundred cases of conscience. Accounts of authentic conversion would be presented to counter charges of enthusiasm and error, and religious melancholy played a central role.

Edwards's *Faithful Narrative* distills the evangelical morphology of conversion from the cases under his review. He identifies three parts to the experience of salvation: (1) the legal conviction of the sinner prostrated before the tribunal of justice of an angry absolute sovereign; (2) the selfless agony of the believer who humbly waits for divine mercy; and (3) the joyful, rapturous infusion of grace and forgiveness of sin that marks conversion. Edwards acknowledges a "vast variety" that differentiates the experience of believers, the protracted terror of some leading to religious melancholy.

> Some have had such a sense of the displeasure of God, and the great danger they were in of damnation, that they could not sleep at nights; and many have said that when they have laid down, the thoughts of sleeping in such a condition have been frightful to them, and they have scarcely been free from terror while they have been asleep; and they have awaked with fear, heaviness, and distress still abiding on their spirits. It has been very common that the deep and fixed concern that has been on persons' minds has had a painful influence on their bodies and given disturbance to their animal natures.[116]

Attributing melancholy in part to Satan's handicraft, and in part to humoral imbalances brought on by protracted religious terrors, Edwards recognized the affinity between experiential religion and mental alienation. He himself suffered from bouts of religious melancholy, and he witnessed the sufferings of many during the revival.[117] Edwards shared Benjamin Colman's understanding of the prevailing frequency of melancholy among the saints, and its cause from Satan's fiery darts sent into the hearts to afflict the godly.

Ever the champion of the awakening, Edwards could not leave the reader convinced that revivals promoted epidemics of religious melancholy—a conclusion that ineluctably followed from his distillation of the cases of conscience. His next paragraph offers an apologia noting that fewer cases of melancholy appeared than in previous revivals. Surprisingly, the revival had the salubrious effect of restoring melancholiacs to health.

> But it has been very remarkable, that there has been far less of this mixture in this time of extraordinary blessing, than there was wont to be in

persons under awakenings at other times; for it is evident that many that before had been exceedingly involved in such difficulties, seemed now strangely set at liberty. Some persons that had before, for a long time, been exceedingly entangled with peculiar temptations of one sort or other, and unprofitable and hurtful distresses, were soon helped over former stumbling blocks that hindered any progress toward saving good; and convictions have wrought more kindly, and they have been successfully carried on in the way to life.[118]

Edwards finished a second defense of the awakening in 1742, in *Some Thoughts Concerning the Present Revival of Religion in New England,* maintaining that the awakening was "a glorious work of God." In the concluding section of the first part of his treatise, Edwards introduced "An Example of Evangelical Piety," derived from the spiritual exercises of his wife, Sarah Pierrepont Edwards, demonstrating how true religion originated in the heart of each believer as the Holy Spirit acted to renovate the heart with God's grace. Sarah Edwards experienced "high and extraordinary transports" of rapturous union with God attended by bodily manifestations of complete prostration, the inability to stand or speak, the "flesh cold," nature overwhelmed under the burden of divine presence, the "animal nature often in a great emotion and agitation."[119] Edwards describes these high transports as the soul

> perfectly overwhelmed, and swallowed up with light and love and a sweet solace, rest and joy of soul, that was altogether unspeakable; and more than once continuing for five or six hours together, without any interruption, in that clear and lively view or sense of the infinite beauty and amiableness of Christ's person, and the heavenly sweetness of his excellent and transcendent love . . . . The soul remained in a kind of heavenly Elysium, and did as it were swim in the rays of Christ's love, like a little mote swimming in beams of the sun . . . .[120]

Edwards defends his wife's inner-worldly mysticism by contending that she did not fall prey to enthusiasm or hypocritical religious excitement. For many years preceding the first awakening in 1735, or the current revival of 1742, Sarah Edwards had lived as a woman devoted to the life of progressive sanctification and glorification of God through the cultivation of an intensive and abiding piety. Edwards describes this as a "weanedness from the world," a mastery over sin and temptations, created through "constant prayer and labor in religion," and self-denial in meekness, sweetness, humility, and benevolence towards others.[121]

Although Sarah Edwards, like her husband, had been subject to periods of religious melancholy in early life, Edwards argues that the evangelical piety and high transports of contemplative union—the out-of-body raptures—in the awakening effectively ended this spiritual despondency. Referring to his wife as "the person," he writes:

> The person had formerly in lower degrees of grace, been subject to unsteadiness, and many ups and downs, in the frame of mind; the mind

being under great disadvantages, through a vapory habit of body, and often subject to melancholy, and at times almost overborne with it, it having been so even from early youth: but strength of grace, and divine light has of a long time, wholly conquered these disadvantages, and carried the mind in a constant manner, quite above all such effects of vapors. Since that resignation spoken of before, made nearly three years ago, everything of that nature seems to be overcome and crushed by the power of faith and trust in God . . . without one hour's melancholy or darkness.[122]

Edwards concludes his defense of Sarah Edwards's evangelical piety by the exclamation, "Now if such things are enthusiasm, and the fruits of a distempered brain, let my brain be evermore possessed of that happy distemper!"[123]

Edwards's two final justifications of what Goen calls the "emotional extravagances"[124] of the awakening included *A Treatise Concerning Religious Affections* (1746) and *The Life of Brainerd* (1737). These works systematized a theology of grace and assurance that grounded the *ordo salutis* in the holy affections of love for God and a cosmic love of all humanity. Edwards' disclaimers notwithstanding, new forms of religious melancholy appeared in the awakening. The white heat of holy affections might prove indispensable to authentic conversions, but many believers failed to sustain these high and extraordinary transports of contemplation and lapsed into what Edwards understood as a dangerous despair.

As Barbara Lacey has found in her study of spiritual diaries and religiosity among men and women of the awakening, women were held to much higher, exalted spiritual standards than were men in the congregations. Not infrequently, virtuous women of exemplary piety felt themselves inadequate to the standards of progressive sanctification, self-denying love, and other holy affections. They thus suffered from religious melancholy.

Offered to society as life-long models of humility, meekness, and submission, women struggled with feelings of worthlessness, or low self-esteem, which ministers called "religious melancholy." Some women failed to find peace both in life and at death as they measured themselves by the standards of perfection set for them by society. The calling to a spiritual life, which initially raised women to a revered position in society, was a difficult and arduous call to follow, and for some women it proved exhausting.[125]

As we shall consider in the next chapter, all too frequently the modal conversion narrative depicted a protracted evangelical humiliation, charges of blasphemy and commission of the unpardonable sin, excessive fasting, and a belief that it was sinful to eat. I have called this religious melancholy "evangelical anorexia nervosa." Ironically, the thrust of evangelical piety that intended to resolve the religious melancholy—the ontological status of sinful and unconverted who languished in permanent half-way status—introduced in the first revival a form of religious melancholy that for some in the nineteenth-century awakening involved attempts at fasting unto death.

Wherever the elements of evangelical Pietism fused with the social movement of religious awakenings and revivalistic technique, wherever collective forces mobilized communities of men and women to undergo the self-torturous travail of the *ordo salutis*, wherever the antimonies of the evangelical self received full support and encouragement, we shall encounter the spirit of melancholy and special affinities for religious melancholy and madness.

The Evangelical Grieving of Mary Fish

Mary Fish (1736–1818) suffered a prolonged episode of melancholy at age thirty-four in 1770. Because she could not care for herself, her children, or her household, she closed her New Haven home and returned to her parents' house in Stonington, Connecticut, on November 5, 1770. Her father, Reverend Joseph Fish, requested that she keep a spiritual diary in this crisis, and this firsthand account reveals her inward journey from despair to rekindled faith and health. Before examining this journal, a discussion of Fish's early life and adversity will set the stage for her subsequent religious melancholy.

Mary Fish was the first child of Joseph Fish and Rebecca Pabodie. Her father, an Old Light Congregationalist minister, settled in North Church at Stonington, and reared his daughter to the standards of evangelical piety. Reverend Fish imposed a regimen that included daily prayers, family Bible reading, strict observance of the Sabbath, and the obligations of filial piety. The virtues of humility, self-examination, private prayers, and study of the Word, and the centrality of diligent work completed the organization of family government for the Fish household.[126]

In later life, Mary Fish would reflect upon her parents and childhood:

> They taught us early what our state is by nature, and the necessity of being born again, and that there is no salvation but by the merits of our redeemer. They taught us also to call ourselves to account every night—How we had spent the day and to ask God's forgiveness for whatever we found we had done amiss, and to pray to him to make us do better in the future. They taught us that without divine assistance we could do nothing and should be liable to fall into great follies.[127]

In 1751, Joseph Fish sent his daughter, at age fifteen, to Sarah Osborn's school in Newport, Rhode Island. Osborn's life and practical piety represented the apotheosis of the New Divinity, the emerging theology that justified the Awakening. Under her tutelage, Mary Fish came of age as a submissive, virtuous, evangelical young woman. She completed her education in 1755, made her first profession of faith in Reverend Fish's church in November 1758, and married Reverend John Noyes four days later, on November 16.[128] She represented the ideal of evangelical culture—a pious, churched young woman eager to embrace "the way of duty" of marriage and motherhood as a reflection of her vocation.

For the next twelve years, Fish's adult life was fraught with adversities. She bore four children in her marriage to Noyes. The first child died in infancy in 1760. Reverend Noyes suffered from consumption, and the disease prevented him from ever taking full employment as a minister. He died in 1767, leaving his wife with slender means and three small children to rear. In a succession of trials in 1770, Fish lost her youngest child and her beloved mother-in-law. To compound her troubles, she was perplexed and mortified by her conduct toward an unnamed suitor with whom she had made a promise of marriage, yet wanted release from this engagement. "The loss of her little daughter broke Mary's spirit. She lapsed into depression, and felt that her faith had died with the child. That autumn, afraid for her sanity, Mr. and Mrs. Fish suggested that she and the boys remove to Stonington for the winter."[129]

How did evangelical Protestants like Fish accept the irreparable losses of death? If the fate of each human life, and untimely death, rests in the hands of God's providence, would not evangelicals rise up in anger toward a God who would take a loving husband or sweet babe. Cotton Mather's well-known sermon, "Insanabilia: An Essay Upon Uncurables" addressed these questions. Mather advised believers that some forms of adversity and grief could not be cured, the dead were forever lost to this world. "The *Grief* of many People are *Incurable . . . Grief* hopeless of any *Cure* in this World; there is nothing that can be done to *Cure* them."[130] However, a capricious God cannot be blamed for adversity and the untimely deaths of loved ones. Mather explains that our sin is the cause of these misfortunes: "Our *Sin* has made us *worthy* of *Grievous Things.* 'Tis to chastise us for our *Sin,* that the *Justice* of Heaven dispenses to us all our Grievous Things."[131]

The grief of death cannot be cured and must be endured. Mather advises Christians to bear grief in patience and with prayer; in silence and humility to reaffirm their faith in God and to see this as an opportunity for continued spiritual growth. However, evangelical personalities were directed by practical theology to turn the anger toward God inward in psychomachy against the self. Grieving would necessarily involve melancholia.

Through the long winter of 1770–1771, Fish undertook what might be termed evangelical "grief work." She needed to interpret the adversity, ill fortune, and untimely deaths of loved ones through an evangelical theodicy that explained the hidden meanings, portents, and opportunities of these sad times. Looking back upon her melancholy from the maturity of old age, Fish embraced this evangelical theodicy. She understood that God visits people with adversity to mortify their pride, to admonish them for worldly concerns, to break a false autonomy and return them in helpless surrender to their creator. The sinner's actions bring the workings of God's providence. Sinners must hold themselves alone accountable for their misfortunes and view them as opportunities to turn again to God and undergo spiritual growth.

Evangelicals who would undergo the arduous work of grieving were first required to acknowledge their anger toward God. Fish directed her enmity against God for taking her loved ones inward in the religiously prescribed godly sorrow and humiliation. In Fish's case, the internalized anger directed against self resulted in protracted and excessive religious melancholy that she interpreted as the work of Satan. Reflecting on this melancholy, she writes from the perspective of old age:

When our character rides high in the world, pride, that worst of weeds is apt to grow, and we ought to be thankful for whatever means providence may employ to destroy or mortify our pride although the operation may be painful. When things appear to work against us, the Tempter steps in and wishes us to let go our hold of God—saying that if God were your friend, such and such things would not have happened to you. If we lose confidence in God we are apt to be driven about with every wind.[132]

Fish read the pastoral work of John Flavel in an attempt to understand her afflictions. Flavel's *Divine Conduct Or, The Mystery of Providence* (1677) introduced her to evangelical pastoral care. He maintained that a special, afflictive providence visits the lives of God's elect to purge and cleanse them of sin and temptation, to mortify their pride and redirect them to God's will.[133] Flavel comforted the troubled by explaining that godly sorrow and humiliation accompany adversity and are caused by the special afflictive providence of a God who chastises wayward saints. The evangelical self, in the commission of sin, has invited God's afflictive and corrective providence in the form of ill-fortune, death, and adversity. The grieving evangelical has only herself and her depravity to blame for the death of loved ones. Fish's reading of Flavel deepened her anguish and then brought temporary comfort. He counseled, "Consider that all your troubles, under which you complain, are pulled down upon your head by your own sins. You turn God's mercies into sin, and then fret against God because he turns your sins into sorrow. Your ways and doings procure these things to you."[134]

Flavel comforted the afflicted by suggesting, "Consider how near you are to the change of your condition. Have but a little patience, and all will be well with you as your hearts can desire."[135] Thus began Fish's crisis of faith in her father's home on January 16, 1771. She enters into her diary:

> Found some comfort in reading God's word—but all the day pensive, fearing it was all wrong with me, and after saying "if it be too with me, why am I thus"—if I am a child of God why has he not given me more wisdom? My conduct has given people reason to suspect my stability of mind—although I have had an eye to the leadings of providence yet I fear that I have been disowned and I am now in a troubled ocean.[136]

She continued in anguish for several days, troubled by religious doubt, guilt-ridden over her dealings with the spurned suitor, and filled with self-loathing. On January 21, she writes:

> In the morning distressed with an unresigned frame of mind & a proud heart—not willing to bow, not willing to have my character roughly handled, but blessed God before noon found relief in meditating on my dear redeemer's agony in the garden—was enabled I hope in a measure to say thy will be done—in that frame I am now and may it continue—O for greater and greater humility.[137]

Her anguish returned the next day as her diary records: "unwell and sorely distressed in mind . . . . "[138] and she continued alternating between hope and despair for six weeks. Her melancholy subsided in April after she ended the engagement with her suitor, mortified her pride with godly sorrow, and became a child of God again. Fish and her two sons returned to their home in New Haven. She writes:

> For a time back I have been at times distressed and sometimes comfortable. This day calm and resigned. The testimony of a good conscience that I have desired and do desire to do the thing that is right and best is a great comfort to me; the same heart that has cast down in months past, I find lifts up and I hope shall arrive to a settled state of peace.[139]

Fish writes that she will never forget her previous distress, "the wormwood and gall." She will conduct her life as a humbled child of God in submission to his will.[140] She enters the following devotion in her journal for July 1, 1772:

> I am guilty of being over charged with the cares of this world—I am resolved—God helping me, that I will live better and strive to keep my heart well all diligence, O Lord . . . . I long for a discovery of divine things! May I never more resist the strivings of God's Spirit, lest I be given over to a reprobate mind, which God forbid of his infinite mercy on Jesus Christ, my Lord.[141]

Mary Fish lived another forty-seven years and in that time suffered many adversities. She buried two more husbands, a son, two grandsons, and many other family members and friends. She endured the travail of the American Revolution and her husband's imprisonment by the British. In all her trials, she was sustained by a maturing faith, a trust in God's mercies, and an evangelical temperament.

Writing almost eighteen months after the onset of her melancholy, she records her assurance of faith and renewed health in a journal entry dated February 11, 1772.

> O strange creature that I am! For I every day this winter experience in my mind what I would have given the world to obtain last winter—that is resignation to God's will. I now view myself and the world in a different light from what I have sometimes before—for great peace have they that love his law and nothing shall offend them . . . I long for greater discovery of divine things.[142]

3

Evangelical Anorexia Nervosa

The evangelical anoretic was a Protestant whose experience of self, other, and world was informed by the vocabularies of an inner-worldly, mystical, pastoral theology. Those who attempted excessive fasting, or even fasting unto death, did so as part of a directed spiritual exercise that was to purify sin in a moment when God had withdrawn his love. The Protestant mystic fully expected that these obsessive rituals of purification would lead the soul through the inward progression of stages culminating in the state of mystical union. Since the *unio mystica* experience proved evanescent, the Protestant mystic understood religious life to be a continual repetition of these spiritual cycles. Anne Fremantle describes this experience as a journey from the ". . . dark nights of the senses, of the soul—the purifications, the progress from petitionary prayer to meditation to contemplation, from contemplation to infused prayer, and thence—for the proficient—to unitive prayer, to the mystic marriage, and finally, to a state of union."[1]

The evangelical anoretic, unlike the pattern previously indicated, remained trapped in a seemingly interminable dark night of the senses, convinced of having committed sins beyond God's pardon, obsessed with personal rituals of purification. Fasting provided a means to repent, to humble the self before God, and to mortify the body so that the spirit could live and petition for forgiveness. But the evangelical anorectic found no easy forgiveness. God had removed his love and countenance, and with it the assurance of salvation. Believers persevered, redoubling efforts of private prayer, meditation, and fasting, hoping that eventually the rapture of divine love would break through their melancholy. Yet God remained absent, and the evangelical anoretic was forced to conclude that sin caused this alienation from God's love. In this state, all human effort and conduct, including eating, compounded the ontological pollution of the sinner. It was a sin to eat.

The saint was enjoined to dedicate eating and drinking to satisfy only minimally the body's natural appetites. Eating ultimately was directed towards the higher ethical purpose of glorifying God. The sinner knew that such glorification proved impossible for him or her. Thus, eating only exacerbated his or her plight. In the fleeting hope of receiving evidence of God's love, yet increasingly convinced in their hearts of their own damnation, evangelical anoretics fasted.

82

The behavioral manifestations of this syndrome include food refusal, generalized anxiety, sleep disorder, and obsessive-compulsive conduct or repetitive neurotic ceremonials designed to alleviate feelings of personal sinfulness. The inner subjective meanings associated with these symptoms, the expressions of hopelessness and the certainty of eternal damnation reflect important theological contradictions of evangelical Pietism as enacted in the lives of believers who attempted and failed to forge a religiously grounded personality. The evangelical anoretic waged a lifelong battle against the self in search of self-denial. Religionists most frequently suffered this type of melancholy during youthful first conversion, or during the mid-life period in the fourth decade. The evangelical anoretic abandoned all hope of grace and stood before the bar of judgment with self-accusations of hypocrisy, blasphemy against the Holy Spirit, and the commission of the unpardonable sin. All conduct added to the debt of sin; it became a sin to eat. Despairing of hope regarding otherworldly salvation and forced to endure unrelieved torment as God-forsaken, the sufferer refused all food and began self-imposed starvation.

William James understood that the religion of "saintliness" promoted a tendency among believers to take the ascetic ideals of purity and moral consistency to scrupulous and fantastic extremes. He aptly describes the internal logic of the evangelical anorectic.

> . . . ascetic mortifications and torments may be due to pessimistic feelings about the self, combined with theological beliefs concerning expiation. The devotee may feel that he is buying himself free. . . . In psychopathic persons, mortifications may be entered on irrationally, by a sort of obsession or fixed idea which comes as a challenge and must be worked off, because only thus does the subject get his interior consciousness feeling right again.[2]

Evangelical anorexia nervosa emerged as a prevalent distinctive expression of religious melancholy among evangelical Pietist sects in England and New England from the seventeenth through the mid-nineteenth centuries. As an interrelated set of subjective meanings, experiences, and conduct informed by one variant of Protestant sectarianism, evangelical anorexia nervosa represents a psychopathology peculiar to certain cultural groups in a limited historical period. It is a "culture-bound syndrome," "a collection of signs and symptoms which is not to be found universally in human populations, but is restricted to a particular culture or group of cultures."[3] From this perspective, cultural meaning systems provide the central orientations for the formation of self and personality, and for elaborate culture-specific forms of stress, conduct, interpretation, and psychopathology.[4] In this manner cultural forces are seen as an axial variable in the causation and articulation of culture-bound syndromes.

Evangelical anorexia nervosa represents a historical and culture-bound syndrome produced by the confluence of three developments during the Reformation: (1) the ascetic rationalization of the body; (2) the de-magicization and disenchantment of religion and world; and (3) the vicissitudes of self that required saints to create a religiously grounded personality, mixing and balancing elements of inner-worldly asceticism with inner-worldly mysticism. These themes retrace the now-familiar concepts first introduced by Max Weber.

Ascetic Protestantism imposed strict ethical discipline upon the conduct of daily life, requiring that all believers resist any sensuous surrender to the pleasures of the flesh. Glorifying God in all things remained the highest ethical maxim that would direct the conduct of saints. In this believers viewed themselves as an instrument of God, as Christian soldiers inwardly battling against the carnality of the natural man, and outwardly in tension against the snares of the secular world. This *auto-machia*, or *anfechtung*, required continual and systematic self-control of the natural appetites. Moderation and temperance in the passions, eating, sleep, and exercise were required to keep the religionist ever alert to his or her duty of glorifying God. The pilgrimage of the spirit during conversion required constant vigilance and dynamic tension against human embodiment symbolized by the term "flesh."[5] The inner-worldly ascetic achieved a religious personality through unending mortification of the flesh so that the spirit might grow in grace. Fasting assumed a central role in Protestant ascetic discipline of the body.

In archaic religions that rely upon magical and sacramental means whereby believers coerce or influence the deity, fasting allows direct identification with and participation in the sacred. "Fasting was associated with purification and preparation for receiving sacred power."[6] Through ritual praxis and sacramental and magical techniques of the body—fasting, dancing, and ingesting intoxicants and other drugs—religionists achieved personal and collective purity, powers of healing and leadership, and mystical possession of the Godhead. Contemporary Native American Sun Dance ceremonies exemplify this sacro-magical religious practice.[7]

In classical and medieval Christianity "fasting was considered a mortification, an act of penance for one's sin. Because food was attractive, it could be a distraction. So one fasted to discipline desire, attain attachment from daily life, and focus on the religious quest."[8] The Protestant Reformation required that all believers struggle to achieve religious virtuosity—a magnificent consistency with God's will known only to medieval Catholic saints and monastics. "Ascetic disciplines in both Catholicism and Protestantism were a system of rules of conduct to control the flesh by starvation and renunciation."[9] John Cennick, the first Methodist lay preacher, exemplifies the fact that Protestant ascetics were required to adopt monastic regimens of the body in their everyday lives. "He fasted long and often, and prayed nine times a day. Fancying dry bread too great an indulgence for so great a sinner as himself, he began to feed on potatoes, acorns, crabs, and grass; and often wished that he could live on roots and herbs."[10]

Protestantism tried to rid religion of all magical and sacramental elements, rejecting the seven Catholic sacraments, with the exception of a modified form of baptism and celebration of the Eucharist. By placing each individual in a direct ethical relationship with God regarding the promise of salvation, Protestant groups diminished the role of the church as a dispenser of institutionalized grace. The medieval Catholic church was a repository of supernatural grace. The worship of saints; pilgrimages to holy shrines; the powers of icons and holy relics; the exorcisms of the devil; the blessing of houses, livestock, crops, and tools; the use of ecclesiastical talismans and amulets—all these were employed to assuage the anxieties of the masses about their health and well-being. The church continually struggled against pagan heterodoxy among the laity and introduced magic to bind people to religion and God.[11] As Keith Thomas argues in *Religion and the Decline of Magic*, Protestantism formally rejected the resort to magical praxis. "Protestantism thus presented itself as a deliberate attempt to take the magical elements out of religion, to eliminate the idea that the rituals of the Church had about them a mechanical efficacy, and to abandon the effort to endow physical objects with supernatural qualities by special formulae of consecration and exorcism."[12]

However, Protestants in the sixteenth and seventeenth centuries continued to face misfortunes such as natural disasters, fires, plague, and epidemic illness. Thomas asks how people could renounce magical and sacramental solutions to these vexing concerns before the modern institutions of insurance, government social welfare, and medicine had developed technical means of protection. Protestants were forced to reintroduce some forms of magic under the guise of devotional piety.

The Protestant world picture in seventeenth-century New England included the idea of a shadow, or invisible, world that existed behind the mundane reality. In *Wonders of the Invisible World*, Cotton Mather writes of this enchanted domain, exploring the terrain of Satan, witches, and other followers of evil. Without a Newtonian-clockwork mechanics and physics to explain the workings of nature, the meanings of events appeared as marvelous evidence of God's providence and admonition through omens and signs. Storms, lightening, comets, monstrous births, freakish happenings in nature, earthquakes, epidemics, wars, fires, explosions, and shipwrecks all were rendered meaningful as "wonder stories" freighted with portents of communal safety, danger, and God's providences toward his people.[13]

Protestantism interpreted misfortune and adversity as part of God's plan, the special providences that punished the wicked and tested the elect. For saints, temporal afflictions represented God's affections calling believers to examine their consciences for the evidence of sin that had provoked divine wrath. Collective and individual guilt was an explanatory principle for the impenetrable workings of divine providence. Only the repentance of sin would protect believers.

In England and colonial New England, public fast days set aside for repentance, humiliation, and petitionary prayer addressed the vexing concerns of communities. In *Worlds of Wonder, Days of Judgment*, David Hall argues that petitionary prayer and fasting assumed central importance in the public, ritual life of early New England. The fast day, like the witch hunt and trial, the confession of criminals, public executions, and covenant renewals, was a social ritual of reaffirmation and renewal of the sacred solidarities in these covenanted communities. "Always the purpose of the ritual was to enact a reversal, as in turning sickness into health, providing passage out of danger, or making visible the hidden. Ritual was a formalized procedure, a patterned means of connecting the natural and the social worlds to supernatural power."[14]

Fast days, as rituals of collective humiliation before God, provided opportunities to repent of the inroads made by apostasy and declension. Fast days made appeals for divine assistance in saving crops from drought or insects. Ritualized fasts sought God's blessing and protection for the voyages of ships and the military campaigns against Indians. New Englanders held fast days to purify the body social and heal the wounds caused by contention among brethren and for the polluting crimes of murder, infanticide, and witchcraft.[15]

During epidemics, fasting and petitionary prayer were employed to protect the community. Certain diseases, such as melancholy, or possession, had natural and supernatural causes for which rituals of fasting and prayer had special healing efficacy. An afflicted believer was urged to employ extraordinary regimes of fasting and supplication until the crisis abated.[16] Hall recounts the case of Elizabeth Knapp, a young woman troubled by fits ascribed to demonic possession. Physicians, in cooperation with a team of ministers, treated her by prescribing various drugs combined with increasingly severe, "extraordinary" regimens of ritual prayer and fasting. The pastoral and medical care administered to religious melancholiacs counseled the perseverance and redoubling of personal rituals of fasting and prayer. In this way they were methods of recovering assurance, and of quieting religious doubts or satanic assaults. Fasting was one of the most important healing rituals available to Protestants in times of sickness, personal perplexities, and transition in the lifespan. Crisis-related fasting could become obsessional, what Freud termed private neurotic religious rituals, designed to purify the believer of sin, guilt, and pollutions. As such, the quest for spiritual consolation in times of personal crisis frequently resulted in the continued obsessive-compulsive use of ritualized fasting, or what I term evangelical anorexia nervosa.

Hall examined the life of Samuel Sewell, a seventeenth-century Boston merchant, magistrate, and diarist, as representative of a life in early New England. Sewall participated in nearly one hundred fasts associated with public adversity and family troubles. Private fasts and petitionary prayers helped Sewall confront the uncertainties of life, transforming anxieties into the assurance of God's blessing and love. By his own account, he performed these magical rituals "incessantly," fasting in a variety of circumstances, from the trivial move to a new house, to times of family illness and death. "Ever anxious to increase his family's share of blessings, Sewell arranged for private fasts at key moments of transition. The change to new quarters in his house was a step completed by a fast that included three ministers and several members of the Council [the upper house of Massachusetts government]."[17]

Thomas notes the growing importance of fast days among Puritans:

. . . it was among the Puritans that this primitive rite was most extensively employed. The strict doctrine of the fast required participants to forego meat and drink, to refrain from their daily labour, to take less than their usual amount of sleep, to wear sober clothes, and to abstain from sexual activity. In this ritual condition, they were to pass the day reading the Word, singing psalms and offering prayers.[18]

Public fast days helped purge community members of collective guilt and guide them along the path directed by their covenant with God. Private fasting, on the other hand, expiated individual guilt and gave special efficacy to petitionary prayer. Saints fasted and prayed for protection, healing, and divination, seeking supernatural guidance when beset by controversy or the burden of choice.[19]

Evangelical anorexia nervosa, so closely related to the cultural significance given to fasting in English and American Puritanism, characterized the *ordo salutis* of the pilgrim, and became a familiar landmark of religious melancholia. The evangelical child who grew to adulthood haunted by fear of the loss of God's love and beset by the repetitious rituals of self-maceration in evangelical humiliation, employed fasting as a private neurotic ritual. The childhood of evangelical nurture produced an adult personality prone to guilt, shame, and a scrupulous conscience. Through private rituals of fasting, believers might find fervency in prayer, self-annihilation, and transcendence. Absent this relief from sin and suffering, evangelicals reapplied themselves with obsessive repetition, fasting again and again until they enjoyed the inner illumination that told them God had forgiven their sins. If they could still not find relief, many became convinced that they had committed the unpardonable sin and began fasting unto death.

Hannah Allen's Travail

Private fasting associated with religious melancholy was also prevalent among seventeenth-century English nonconformists. Hannah Allen's spiritual autobiography, *Satan his Methods and Malice Baffled* (1683), provides an early account of this variety of religious melancholy. Allen presents her early life as a time marked by intense melancholy, which she interprets as a physical disease that left her vulnerable to the fiery darts and attacks of Satan. From the perspective of recovered physical health and spiritual assurance of God's love, she recounts her years of affliction as admonition and encouragement to others beset by religious melancholy.[20]

Allen's first conversion crisis in the 1650s was marked by self-accusations of committing the unpardonable sin. In 1662, a series of economic and family misfortunes, including the death of her seafaring husband, initiated a second period of protracted melancholy. Satan filled her mind with temptations, blasphemous thoughts, and obsession with hypocrisy. During a thunderstorm she heard the voice of God proclaim, "There remains no sacrifice for sin," which she interpreted to mean that God had chosen her for damnation.[21]

In this state of confirmed religious melancholy, Allen went to live with family in London. There she attempted suicide on several occasions by regimens of starvation. She went to live with an aunt in Derbyshire in 1665, and again starved herself. Of this wasting away Allen writes:

> Towards winter I grew to eat very little, much less than I did before, so that I was exceeding lean, and at the last nothing but skin and bones. (A neighbouring gentlewoman, a very discreet person, that had the greatest desire to see me, came in at the back door of the house unawares and found me in the kitchen. Who, after she had seen me, said to Mrs. Wilson, "She cannot live; she hath death in her face.") I would say still that every bit I did eat hastened my ruin and that I had it with a dreadful curse, and what I ate increased the fire within me, which would at last burn me up, and I would now willingly live out of hell as long as I could.[22]

During the spring of 1666, she received pastoral and medical care from a cousin by marriage, himself a minister who, by increments, nurtured her starved body and despairing heart until she recovered health and religious consolation. Allen's spiritual narrative recast her years of desolation as the physical disease of melancholy that permitted Satan to invade her mind with obsessions, including the determination to fast unto death, confirmed as an unpardonable sinner.

Hannah Allen's spiritual travail needs to be seen in the context of a representative and successful Christian life consistent with other seventeenth-century accounts by Bunyan, Baxter, Perkins, and Ames. Indeed, the genre of spiritual biography and pastoral theology identified the typicality of Allen's religious melancholy. In a sermon preached on March 6, 1691, John Moore sought to guide and sustain those afflicted with scrupulous consciences and overwrought with self-accusations. "For they, feeling no present Comfort from their long and strict Fasts, nor from their lament and often repeated Prayers, do conclude, That whatever they do in it will neither please him, nor profit their souls."[23] Moore identified the three typical obsessions of the melancholy as (1) a belief that reformation and conversion proceeded due to fear of punishment and not love of God; (2) flatness of mind, want of zeal, and fear of spiritual inadequacy; and (3) fear of blasphemy against the Holy Spirit tantamount to commission of the unpardonable sin.[24]

Reverend Moore counseled perseverance, even if spiritual trials continued unabated.

> . . . persevere in your Duty and confide in his infinite goodness, and at length the Cloud which now darken your Minds shall all vanish, and be succeeded by steady and pure light, your fears shall be turned into full Assurances of inconceivable happiness; and the Disorder, Tumults, and Confusions in your Souls, shall be changed into Eternal Peace, and undisturbed and endless Joy.[25]

Reverend John Langhorne authored another work in this literature of spiritual assurance and consolation. *Letters on Religious Retirement* (1762) were addressed to a young woman named Cleora, advising her that the path of true religion involved moderate, rational piety. In a collection of twenty letters, he instructed the silent Cleora to avoid above all the excesses of fanaticism and enthusiasm that for Langhorne were synonymous with Catholic monasticism and mysticism, Methodism, and conventicles of evangelical Pietism.

Cleora had read Reverend William Romaine's *Triumph of Faith* and meditations upon the songs of Solomon, and she longed for the ravishing inward experience of God in her soul. She retreated into her secret chamber, praying, fasting, and in contemplation, so that her soul could become a vessel for God's spirit, waiting for the rapture. Langhorne admonished that this path could only lead to enthusiasm and religious melancholy. He had witnessed countless cases, especially the lamentable instance of "Eleanora," a person of mutual acquaintance, who had succumbed to melancholy.

> She spent her days in mortification, and her nights in terror; for she was taught to believe, that her Devotion would be acceptable to God, in proportion as it was distressful to herself. From that persuasion, she passed the greatest part of her life in penal austerities: but, as she was a child of ENTHUSIASM, she was sometimes visited with a gleam of fanatic joy, which shone through the gloom of her cell; and, during those intervals, she asserted that she was in Heaven. Those intervals, however, as they were too powerful for a mortal mind, were very short and very rare: her exhausted spirits were afterwards reduced to the lowest languor; and she, who, the last moment, was exulting in the ecstasies of Heaven, was now aghast on the brink of Hell.[26]

Langhorne advocated avoiding the delusion that one's whole life should center around self-denial and mortification. Rather, he said, the Christian should, in moderate love toward God, fulfill her traditional duties as wife, mother, and mistress of household. Langhorne realized that Cleora and other women who responded to the call of Protestant mysticism sought freedom in the paradoxically self-destructive mortifications and fasts of evangelical anorexia from their limited opportunities. Langhorne redirected these women, suggesting that they might find realization of their desire to serve God by resignation to the spheres of domesticity. Nurturing their children and attending to the needs of their husbands "will leave you no languid vacuity either in your time or thoughts."[27] Consistent with the duty of Protestant inner-worldly ascetics to make active contributions to the commonweal, as opposed to world-rejecting monasticism, he advised Cleora, "is not this to serve your Creator as he ought to be served? Is it not preferable to the life of those *unprofitable servants*, who spend their days in monastic dullness . . . ."[28] His advice was to resist the wish to be free and the temptations of enthusiasm, and cleave to the order of proper domestic influence.

Evangelical anorexia also typified the religious experiences of many leaders and followers of the First Great Awakening in eighteenth-century New England. These champions of Pietism and heart religion wrote spiritual guides of their own travail for others to follow and helped legitimate the theology of the awakening. In New Divinity theology, by implication, fasting was heralded as a tried and proven method of humiliation that brought great spiritual harvests. We see this in the life and work of David Brainerd, William Tennent, Jr., Samuel Hopkins, Susanna Anthony, Sarah Osborn, and Mary Moody Emerson. They each suffered religious melancholy and evangelical anorexia nervosa. These published memoirs and spiritual pilgrimages became the evangelical classics, the exemplars of spiritual success that so many eighteenth-century New Englanders would emulate.

The Near-Death Experience of William Tennent, Jr.

In 1806, Elias Boudinot published the "Memoirs of the Reverend William Tennent." Tennent (1705–1777) was a Presbyterian minister who served forty-six years in Freehold, New Jersey, and who championed the cause of the evangelical New Light religion in the Great Awakening.[29] William Tennent's older brother, Gilbert, together with George Whitefield, spread the fire-and-brimstone message of evangelical Pietism throughout the middle colonies in the 1740s. In Neshaminy, Pennsylvania, William Tennent, Sr., established Log College, a ministerial training center that preceded the New Divinity movement's education of pastors in the frontier settlements of western New England.

In 1731, at age twenty-six, William Tennent had completed his preliminary education and left his father's home to prepare for the ministry, residing with Gilbert, who was serving as a pastor in New Brunswick, New Jersey. As a prerequisite to acceding to the call of the ministry, each candidate first needed to experience the inner journey to conversion. Gilbert Tennent acknowledged the influence of the Dutch Reformed theologian Frederick Frelinghuysen in delineating the stages of the *ordo salutis*—law work (evangelical humiliation and repentance), rebirth (the searing cathartic experience of selfless surrender to the sovereignty of God), and the practice of piety.[30] Gilbert taught these principles of Pietist, experimental religion to his brother. Here, the term experiment refers to the demonstration of a known and true theological principle revealed in the direct observation of the predicated changes in an individual case. William Tennent applied his brother's principles and experienced the anticipated evangelical humiliation and melancholy.

Many of Gilbert Tennent's sermons from his early career in the 1730s and the Awakening of the 1740s resonate with a contemplative exegesis of inner-worldly mystical themes found in the Song of Solomon. Two sermons, *"De amore Christo,"* and *"De nuptiis cum Christo,"* seek to instill religious affections by exhorting believers to harken to the love of Christ, accept the invitation to the wedding, and enjoy the spiritual gifts that Christ the bridegroom offers his bride.

> Sinners, if you marry him all is yours. All his riches are yours forever. If you are in debt even a thousand talents, he has enough to pay all. All he asks is your consent. Will you come to the King's supper? Will you

embrace him, accept him for your all? What do you say? What answer shall I return to the great king who sent me to you?[31]

The inward, contemplative love for Christ served as the foundation of Tennent's preaching and devotional piety. As one recent commentator has written, "he had an astounding spiritual vitality, a trait he has bequeathed to the whole of American Christianity."[32] Gilbert conveyed this contemplative and experiential religion to William.

Gilbert Tennent was known for a style of direct, emotive, and powerful preaching that struck down the unconverted and coldhearted alike, awakening them to the perils of their condition. Those who came under his masterful rhetoric felt that he spoke directly, intimately, to the personal state of their souls. Although we can never know with certainty the conversations and exhortations between Gilbert Tennent and his brother, we can speculate that Gilbert's preaching and appeal to unregenerate sinners during the awakening of the 1740s resembled his earlier appeals to William. Tennent's sermon, "*De Impotentia Hominis*," preached on July 22, 1746, recreates the total inability and powerlessness of the unregenerate to redeem themselves from sin. The sermon is an exhaustive catalog of the weaknesses and insufficiencies of the natural man—impotent and compounding his plight by adding sin to sin. All of man's thoughts, perceptions, and volitions resemble the tainted fruit of a poisoned tree. The unredeemed possess an aversion to spiritual goodness and a proclivity for evil and sinful action. Acts of duty, good works, and exercises of piety performed by a corrupted heart do not fulfill the demands of the law—a perfect and perpetual obedience to God's will. Sinners cannot repent and hope in Christ's mediation and mercy. They live as "aliens from the commonwealth" and "strangers from the covenant."[33] Should they come to a realization of their plight, unable as Arminians to work their way to salvation and by human agency remove the wrath and curse of God, unable by antinomian experience to atone and find salvation in direct communion with God, the unregenerate enter into what Tennent conceptualized as the necessity of despair of self. In this movement towards despair, the sinner began a helpless surrender to the absolute sovereignty of God. Some sinners viewed suicide as an escape from their plight. Tennent knew of the unregenerate who, in their descent went to the extreme of suicidal starvation.

A decade earlier, William Tennent had stopped eating in a conversion crisis. In his sermon, Gilbert Tennent argues that "it is unreasonable to conclude that [the] graceless sinner should leave of [sic] eating & drinking because they sin therein, for if they do they would murder themselves which is a greater evil."[34] Gilbert knew firsthand of this unreasonableness. In exhorting his brother to enter the stage of despair as part of the passage into selfless surrender to God, and in urging upon William the visage of the contemplative as an adopted child of God, Gilbert did not anticipate the ensuing starvation and near-death experience. Thus begins an extraordinary narrative of William Tennent's conversion crisis, starvation, and prolonged period of coma.

Boudinot and Alexander provide this account:

After a regular course of study in theology, Mr. Tennent was preparing
for his examination by the presbytery as a candidate for the gospel ministry. His intense application affected his health, and brought on a pain in
his breast, and a slight hectic. He soon became emaciated, and at length
was like a living skeleton. His life was now threatened.[35]

Commentators on Tennent's life have interpreted this condition of inanition and marasmus as the result of a respiratory infection that produced these
symptoms resembling a hectic. However, some fifty years earlier, Cotton
Mather described his own conversion crisis and period of starvation at the
age of fourteen as a hectic condition. An alternative eighteenth-century usage
for hectic defined this condition as "belonging to or symptomatic of the bodily
syndrome or habit,"[36] not necessarily accompanying consumption or a physical
disease. It is quite likely that William Tennent, like Cotton Mather, refused
food in the context of his vocational crisis. Since Tennent's journal does not
explain the motives for his food refusal and emaciation, any interpretation
hinges on which meaning of hectic one employs. Tennent's biographers,
working in the genre of hagiography, wrote that hectic signified physical disease. No hero of experimental religion memorialized as an exemplar for succeeding generations could succumb to religious melancholy and fasting unto
death. No authentic account of true and vital piety operating in a believer's
life could portray religion as associated with mental aberration and alienation.
The account of his crisis continues:

> He grew worse and worse, till little hope of life was left. In this situation,
> his spirits failed him, and he began to entertain doubts of his final happi-
> ness. He was conversing, one morning, with his brother, in Latin, on the
> state of his soul when he fainted and died away.[37]

Presuming him to be dead, William Tennent's family placed his body upon
a board and prepared for the funeral. However, Tennent's physician, who had
just returned from a trip, refused to accept this death. He examined the cold,
stiff corpse, its eyes sunken and lips discolored, and found a slight warmth
under the arm. The physician remained with the comatose patient for three
days, until he was able to revive him by softening the tongue with oil. Gilbert walked in upon this scene and was reported to have exclaimed, "It is
shameful to be feeding a lifeless corpse." Gilbert insisted that he proceed with
his brother's burial. "At this critical and important moment, the body, to the
great alarm and astonishment of all present, opened its eyes, and gave a dreadful groan, and sunk again into apparent death."[38] Within two hours, William Tennent regained consciousness. He convalesced for six weeks, suffering almost total amnesia about his previous religious training and crisis. He
had lost his capacity for language and could not speak, read, or write. After
three years, Tennent recovered from the coma and provided this account of
his out-of-body and near-death experience, describing meeting God and the
heavenly hosts. He lost consciousness when speaking with his brother on issues
of salvation and the state of his soul.

. . . I found myself, in an instant, in another state of existence, under the
direction of a superior being, who ordered me to follow . . . I felt joy
unutterable and full of glory. I then applied to my conductor, and requested
leave to join the happy throng. On which he tapped me on the shoulder,
and said, "You must return to the earth." This seemed like a sword through
my heart. In an instant, I recollect to have seen my brother standing before
me, disputing with the doctor.[39]

William Tennent was ordained as pastor of a Presbyterian church in Freehold, New Jersey, in October 1733. He assumed the vacancy caused by the
untimely death of his brother, John, in 1732. William Tennent remained in
this service until his death in 1777. His memorial recounts other extraordinary religious experiences during his pastorate. Tennent enjoyed taking long,
meditative walks and during one such exercise, he was struck down in rapturous surrender to the Spirit of God. A flood of light irradiated his soul:

. . . and the infinite majesty of Jehovah were so inexpressibly great, as to
entirely overwhelm him, and he fell, almost lifeless, to the ground. When
he had revived a little, all he could do was to raise a fervent prayer that
God would withdraw himself from him, or that he must perish under a
view of his ineffable glory. When able to reflect on his situation, he could
not but abhor himself as a weak and despicable worm. . . .[40]

Concerned church members searched for and found Reverend Tennent in
this stupor. He was brought back to the church and revived. Despite protes-
tations of his unworthiness to preach, Tennent inspired new levels of evangelical religious affections among his flock that Sabbath day.

The near-death trance and subsequent ravishing accounts of the Holy Spirit
delineated in Tennent's memorial affirmed the peculiar workings of God with
his chosen and were urged upon succeeding generations, who sought direction and comfort, who found themselves "groaning under the pressure of the
calamities which they often have to endure in their pilgrimage through the
wilderness of this world."[41] Indeed, Boudinot felt himself duty-bound to publish the memorial to Tennent as a model and invitation for all to imitate. He
begins this work with the rationale, "Among the duties which every generation owes to those which are to succeed it, we may reckon the careful delin-
eation of the character of those whose example deserves, and may invite,
imitation." [42]

William Tennent's "slight hectic" was an apologia for evangelical
anorexia, an attempt to fast unto death in the course of a conversion crisis.
This remarkable near-death experience, memorialized by Boudinot, provides
a historical case study of a culture-bound syndrome tied to the structure of
New Divinity theology and religious experience that was to characterize the
emerging evangelical movement in the First and Second Great Awakenings.
Boudinot extolled and valorized the vital piety of William Tennent and invited
all discerning Christians to imitate this spiritual pilgrimage. Not surprisingly, many
who labored in his spirit encountered their own "dark nights of the soul.

David Brainerd's Devotional Piety

In 1749, two years after David Brainerd's untimely death from tuberculosis, Jonathan Edwards edited, annotated, and published Brainerd's spiritual diaries. Brainerd was born in Haddam, Connecticut, in 1718, entered Yale College in 1739, but was expelled in 1742 for his participation in New Light enthusiasm and for questioning the grace of a college tutor. In the remaining six years of his life, Brainerd completed his preparation for the ministry, was ordained, and worked as a Presbyterian missionary to tribes in New York, Pennsylvania, and New Jersey. He preached to, catechized, and organized a Native American congregation, baptizing thirty-eight converts among the Delaware.[43] The dying Brainerd relinquished his itinerant ministry and spent his last months as a guest in the Northampton home of Jonathan Edwards.

For Edwards the spiritual diaries represented an extended case history of the evangelical *ordo salutis*, of the inward journey of the soul's ceaseless striving to forge an authentic Christian life, and of the operation of religious affections. Edwards's *Life of David Brainerd* needs to be read as a life history that exemplified the systematic theological claims first introduced in Edwards's treatises on *Religious Affections* and the *Faithful Narrative*. In appended reflections to the memoirs Edwards states, "We have here the opportunity, as I apprehend, in a very lively instance to see the nature of true religion; and the manner of its operation when exemplified in a high degree and powerful exercise."[44] The nature of true religion validated by Edwards and published as an example for all Christians to emulate would include a life punctuated by self-torture, mortification of the body, fasting as a ritual of purification, and religious melancholy.

David Brainerd experienced conversion in October 1740 while a student at Yale, following several years of religious anxiety and preparation. After so prolonged a struggle with his carnal heart, in repentance and evangelical humiliation for his sinfulness and utter depravity, he found helpless surrender to the all-powerful sovereignty and majesty of God. Brainerd could finally turn toward God in selfless ecstasy, filled with self-denying *caritas* for all humankind. He recorded the following passage:

> Saturday October 18. 1740. In my morning devotions my soul was exceedingly melted for and bitterly mourned over my vileness and exceeding sinfulness. I never had then felt so pungent and deep a sense of the odious nature of sin as at this time. My soul, I trust, mourned truly after a godly sort while I had very lively apprehensions of God's love to me and my soul going out in love to him and this love and hope at that time cast out fear.[45]

Conversion proved to be only the beginning of Brainerd's lifelong striving after the elusive ideal of spiritual perfection in holiness and the maturing "progressive sanctification."[46] Edwards extols Brainerd's exercise of religious affections: the sorrow for sin, "love to God," and rejoicing to Christ. Edwards explains that religious affections and the quest for holiness necessitated continual evangelical humiliation, which for Brainerd consisted of "a sense of his own utter insufficiency, despicableness, and odiousness."[47] Through devotional piety, daily secret prayer, meditation, and self-examination, Brainerd fostered these religious affections and self-consciously employed techniques of evangelical humiliation, seeking evidence of his vileness and pollution. Only through this self-induced torture, what he termed "wrestling with God," could he enjoy transient seasons of communion with the Holy Spirit, contemplative oneness with Jesus, assurance of adoption and love as the child of God, and self-denying benevolence and love toward all humankind. Paradoxically, only in the desolation of melancholy and the odious evidence of his pollution dredged up from the exercise of evangelical humiliation could Brainerd find assurance of God's love. The heights of rapture, of God's love ravishing the heart, came from the depths of religious melancholy. Melancholy was that "pleasing pain" that augured a transient season of consolation. Brainerd writes:

> . . . God has been pleased to keep my soul hungry, almost continually; so that I have been filled with a kind of pleasing pain: When I really enjoy God, I feel my desires of him the more insatiable, and my thirstings after holiness the more unquenchable; and the Lord will not allow me to feel as though I were fully supplied and satisfied, but keeps me still reaching forward; and I feel barren and empty, as though I could not live without more of God in me; I feel ashamed and guilty before God.[48]

In the ceaseless quest for spiritual perfection, or "thirsting after holiness," Brainerd embraced melancholy, fasting, and mortification of the body. Brainerd made the devotions of the closet into daily repetitive personal rituals like the neurotic ceremonials of Cotton Mather. He transformed the evidence of sin and spiritual deadness revealed in self-examination and evangelical humiliation from occasions of doubt to indications of a maturing thirsting after holiness. He is led to exclaim, "Oh, this pleasing pain! It makes my soul press after God."[49]

He lapsed into spiritual coldness especially when pressed by a daily schedule of travel and ministerial work. Writing on January 2, 1744, he speaks of his solitary way as a pilgrim in temporary sojourn in this world, at peace only when he can retire from his public role and devote himself, obsessively, to the secret duties of the closet: "Those weeks that I am obliged now to be from home, in order to learn the Indian tongue, are mostly spent in perplexity and barrenness, without much sweet relish of divine things; and I feel myself a stranger to the throne of grace, for want of more frequent and continued retirement."[50]

Brainerd invariably employed rituals of purification in private or "secret" devotions as techniques endowed with special efficacy to produce evangelical humiliation. Continuing his journal entry for January 2, he writes:

> When I return home and give myself to meditation, prayer, and fasting, a new scene opens up to my mind, and my soul longs for mortification, self-denial, humility, and divorcement from all the things of the world. This evening my heart was somewhat warm and fervent in prayer and medita-

tion, so that I was loath to indulge sleep. Continued in those duties till about midnight.[51]

Not infrequently, Brainerd believed that through sinful acts he grieved the Spirit, and thus the countenance of God would not illuminate his heart. Brainerd suffered continued episodes of melancholy when he felt God had forsaken him. Brainerd possessed a "tender conscience" that recounted the sins of his youth in unending repetition. He could not forgive himself and cease the relentless self-chastisement, the self-torturous litany of his sins against man and God. Could God forgive him? Could his indwelling faith and grace offer evidence of the remission of these pollutions? Only in the repetitive cycle of evangelical humiliation and self-denying ecstasy could Brainerd find temporary assurance that God had indeed done so. Throughout the scores of dark seasons recorded in the diary, he resorts to private fasts, prayer, Scripture reading, meditation, and self-examination to renew his inward assurance of God's love. Less than a week had passed from the warmth of heart quoted previously, when Brainerd would lament on Friday, January 6, 1744:

> Feeling and considering my extreme weakness and want of grace, and pollution of my soul and danger of temptations on every side, I set apart this day for fasting and prayer, neither eating nor drinking from evening to evening, beseeching God to have mercy on me. And my soul intensely longed that the dreadful spots of sin might be washed away from it.[52]

For Brainerd, fasting assumed heroic proportions like that of Kafka's Hunger Artist. Brainerd employed private fasts for one or two days each week, typically Thursday and Saturday. He felt that fasting increased the fervency of his prayers and devotions to God. Only when the body was quiet, denied, and suppressed could the spirit grow. Writing in preparation for the Sabbath on March 3, 1744, he states that "Prayer was so sweet an exercise to me, that I knew not now to cease. lest I should lose the spirit of prayer. Felt no disposition to eat or drink for the sake of the pleasure of it, but only to support my nature and fit me for divine service."[53]

He spontaneously fasts rather than end his devotions. Here the pilgrim thirsting after holiness needs only God's love for sustenance. Meditating upon verses from the Book of Job ("I have treasured up the words of his mouth more than my necessary food."), Brainerd writes on January 9, 1745: "My soul so much delighted to continue instant in prayer, at this blessed season, that I had no desire for my "necessary food" [Job 23:12]: even dreaded leaving off praying at all, lest I should lose this spirituality and this blessed thankfulness to God which I then felt."[54]

The years of fasting and mortification, the thousands of miles traversed on horseback as an itinerant preacher, and the disease of consumption exacted a great price on Brainerd's body. Lean, wasted, near emaciation, he used even this attribute to promote ever greater evangelical humiliation. He selected the passage from Job 16:8: "And Thou hast shrivelled me up, which is a witness against me; And my leanness riseth up against me, it testifieth to my face."[55]

Brainerd views his wasted body as further evidence of God's wrath, as cause for yet another occasion for evangelical humiliation in search of spiritual consolation.

David Weddle argues that "Brainerd's entire life seems to have been a process of dying, of 'mortification,' in order to serve God without vanity."[56] Through tuberculosis, fasting, and hard use in the service of God "the spirit devours the flesh" and "the dissolution of his body would release him into the only air his soul could breathe: the atmosphere of heaven."[57]

In the appended commentary on Brainerd's journal Edwards saw fit to include a brief section devoted to the duty of secret fasting. Brainerd had demonstrated the "right way of practicing religion," Edwards argues, and ministers in their pastoral duties to anxious and private Christians could discover a model of living "free from disquieting doubts and dark apprehensions about the state of their souls."[58]

> The reader has seen how much Mr. Brainerd recommends this duty, and how frequently he exercised himself in it. . . . Among all the many days he spent in secret fasting and prayer that he gives an account of in his diary, there is scarce an instance of one but what was either attended or soon followed with apparent success and a remarkable blessing in special incomes and consolations of God's Spirit; and very often before the day was ended.[59]

In *The Life of Brainerd*, Edwards had the ideal vehicle to demonstrate that the outward person of self-denial devoted to the causes of benevolence and Christian activism was founded upon the inward growth of evangelical piety. Edwards warns that good works and a sanctified life alone did not distinguish the bona fide Christian. The Arminian way to grace was rejected. Edwards also found in Brainerd's journals the rejection of enthusiasm—a denial of the sudden, violent extremes of revivalistic conversions. Brainerd exemplified the middle path between these positions: the lifelong repetitive, obsessive devotional piety of the evangelical in warfare with the self and questing after the holy religious affections of contemplative mysticism. As the evangelical hero, Brainerd set on an inner spiritual pilgrimage that displayed equal ascetic self-discipline directed towards transforming the world according to the values of benevolence and winning souls for Christ as a missionary to the heathen. Edwards extolled the simultaneous pursuit of inner contemplative mysticism and outer vocational asceticism as the authentic balance of Christian living for all to follow.

Edwards's publication of Brainerd's journals became an evangelical classic and reached large audiences in the Second Great Awakening, particularly following the American Tract Society's 1833 edition.[60] Joseph Conforti maintains that this was Edwards's most popular and widely read work, which influenced John Wesley and American Methodists and the training of generations of ministers and missionaries at Yale and Andover Theological Seminary. Brainerd became a part of the evangelical oral tradition as ministers preached on his life, parents made tales of his piety a part of evangelical child-rearing, and private individuals looked to Brainerd's heroism as guideposts during their own struggles in the morphology of conversion. Conforti argues:

> Both Brainerd himself and Edwards's *Life of Brainerd* need to be restored to their central place in American religious history. First of all, by the early nineteenth century Brainerd had secured an exalted position in evangelical hagiography, and Edwards's *Life* had become an immensely influential devotional-inspirational work among evangelical clergy and laity.[61]

The spiritual diaries kept by college and seminary students and missionaries coming of age during the second decade of the nineteenth century invariably cite Brainerd as they model their own spiritual pilgrimage upon the tried and tested exercises revealed in the *Life*. Most notably, the values of selfless benevolence, Christian activism, and the missionary spirit combined with the inner spiritual exercises of evangelical humiliation provide the abiding themes through which these evangelical youth forged their spiritual identities. We see how Edwards's *Life* valorized melancholy and the secret devotions of the closet, including fasting, as neurotic ceremonials that would lead the soul to God's love and the possession of the Holy Spirit. Edwards's *Life of Brainerd* provided the pastoral model of evangelical anorexia nervosa that religionists in the midst of their conversion crises would embrace with varying degrees of severity.

Isaac Bird (1793–1876) is a case in point. In 1813, at the age of twenty, Bird began his freshman year at Yale College (he was in the same class as Benjamin Noyes, whose case we will encounter in Chapter 4). Bird was an older student and had not yet experienced a saving grace when he began his college studies. His college journal records the protracted, two-year struggle with sin during this first conversion crisis. Recounting his selfishness, vanity, levity, worldliness, and deceitful heart, he alternates between moments of submission to God and long interludes of desolation. Like so many other evangelicals, he waged war with the self and employed the exercises of devotional piety to vanquish his pride. Writing on November 13, 1813, he laments:

> I have made late discoveries of such pride, envy, & hypocrisy reigning in my breast that I am sure I ought to be alarmed for my state. I attend to secret prayer but slightly in the morning. I at length in the evening, but this appears not sufficient. My corruptions are gaining. I fear their ascendancy.[62]

Through his many conversations with students and tutors and his correspondence with friends on religious matters, Bird perseveres in his strivings for grace. He reflects upon the sudden death of two of his roommates during the first term, the hovering presence of death, and the chief task of this life in preparation for the soul's salvation. Writing to James Winchell after hearing of his friend's conversion, Isaac recounts attending a prayer meeting with Winchell in Lenox, Massachusetts, during their summer recess. "My heart was often wrung within me, & the tears gushed involuntarily from my eyes. To be particular, recollect the affectionate manner in which you more than once conversed with me, & entreated me to consider the amazing length of eternity, the uncertainty of life, & the happiness of Christians."[63]

He opens his diary on January 1, 1814, with the agonized awareness of the shortness of time: "Another year nearer the grave."[64] Bird begins reading the journals of Brainerd and undertakes a regime of ascetic mortification of the body. Citing Jonathan Edwards, he notes "I am sensible that we ought by no means to eat for the mere enjoyment it produces but chiefly that we may be supported in life. Therefore Resolved To be particularly cautious in suffering myself to eat (no) more than what nature requires."[65]

In the spirit of Brainerd, he ardently seeks evangelical humiliation, social withdrawal to practice devotional piety, and a sober, somber demeanor, stating "Christ never laughed, therefore, let his followers be sober."[66] By February, Bird adds private fasts to his devotions, citing the authority of Brainerd and Edwards.

> Sunday 6. Neglected to attend meals in the morning & at noon spending the time in prayer while my roommates were gone. At noon found much more fervency & enjoyment in prayer than for a long time before. I was led to the determination of fasting from the recommendation of Brainerd & Edwards.
>
> I find it one of the most blessed means of increasing fervor of spirit. I found the same result on the first trial, at home, in the vacation.
>
> It is a denial of our service to the God our appetite (which I have long served as such without knowing it) & substituting the glorious service of the Living God.[67]

In the course of these private fasts, conducted two or three days each week, Bird mortified his flesh so that the spirit could live and grow. Solitary fasting intensified his humiliation and devotions. He reported feeling purified of sin. He gained the assurance of obedience to God and a sense of independence and separateness from a sinful world. In rapture, he exclaimed, "O how glorious it be if I could not sin and thus grieve the Holy Spirit to leave me."[68] Bird had discovered the experimental piety of Brainerd: fasting amplified the fervency of prayer and induced the white-heat of God's love in his heart.

In this case, "successful" fasting was a devotional technique employed to amplify the power of private piety usually attended, as Edwards noted, by the renewed possession of the inner psychological evidence of spiritual growth. Bird could testify that from the depths of self-induced humiliation augmented by fasting he experienced the holy affections of Edwardsean conversion. He discovered, in the secret duties of the closet, the workings of experimental religion in his own heart. He applied Brainerd's principles of piety in his secret devotions and experienced the anticipated humiliation, mortification, melancholy, and rapture. Thus, Bird's spiritual travail held the promise of conversion and progressive sanctification if he would only persevere in the experimental principles set forth by Edwards and Brainerd.

He attended a prayer meeting on February 20 and shared his newfound assurance with his college brethren. Bird proposed that they pray and fast together. His request was summarily rejected and he responded with impatience and anger. Bird relates that "I was sinfully impatient because my counsel was not received, so wicked is my heart. How must Christ despise such a spirit exercised towards his followers. May such repeated instances of sin make one more watchful."[69]

Like Brainerd, Isaac Bird fostered a tender, scrupulous conscience, directing anger caused by rejection from his classmates inward as renewed evidence of a vile self. Yet this inwardly turned anger that unfailing produced melancholy created "that pleasing pain" of evangelical humiliation that Bird interpreted as necessary for spiritual growth. He would write, "I have wished to be like Brainerd from reading his life & Journal."[70] This wish, when granted, brought an unending cycle of self-imposed humiliations and fasting, melancholy as a constant companion, and the all-too-brief respite of spiritual consolation. With a renewed heart, Bird made a profession of faith and entered the covenant of the Yale College Church on March 6, 1814. However, by March 10 he began anew this cycle of doubt and self-flagellation: ". . . I have to confess a criminal propensity to relaxation in my exertions after holiness. I want more enlarged views of the character of God. I want a habitual soberness of mind. . . . I see no Christian examples worth following. None are sufficiently engaged. But I know not the heart of others. I however, see no Calvins, no Whitefields, Luthers or Brainerds."[71]

Through the close of the spring term, Bird self-consciously emulated the character of Brainerd, seeking to become a morose, solitary pilgrim who walked in the world unaffected by worldliness. He avoided the company of others in favor of his private devotions. In public prayers and evening religious meetings he comported himself with a dour seriousness that prompted admonition from peers and tutors. In walking Brainerd's path, he suffered months of seemingly unrelieved melancholy. Returning to his father's farm during summer recess, Bird persevered in his piety and fasts but his scrupulous conscience knew no release from this spiritual torment.

> When the wind blows heavy against the house I fancy I hear the voice of God speaking in this manner "I can prostrate the dwelling you inhabit & bury you in the ruins—fear my power & remember when the wind shall cease & all its tokens of my anger vanish, that I am still the Lord."
> Can I say in my heart that I feel heightened to God at the end that I did at the beginning of the week. O have been an unprofitable servant. O Lord who hast the hearts of all men in thy power help me to resign more into thy hands & may not another week pass . . . which shall not add fervor to my soul & brightness to my hopes.[72]

Isaac Bird stopped keeping a private spiritual diary and record of his soul's pilgrimage on August 14 after his return to Yale and conversation with Elias Cornelius. Cornelius explained that diary writing was an exercise in self-indulgence and pride. Bird countered that "I live most devotional when I thus bring myself to account at stated periods" by writing in his journal each morning or upon retiring for the evening.[73] However, after this entry his journal contains public events, accounts of his travels, and lecture recitations, not the inward struggles of the *ordo salutis*.

Isaac Bird left no evidence of how he resolved his scrupulosity and tempered the practice of Brainerd's model of self-flagellation. His regimes of piety and fasting did not reach the extremes of self-accusation of committing the unpardonable sin and fasting unto to death.

He did join a college literary fraternity and pursued his studies with renewed energy. Although he recorded the public events of the college revival of 1815 (omitting the suicide of Benjamin Noyes), Bird reveals little of his own heart except to state, "As for myself, I have been sinfully sluggish, dull, proud, & vain. During this awakening my conduct has been unworthy of a christian."[74]

Isaac Bird never relinquished Brainerd's model of experimental piety, as evidenced in a farewell sermon preached before his Yale classmates on April 2, 1816, prior to graduation. Entitled "The Importance of Sincerity," it depicts true Christian sincerity as public, self-denying benevolence, the lifelong pursuit of the missionary spirit, and domestic friendship and love. Most interesting of all, he claimed that authentic sincerity rested upon the evangelical piety of the renewed heart, ever striving for the illusive ideal of perfection, daily immersed in the exercises of secret devotion. For Bird, the sincere man's public persona was founded upon an abiding piety.

> Behold him in his closet, holding communion with the Father of his spirit. Here he appears to *himself* indeed the humblest, but to *us* the most exalted of human beings. Here he seems endowed in a manner with a supernatural power. He lays hold with effect on the promises, "ask & ye shall receive," "Seek & ye shall find." *This* is " *the inwrought fervent* prayer of the righteous man." Here he, in effect heals the temporal diseases of man, rescues their souls from future misery . . . .[75]

Isaac Bird taught school for a year before entering Andover Theological Seminary in the fall of 1817. From his lecture notes and diary, we know that he again read Brainerd, participated in the school's public fast days, and embraced the student code of diligence in studies, humility, brotherly watchfulness, and reproof. He writes: "utmost importance, seek illumination of the Holy Spirit."[76] At the seminary, Dr. Leonard Woods instructed the students on the duty of temperance and fasting. Bird's lecture notes state: "Strict temperance—in eat and drink & c. He who eats too full & makes this a great part of his enjoyment perverts (the) design of God—takes most direct course to clog his mental processes."[77]

Isaac Bird completed his studies at Andover in 1820, received ordination and appointment from the American Board of Commissioners for Foreign Missions (A.B.C.F.M.) in 1821, married Ann Parker in 1822, and embarked as a foreign missionary to Beirut. His early conversion crisis resolved, he found a careful spiritual titration composed of outward benevolence and activism in the missionary spirit that was founded upon inward piety and religious affections. For Bird, the brief encounter with evangelical anorexia nervosa resolved into a temperate life of self-control.

Many other Andover students embraced the experimental piety of Brainerd during their early conversion crises. Levi Parsons, a member of the class of 1817 and missionary to Palestine, writes to his mother from Andover in July 1816.

> O for the spirit of Baxter and of Brainerd—for that ardour of piety, that tenderness of soul, that deadness to the world, that concern for sinners, which were so conspicuously manifested in their daily conversation. Never, never may I cease to struggle and fight till every sin is subdued.[78]

Parsons's diary records repetitive private fasts, repentances for sin, and humiliations. During December, he lapsed into a prolonged melancholy that lasted through the following November of 1817. The model of fasting, prayers of repentance, self-abasement, and other ceremonials proven by Brainerd to prepare the heart to receive God's love failed to produce the desired outcome. Parsons laments:

> November 29. Saturday evening.—Have suffered much the past week from an evil heart of unbelief. I dare not expect a blessing to accompany my exertions. God has cast me from his presence, and taken his Holy Spirit from me. My only plea is, Lord *remember me a miserable sinner*.

> After serious examination, fasting and prayer, I have obtained clearer discoveries of my own defilement. I am certain of a spiritual declension. I will return to him, who *has* delivered me from trouble.[79]

Daniel Morton, who edited Levi Parsons' journals and letters for publication, deleted many of the details of this conversion crisis. We cannot know the frequency and severity of these fasts, or whether Parsons felt so bereft of God's spirit as to consider himself beyond all hope, an unpardonable sinner. The published *Memoir* does depict a man who self-consciously emulated the life and character of David Brainerd, who suffered recurrent episodes of religious melancholy when he felt God withdrew his countenance, and who fasted twice weekly when health allowed. He understood the continued importance of fasting, as his journal entry of September 25, 1819, indicates: "Why should we fast? Because sin reigns in our mortal bodies, because our faith is weak, our vision of heaven obscure, our love for souls languid; because our temptations are fiery, our work arduous and responsible, our enemies numerous and powerful."[80]

Parsons also fasted and prayed with his missionary companion in Palestine, Pliny Fisk. They consecrated their efforts to God, rendering mutual support and admonition, and fostering brotherly affection and harmony. "We are to live in love; to maintain the most perfect harmony of feeling, of design, and of operation; to unite our strength, our talents and our influence, for the conversion of the heathen."[81] Parsons and Fisk continued the tradition of public fast days and communal fasting in small prayer groups characteristic of Andover.

The evangelical anorexia of Bird, Parsons, and Fisk, from the evidence extant, did not reach the extreme proportions of other persons in the throes of a conversion crisis, who fasted excessively, day after day, in a repentant search for the inner assurance of God's forgiveness. Realizing no relief and in abject hopelessness, they declared themselves to be damned, having grieved the Holy Spirit forever and thus having committed the unpardonable sin. In this state, they attempted to fast unto death in the belief that eating only compounded their sin. Successful religionists resolved their conversion crises and pursed a life of spiritual growth in temperate, moderate fasting and devotional piety. Those who failed to resolve their conversion crises suffered an excessive evangelical anorexia that frequently lead to attempted suicide by starvation. In principle, every evangelical was called upon by God to undertake a spiritual pilgrimage, appropriating Brainerd's experimental model of a Christian life and risking succumbing to scrupulosity. In principle, each pilgrim faced the possibility of falling into the excesses of evangelical anorexia.

Nearly fifteen hundred young men received their theological training at Andover in the period from 1808 to 1840.[82] Andover graduates went on to serve as missionaries for the A.B.C.F.M. and in Baptist missions, but the majority of the graduates who received ordination as ministers settled in New England or led western congregations. Andover graduates carried with them the legacy of Brainerd and Edwards's model of experimental piety. As they had forged an evangelical temperament through the crucible of conversion crisis and devotional piety, so they labored in their foreign missions and domestic congregations to win souls to Christ by proselytizing Brainerd's model for making a Christian life.

Samuel Hopkins and the New Divinity Movement

Samuel Hopkins (1721–1811) articulated the first American system of theology, inspired by the evangelical piety of the New England Awakening of the 1740s. A disciple of Jonathan Edwards, Hopkins rationalized Edwards's work on religious affections, virtue, and freedom of the will, producing a systematic theology that championed human freedom in the context of divine sovereignty, and the individualistic pursuit of life, liberty, and property consistent with a social ethic of selfless surrender to God and universal disinterested benevolence.[83] By mediating between the dialectical tensions of Arminianism versus antinomianism, free will versus the determinism of God's will, and modern individualism versus self-denial and self-abnegation to God, Hopkins forged a renewed Calvinistic doctrine that addressed the concerns of persons caught within the political and economic changes of the Revolutionary War and nascent industrialization. Hopkins became the principal minister whose name and doctrines were associated with a religious movement, initially termed "New Divinity" by its detractors. In *Samuel Hopkins and the New Divinity*

Movement, Joseph Conforti has written that "New Divinity was a movement of a particular group of pious, young New England men, students from small settlements in rural Connecticut who were converted either in the mid-century revival, in subsequent local revivals, or in the Second Great Awakening."[84]

The New Divinity movement articulated a systematic theology that legitimated the breakthrough of evangelical Pietism during the Awakening in the 1740s, defending the authenticity of mass conversions and the sudden and complete experience of rebirth during revivals.

The New Divinity movement required men to undergo conversion before preparing for the ministry. In the western settlements in Connecticut's Litchfield County and in Berkshire County in Massachusetts, Hopkins, Edwards, Stephen West, Joseph Bellamy, Nathanael Emmons, and other ministers opened their parsonages and received candidates to study in what came to be known as "Schools of the Prophets." The conversion experience, ministerial training, and early career of Samuel Hopkins served as the model for New Divinity men.

Born in 1721 in Waterbury, Connecticut, Samuel Hopkins enjoyed the benefits given to the son of a wealthy and influential farmer and landowner. The elder Hopkins informed his son at age fourteen that the youth would prepare for the ministry. Hopkins went to live with a tutor, the Reverend Graham of Woodbury, Connecticut, who prepared the boy for Yale's college entrance examinations. In 1732, Hopkins enrolled in Yale at the age of sixteen, returning to Waterbury each summer to assist in farm work. He made a profession of faith during his junior year and found himself swept up in the Great Awakening during his senior year.

During October of 1740, George Whitefield preached at Yale, which proved the beginning of many months of religious enthusiasm and contention. New Light itinerants and exhorters came to the college with the purpose of extending the work begun by Whitefield. During the winter term, routine college life proved impossible, as private prayer meetings took the place of classes and recitations. David Brainerd, then a sophomore at the college, questioned the piety and conversion of college tutors and was expelled by the end of the term. Armed with a newly found inspiration, students undermined college authority. "Conversions multiplied and so did emotional excesses. Weeping and shrieking accompanied visions of damnation. Once awakened to a conviction of sin, individuals shouted and screamed for relief. Spiritual agony expressed itself through bodily contortions. . . ."[85] Gilbert Tennent arrived at Yale in March 1741, preaching seventeen times and amplifying the force of New Light enthusiasm. Tennent's fire-and-brimstone rhetoric moved Hopkins, who writes: "when I heard Mr. Tennent . . . I thought that he was the greatest and best man, and the best preacher that I had ever seen or heard. His words were to me 'like apples of gold in pictures of silver.'"[86]

Tennent so inspired New Light students at Yale that in their zeal they defied college rules by visiting individual students in their dormitory rooms, inquiring after the state of their souls and exhorting and evangelizing unconverted classmates. David Brainerd's visit to Hopkins had a devastating effect, plunging Hopkins into the depths of a conversion crisis of evangelical terror and humiliation as a sinner in the hands of an angry God. With the passing of the immediate crisis, Hopkins languished for more than a year in religious melancholy. He writes in his memoirs:

> After I had taken my first degree, which was in September, 1741, I retired to my father's, in Waterbury; and being dejected and very gloomy in my mind, I lived a recluse life for some months. Considering myself as a sinful, lost creature, I spent most of my time in reading, meditation, and prayer, and spent many, whole days in fasting and prayer. My attention turned chiefly to my own sinfulness, and as being wholly lost in myself, of which I had an increasing conviction.[87]

Hopkins was licensed to preach in October and assisted in exhorting, fasting, and praying with the unconverted in a local revival. Still his melancholy persisted as he personally confronted a central doctrinal issue of New Divinity—the insistence upon converted ministers whose inward lives of exemplary devotional piety supported their public efforts of promulgating the Gospel. How could he pursue his ministerial vocation without the assurance of grace, being guilty of the same errors as the Old Light Calvinists that New Lights charged with hypocrisy? Hopkins decided to study with Jonathan Edwards to search through this perplexity.

Edwards had delivered a commencement address, "The Trial of the Spirits," before Hopkins's graduating class in September 1741. Hopkins decided against going to study with Gilbert Tennent in favor of living with Edwards in Northampton. In December 1741, Hopkins left Waterbury, making the eighty-mile trip by horseback to Edwards's parsonage. He arrived to find his mentor abroad on a preaching tour. Mrs. Edwards received him but found her young charge languishing in spiritual desolation, keeping to his chamber during the day. Hopkins writes:

> After some days, Mrs. Edwards came into my chamber, and said, 'As I was now become one of the family for a season, she felt herself interested in my welfare; and [as] she observed that I appeared gloomy and dejected, she hoped I would not think she intruded by desiring to know, and asking me what was the occasion of it'. . . .[88]

Hopkins told her that he was "in a Christless, graceless state, and had been under a degree of conviction and concern for a number of months, [I] got no relief, and my case, instead of growing better, appeared to grow worse."[89] Upon his return, Edwards guided Samuel through the inner journey of the recast evangelical *ordo salutis*, posing a series of questions regarding the religious affections of the regenerate. Thus, Hopkins found the assurance of his heart's regeneration.

> . . . for why doth that God that is described in the Bible appear the most desirable to me, unless I have seen him and do love him? Why do I long to behold a great, a holy, a powerful, a just, a true, an eternal, an omniscient, omnipresent, all-wise, and sovereign God . . . . And why doth every Chris-

tian grace, as it described in the word of God, appear beautiful and lovely
to me, considered in themselves, considered without their consequence,
(even eternal life and happiness,) unless I have seen the beauty of holiness?[90]

Hopkins characterizes his melancholy as an inward, reclusive solitude, as
a person lost in himself with no evidence of God's love, no assurance of having experienced a saving grace. These qualities of solitude, combined with
contemplations of divine love in exercises of private prayer and fasting, would
become the distinguishing traits of the melancholic quest for rapturous assurance. Hopkins's successful resolution of this conversion crisis would validate
the theology of the Awakening and a new organization of Christian life and
piety. Only the candidate who embraced a continual regimen of evangelical
humiliation, on his knees in the secrecy of the closet in prayer, meditation,
Scripture reading, and solemn conversation with God, could hope to find God's
love. Hopkins set aside each Saturday as a day of fasting and private devotion and continued this piety for sixty years. Paradoxically, the humiliated
saint reviled as a vile worm, in the depths of helplessness and dependency
upon the absolute sovereignty of God, could, in this moment of selfless,
ecstatic surrender, find the ravishing inner illumination of God's spirit. Writing on August 7, 1742, Hopkins records the resolution of his conversion crisis.

> Seeing Christ requires that I deny myself, take up my cross, and renounce
> all for him, taking him for my only portion here and forever, I do now
> afresh dedicate myself to the Lord, solemnly promising to renounce all other
> lords, and take him for my portion. I call heaven and earth to witness,
> that I now take the God of heaven and earth for my God. I now make
> myself over, with all that I have or ever shall have, to him.[91]

Hopkins's system of theology and the New Divinity movement were formalized and institutionalized renderings of his personal conversion experience
and contemplative practice of piety. Hopkins rationalized his own life experience as a guide for all who would know God. In *Enquiry concerning the
Promises of the Gospel; Whether any of them are made to the exercises and
doings of persons in an Unregenerate State* (1765) Hopkins repudiated the
Arminian doctrine of works. Following his own morphology of conversion,
he argued that sinners are under an urgent moral compulsion, immediately,
to choose God as their portion. Hopkins reflected upon and liberalized
Edwards's doctrine of human agency, arguing that all people are born into
this world as sinners with unregenerate hearts or wills. Sinners habitually chose
sin over sanctified conduct. However, all other faculties of the mind remained
intact—reason, understanding, perception. Where Edwards maintained that
the unregenerate had a natural inability to use the will because of the pollution of their faculties, Hopkins's theology restored these faculties to the natural
man. Sinners remained under an urgent moral duty to use their intellectual
faculties in an ethical manner. Thus, sinners must read the Word, listen to
preaching and sermons, receive instruction and exhortation, and immediately
repent. Through the action of the will, sinners repented and gave themselves

up totally to the absolute sovereignty of God. Failure to exercise the will for this holy purpose meant that all human agency—good works and outwardly ethical conduct, including the means of grace—were wicked and despicable in the eyes of God.[92] Before regeneration, all action by the sinner was wicked and completely unacceptable to God.

Hopkins rejected the idea of the Old Calvinists, that through gradual preparation, in response to the conditional promises of the covenant of grace, a sinner might use the means of grace—works and religious devotions—to move closer to holiness. The reformed evangelical morphology of conversion demanded that the sinner choose God and in the sudden passage of this moment of volition experience conversion. As William Breitenbach has argued:

> The Hopkinsians could deny the value of unregenerate doings because they had so fully established the natural ability of sinners to repent and be holy. Since the unregenerate were under no natural necessity to sin, and since the only obstacle to their acceptable obedience was their voluntary unwillingness to obey, they should be pressed into immediate repentance.[93]

Although Hopkins granted the free volitional power of the sinner's heart to repent and love God above all else, this choice involved a veritable transvaluation of self. The envisioned spiritual itinerary included relentless exercise of self-denial. The sinner who would freely choose to be holy needed to state a willingness to forge a life consistent with the ethical maxim, "thy will be done"—for the greater glory of God. The sinner had to state a willingness to suffer damnation for God's glory. Only this would evidence an end of self-love. In a "Dialogue Between a Calvinist and Semi-Calvinist," Hopkins states that "No man can know that he loves God until he does really love him; that is, until he does seek his glory above all things, and is disposed to say, 'Let God be glorified, whatever may be necessary in order to it,' without making any exception; and this is to be willing to be damned, if this be necessary for the glory of God."[94]

The willingness to suffer damnation and serve for eternity in hell as a monument to the glory of God represented the ultimate in self-denial and selfless love to God. The regenerate would prove their love to God despite their personal fate and not out of gratitude for Christ's mediation or pardon for their sins. All believers who would freely choose God as their only portion declared an unceasing warfare against the self. Children of God waged their *auto-machia* armed with the devotional exercises of evangelical humiliation.

Only through humiliation could the believer hope to progress through the morphology of conversion: faith, justification, adoption, sanctification, and glorification.[95] Reverend Joseph Bellamy, another New Divinity leader, who established a school for prophets in Bethel, Connecticut, defines evangelical humiliation in "True Religion Delineated" (1750) as a:

> sense of our own sinfulness, vileness, odiousness, and ill desert, and in a disposition, thence resulting to lie down in the dust full of self-loathing

and self-abhorrence, abased before the Lord, really accounting ourselves infinitely too bad ever to venture to come into the divine presence in our own names, or to have a thought of mercy from God on account of our own goodness.[96]

Humiliation was an exercise in self-denial, a time of repentance, a mortification of the body, and a reaffirmation that only through the inner mystical reception of Christ the mediator and the infusion of God's love could the regenerate maintain their hope for salvation.

Through the travail of humiliation the saint glorified God. Nathanael Emmons's sermon, "The Duty of Perfect Holiness in This Life," enlarged upon the writings of Hopkins and Bellamy and sounded a theme that would characterize New Divinity devotional piety. Emmons writes, "Those precepts which require saints to do every thing from love to God, require them to be constantly holy and free from sin. Paul, speaking to the saints at Corinth, says, 'Whether therefore ye eat, or drink, or whatever ye do, do all for the glory of God.'"[97] Emmons enjoined the Christian to contemplate the perfection of God's moral government and the promise of the blessedness of heaven made possible by Christ's mediation. As the saint would grow in grace with a heart infused by the love of God, so, in equal proportion would believers grow in humiliation. "There is no Christian grace they find more occasion to exercise, than humiliation and self-abasement."[98]

The principle of love of God and self-denial resembled the seventeenth-century French Catholic mystical teachings of François de Salignae de la Mothe-Fénelon and Jeane-Marie Bouvier de la Motte Guyon, who annihilated the self in the inward possession of a pure love for God.[99] Cotton Mather's contemplative ideal of *resignatio ad infernum*, or the willingness to love God even if God has chosen one for damnation, is a parallel and independent ideal in Mather's evangelical Pietism.[100] Hopkins urged upon each believer such mystical infusions of God's love, the hard-won evanescent times of ravishing and rapture following the secret devotional exercises of the closet in evangelical humiliation. The sermon "On Christian Practice" details the saint's way to God. Loving God with all their hearts and loving neighbors as themselves involved public and private devotions. Public worship, Sabbath-keeping, support of the Gospel and institutional religion, brotherliness, and acts of charity constituted public Christian practice. Equally important was private piety. Hopkins enjoined the selfless, humble child of God to serious and pious conversation, daily Scripture reading, secret prayer, meditation, and fasting. Through these secret acts of humiliation, the saint drew closer to God and enjoyed special times marked by the inner-worldly mystical possession of God's love. Fasting proved especially important in achieving these seasons of rapture. Hopkins writes:

Religious fasting consists in abstinence from common food and drink for a certain time, longer or shorter, as shall be found most convenient and best suited to answer the ends of fasting, which are to promote and express engagedness of mind in prayer and devotion; especially to express humiliation, contrition, and concern of mind, and a readiness to crucify the flesh, with the affections and lusts, and mortify the body. This is to be practiced, especially when under any particular or great calamity, spiritual or temporal; or when such a calamity is threatened, and persons set themselves to seek of God deliverance from the evil that is upon them, or that the threatened evil may be averted. Also when any great and special mercy is sought, it is proper to do it with fasting and prayer.[101]

This passage on fasting reflected the experimental religion that Hopkins practiced. He urged that religious fasting was to be employed as a means of humiliation for as long as necessary to achieve the desired spiritual results. In principle, the saint would fast indefinitely until the renewal of God's love brought this season of humiliation to a successful resolution. In the routine of religious life, the private fasting for a day each week and the observance of public fast days limited the duration of humiliation to one day. Hopkins intended moderation in the use of devotional piety and in the management of the appetites and passions.

Hopkins prescribed fasting in times of adversity when the special providences of God afflicted saints with spiritual and temporal trials. Fasting protected against impending evil, and gave believers the assurance of deliverance, special mercy, and the infusion of God's love. Should God continue to withdraw his countenance from the believer, the logic of humiliation urged perseverance and continued fasting. The saint could not command God's presence through magic or sacrament. The bridegroom experience did not result from a formula that specified only a certain degree of fasting and humiliation. In principle, self-denial was absolute, fasting was for an indefinite period, and once begun, the evangelical humiliation was continued until God chose to shower the penitent with love. This could result in excessive fasting, even fasting until death, as we shall encounter in several psychiatric case histories and the case of Sarah Osborn, a congregant in Hopkins's Newport, Rhode Island, congregation.

The act of free will that chose God, paradoxically began a new life of radical self-denial where each saint exercised evangelical humiliation and mortification of the body through fasting. Fasting was thus inextricably tied to the process of progressive sanctification and making the godly life. Fasting assisted the saint in becoming a selfless, empty vessel, a receptacle for God's spirit and love. In addition to this inner-worldly mystical dimension of evangelical Pietism, Hopkins also expounded a social ethic of virtue, an inner-worldly asceticism of public Christian activism.[102]

William Breitenbach interprets Hopkins's theology as an attempt to orient Christians in this unfolding modern world order. Hopkins affirmed absolute standards of right and wrong, rejected forms of self-interest that contributed to disorder or anarchy, and redefined self-interest through a social ethic of virtue and benevolence. Hopkins's system of theology envisioned the Christian saint as a free and active moral agent who chose God and holiness. The saint crafted a life to achieve the religious value of glorification of God through self-denial and Christian activism motivated by universal disinterested benevolence.

Hopkins and New Divinity theology provided the ethical validation of fasting and lent support to a logic of bodily mortification that produced the unintended consequences of evangelical anorexia nervosa.

The success of this popular theology in the revival campaign in the frontiers of New York and Vermont brought new criticism of Hopkins's notion of radical self-denial. Nathan Bangs, a Methodist minister, published a scathing criticism of this doctrine in his 1815 work, *The Errors of Hopkinsianism Detected and Refuted*. He argues that "the Hopkinsian idea of disinterested benevolence, which declares that a man must be willing to be damned, in order to be saved, teaches us to hate our own flesh."[103]

Bangs understood the contradictory nature of a theology that taught redemption through absolute self-denial, a way to grace by hatred and mortification of the body. Hopkins ensured that these lessons of practical theology would reach the widest audience by sponsoring the publication of the spiritual diaries and life histories of two congregants in his Newport church. Like Edwards's *Life of Brainerd*, Hopkins's accounts of Susanna Anthony and Sarah Osborn gave nineteenth-century readers evangelical classics depicting the champions of devotional piety in their ceaseless warfare against the self.

Susanna Anthony

Samuel Hopkins envisioned the publication of the biographies of two members of the First Congregational Church in Newport as an enduring testimony to the vital experiential piety of adherents of the New Divinity movement. These memoirs were intended as detailed case studies of the work of religious affections in converting sinners to God. Susanna Anthony and Sarah Osborn dedicated their efforts, in full measure, to shaping lives consistent with the principles of self-denial, disinterested benevolence, evangelical humiliation, and progressive sanctification. Here Hopkins depicted model lives, exemplars for all to emulate. Published as guides to the perplexed, as hortatory literature, as inspirational narratives of saints' victories in this world, these devotional exercises of evangelical anorexia were valorized by Hopkins for succeeding generations of religious seekers.

The genre of spiritual autobiography begins with the subject's early life and proceeds to the critical turning point, the moment of awakening to sin and the first conversion crisis. At the age of fourteen Susanna Anthony (1726–1791) suffered a prolonged crisis of conversion during the 1740 Great Awakening in New England. Her travail entailed the relentless effort to subdue her growing sense of personal autonomy and agency, symbolized by allusions to her prideful and vile self. Only by vanquishing all worldliness could she turn to God and experience conversion in a moment of selfless, ecstatic surrender. However, Anthony, like many other evangelicals in the eighteenth- and nineteenth-century revivals, did not easily travel the spiritual itinerary from the first awakening of sin through doubt and then faith and assurance of grace as a child of God. Anthony struggled for more than two years, obsessed with blasphemous thoughts and rebellion against God's sovereignty, alternating between times of hope and seasons of despair, weary of the incessant struggle with Satan and anxiety over her eternal state. In her journal she records the unfolding crisis. After attending the fire-and-brimstone preaching of Whitefield, she writes: "O! How many hours have I spent bewailing a loss of God, and a loss of heaven; crying out, "I am undone! I am undone! condemned already, and shall be damned!" . . . For Satan began to persuade me that I was a devil incarnate, that God had raised me up as a monument of his wrath and vengeance . . . ."[104]

As Anthony's crisis deepened, she began more desperate acts of self-abuse and mortification, including biting her flesh, twisting her arms, and wringing her hands, culminating in a stated wish to end her life by a refusal to eat. In her own words she recounts the special meaning of this evangelical anorexia nervosa.

> My distress increased on me, until the necessaries of life grew tasteless. And here Satan set in to persuade me I had sinfully indulged my appetite. And when I was under this temptation I met with the words, Rom xiv.23, "he that doubteth is damned, if he eat" . . . I had been so long harassed and terrified with the dismal apprehension of certain, unavoidable damnation, that though I took only enough to preserve life, yet every mouthful seemed to seal up my condemnation. And therefore I seemed ready to give up, and wholly abstain, rather than endure the distress of every mouthful I took filled me with.[105]

After two years of inner torment, Anthony's fasting and self-torture brought her to a moment of ecstatic surrender to Jesus and the resolution of this first conversion crisis. She ended her starvation and entered a life of service to God. She was greatly moved by the preaching of the more gentle Old Light pastor, Joseph Fish, of Stonington, Connecticut. Fish counseled that "here none were excluded but such as had committed the unpardonable sin. It was a sermon full of encouragement. But Satan set in to persuade me that was my case; and therefore there was no hope for me."[106] After much pastoral care, Fish quieted her doubts and Anthony was baptized on October 24, 1742, at the age of sixteen.

Baptism and first conversion did not inoculate her from despair. She suffered from repeated episodes of religious melancholy and invalidism for much of her adult life. Nearly thirty years later, she would confide to Reverend Fish her unrelieved melancholy and desolation.

> I know not what I shall bear. I fear I am sinking into great stupidity, yea, that I am farther gone than I was aware. I have indeed had relief from distressing conflicts; But I have misused and abused the mercy; and am ever ready to covet them again . . . conflicts often stir up the polluted fountain, and cause me to loath and abhor myself for all my abominations. But I fear my heart has since grown like a standing sink, which is not purged but its scum remains.[107]

Known as "Susa" to her dear friend, Sarah Osborn, Anthony maintained a correspondence with her for forty years, from 1740 to 1779. Published post-humously in 1807 as *Familiar Letters Written by Mrs. Sarah Osborn and Miss Susanna Anthony*, these letters reveal a close friendship between two women who offered each other mutual edification, religious instruction, and messages of spiritual refreshment intended to quiet doubts, allay fears, and foster growth in vital piety. Osborn exhorted and criticized any blemish of pride or self-love in her friend. Together they kept a sisterly watch against the inroads of sin. This correspondence is even more remarkable because they both resided in Newport, Rhode Island, and visited with each other several times every week in special prayer groups or in the Saturday afternoon sessions reserved only for themselves.

Anthony writes: "In your last, [*sic*] you have showed me how much more the hateful principle of self-love reigns in me, than love to God."[108] In concert, Anthony and Osborn maintained constant self-examination and evangelical humiliation—praying, meditating, and fasting. Anthony's letters frequently relate self-abasement: "I am this moment melted down, and confounded; inexpressibly abased and ashamed. Under a just, though *inadequate* view of myself, of my amazing wretchedness and vileness before a holy, gracious, infinitely amiable God!"[109]

Self-abasement would lead to reappropriation of the sense of total dependence upon the absolute sovereignty of God, ecstatic surrender, and the inner-worldly mystical recovery of God's love. Anthony speaks of the resolution of self-abasement when the Holy Spirit "broke out as a sun-beam—Bodily strength was directly exhausted, and I could not pursue the delightful exercise, yet somehow, through much darkness and dejection, the glorious character of the divine omnipotent Redeemer, has been a support and stay to my mind ever since!"[110]

Anthony cherished the weekly meetings of the Female Religious Society, held in the 1740s and renewed in the 1760s, where twenty to thirty congregants of the First Church met in Sarah Osborn's house for prayer. In a letter to Reverend Joseph Fish, on December 26, 1760, Osborn writes, "I bless God I have the Privilege of having a society of women meet at our house every Wednesday evening of which dear Susa is one . . . ."[111] Less than a year later she writes, "Susa wrestles with the spirit of God"[112] during a prayer meeting. In this atmosphere of a spiritual hothouse, the Reverends Samuel Hopkins and Joseph Fish, by letter and pastoral visit, exhorted both friends to ever greater virtuosity. The intensity of prayer, public confession, meditation, and fasting of the female religious society produced great trouble for Anthony, a frail, sickly woman. Osborn proclaimed, "Oh yet our society may in deed [*sic*] be a Nursery for Piety."[113]

The published *Life of Miss Susanna Anthony* found a wide readership in New England during the Second Great Awakening. The Yale College chapel library included a copy of this work. Students read and emulated Anthony's spiritual battles during the college revival of 1813. The conversion of Elias Cornelius is a case in point. As an undergraduate at Yale, Cornelius acquired a reputation as a thoughtless young man. His biographer characterized him in spiritually unflattering prose: "Of prepossessing personal appearance, of a generous, frank, and sociable disposition, fond of company and amusement, his society was coveted by the inconsiderate and irreligious portion of his fellow-students."[114]

In 1813, upon returning from January vacation for the beginning of his final term as a senior, Cornelius experienced his spiritual awakening just as the college entered into a revival. The narrative of his conversion continues:

> ... I perfectly recollect his making his first entrance into the Moral Library, of which I was librarian, and selecting the 'Memoir of Susanna Anthony' .... From this time I do not believe a smile appeared on his countenance, till his conversion. He lost flesh rapidly, and the effect of this external change was irresistible upon the most irreligious of our class. I have no remembrance of ever witnessing so visible and affecting an alteration in one's external demeanor.[115]

Cornelius found his ecstatic, rapturous moment of conversion in March, after having embraced a regimen of fasting, repentance, meditation, and prayer. Consistent with his instructions, his diary and correspondence were destroyed after his death. We do not have more detailed and intimate first-person accounts of this evangelical anorexia and the resolution of the conversion crisis. Cornelius completed both undergraduate and divinity degrees at Yale, dedicating his life as an ordained minister to the principles of disinterested benevolence. His work as a pastor, Secretary of the American Education Society, and with the A.B.C.F.M. involved a life of Christian activism with roots nourished by the evangelical piety of the New Divinity movement. When Cornelius in his work for the American Education Society, awarded scholarships to indigent youth to prepare them for the ministry, he interviewed and guided each candidate. Upon acceptance for scholarship, each recipient was given a copy of Edwards's *Life of Brainerd* as a model for the making of an authentic Christian life. One young man offered the following testimonial concerning Elias Cornelius and any young man who manifested doubts and "spiritual darkness":

> Such was his manner that they could unbosom themselves without reserve; and his ability to advise in such a case none will question. Were they in doubt as to what part of the field called most urgently for their labors? His acquaintance with the wants of the world, and his liberal and impartial feelings with reference to every branch of Christian effort, made his remarks on this point exceedingly valuable. Before separating, he presented us with a copy of *Brainerd's Life*, and then offered a short prayer. Such a prayer as I will not undertake to describe; touching the condition of our souls—the operations of the education society—the glory of the Redeemer—and the wants of the world.[116]

The piety of Brainerd and Anthony—evangelical humiliation, lifelong fasting, and prayer—devoted inwardly to progressive sanctification and turned outwardly to a vocation of disinterested benevolence, was passed across three generations. *Memoirs of Elias Cornelius,* published in 1834, spread these doctrines to the reading public as did the preaching of ministers trained at Andover, Yale, and other New England seminaries.

The Exemplary Piety of Sarah Osborn

Samuel Hopkins's *The Memoirs of the Life of Mrs. Sarah Osborn* (1799) introduced the special qualities of devotional piety and heart religion of the New Divinity movement to a new generation of New Englanders, who would forge a Second Great Awakening, in part, from these evangelical foundations. Born Sarah Haggar in London in 1714, Osborn migrated to Boston in 1723. The family relocated a year later to Freeport, Rhode Island, and in 1729, to Newport, where she remained until her death in 1796.

Osborn's detailed memoirs were completed in 1743, when she was thirty years old. Her narrative was reprinted with extensive editing, and depicted her years of spiritual trial that culminated in conversion during the revival of 1741 and her embrace of the preaching of Gilbert Tennent and George Whitefield. The young woman's first awakening was prompted by the pastoral direction of Reverend Clap in 1737. She experienced terror before God, naming herself as a sinner who stifled the Holy Spirit and resisted the invitation of the Savior. In utter desolation she labored under the conviction of having committed the unpardonable sin. In her diary she writes: "And it was suggested that I had committed the unpardonable sin because I had sinned against the light and knowledge, even against the conviction of my own conscience. This I knew I had done; and therefore believed I had committed that sin which could not be forgiven."[117]

Thus began her week of continual torment. She languished in desolation, bereft of hope as one who had grieved away the Spirit, who had blasphemed against the Holy Spirit and indeed committed an unpardonable sin. She faced the terrible certainty of eternal damnation in the next world, the knowledge of which brought unrelieved anguish. In this state of conviction, she could not sleep and refused all food. She fasted as part of her humiliation before God and wrote "it was the same with my necessary food. I thought myself so unworthy of the least mercy, that I knew not how to eat."[118] After these days of unending self-torture and fasting she confronted the final temptation, struggling with Satan, who urged her to despair and suicide. Osborn resisted and, in a moment of humiliation and selfless agony, found submission to God through the covenant of grace. Speaking in the terms of the mystic's possession of the Godhead, Sarah writes of being ravished with his love, of a heart melted and eyes overflowing with tears. She could exclaim as the bride of Christ, "But O, what rapture was I in, when I resolved my engagement to be the Lord's!"[119] Sarah Osborn joined the First Congregational Church in Newport on February 2, 1737.

Osborn continues her narrative by admitting that she could not sustain the intensity of evangelical piety and succumbed to years of declension, worldliness, and carnal reasoning. She fills her diary with self-accusations of pride and hypocrisy. In this state of spiritual dullness and stupidity she attended the revival meetings of Gilbert Tennent and George Whitefield in 1740–1741, and repeated her conversion itinerary of unpardonable sin, evangelical anorexia, and rapturous submission to God. At this time she began a lifelong friendship with Susanna Anthony and formed a women's religious society dedicated to nurturing the devotional piety of the unconverted and communicants of the First Church.

Sarah Osborn devoted the remaining fifty years of her life to nurturing this evangelical piety, to the task of progressive sanctification and perfecting herself of sin, worldliness, and selfish pride. She embraced a ceaseless battle with sin and evil, which she personified as the taunting and tempting manifestations of Satan. Her memoirs and letters depict a life punctuated by repeated episodes of religious melancholy, evangelical anorexia, and spiritual growth.

Sarah Osborn modeled her life upon the ideal of disinterested, self-denying benevolence, as manifested in her extensive correspondence with Anthony and Fish. Osborn's correspondence and friendship with Anthony and Fish reveal the unfolding of intimate, confessional, and pastoral relationships. Osborn kept a school for young women and educated Fish's eldest daughter, Mary. Both women maintained their relationship of mutual edification long after Mary Fish left Osborn's charge. Osborn helped inculcate in Mary Fish the special qualities of piety and affinity for religious melancholy.

In the many letters to her correspondents, Fish, Anthony, Hopkins, and Noyes, Osborn examined the state of her soul, sought spiritual guidance in the midst of her perplexities, and created a written forum for her continued self-examination. She cultivated an intense and abiding spirit of evangelical humiliation—self-flagellation and self-torture to remind her of her continued sin, depravity, and vileness in the eyes of God. Paradoxically, only by debasing herself as a dependent child of God, a repugnant sinner deserving of God's wrath, could she feel the inner assurance of adoption by Christ's mercy and forgiven of sin. Writing in 1743 to Fish, after recovering from a time of religious melancholy and crisis, she recounts: "I would just tell you yet he is very gracious to His poor weary Pilgrim. Sin and Satan has rally'd their forces this last year to some purpose. Such conflicts I have had that at some times I have almost been beaten out of health and ready to say I can't hold out no longer but then my glorious Captain appears and puts my foes to flight . . . ."[120]

Throughout her writings, she refers to herself as unworthy, puffed-up with pride—"a worthless worm." In 1755, she published a tract titled *The Nature, Certainty, and Evidence of True Christianity*, reprinting a letter of consolation to a friend laboring under religious concerns. Osborn begins the letter on this note of self-abnegation: "Oh that God will now bless the poor weak Endeavors of a worthless worm to refresh you."[121] In a letter to Samuel Hopkins, written in 1769, she speaks of her unending struggle against indwelling pride and selfishness, "fighting, watching, praying and weeping for deliverance from this monster with a thousand heads!"[122]

She immersed herself in exercises of devotional piety—early morning prayers, meditations, Scripture reading, and writing; family prayer meetings; special Saturday devotions with Susanna Anthony; Wednesday evening prayer meetings with the Female Religious Society; and other evening meetings with unconverted youth and slaves. She kept to this schedule, in addition to the arduous task of keeping a school for young ladies, and in the context of continual financial pressures, caused by her husband's infirmity, which forced her to support the family.

Fasting assumed great importance in Osborn's regimen of piety and evangelical humiliation. The Female Religious Society kept numerous public fast days and met in Osborn's home for fasting, penitence, and prayer on New Year's Day, the first Thursday in April, July, and October, the Saturday before every sacrament, and the last Thursday of every month. Fasting increased the intensity and fervency of these devotions, resulting in "remarkable outpourings of the Holy Spirit."[123]

Sarah Osborn also undertook weekly private fasts in the spirit of self-denial. If she would dedicate her life wholly to the glorification of God, then all thought and action must conform to this ethical purpose. Osborn wrote that eating must somehow further the saint's state of grace and progressive sanctification. "Whether therefore ye eat or drink, or whatsoever ye do, do all to the glory of God."[124] She continues this theme by investing eating and fasting with religious purpose. Writing on March 1, 1764, she states "Lord, rectify the disorder of my appetite, and my views in refreshing my body. I bemoan before God, that I so often eat and drink with no higher view that merely refreshing my body . . . O cure my ingratitude, respecting my food and sleep and now go with one into my calling.[125]

During her frequent seasons of religious melancholy, when she charged herself with hypocrisy and declension, wrestled with Satan, and felt the spirit of God depart, fasting assumed even greater importance. In 1743 she was brought to write to Joseph Fish, "my soul thirsts and is now become melancholy. The glory of God seems to be departed and I scarce ever meet him."[126] Fasting help restore her faith, and God's countenance returned. Consistent with evangelical character, she could not act with agency and confidence, without first submitting to a session of humiliation—fear and trembling—to ascertain whether a course of proposed conduct was indeed consistent with God's will. Ever conflicted and wracked with doubt, she exercised self-examination, meditation, prayer, and fasting to assuage this ontological insecurity. Anxious about her leadership role during the 1741 Awakening, she writes to Fish, hoping to "unburden my perplexed mind." Sarah relates ". . . the weight and concerns that lies upon my spirit at this time Lest I should take any sinning step or encourage others to do so causes my sleep to depart from me . . . ."[127]

She again lapsed into a severe melancholy when confronted by the criticism of some members of her congregation for educating and catechizing slaves and young men and women in the revival of 1766–1767. Osborn was careful not to challenge the authority of slave masters, to not instill independence or pride or social aspirations that would threaten the established order. "Despite

these precautions, by August 1766 Mrs. Osborn found herself being ostra-
cized by those she sarcastically termed the 'Holy Sisters.'"[128] Smitten by an
overly tender and scrupulous conscience, she anguished over her leadership
role in the religious education and evangelization of Newport's African-Ameri-
cans. She fasted continually and excessively in hope of receiving God's guidance. Writing to Fish, she explains, "the pressure is so great that I have lost
six whole nights sleep out of eleven without so much as one wink . . . and
my flesh begins to waste and except God appear for my help, I fear reason
will go next."[129]

In each season of financial, temporal, and spiritual trial Osborn relied
upon the practical devotions of evangelical humiliation and fasting to quiet
the body so that the spirit might live and grow. Osborn harkened to the advice
of her confident, Anthony, who instructed her: "When the Bridegroom is
absent, shall not the children of the bride-chamber fast, as well as pray?"[130]
These techniques seemed to bring consolation and promote spiritual growth.
Indeed, Osborn's unflagging public religious activism and courageous stance
before critics who questioned the propriety of a woman rescuing the souls of
unconverted slaves and white youth was supported by these inward religious
values. Commitment to self-denial and selfless benevolence meant continual
struggle against Satan and standing in tension to the natural propensity for
selfish comfort, worldliness, and pride.

The publication of Osborn's *Memoirs* and letters brought to ever growing publics the texture of a vital piety that had previously been intensely personal and limited to the congregation of the First Church and community of
Newport. Hopkins's sponsorship and imprimatur disseminated and legitimated
the making of a Christian life that was inextricably tied to evangelical anorexia
nervosa. The case histories of Osborn and Anthony represented the hard-won
successes of New Divinity piety, demonstrations of the processes and outcomes
of experimental religion. Each case depicted a conversion crisis that involved
awakening, terror, and the charge of unpardonable sin. In this state of religious concern, Osborn and Anthony fasted and began a regimen of starvation under the conviction that all action only compounded their sin. For the
order of conversion to proceed, candidates needed to understand that they
had not committed an unpardonable sin and that these blasphemous and
obsessive thoughts directing them to suicide and starvation were, in fact, the
temptations of Satan. The moment of ecstatic, selfless surrender to God
brought an inward mystical possession of the Holy Spirit and the evidence of
grace, forgiveness of sin, conversion to God, and adoption as the child of God.
The successful religionist made this progression to first conversion and repeated
these spiritual exercises throughout life's way.

The method of evangelical piety fostered self-abasement and bodily mortification through fasting, but could neither magically coerce the appearance
and evidence of God's love nor, in church sacrament, offer absolution of
sin and assurance of God's continued favor. Too often, as the lives of Osborn
and Anthony reveal, the faithful suffered that "dark night of the soul" when
God's love and countenance were absent. Times of secular trial—interpersonal

conflicts, financial reverses, illness, and bereavement—were often associated with these spiritual crises, because believers interpreted afflictions as the special providence and chastisement of God. Believers needed to submit to ever greater exercises of evangelical humiliation, including fasting, until God's love broke through in ecstatic reassurance. Thus, in the midst of recurring afflictions and controversies, Osborn and Anthony fasted, sometimes continuously, until God intervened in their souls. As Osborn stated in her crisis of 1766, only God's assurance preserved her reason and life, permitting her to end the fast.

Osborn spoke of her daily secret devotions in the closet of her bedchamber each morning before breakfast as spiritual nourishment. She writes, "Thus I redeem an Hour or two for retirement without which I must starve. . . ."[131] Paradoxically, these very devotions fostered a discipline of physical mortification that engendered regular fasting, and the potential for fasting unto death, in times of spiritual crises.

Hopkins chronicles how in 1806 members of the First Church sought to institutionalize the exemplary piety of Anthony and Osborn after their deaths by sponsoring the Religious Female Society (also known as the "Female Praying Society in Newport" and renamed the Osborn Society in 1826). Osborn's house, the site of their original meetings, was purchased by the First Church for use by the auxiliary society. The house held special significance for the congregation. As a private voluntary society chartered by the Rhode Island legislature, the Osborn Society elected officers, solicited funds, and maintained this meeting place. Here a new generation of Christian women would keep alive the evangelical fervor of the New Divinity pioneers.[132]

Mary Moody Emerson

Ralph Waldo Emerson would memorialize his aunt, Mary Moody Emerson, in a biographical essay, likening her quest of contemplative sainthood to the mysticism of Guyon. Ralph Waldo Emerson called Mary Moody Emerson "a representative life, such as could hardly have appeared out of New England; of an age now past, and of which I think no types survive."[133] But because so many aspects of her life appear eccentric and peculiar, how could Emerson support this claim of the representativeness of his aunt's life as "a fruit of Calvinism and New England"?

She was born in 1774 into a family that would produce six generations of ministers in the Calvinistic tradition. Her father served in the Revolutionary War as a chaplain to the American army at Ticonderoga. He died of fever during this campaign, leaving an impoverished widow and five children under the age eight. Infant Mary Emerson went to live with her childless and poor aunt, Ruth Emerson, in Malden and remained there through girlhood and youth until the age of thirty-four. Mary Emerson's early years of poverty, orphanhood, and loss left a permanent sense of bitterness and defiance as "a have-not in a world of American and Emersonian haves."[134]

The conventional women of her generation, born in the era of revolution, chose domesticity and "true womanhood" in marriage, childbearing, and submission to the familial government and authority of husbands. Mary Emerson rejected this domestic surrender and self-abnegation, in its place she shaped her life by an alternative cultural ideal—the cult of single blessedness.[135] As Lee Virginia Chambers-Schiller argues in *Liberty, a Better Husband*, almost 10 percent of Mary Emerson's generation of middle-class, white, New England women never married. They perceived as unacceptable the thralldom of a woman's place in marriage. The legal doctrine of coverture denied wives legal personhood. Thus, in marriage women renounced their rights to property, the control of wages, or the ability to enter contracts as legally competent individuals.

The cult of single blessedness allowed the re-evaluation of spinsterhood as a morally desirable state whereby women could pursue liberty, autonomy, and selfhood, particularly in the domains of economic independence, intellectual development, and spirituality. These ideals of the cult of single blessedness would structure her life. Emerson rejected suitors and dedicated her life to singlehood, devotion to godliness, and intellectual development. With only the most rudimentary education, she emerged as a self-taught lay scholar conversant in theology, English literature, and philosophy, among other areas of her wide reading.

Consistent with the cult of single blessedness, in 1807, at the age of thirty-four, Emerson renounced marriage and rebuffed her suitor, Captain Dexter. She returned his ring, and consecrated her life to divine love. "Henceforth the picture I'll image shall be girded loins, a bright lamp, fervent devotion. My condition in life is singular, and presses me on the throne of my Master with peculiar strength."[136] In celibacy and austere asceticism she would seek a contemplative union with God.

Mary Moody Emerson crafted her representative life from the personal trauma of her childhood loss of father and mother and recast it as the contemplative quest for God's love. The fragments of her almanacs that survive depict the spiritual itinerary of her soul's hunger and thirst for God, voiced in the New Divinity language of self-denial, disinterested benevolence, and redemptive suffering. Emerson relished the solitude of evangelical devotional piety, spending many Sabbaths in her secret closet. Here she prayed, meditated, read Scripture, fasted, and sought the inward mark of the remission of sin. In preparation for these devotions she frequently visited a local graveyard and walked among the gravestones, longing for her own death as a release from worldliness into eternity and immortality. She valorized the trials and sufferings of the good as necessary for the accomplishment of virtue. Only through self-abasement and redemptive suffering could the saint know God. "It is in hearts subjugated by grace and sanctified from the world, where only the spirit of love is triumphant."[137]

Emerson employed fasting as an integral part of her evangelical humiliation in these seasons of solitude. Writing on November 11, 1804, she understood that "no one I don't believe ever attained eminence in virtue who did not deny themselves sleep & food in a degree."[138] Throughout her early almanacs, Mary rejected earthly food and drink so that her soul could hunger and thirst after God. On November 21, 1805, she writes, "Oh may I imbibe his Spirit, and feel an ambition to pursue his path, and aim at possessing His glory . . . . My breath shortens with *hunger and thirst*."[139]

Emerson's spirituality blended the model of New Divinity conversion with the mystical ideals of self-mortification through fasting. She sought perfection though the imitation of Christ and a *unio mystica* experience of feasting upon the spirit of God. Like all inner-worldly mystics, she suffered frequent "dark nights of the soul." Repeatedly, in her systematic exercises of self-examination, Mary found evidence of sins, stains of her failure to attain perfection. By her own account she sinned through acts of pride, vanity, frivolous conversation, a quick temper, and a sharp tongue in her dealings with others. Emerson retreated in solitude to review these failings—her times of backsliding from God's love, what she termed her "negative existence," periods of melancholia that troubled her throughout her life. She referred to religious melancholy in a journal entry about her depression in the spring of 1806, stating "and I think myself sincere when I say that I had rather have died than passed the last three months."[140] She suffered recurrences of melancholy in 1806–1807, 1811, and 1817.

> Mary valued her own despair because it assured her of the existence of God. Being in the wilderness put her on the road to Canaan and gave her life an eternal, Biblical context. Hers was the paradoxical spirit of Calvinism that found in the darkest despair the most arrogant presumption of holiness, that embraced rejection and turned it into an identification with Eternity. For her, the wilderness and Canaan, suffering and ecstacy, the shabby real and the cosmic ideal, were all bound up in the bundle of life together.[141]

In times of melancholy and moments of ecstatic elation when she could proclaim, "I trod on air—I danced at the musick of my own imagination,"[142] she always returned to the theme of self-denial and evangelical humility. Writing on the Sabbath of November 17, 1804, just ten days after she "walked on air," she condemned herself with these words: "I return as the dog to his vomit. I am a poor needy sinner, complete in nothing, lacking in the whole in many things."[143]

Emerson viewed her domestic duties in her aunt's home as punishment and privation, as opportunities for humiliation, as time spent away from meditation and solitude. She hungered for the spirit of God in the midst of "scenes of dirt, vulgarity, misery & unqualified ignorance."[144] As another test of her growing virtue and disinterested benevolence, Emerson assumed responsibility for the care of her aunt's sister, Rebecca Brintnall, who in 1802 came to Malden suffering from insanity. Phyllis Cole explains, "caring for the sick—in Mary's eyes, woman's dirtiest and most holy duty—brings out in Mary her strongest gestures of duty and avoidance, self-punishment and cosmic arrogance."[145]

Only through such self-punishment that produced redemptive suffering could Emerson prove herself worthy of religious solitude. In seclusion, prayer, and purifying fasts she received inward evidence of God's forgiveness and love. She speaks of her religious devotions and solitude as:

> ... a day of penitence & prayer for the past failures. How strongly impressed my mind with what a few hours before ap'd trivial. How important (indispensably so) for a xian [Christian] to set apart such seasons. Never a more sad one—never one endured so warmly in faith & hope. I blessed God I was out of punishment . . . .

> An endless seclusion from nature and society with thy presence, Oh source of all nature & beings who art connected with every event & passeth thro' all existences, would forever render myself dear and valuable![146]

The surviving almanac fragments do not reveal just how extensive and severe were Emerson's fasts and mortifications. It remains doubtful that these austerities ever threatened her life. She did fast at least one full day each week in preparation for the spiritual communion with God in her Sabbath day solitude. She would write on February 12, 1807, that "the richest joys are those of communion," and "I swear in the name of Him who is my Mediator to renounce every pleasure & connection which would interrupt my communion—marr [sic] the grandeur of my prospects—and defile the purity of the xian [Christian] light. That character must be misguided who professing Christ is not humble."[147]

Emerson's fasts and asceticism allowed her to reject the snares of worldliness, seek purification from sin, and attend to the ways of godliness and sanctification. Throughout her journals she noted that eating proved a suspicious distraction from the path of true virtue. In April of 1807 she writes, "It is an awfull symptom if we cannot renounce every indulgence of eating, sleep, dress, recreation, reading, study & friendship which appears suspicious! Oh, what awfull hazards attend us ere enter on our rest."[148]

Speaking in the tradition of the Calvinist devotional theology of Hopkins, Emmons, and Edwards, Emerson understood that God charged Christians with the duty to practice virtue independent of the promises of salvation and future rewards. The soul turned away from sin and toward God would seek selfless love and disinterested benevolence. Through the practice of evangelical humiliations, in fleeting moments of rapture, Emerson enjoyed a mystical union with God, assured that "with loving kindness truth he covereth me."[149] Thus, Emerson dedicates her almanac in December 1806 to a life shaped in the struggle to realize a central organizing ultimate value—the perfection from sin and the imitation of Christ. "Nothing short of standing *complete & perfect*—of imitating Jesus Christ in every part of his inimitable & sacred character shall hence forth be my object."[150] Emerson saw perfectionism and the *imitatio Christi* as the critical turning point of her life. Now her almanacs would record the history of this pilgrimage: "It is the record of virtue—the beginning of a portion of the history of a *soul*—struggling with weakness & ignorance & opposite appetites to the pure state of Heaven! God of infinite power & love, aid the being before thee to honor thee & herself in this little history."[151]

During 1807, Emerson's perfectionism and imitation of Christ would receive a severe test. She would break off an engagement, arrange to sell her interest in the Malden home, and remove to Maine. In the midst of these upheavals, she witnessed the deathbed scene of a seven-year-old, John Clarke. This travail awakened profound childhood memories of her own traumatic losses. How could a benevolent and loving God, who ordered the world with a just moral government, allow a pious youth to suffer so terribly? The travail and mystery of Christian faith pertains to a God who would permit the suffering of children.[152] Emerson had no easy answer to this question of theodicy.

She fasted and offered petitionary prayers for the recovery of the boy. But God did not confer his blessing upon these efforts and the child died. Clarke's death was paradigmatic of her own abandonment and evangelical nurture as a child. No one had protected her from suffering and loss, and she in turn could not protect Clarke. In May 1807 she wrote:

> I erred—folly, vanity, impatient indignation had their turns—at first—but I became reflective and took less interest in what past *and I did fail;* after a fortnight of watching, fasting, and every holy charity, *I failed.* It will imbitter memory. Tho' the tenor of my time was devoted, yet at moments *I failed.*[153]

Edwards's treatise, *Freedom of the Will,* offered a theological resolution to these problems of theodicy and individual moral agency. Emerson read and re-read Edwards throughout her youth and later life, as her journal entries reveal.[154] Edwards discounted the Arminian claims of the "self-determining power of the will." Instead of contingent and unrestricted human freedom, believers faced the burden of moral choice in the context of divine sovereignty, or God's "universal determining providence." By availing themselves of evangelical means, the faithful, in a sudden transformation experience regeneration of their hearts, could recover the moral ability and moral necessity to perform God's will in a life shaped by the *ordo salutis* of progressive sanctification and glorification. The saint whose regeneration provided the grounds for moral ability and adoption as the child of God accepted the workings of God's providence in his or her life as just and benevolent, even if this meant the seemingly senseless suffering and death of children like Clarke or the young Emerson.

Emerson might rejoice in her conversion as twice-born and flee in contemplative solitude to await the bridegroom. She embraced the doctrine of true virtue found only through evangelical humiliation that removed self-love and in its place brought universal disinterested benevolence. As a child of God she glorified his providence, accepting even the mystery of the unmerited suffering of children. Yet, somehow the devotional edifice of New Divinity could not satisfy her spiritual longings for release from mortal existence. Despite her solitude, celibacy, fasting, and contemplations, she failed to sustain the inner-worldly mystical unity with God. What remained for Emerson was her prodigious intellect that probed matters of moral philosophy, her retreat into nature and the wilderness of rural Maine, and her obsession with death as the gateway to eternity and release from the prison of mortality.

For more than fifty years, the thought of death and eternity obsessed her. Ralph Waldo Emerson noted her eccentricities—wearing funeral shrouds and using a coffin as a bed.

> For years she had her bed made in the form of a coffin; and delighted herself with the discovery of the figure of a coffin made every evening on their sidewalk, by the shadow of a church tower which adjoined the house. . . . She made up her shroud, and death still refusing to come, and she think- ing it a pity to let it lie idle, wore it as a night-gown, or a day-gown, nay, went out to ride in it, on horseback, in her mountain roads, until it was worn out. Then she had another made up, and as she never travelled with- out being provided for this dear and indispensable contingency, I believe she worn out a great many.[155]

Mary Emerson's longing for the infinite moved her spirituality beyond the consistent Calvinism of the eighteenth century, away from the evangeli- cal anorexia and humiliation of the contemplative. This spiritual itinerary brought her into the realm of her nephew's idea of the self-reliant individual attuned to the transcendentalism of nature and nature's God. In July 1826 she writes without sentimentality of her prayer for death, of the depredation of vultures upon her executed body and the soul's reunion with the infinite.

> If one could choose, and without crime be gibbeted,—were it not altogether better than the long drooping away by age without mentality or devotion? The vulture and crow would caw caw, and, unconscious of any deformity in the mutilated body, would relish their meal, make no grimace of affected sympathy, nor suffer any real compassion. I pray to die . . . .[156]

Emerson's devotionalism in the Malden years was that of a Puritan con- templative founded upon a childhood of suffering and loss—a representative life in an era of social transformation that "marks the precise time when the power of the old creed yielded to the influence of modern science and humanity."[157]

Conclusion

In the eighteenth century, public religious fasts formed an integral part of community ceremonial life, providing a ritualized praxis that brought believ- ers out of their mundane, work-a-day lives into sacred time and participa- tions. Public fasts preceded elections, ordinations, and times of thanksgiving, repentance, and collective renewal.

Private fasting also assumed an integral part in the routine practice of devotional piety, bringing an enhanced fervency to petitionary prayers, assisting in evangelical humiliation and repentance for sin, and facilitating the con- templation of God. Fasting produced the desired irradiations of divine love and the ravishing possession of the Holy Spirit. In times of spiritual desola- tion and predicament, the pious fasted to recover the love and countenance of God. Fasting proved an effectual remedy for the religious melancholiac who felt forsaken by God. However, for evangelical Pietists private fasting became a neurotic ceremonial, an obsessional ritual to relieve the burdens of sin and melancholy. Private fasts assumed heroic regimens of food refusal—hectic wasting away in the service of religious ends.

Mother Ann Lee, the English visionary, received a direct revelation from Christ while sojourning in New York in the 1770s. From this vision she discovered the secrets of perfectionism, and freedom from sin and alienation from God's love. Christian communitarians, who held all things in common and who practiced sexual celibacy, instituted this vision through their early Shaker ecstatic, charismatic devotion. Mother Ann Lee received this prophecy after a decade of religious melancholy, bodily mortification, and extreme fasting. In a hagiographic account of her life, she reportedly testified about evangelical anorexia nervosa during her sojourn in this spiritual desert:

> Thus, I labored in strong cries and groans to God, day and night, till my flesh wasted away and I became like a skeleton, and a kind of down came upon my skin, and my soul broke forth to God, which I realized with the greatest precision. Then, I felt unspeakable joy in God, and my flesh came upon me like the flesh of an infant.[158]

Inquire into the narratives of conversion and theology of religious leaders, congregants, and visionaries, and one encounters fasting in its myriad dimensions, including the evangelical anorexia nervosa of those tortured souls, like Ann Lee, who felt forsaken by God.

4

What Hath God Wrought?
Religious Melancholy in
the Second Great Awakening

The Evangelical Morphology of Conversion

This chapter will explore the case of Benjamin Noyes, a Yale College under-graduate enthralled by the promises and antimonies of evangelical religion in an age of wondrous visitation by the Holy Spirit—an age of revivals. Noyes's life and untimely death need to be viewed against the wider context of how evangelicals were enjoined to fashion a life and personality consistent with evangelical values.

Evangelical culture, that complex of values, beliefs, and models for living that developed during the Second Great Awakening, represented the mainstream of American Protestantism and claimed the allegiance of between one-third to one-half of all Americans living in the antebellum period. Masses were brought to conversion.[1] Those who embraced evangelical culture committed themselves to the realization of an evangelical life-order, with personal conversion as the foundation for Christian activism. They grappled with the at times overpowering burdens of Protestant spirituality and the contradictions of the evangelical morphology of conversion.

Richard Rabinowitz's *The Spiritual Self in Everyday Life* examines the structure and practice of evangelical religion in New England from 1790 to 1860. He identifies three ideal-typical forms of personal religious experience in this era: the doctrinalist, the moralist, and the devotionalist. Each type of evangelical character or personality was organized around key questions about the alienation or intimacy of the believer to God, the tests of authentic religiosity, and the changing roles of intellect, will, and religious affections in religious experience.[2]

Doctrinalists, as consistent Calvinists, lived in utter alienation as sinners before the unknowable, metaphysical presence of God, whose divine will was manifest in law and the order of the Gospel plan. By the faculty of the intellect and the understanding, the sinner who stood before God's law with a troubled conscience needed to relinquish pride and self-reliance, accept human inability, and submit to God. In progressive stages, by degrees, believers came to understand that individual sin reflected "a general condition of sinfulness; it was not enough that they did not love God—they needed to acknowledge that they were nothing but enemies of divinity."[3] Rabinowitz identifies a stillness marked by intellectualization of Hopkins's systematic Calvinism in the doctrinalist conversion narratives. These early revivals publicly rejected the religious enthusiasm and emotional excesses of the camp meetings. The conversion narratives "seemed to contain no excitement, no peaks of particularly intense love or pain, but only a succession of still points from which one could reflect on the irony and futility of one's previous exercises."[4] The faithful took the conversion journey and proved their solid knowledge of theology when examined for admission to church membership. In this manner, after the American Revolution, men and women adapted an evangelical version of the covenant of grace and the church covenant of first-generation Pilgrims.

Moralists emphasized the active, self-determining powers of volition or will, "the power of positive human willfulness," as the key mental faculty in conversion.[5] In place of human inability, moralists stressed human capacity to choose either God or worldliness and sin. In place of the *deus absconditus* of doctrinalists, God became a benevolent moral governor who acted with justice and mercy toward the faithful. With confidence in the moral character of God, believers found confidence in themselves. Moralists encouraged risk-taking by making each person solely responsible for his or her own conversion and character. Confidence legitimated Christian activism—moral reform and the institutionalization of benevolence in the social world. In this manner, moralists championed the inner-worldly asceticism of Protestantism and developed character fashioned as a behavioral self in obedience to the standards of public morality: rectitude, probity to contract, and benevolence.

By the 1850s, Devotionalists had made the inner-worldly mysticism of evangelical Pietism the distinguishing mark of religious experience by promoting an intensely emotional, loving, sentimental relationship with God personified as Jesus. Through the daily practice of devotional piety—meditation, private prayer, attention to the closet—believers experienced an ecstatic intimacy with God as they "came to Jesus." "Now feelings, temperaments, manners became the very stuff of religious life, and men and women had no place in the world other than the psychological and physical conditions of their ordinary lives."[6] Devotionalists consecrated their daily lives in the image of Christ. Failure or personal inadequacy to meet this standard of perfection did not promote a sense of sin, only a need. The atoning sacrifice of Christ not only redeemed all believers, but for devotionalists, satisfied all physical, psychological, and social needs. Devotionalism downgraded conversion crises by viewing the continuity and development of religious life-history as central, not the momentary work of regeneration that turned the sinner to Christ.

These three historical ideal types represent "streams of religious experience," each accentuating one aspect of evangelical Pietism. Doctrinalists emphasized the magnificent logical consistency and precision of orthodox Calvinism. Moralists encouraged inner-worldly asceticism and activism in a setting of growing Arminianism, but attenuated the inner-worldly mysticism of heart religion. Devotionalists built their system around the universality of grace and the psychology of the inner-worldly mystical aspect of evangelical heart religion. Although Rabinowitz wishes to trace the progression to Devotionalism from 1790 to 1860, he does recognize the overlap and inter-relatedness of the ideal types. Indeed, in the lives of evangelicals in the first half of the nineteenth century, men and women mixed and balanced these various streams of religious experience, shaping a praxis of religion that juxtaposed the seemingly contradictory elements of doctrine, asceticism, and mysticism. In the same conversion narrative one finds the torturous, emotionally harrowing struggle to submit to a sovereign deity (Doctrinalism), the risky venture of making the behavioral self solely responsible to choose holiness, conversion, and Christian activism (Moralism), and the inner search for intimacy and communion with a personal God as the warrant of grace in the heart (Devotionalism).

Rabinowitz makes a compelling argument that the varieties of religious experience are structured and informed by three distinct religious praxes. However, in these experiences exists another dimension that complements the stillness for Doctrinalists, confidence for Moralists, and rapture for devotionalists. What Rabinowitz does not include are the emotionally searing episodes of melancholy in conversion crises for each type of religious praxis: the crushing self-condemnation of the Doctrinalist as an enemy of God, the unrelenting self-torture arising from charges of hypocrisy made by Moralists who lacked the strength of character to fulfill their resolutions, and the desperate dark night of the soul for Devotionalists, who are alienated from intimate walks with a personal savior. Absent the powers of a personal savior, their needs became sins; their hearts filled with a paralyzing recognition of pollution. The discussion that follows explores these melancholy dimensions of religious experience for nineteenth-century evangelicals.

Religious leaders in the early New England revivals adopted Jonathan Edwards's *A Faithful Narrative* and *Treatise Concerning Religious Affections* to guide the work of bringing souls to Christ. Edwards identified the steps of the *ordo salutis*, where sinners awoke in terror and humiliation from their cold-hearted slumber of sin. Convicted before God's law, unable to secure salvation through any human action, they first rebelled and then with frightful anguish came to accept the absolute divine sovereignty over them. Sinners proceeded from legal terror and humiliation to the next stage of repentance and atonement. Finally, they experienced abject surrender, falling into the hands of a merciful God, selfless, ecstatic as the inner illumination of the Holy Spirit infused them with grace, remitting sin and renewing the heart.

Edwards argued that powerful preaching designed to awaken slumbering sinners, to prick their hearts and arouse their religious affections, would promote the work of conversion and revivals. Religious affections motivated believers to act, directed them to the power of godliness—love of Christ and joy in Christ. The promotion of true religion necessitated the excitation of religious affections—a love of God that produces terror, anguish, hopelessness, grief, and rapturous joy.

From a vigorous, affectionate, and fervent love to God, will necessarily arise other religious affections; hence will arise an intense hatred and abhorrence of sin, fear of sin, and a dread of God's displeasure, gratitude to God for his goodness, complacence and joy in God, when God is graciously and sensibly present, and grief when he is absent. . . . And in like manner, from a fervent love to men, will arise all other virtuous affections towards men.[7]

The orthodox Congregationalist and Presbyterian promoters of the nineteenth-century Awakening adopted Edwards's work as a model, stressing divine sovereignty and human inability. Persons laboring under religious convictions were urged to look to Edwards's works for guidance and comfort; no other author was as widely read or as influential. His writings reassured anxious souls that their emotional torment was indeed the mark of the Holy Spirit, that no true religion was possible without these religious affections. Edwards described the steps of the morphology of conversion, delineating clear mileposts in each pilgrim's journey. He stressed, however, that each individual undertakes a special and unique spiritual passage, that variety, not uniformity, characterizes the way from sin to regeneration. Some souls encounter great fear and trembling, protracted anguish and despair, whereas others find quick passage to grace.

Edwards's works gave legitimacy to evangelical methods and the heart religion of the Great Awakening and found direct pastoral application in the Second Great Awakening by ministers who, like Edwards, avoided the excesses of religious enthusiasm, yet desired to authenticate the awakening as the visitation of the Holy Spirit. The nineteenth-century revivalists, while conducting prayer meetings with congregations, beseeched God to visit them with the Holy Spirit and initiate an awakening. However, revivalists came to rely upon Edwards's formalism as proven evangelical techniques by which men and women could, through human means, promote revivals in cooperation with the Spirit. Given the changing mix of human and divine agency in promoting the awakening, religious leaders legitimated their efforts by appealing to Edwards's prescriptive model of conversion and religious affections.

William Sprague's *Lectures on Revivals of Religion* (1832) declares "the Spirit is active in convincing men of sin" plunging the awakened sinner into godly sorrow ". . . uniformly attended by remorse; and not infrequently so pungent as to amount to agony. Hence too, convinced sinners are said to be 'pricked to the heart';—an expression which denotes the most excruciating pain."[8]

Reverend Asahel Nettleton, the only itinerant permitted to evangelize during the early revivals in Connecticut, reprinted his sermons and exploits during 1819–1822, and reiterated the Edwarsean morphology of conversion. The awakened sinner "realizes that he is condemned by the divine law. He knows that he has broken the law in times and ways to him innumerable; and that not a single sin is pardoned."[9] Reminiscent of Edwards's "Sinners in the Hands of An Angry God," where the vile sinner is compared to a spider held in God's hands over an abyss, Nettleton reminds those laboring under religious concerns that the Holy Spirit may cease to strive for their salvation. "Again—he realizes it is altogether uncertain how long the Spirit will strive. He knows that he has resisted his strivings, and that God may justly at any moment take his Spirit from him."[10]

Dr. E. Porter published excerpts from the diary of a congregant who reacts with anger and rebellion—enmity toward God—an important Edwardsean theme.

> Never before had I such an idea of the plague of my heart, or of the sensible enmity against God which an awakened sinner may be subject of. My distress was such that I thought I could not endure it. I slept but little, and, whenever I awoke from sleep, my distress and anguish came upon me in a moment.[11]

In the manner of Edwards's *Faithful Narrative*, the works of Sprague, Nettleton, Porter, Joshua Bradley, Bennett Tyler, and Heman Humphrey collected and disseminated model conversion experiences to educate and guide believers. In addition, religious periodicals such as *The Connecticut Evangelical Magazine*, *The Religious Intelligencer*, *The Christian Spectator*, *The Christian Advocate*, *The New York Evangelist, and The Methodist Magazine*, among others, published conversion narratives. Ministers or pseudonymous converts submitted for publication "stylized renditions of the act of conversion," conforming to an idealized prescriptive portrayal of evangelical religious experience.[12]

The model conversion narrative told by the successful, regenerate Christian recounted the spiritual itinerary of awakening, stressing the difficulty of many Christians in accepting the absolute sovereignty of God and destroying the prideful self in surrender to God. Nineteenth-century conversion narratives depicted the awakened sinner stuck in mid passage, laboring in despair, open rebellion, and enmity toward God. As recounted so frequently, men and women suffered intense spiritual turmoil, at times ranting and blaspheming against the Holy Spirit. Frequently, in enmity toward God, individuals were beset with suicidal impulses. One tortured soul writes:

> I questioned whether the Bible was the word of God, and I even sometimes harbored the thought that there was no God. . . . I viewed it as evidence that I was left of God. . . . I now began to despair of ever being brought to repentance. And for a considerable time, except at intervals, I chose death rather than to continue life. I thought there was no happiness for me in this world, nor in the next—and that the longer I lived the more intolerable would be my future misery. In these dreadful moments of despair, the most shocking temptations would rush upon me urging me to destroy myself.[13]

For those who initiated the Edwardsean formalism of the morphology of conversion, expecting an ultimate submission to God as the mark of their renewal, success was not inevitable. Although revivalists and those who published conversion narratives emphasized optimism and implicit faith that the Holy Spirit directed the work of revivals and would eventually bring sincere

Christians through the torturous journey into a conversion relation, many persons failed to win the inner assurance of grace. Failure, rarely publicized, proved an all-too-common experience during the revivals.

> The generally cheerful autobiography of a Lyman Beecher must be read against the background of numerous cases of intense melancholia, occasional suicide, and despairing libertinism and alcoholism that marked the age of the revivals. These were the years of serious trial in which by no means all came to a happy submission to the sovereign God.[14]

How can we account for these failures? What issues in the *ordo salutis* proved most vexing for evangelicals? Philip Greven reminds us how struggle over issues of autonomy and personal agency tormented evangelical people as they sought to suppress the prideful, worldly self and return in humble submission. Evangelicals, even after conversion, never completely resolved the issues of autonomy and agency, ever waging an *auto-machia,* empowered to act only after repeating the paradigmatic moment of surrender to the divine will. In Greven's estimation, this lack of resolution and personal integration formed the crux of the evangelical persona. Will-breaking and the crushing of the child's personality so that the evangelical could become more pleasing to God was at the very center of evangelical nurture. These children became adults plagued by religious melancholy, and the question of submission to the sovereignty of God versus hatred of God paralyzed them in their *ordo salutis*.

Barbara Epstein's consideration of conversion narratives supports Greven's findings. Epstein argues that evangelical women experienced a unique, gender-specific conversion. She encounters women in anger, anguish, and guilt over the central drama in their conversion—rebellion and enmity toward God. Susan Juster finds convergence in the narratives of both men and women in their struggle with submission to divine authority. "This process of repudiating independence of will and free moral agency was often painful, at times unbearable, for both men and women. While the level of emotional intensity was perhaps greater in women's accounts than in men's, issues of authority were central for both sexes."[15] For both men and women alike during the revivals, failure meant halting one's spiritual itinerary over the issue of submission to divine sovereignty.

The ubiquitous published conversion narratives of the early New England revivals represent exemplars of the expected, authentic spiritual exercises of successful converts. Readers of the popular religious press could not fail to encounter these didactic accounts when seeking guidance in their lives. The exemplars simultaneously validated their own experiences and constituted a prescriptive conversion model. If the awakened too felt enmity toward God and struggled with anger, guilt, suicidal inclinations, and obsessive blasphemous thoughts, then these religious affections were the authentic marks of the work of the Spirit that had visited others who eventually succeeded as saints. The exemplars demonstrated a well-traveled path that augured success for the individual under religious convictions. Constitutive of religious experience and validating the self-torture of heart religion, conversion narratives externalized the internal conflict of believers during the early New England phase of the revival.

The Great Awakening of the 1740s introduced evangelical Calvinism, as the revivalists proclaimed that the sincere repentance of the awakened soul wins God's mercy and grace. Revival preaching brought sinners into the conviction of their sin, and seared them with the white-hot truths of divine sovereignty and the utter inability to save themselves. However, God recognized the religious affections of godly love as the motivating source of true repentance. A gracious and merciful God bestowed redemption and renewed the hearts of those who prostrated themselves in ecstatic surrender. In this manner, the awakened fulfilled the covenant of grace, a covenant that placed stipulations and limitations upon divine action.

The Second Great Awakening transformed evangelical Calvinism into evangelical Arminianism, expanding the notion of the freedom of the will and emphasizing the active, volitional agency of believers to choose for God and reject worldliness and sin, symbolized in the persona of Satan. Individuals gained freedom to choose at the expense of the Edwardsean conception of human inability and the absolute sovereignty of God. "In philosophical terms it meant that if immediate conversion is available by an act of the human will, then, through God's miraculous grace, all things are possible: human nature is open to total renovation in the twinkling of an eye and so, then, is the nature of society."[16]

Nathaniel Taylor, a professor of divinity at Yale, championed this New Light theology known as Taylorism, New Haven theology, or New School Presbyterian thought. Taylor taught that God bestowed persons with free moral agency so that believers could choose holiness over sin, salvation over damnation, the way of God over the path of Satan.[17]

The Arminianism of Taylor's theology found ready acceptance with the Oberlin School and Charles Finney's revivals in the West and throughout evangelical culture in New England. Taylor depicted the way of the Christian as the intentional making of a life through the self-determining power of the will. Each person needed to confront the existential choice of holiness or selfishness, of benevolence or worldliness. Taylor termed the choice of either organizing ethical principle "the predominant volition." The willing of a predominant volition for benevolence and holiness turned the believer's life toward the fulfillment God's will, placing each subsequent act within a system or coherently organized life plan dedicated to the realization of religious values.[18] In principle, Taylor conceived that each person needed to make an antecedent choice of a predominate volition—the unifying ethical system that would bring coherence and purpose to their lives—and then shape their lives to make them consistent with the ultimate values of that predominate volition.

Taylorism presented two practical difficulties for persons who adopted this theology. First, by devaluing the importance of the Holy Spirit's power in affecting conversions and by recasting the concept of slow, gradual preparationism into an immediate revival conversion effected by human action (revival techniques and individual volition), Taylor made each believer responsible for his or her conversion. Should the person fail in this effort, effectively failing to will for God, holiness, and benevolence, then the individual alone shouldered the responsibility for the inability to find grace. In Taylor's theology, God endowed each believer with moral agency, the self-determining power of the will, and the capacity to choose sin—-contrary of divine law. Each person's capacity to choose made him or her an omnicausal agent of either holiness and benevolence or damnation and sin.[19]

Second, even Christians who successfully adopted holiness as their predominate volition remained imperfect creatures who, at times, succumbed to acts of sin, selfishness, and worldliness. Time and again they concluded that their inconsistency had the effect of renouncing their state of grace, suspending their predominate volition. Taylor recognized the extreme inner turmoil of religionists over this issue and attempted to assuage their fears. He argued that the imperfect holy principle of believers who willed for God but later sinned did not secure their condemnation by God. A benevolent and merciful God would forgive the sincere and penitent person who reaffirms his or her dedication to holiness. However, many believers condemned themselves as hypocrites, as guilty of self-delusion in ever considering themselves as children of God. Even if God could forgive them, in principle, they could not forgive themselves, in actuality. Here the structure of the omnicausal self promoted a distinctive form of religious melancholy.

The successful Christian resolved the crises of autonomy and moral agency and turned toward God in conversion, reborn through Christ's atoning sacrifice. Whether by appeal to private prayer and the secret meditations of the closet or the public standards of rectitude and benevolence consistent with God's moral government, the Christian ever looked for godly direction in the conduct of his or her life. Christian's relationship with the divine needed to be warm, personal, and constant. By mid-century this inner-worldly mysticism became the predominate element in evangelical religion.

The commission of sin or the believer's heart growing cold and distant to the purposes of religion would cause God to withdraw his countenance, replacing the assurance of love with doubt, the rapture and comfort of communion with despair and melancholy. This alternation of inward possession of communion with God and the withdrawal of God's presence has characterized evangelical Pietism, especially during the Second Great Awakening. Here the logic of evangelical Pietism again structured another modality of religious melancholy.

The evangelical morphology of conversion combined the older Edwardsean elements of divine sovereignty and the freedom of the will to accept human inability and choose surrender in selfless ecstacy to God with the Arminianism of the self as omnicausal agent and the inner-worldly mysticism of communion with God. (See Appendix A, "Pastoral Care," for a discussion of evangelical and moderate modes of guidance that were provided for perplexed believers in the Second Great Awakening.) Yet each element of conversion could constitute a trap for the Christian: the refusal to surrender to God occasioned by rebellion against God's law, blasphemy and commission of the unpardonable sin sealing one's eternal destiny; the continued sin of the omnicausal self prompting accusations of hypocrisy and a return to enmity toward God; and the dark nights of the soul occasioned by the withdrawal of God's loving communion. Each trap produced a spiritual crisis and an episode of religious melancholy. For those whose childhood and youth had been marked by evangelical nurture, religious melancholia provided one way of covert rebellion: through disabling illness.[20] Melancholy was one way to sidestep the intrapsychic crisis pitting the issues of autonomy against the counterclaim of living to fulfill the imposed purposes of parents and submission to the divine will. Now the despairing believer could not be expected to fulfill the agenda of evangelical character and annihilate the self in service to divine mandate. Invalidism, mental distraction, and the hopelessness of mental alienation immobilized the sufferer. The religious melancholiac ultimately satisfied neither side in the war. Not infrequently, this covert rebellion assumed self-destructive proportions, as in the case of Benjamin Noyes.

The Suicide of Benjamin Noyes

On April 22, 1815, after several months of fervent work in a revival of religion at Yale College, Benjamin Noyes, a junior, abruptly left school in the middle of the term. He traveled by stage from New Haven to his maternal uncle's home in Saugatuck (Westport), Connecticut. Later that evening, Noyes left by climbing out a window from his bedchamber while the family slept. He wandered about the Connecticut shoreline for three days and was last sighted on a bridge over the Saugatuck River on April 25.

Noyes's disappearance prompted alarm and a concerted effort by his family and his associates at Yale to find him. Benjamin Silliman, a distinguished professor of mineralogy and chemistry at Yale, and himself a maternal uncle of Noyes, took a personal interest in the youth's education and welfare. Professor Silliman helped organize a group of students to search in Saugatuck, and alerted the extended family network regarding Noyes's mental state and peril in a letter to Mary Fish, the youth's maternal grandmother: "Benjamin is in a very unhappy state of extreme religious despondency joined with a good deal of bodily indisposition occasioned by influenza, [and] I am endeavouring to persuade him to go home."[21]

William Channing Woodbridge, an 1812 Yale graduate who returned in 1815 to pursue a year of graduate theological studies and who befriended and provided religious guidance to Noyes, joined Silliman in the search, and entered the following account in his diary.

> April 24, 1815 Heard a distressing account of Benjamin Noyes who has been a very exemplary member of the church for several years. He has always appeared remarkably pleasant and cheerful and uniformly the same and has given the best evidence that he was a christian. Three weeks since after a meeting of the church in which some of the members had expressed very ardent feelings in this subject of the revival, he went to converse with Mr. Safford, [a tutor at the college] trembled very much, and said he could

not be a christian. Mr. Safford talked with him until one o'clock, told him these were probably the suggestions of Satan. He mentioned that he had been prevented by fear and doubt for two or three days from visiting two or three friends . . . . I conversed with him afterwards and found him repeatedly doubting very much and at last settled in the belief that he was an enemy of God. No reasoning seemed to have any effect. All were good until applied to his own case. Mr. Goodrich silenced him, but did not convince him. Mr. Safford found him wringing his hands in despair and agony. On Wednesday evening last, he asked Mr. Emerson to talk with him and was greatly agitated, talked very incoherently and looked wild, and led Mr. E. to suspect him a little insane. Mr. Hickock his tutor thinks his mind has been growing shattered.[22]

Silliman's efforts to convince Noyes to return to his parents' home in Norfield failed, as did pastoral care and reassurance by faculty, students, and friends. He condemned himself as an enemy of God, as a helpless victim of Satan's evil and temptations, as deserving of annihilation.

On May 6 searchers discovered Noyes's decomposed body floating upright in the Saugatuck River near the bridge where he was last sighted. A note found in his pocketbook, a slash wound on the throat, and final entries from his diary presented clear evidence of suicide. Woodbridge relates the details of his associate's melancholy.

> May 6, 1815 Read Benjamin's diary in part. He mentioned the Wednesday before he left N.H. that he attempted to cut his throat but the 6th commandment prevented it. What agony he endured. At night however he has a happy season, all was bright. He felt entire submission and was calm and a few triumphant expressions are the last he ever wrote. The next day however, it seems he lapsed into darkness. He seems to have had doubts and fears about a month gradually increasing. On his body was discovered a gash, on his throat, probably an attempt made on his body before plunging.[23]

The suicide note serves as a last will and testament for a soul in extremis. Even as he prepared for a self-inflicted death, Noyes continues the evangelical efforts of winning souls to Christ that he had so diligently pursued among his college classmates during the spring revival at Yale. He exhorts family members to find salvation and avoid his errors, disposes of his books, gives advice, and bids a last farewell to loved ones.

> Pa & Ma do not grieve—be extremely careful to instruct your children in the great concerns of eternity—use your utmost endeavours that they all know Jesus Christ & him crucified. Be very careful that they do not deceive themselves in the great matters of religion—I wish Burr to have a religious & liberal education, my books will serve him—Sister Mary be careful not to destroy yourself—The Devil is very active & artful. He has got fast hold of me so that I am entrapped. Fight the good fight of faith & you shall at last receive a crown of glory. Tell Aunt Grace that God did not make mankind to damn them but that they voluntarily damn themselves. Tell William & his wife—Samuel & his wife & John & his tell them all to be

exceedingly careful with respect to their good estate. Charles seek Christ immediately—kindly thank you Uncle Benjamin for all your favors to me. Aunt likewise I would be grateful to. Be very careful each of you that you deceive not yourselves. I know my ruin was owing to my great negligence in the great matters of the soul. I feared when I ought to have loved. I have been too dependant on others, not looked so well to my own estate as I should have done. Be careful that you come not to this place of torment ——— I do not realize my own situation.[24]

Mary Fish, Benjamin's grandmother, offered solace to her grieving extended family, charging her "dear Children" to remember Benjamin Noyes ("that you have so much satisfaction in his life") and trust in his eternal salvation ("tho his exit was dreadful we have reason to think he was not in his right mind and therefore not accountable for that his last act").[25] Reverend John Noyes, his father, interpreted this family tragedy from the pastoral framework of adversity as a manifestation of divine providence, as an invitation for believers to reappropriate humility—submission as God's children—and as an opportunity for spiritual growth. He writes to his mother, Mary Fish, on May 7, a day after discovering the body.

Dark and distressing is the Providence which causes our hearts to bleed, & our eyes to flow with tears. But we desire to justify God, and to realize that his way is perfect.

From the evidence which our dear departed gave of general piety, we still hope that he is gone to a better world; and if so, we have reason to rejoice on his account.[26]

Apart from a compelling narrative of a Noyes family tragedy, why reconstruct the suicide of Benjamin Noyes? What larger socio-historical significance does this particular case illustrate? How does this life history relate to the central issues and contradictions of the culture of evangelical Pietism during an era of religious awakening?

Benjamin Noyes's life reflected the highest ideals and cultural imperatives of evangelical Pietism—the self-reflective, continuous shaping of life's pilgrimage to find the inner certainty of grace and the outer activism of a vocation dedicated to the service of the Lord. His early life and character were hammered on the anvil of evangelical child-rearing to produce a modest, gentle youth, who had internalized the strictures of parental discipline and filial piety. Ever obedient to the will of his earthly and heavenly fathers, he possessed an extremely sensitive conscience, frequently overwhelmed with anguish and guilt for sins or unbrotherly thoughts. He suffered the typical life crisis of evangelicals as he made the transition from childhood to youth: the war against the self as symbolized by the sin of pride, requisite to a total submission to the will of God and regeneration of his heart. His daily, methodical, and unrelenting employment of devotional piety, notably self-examination, produced torturous seasons of religious melancholy punctuated by brief interludes of peace.

Finally, Noyes was a child of the Second Great Awakening. He fervently understood that his own salvation and spiritual well-being required the conversion of his family, friends, and classmates. Indeed, nothing less than the tireless efforts of reborn Christians, working through the agency of the Holy Spirit in the revival, were required to usher in God's kingdom in America during their lifetimes. Seen from this light, Noyes's spiritual itinerary from sin to salvation, and the maturing evidence of grace after his conversion, represented an inner journey and a publicly enacted drama of soteriological and eschatological significance. The salvation of mankind and the possibility of the millennium were inextricably linked to each conversion during revivals of religion. Benjamin did not suffer his melancholy in silence. His public, open weeping, groaning, handwringing and other histrionics dramatically enacted the godly sorrow marking the soul's progression toward selfless surrender in God's mercy. Benjamin's dramatic victory, and later his ultimate failure, were perceived as elements in a cosmological struggle against the forces of evil and sin, symbolized by Satan. The renewal of each new soul, and the subsequent efforts of each new convert to win other souls, gave hope for the coming of the kingdom of God in America.

He devoted himself to the realization of these ultimate values, as an exemplar of evangelical piety. How explain the fact that Benjamin Noyes, a full communicant and professor of religion, single-mindedly employed in service to the Lord, lapsed into intractable religious melancholy, choosing suicide? How did he arrive at the sorrowful conclusion that he was an enemy of Christ, a deluded hypocrite who never had been a child of God? How did his faith turn into despair?

Fortunately, many personal documents—diaries, letters, and memorials—exist, and provide access to the inner thoughts, feelings, and experiences of Noyes, his parents, uncles, and Yale classmates. Ultimately, his own diary documents the precise logical argument of an undergraduate recitation, proving true and certain the realization of his worst fear—he had committed secret sin that permanently transformed him into an enemy of God. Without recourse to the saving pardon of divine mercy, unable to endure the torment of life in this world, and contemplating an eternity of damnation, he chose suicide.

An examination of these personal documents, his family background, conversion and covenant with God (1812), acceptance as a communicant at Yale College Church (1813), and participation in the college religious revival of spring 1815 will reconstruct the life and melancholy of Benjamin Noyes.

Family Background and Evangelical Childrearing

Benjamin Noyes was born on February 5, 1796, the sixth of nine children of Reverend John Noyes and Eunice Sherwood Noyes.[27] He grew to maturity in a remarkable family marked by evangelical piety.

John Noyes, like his father and grandfather, was a Yale graduate (1767) and a Congregationalist minister, receiving his license to preach in 1784. After a period of itinerancy he accepted an offer to settle at Norfield (Weston), Connecticut, and was ordained on June 5, 1786.[28] That same year, he married Eunice Sherwood, the daughter of his predecessor, and together they raised a large family on his slender salary, supplemented by farming. Reverend Noyes provided twenty-two years of faithful service in Norfield until a doctrinal controversy over infant baptism, pecuniary difficulties, and the total loss of his voice in 1806 convinced him in 1807 to seek dismissal from his appointment.[29] It appears that Reverend Noyes suffered a conversion hysteria where the instrument of his pastoral service—his voice—suddenly, and without apparent physical injury or disease, was rendered useless. He could no longer preach.

His voice returned when he left the Norfield church, and in 1808 he accepted "supply" or temporary preaching responsibilities to fill the vacancies of neighboring churches. He remained in Norfield and for the next eighteen years offered supply preaching until his retirement from the pulpit.[30]

Reverend Noyes could not afford to send Samuel and John, his oldest children, to Yale, or settle them in a profession or business when they came of age in 1805. This financial embarrassment vexed him and explains some of the concerns that attended his hysterical loss of voice and vocational crisis. John Noyes remembered when during the American Revolution his mother, faced with deflated currency and financial reverses, risked debtors' prison to send her three sons to Yale. He could not offer this benefit to his own sons.[31]

Seven years later, however, with considerable sacrifice, he did pay the costs of tutors, college preparation, and tuition for Benjamin Noyes. In a important sense, the Noyes family traditions scripted his life and justified the considerable costs of a liberal education. Of the seven sons, Benjamin Noyes was selected to receive a Yale education as preparation for the ministry, to continue as the fourth successive generation in this vocation. Although, the details of his selection remain unknown, he clearly felt the awesome responsibility and burden of this legacy, of proving himself worthy. It added yet another burden to the morphology of conversion and transition to adulthood.

John and Eunice Noyes were model parents in their endeavors to shape the evangelical character and temperament of the children. Near the close of his life in 1844, Noyes published a selection of letters of moral and religious advice. In this volume he presented his views and experiences about evangelical child-rearing. The selection, "To a Young Married Lady on Her Requesting Advice How to Bring Up Her Infant Son," Reverend Noyes prescribes will-breaking, filial piety, and obedience. "The sooner children are made to submit to the will of the parent, on being capable of knowing that they are under his control, the better."[32]

Noyes prescribes a regimen that he had implemented in his own family—one of strict moral discipline requiring careful observance of the Sabbath, self-control, and the requirement that children display humility, meekness, and unquestioning submission to parental authority. Children must employ a formal address of "sir" or "ma'am" when speaking to their parents. Above all, he charged parents with the duty of instructing children in the great matters of the soul.[33] "They should be taught the way to the throne of grace, and the duty and privilege of coming to it day by day with a humble and believing heart. They should be frequently reminded of their dependence on God, and accountability to him, and of the uncertainty of life . . . ."[34]

Reverend Noyes's advice to parents and guidance to his son was a prescription for evangelical nurture. The younger Noyes came of age obsessed with feelings of guilt and shame, unable to win the love of his earthly or heavenly fathers. As Benjamin Noyes approached adulthood and needed to make a confession of faith, own a church covenant, complete his studies in preparation for a life of public service in the ministry, and resolve the issues of sexuality, he foundered on these questions of adult autonomy. Equating self with autonomous agency, he felt compelled to quash this issue by self-torture, self-denying evangelical humiliation, and selfless surrender into the bosom of Christ. Yet, these spiritual exercises led him into desolation and self-destruction. Religious melancholy and suicide provided Benjamin Noyes with an indirect, covert rebellion against his father and the regimen of evangelical nurture that had overwritten the youth's persona and aspirations with those of his father and ultimately of God's will. After all, how could the young man proceed in this spiritual itinerary and ministerial vocation if he had never experienced authentic saving grace, but lived as a hypocrite? What should he do if he had sinned away the day of grace? But these observations anticipate the end of the story.

Noyes became an obedient, loving son, a pleasant and cheerful youth, eager to please. He possessed a keen analytic mind, a tender heart open to religious sentiments and affections, and a harsh, exacting conscience. He accepted, without protest, the central mission of life: to know himself and his state of grace as a basis for conversion and subsequent sanctification through vocational devotion to the cause of the Redeemer.

The piety and evangelical milieu of the Noyes family that encouraged the son to walk in the path of his forbearers by attending Yale and preparing for the ministry also brought him into direct contact with religious despair and mental alienation. Mary Fish suffered a debilitating religious despondency (1770–1772). John Noyes lost his voice in a hysterical illness in 1806. Uncle Joseph (Jose), also a minister who failed in every occupation (minister, surveyor, farmer, and lawyer), became the family ne'er-do-well. He migrated to the frontier in the Ohio Western Reserve and there claims to have received direct illuminations of divine prophecy that he recorded in his "Dream Books."[35] Jose's son, Joseph Fish Noyes, aged eighteen, went mad after suffering a disappointing love affair. On May 19, 1803, he left his father's home and set out on foot to return east to Connecticut. Benjamin Silliman recounts how the young man traveled over four hundred miles in eighteen days.

> . . . without money, without friends, often for a whole day without food, once lodging in the woods on the ground, obliged to sell every article of clothing except what he wore, often ridiculed & abused, suspected of entertaining a design on his own life, taken up and carried before a magistrate and about to be committed to prison as a suspected character, often worn down with fatigue & hunger, with blistered feet and ready to sink under such accumulated suffering, but at last arriving in Phila [delphia] . . . .[36]

Through the help of family friends, Joseph Noyes was sent to Connecticut, where he visited his grandmother in Fairfield and uncle in Wallingford, and in August, spent a month on the Noyes farm. Joseph Noyes returned with his father to Ohio later that fall, and disappeared in 1805.

Benjamin Noyes's family brought him into intimate contact with mental alienation. He knew, from direct experience, the dangers attendant on religious enthusiasm: melancholy, derangement, and suicide. The experiences of living with a mentally ill parent, uncle, and cousin may have contributed to his later alienation.

Questing After the Grace of God

Benjamin Noyes emerged from boyhood as an exemplary evangelical personality. His diary entries, quoted extensively in this section, reveal a youth who actively and warmly embraced the ideals of evangelical Pietism: (1) the mortification of self and surrender to the will of God; (2) the routine practice of devotional piety in fasting, secret prayer, self-examination, Sabbath keeping and public worship; (3) a tender-hearted personal relationship with God; and (4) a generalized benevolent concern for the salvation of all people as part of the labor to create God's kingdom in America.

Benjamin Silliman wrote a private "memoir" recounting the life and character of his nephew in an attempt to console and reassure the family that Noyes indeed possessed a vital piety that could not be tarnished by a single desperate act. Silliman provides a biographical sketch of the young man. In the fall of 1808, at the age of twelve, he left Norfield to live and work in New Haven for a mineral water company. Silliman invited Noyes to live and work with his family in September 1809, where he remained for three years until leaving for Yale.[37]

Boys first left home at the age of eight and began the semi-dependence of youth, no longer dependent upon their families of orientation for support, yet unable to make major adult transitions in marriage or vocation. Youths in semi-dependence remained emotionally tied to their parents, often seeking approval or permission as if they lived in their parents' household.[38] Semi-dependent young men entered apprenticeships or received board and tutoring in exchange for service in their master's household.

Noyes would return to his parents' home in Norfield periodically for visits and to assist his father on the farm. He too remained emotionally tied to his parents, seeking their advice, approval, and support, although removed from their direct supervision.

During his residence and service in the Silliman household, Noyes displayed "an uncommon sweetness of temper," diligence in work, and careful attention to college preparation, guided by Chauncey Goodrich.[39] Silliman adopted an evangelical family government marked by family worship, Sabbath exercises, and religious instruction. Noyes actively joined his uncle's family in the practice of piety. Silliman notes that "His observance of the duties of religion was exemplary; he was punctual—attentive, & apparently, devout in joining the family worship; & he spent the Sabbath exclusively in his appropriate duties ———— always seeking instruction from religious books in the intervals of public worship."[40]

However, during the summer of 1811, he experienced his first episode of religious melancholy, his first realization of the ambiguous status of semi-dependence that allowed the dangerous possibility of greater self-assertion, agency, and independence. He needed to smother this nascent sense of self, a requirement prescribed for all evangelical youth. His uncle relates that ". . . his cheerfulness forsook him—he seemed to have lost his satisfaction in everything around him, and, at times, seemed as if he would sink under it. I know not how it was, that in a mind like his, constitutionally bright, & cheerful, an increasing interest in religious subjects seemed to produce correspondent depression and distress . . . ."[41]

Noyes could not find comfort and spent many evenings, as his uncle noted, in uncommon distress,

> going to bed at midnight, or perhaps, later—nor was this all—we could often hear him at his devotions for a long time after he had retired to his chamber; his tone of voice, accompanied by groans & ejaculations, discovered a mind in anguish, & his countenance in the morning often indicated extreme exhaustion & wretchedness.[42]

Noyes's diaries recount his secret devotions in the closet—prayers and daily self-examinations—that revealed evidence of sin, pride, levity, coldheartedness, and the self-accusation of manifesting too little devotion to the cause of the Redeemer. He would invariably enter resolutions to reform, beseeching God for guidance and strength. Writing in an early entry on August 18, 1811, he completes the cycle of self-examination and self-accusation by the plea, "O Lord wilt thou be pleased of thine infinite mercy to help an unworthy Servant to amend his way. Wilt thou assist him in turning from sin unto thee."[43]

One particular sin proved most difficult to overcome. The guilt associated with the realization of the enormity of his betrayal of God's will triggered episodes of religious melancholy in 1811–1812, April through July of 1813, February through March of 1814, and March and April of 1815.

Noyes had great difficulty understanding his awakening sexual impulses and needs. Evangelical culture provided no satisfactory expression of adolescent sexuality, prohibiting premarital intercourse and masturbation as acts of moral depravity, demanding the systematic repression of sexual thoughts. His sexual thoughts and masturbation, as noted in his journal, filled with him an overpowering awareness of sin, prompting him to make resolutions that he failed to keep. He suffered doubts that such a sinner could ever enter the Kingdom as a child of God. He pledged, during his first religious melancholy:

> August 16, 1812 I do at this time with the presence of the God who searches the heart & trys the reigns of the children of men, solemnly resolve to do all that I am able through God's grace assisting me to check every lewd & unclean thought & more especially to repress, shun, and abstain from the

filthy act of uncleanness . . . I am now around the age of 16 and onward
———— I have always been very sinful but in an especial manner so for a
year past. I have had all the offers of mercy, but my hard & stubborn
heart has resisted & refused them all.[44]

With precise logic, Noyes employed the rules of self-examination. In
reviewing his sexual conduct, he found evidence of sin. This was inconsistent
with Christian character, where inward grace and renewed heart empowered
the true believer to shun things of the flesh and of this world, and work with
unfaltering resolve to fulfill God's will. Time and again, Noyes found himself driven, ineluctably, to the conclusion that he had deceived himself in daring
to believe in the possibility of salvation. In his melancholy he accepted the
inward revelation of his "true" self and state: "I feel as if I was not a true
subject of the redeemers [sic] Kingdom. My heart is filled with sin . . . ."[45]

Noyes's uncle and father tried to guide the youth, although no evidence
exists that they knew of the sexual nature of his perplexity. Silliman counseled patience, that those under religious concerns only gradually find evidence of grace. John Noyes sent a detailed letter of advice to his son, yet the
father inadvertently reaffirmed the dangers of self-delusion and hypocrisy, the
very charges that would lead to the young Noyes's suicide two years later.
Writing on November 4, 1812, John Noyes seeks to comfort and sustain his
son in this time of religious concern.

> We are glad to have you open your mind so freely & fully on the subject
> of your spiritual concerns—And tho' we feel tenderly affected with the rep-
> resentation which you give of yourself, yet we had rather have you in such
> a state of mind, than in a state of insensibility; or than that of one who
> flatters himself that he is a child of God while he knows not experimen-
> tally what it is to be born of God.[46]

Noyes reiterated the standard spiritual itinerary of conversion: sinners awakened to legal terror of their sin, prostrated in godly sorrow by the realization
of the sovereignty of God, affirming their complete dependence on God and
their "utter insufficiency to change their own hearts," finally, experiencing a
selfless anguish and ultimate surrender into the hands of a merciful God who,
through the intercession of a dying savior, redeems their sin and renews their
hearts. He concludes by posing several questions to plumb the nature of his
son's soul, advising him to seek the guidance of Timothy Dwight, president
of Yale.

> I hope my dear son that you will be on your guard against a despairing
> frame: and believe that Godly grace is as sufficient for the renewal and
> sanctification of the hearts of sinners as it is for the pardon of the true
> believer ———— I do not find that you are quarreling with the decrees of
> God & with his sovereignty as sinners under awakenings are prone to do—
> I would ask you are you willing that God should reign; and is it not a
> satisfaction to you that he is such a being as declares himself to be in his
> word! And can you not cast yourself on his mercy thro a blessed Redeemer
> as he is encouraging you to do?— . . . . I have written to Dr. Dwight in

your behalf, requesting him to attend to your case—open your mind freely
to him: and as your parents have before enjoined, do not keep your burden to yourself, but let it be known to us, & to some Christian friend that
may be at hand.[47]

In a letter dated November 17, Benjamin Noyes responded, stating that he
feels fear and dread over the growing evidence of his "treacherous heart" that
has never been "truly humbled. . . . I pray to God for a change of heart: but
it is such a prayer as is not worthy of acceptance: not coming from improper
heart dictated from, perhaps, altogether selfish motives." He continues by
answering his father's questions:

> You sir put the question to me "Are you not willing that God should reign"
> and "can you cast yourself on his mercy through a blessed Redeemer." I
> think I have no hesitation in saying that I am willing that God should reign
> while, yet I don't mean to convey the idea that I can repose on him &
> confide in Him with all the heart. . . . I cannot neither cast myself on God
> with that sorrow for sin . . . . I have read Edwards, & been to Doctor
> Dwight. He gave me the sermons to read on the evidences of regeneration,
> which I have read & am to go there Thursday to converse with him. I
> shall endeavour to open my mind to him fully. I need to have a deep humil-
> iating sense of my sin & a truly broken heart. My great difficulty is that
> I do not feel my sins as I ought to . . . .[48]

Noyes understood the crux of his perplexity as a personal failure to accept
the abundant mercies of divine grace, freely proffered; as an inability to profit
from those ardent Christian friends who endeavored to assist him in this conversion. He read Edwards's *Treatise Concerning Religious Affections*, seeking guidance in differentiating between natural feelings of dread and the distinguishing marks of a soul turning to God with a renewed heart—"Love to
Christ" and "Joy in Christ." Edwards defines and clarifies just exactly those
inward exercises of the heart that offer proof of true religion and the power
of godliness in one's heart: ". . . every one that has the power of godliness in
his heart, has the inclinations and heart exercised towards God and divine
things, with such strength and vigor that these holy exercises do prevail in
him above all carnal or natural affections, are effectual to overcome them.
. . ."[49] In a letter of December 26, 1812 he confides to his father "I find that
the greatest and only difficulty is in myself."[50] With the assistance of his teach-
ers, family, and the works on regeneration and religious affections, Noyes
discovered the first signs of the power of godliness in his heart.

However tentative and troubled by doubt, his melancholy lifted and he
mustered the courage to make public his profession of faith by entering the
covenant of grace on March 15, 1812, at the age of sixteen. In a written
contract, he affirmed the contents of his faith, acknowledging the majesty of
God's sovereignty, and "the bountiful provision made in the gospel through
Jesus Christ . . . wilt the Lord blot out my numerous sins, & remember not
against me my former iniquities." After making this written profession of faith,
he stated: "I do therefore . . . with utmost solemnity surrender myself to the
O Lord in a Covenant never to be broken."[51]

In the concluding paragraph of the covenant, Noyes stipulated the terms of his surrender and humility in God's service as a contractual exchange for the remission of sin and the seal of grace and salvation. He places his life in God's hands, petitions God to shower mercies upon him, never to remove the Spirit, always to persevere in this vocation:

> Now O Lord I am thine if thou wilt receive me. Use me and all that thou has given me as thou seeist fit. I will always strive to acquire in all these allotment O Lord of whatsoever temporal mercies thou mayest see fit to deprive me, take not I humbly beseech thee thine holy Spirit from me. Suffer me never to fall from thee. Let me never forget this solemn & interesting transaction. Give me deeply to resolve that "he that putteth his hand to the plough and looketh back is not for the Kingdom of Heaven."[52]

John Noyes routinely sent a letter of admonition to persons who made a public profession of religion. Although his communication with his son has not survived, Noyes did publish an admonition to another family member in his collected *Letters*. Most important, he warned the youth about the perils of Satan, a theme found throughout his son's own diary and in the suicide note. Benjamin Noyes had internalized these admonitions and remained vigilant, ever beset by the perils of worldliness, sin, and the personification of evil in this world—Satan. His father states:

> The Christian lives in an ensnaring world, which is continually courting his attention, to draw him from his duty, and to plunge him into sin. He also has his own corruption to struggle with. . . . And Satan is a very busy adversary, seeking whom he may devour. He is cunning as well as malicious; and if he cannot succeed in destroying the Christian, he will tempt and worry him, and ply all his arts to hinder his progress in the Christian course. We need to be sober and vigilant from the consideration of our danger from the grand adversary.[53]

These admonitions of backsliding, of the ever-present snares of Satan, and his earlier warnings about insensibility of heart, self-deception, and hypocrisy about one's state as a child of God, would later form the basis of the son's final melancholy and suicide.

Benjamin Noyes reviewed his ownership and progress in this covenant every six months and duly noted his continuance on the back cover of the document at New Year's Day of 1813. He reaffirmed the covenant when he became a communicant in Yale College Church on April 4, 1813. Noyes reiterates the metaphor of the "hand on the plough," disavows the temptations of Satan, and affirms before the witnesses of the assembled congregation and Jesus that he shall suffer terrible judgments should he fall from grace. In his diary he records:

> I have put my hand on the plough and cannot look back; but am bound to press forward towards the mark for the prize of the high calling which is in Christ Jesus my Lord—Heaven and earth will be the witnesses against me if I forsake the Lord—The assembly before whom I have vowed, will be witnesses against me—Jesus Christ will witness against me—& will be

my awful judge, if I am not found faithful in the most solemn engagements which I have taken upon me this day.[54]

Benjamin Noyes asks for strength to do God's handiwork, to devote himself to the salvation of mankind, and to remain true to the paths of righteousness.

O Lord teach me where my strength must be found, & enable me to place entire confidence in thy promises that thou will keep all those who sincerely commit themselves into *thine* arms of mercy . . . . O be pleased to keep my feet from falling—my eyes from tears, & in all circumstances of life,—may I be enabled to advance thine honor & glory, as well as the *present* & *eternal* welfare of my fellow man. Wilt thou daily lead me by the hand in the paths of righteousness. Be thou the God of my days, & the guide of my youth. May I remember, that, having partaken of the table of Christ, I can no longer partake of the table of the Devil.[55]

Noyes anticipated that terrible punishments would befall him if he did not persevere and continue to grow in grace, should the warmhearted grace of God ever recede and leave a coldhearted doubt.

Religious Melancholy

Conversion, church membership, and the practice of piety offered Noyes little protection from recurrent and severe periods of religious melancholy. He began one such period in June 1813 and remained despondent until October of that year. In what emerged as the pattern for his subsequent depressions, he employed the daily meditation and self-examination of secret prayer in the closet to ascertain his soul's progress and growth in grace. Invariably, he found distressing evidence of renewed sinfulness: levity, pride, inattention to religion, stupidity, insensibility, and hardness of heart. Frequently, he chastised himself for a failure to experience authentic humilation, writing on July 19, "I seemed to be particularly forsaken last night. Could not feel that sense of my vileness which I wished."[56] After he had committed what he considered an act of lewdness or physical uncleanliness, meaning either masturbation or a nocturnal emission, his feeling of sin, self-loathing, and melancholy intensified. His diary entry of August 20 reveals that "This morning I awoke and found myself in a miserable state. Will God be pleased to forgive me, and spare me for mercies [*sic*] sake. May I be formed into the likeness of God . . ."[57]

Few of his friends realized that he suffered such torturous doubt. Noyes's public persona appeared as the exemplary model of a pious, evangelical college student, actively interested in the salvation of his classmates, whom he termed, "dear youths" and "brethren." His daily schedule or "Course for the Day," imposed a routine of disciplined study, devotional piety, exercise, classes, and recitation. He would rise at 6:00 a.m., dress, and attend morning prayers in the chapel. Next came recitation, a walk for exercise, breakfast, secret duties in his room, followed by a full day of class, three additional periods of self-examination, and an evening prayer service or religious meeting. Sabbath days were strictly kept as times of fasting, prayer, and humiliation.[58] Noyes frequently stayed by the bedside of a sick or dying friend, offering comfort and spiritual guidance. He indefatigably engaged his classmates in religious conversation, meeting in their rooms to discuss the weighty matters of salvation and the state of religion at Yale. He understood that an abiding concern for the salvation of others marked the authentic sign of maturing grace in his heart.

Although the public youth comported himself as a model of Christian charity, the private diaries revealed a growing melancholy as he relentlessly charged himself with hypocrisy. Only infrequently did he receive relief and assurance of faith and the abiding comfort of God's love. And, as he states in the following diary entry, how transient and short-lived were these times of peace.

> August 7, 1814 Sabb. 7. I arose this morning at the ringing of the prayer bell—did not return to my room till after breakfast. After I returned to my room I read a chapter in the bible—had prayers with Br. Cornelius and after-wards [sic] when he was absent, had a good season of private prayer. I wished to pray especially for preparations for the solemn duties of this holy day, that I might be prepared to approach the table of the Lord with a right heart—that I might not eat and drink the body and blood of the Lord Jesus Christ unworthy. Oh what a privilege is prayer! I then went up to the house of God. . . . Oh how negligent have I been! How unlike a follower of the glorious Redeemer have I acted! Surely God would be just should he cast me off forever. After the usual exercises—I was permitted with my Christian Brethren to approach the table of the crucified Redeemer. I think I enjoyed the season. My heart was much interested on this occasion and I thought I was willing unreservedly to give away myself into the hands of God—that I was willing to make measured exercises to maintain holiness of life, & that by, his grace strengthen me I would begin a new [sic] to serve him more faithfully. Oh Lord let not these be shortlived feelings . . . .[59]

During the first term of his junior year in 1814, in a letter of December 2, he wrote to his grandmother, Mary Fish, of visiting the bedside of a dying classmate, exhorting and praying. He exclaimed, "Would to God that all youths would live the life—that they might die the death of the Righteous!" Noyes added a prayer of thanksgiving as the principal message in this letter.

> What cause for gratitude and thanksgiving have we my dear Grand Ma that God has been loading us with mercies, not only the past year, but thro' our lives.—mercies have been new every morning & fresh every night! May we in the word, & with the spirit of the psalmist, say "Bless the Lord & my soul; and all this within me, bless his holy name ——— Bless the Lord, O my soul, and forget not all his benefits.[60]

Writing on New Year's Day of 1815, a Sabbath after he received communion, he takes stock of his life and resolves to "begin a new course of life—

or would endeavour to live more as it becomes a follower of the Blessed Redeemer."[61] Noyes elaborates on this resolution by promising to continue his spiritual diary, with the anticipation that his writing

> may be less *dark* in the retrospect—that it may flow from a heart more warm with divine grace! My resolutions to live a holy life have been many since I began to record them. Some of them I have by divine grace been unable to keep. Many furnish matters of deep humiliation. I humbly implore the pardon of all sins—particularly those of the past year—And look to God for grace to enter upon the present year—with more devotion of heart to his service.[62]

Noyes completes this journal entry by rededicating himself to the practice of devotional piety in a series of five resolutions, beseeching God for strength to redeem the pledges made, bowed in humility and surrender.

> And humbly relying on the grace of God to perform them I resolve
> 1st To *attend more strictly to serious self-examination.*
> 2nd To *contend against the lusts of the flesh*
> 3rd To *be more faithful in making the word of God the rule of my conduct*
> 4th To guard against levity—that it not take the place of *cheerfulness*
> 5th in short to live more as becomes a child of God. O Lord enable me to realize that these solemn resolves are indeed binding—Make me to feel my dependence on God for strength to perform them. Lord I am thine by vocation & by voluntary dedication. Oh enable me to live as becomes thine. Without *thee* I can do nothing—Thy grace assisting me I can do all things.[63]

Again he resolves to employ self-control against the lusts of the flesh, a problem that he never mastered and that brought intense feelings of anguish and self-loathing. After the commission of these sins, he felt the presence of God's love withdraw from his heart. Without such assurances, without the prospect of salvation, life would become an unbearable burden.

The Revival and the Final Crisis

The spring term at Yale brought a public revival of religion and the ultimate trial of faith for Noyes. In a journal entry on February 21, 1815, he writes of his continuing spiritual malaise, of feeling insufficient emotional fervor in his prayers and devotions, and makes accusations of deceit and corruption. ". . . I saw much pride much self-righteousness much deceit lurking secretly in my heart. Lord, I desire to be stripped of this *garb* of filthy rags & be clothed with the spotless robe of *Christ's* righteousness. Lord wilt *thou* humble me— expose to view my deformity & bring me to unfeigned repentance."[64]

Noyes resolved that he would know himself and find the answer to his many years of torment. Either he was a child of God, destined for salvation, or a vile hypocrite, deluded and bound for eternal torment. He returned to

Jonathan Edwards's *Treatise Concerning Religious Affections* to ascertain the authenticity of his heart, his sentiments, and his state of grace. Writing on February 22, he commits himself to this struggle for self-knowledge, whatever the consequences: "I see the necessity of knowing myself—I must: and with the gracious assistance of God I will know more of my heart than I have heretofore known . . . If I am a *Hypocrite* than should I be likely to know it—If a child of God—this I might have comfortable evidence of."[65]

Self-knowledge rarely brought Noyes comforting news, as he uncovered the awful truth about his nature. On March 3 he writes: "I have felt more sinful to day [*sic*] than for some few days past. I mean I have had proofs of my sin. I fear I have much reason to suspect my state. Oh how awful a thing it will be to see at the day of Judgment that I have been a hypocrite."[66]

Benjamin Noyes thus began his most severe religious crisis as a collegewide religious awakening took hold at Yale. This revival commenced during the first week of April 1815 at Sabbath evening prayers. Chauncey Goodrich's "Narrative of Revivals of Religion in Yale College," provides a firsthand account of the visitation of the Holy Spirit.

> It was then customary for the members of the senior class, taken categorically, to read on that occasion, a short sermon or other piece, selected by the faculty. The person to whom the duty fell that evening, was very far from being seriously inclined; but the solemn recitals of this narrative which he had never before seen, affected his mind so deeply, that he read with increased emotion as he advanced, and at last ended in a faltering accent and with tears. Such an exhibition of feeling where it was least expected, operated, at once, with a kind of electric power on the whole body of students. Nearly every individual in college, became anxious for the salvation of his soul . . . .[67]

The emotional intensity and enthusiasm of the revival swept through the nearly three-hundred undergraduates at Yale, who petitioned President Dwight for a suspension of classes. Although he refused, Dwight did increase the number of prayer services, and directed theological graduate students to hold inquiry meetings each afternoon.[68] William Channing Woodbridge and Elias Cornelius worked tirelessly, exhorting anxious sinners. In a letter dated April 13, 1815, Cornelius writes:

> Those who were awakened, we requested to assemble at particular rooms— of which one was designated for each *entry*, and proper persons were appointed to take charge of the meetings. The attention to the subject was such, that religion might properly be said to be the general topic of conversation. It seemed at one time, as if a universal solemnity prevailed, and every individual was prepared to hear conversation on the subject.[69]

The graduate students and professors of religion, Goodrich, Fitch, Taylor and others, fomented a milieu of sacred time and agency, creating collective expectations that everyone must seek the soul's salvation, or renew the covenant with God.

William Channing Woodbridge, having found grace after several torturous years of religious inquiry, worked tirelessly with the Yale undergraduates. On May 9, 1815, he writes in his journal that

> I have conversed with about 40 of my acquaintances. . . . I have used the obvious method at first to convince them that they were at enmity with God and were helpless in themselves. . . . I urged them therefore to strain every nerve and struggle for their lives to repent & believe & love God & to continue the struggling until they either repented or were sensible of their helplessness.[70]

As the awakening continued through April, Yale became a crucible of unrelenting pressures for students to make a public renewal of faith or first profession of religion. Goodrich offers the account of one student's fervor and the dangers of religious enthusiasm. This student was a churched, pious, individual, who was completing his studies when the revival began, and when he was struck by melancholy.

> He shut himself in his room, and resolved never to cross the threshold, till he came out a servant of God. His food was carried to him from the Hall; Christian friends visited him, from time to time, for conversation and prayer; and the interests of his soul absorbed all his thoughts and feelings. But he made no progress; nearly three weeks passed away and he made no progress; his mind was only more dark and confused . . . .[71]

These experiences proved all too common during the Yale revival. Noyes shut himself off from friends and normal routine several days before he left the college. He immersed himself in a collective movement that demanded his heartfelt assurance of grace to add his soul to the sum of those brought to God. He spent all his energy in this evangelical effort, neglecting studies and skipping meals to increase his time for secret prayer. Yet, like the youth mentioned previously, his mind too "was only more dark and confused."

Yale college periodically welcomed revivals during the Second Great Awakening, including those "seasons of spiritual refreshment" in 1801, 1807–1808, and 1812.[72] President Dwight, from the beginning of his tenure in 1795 until his death in 1818, championed the doctrinal orthodoxy of Congregationalism against the perceived threats of Universalism, Unitarianism, and Deism, and infidelity. He strongly supported evangelical methods to accomplish the goal of educating a generation of men to lead church and society. Equally as important as a liberal education, Yale students needed to achieve their soul's regeneration as the foundation for their public vocations.[73]

Dwight understood that times of indifference to religion followed seasons of awakening. During this period of spiritual dullness, he initiated measures to reanimate religious concerns among the undergraduates by establishing special Sabbath prayers asking God to visit Yale again with the Holy Spirit. These prayers began on December 5, 1814, four months before the beginning of the April revival. In his diary, Elias Cornelius records: "The state of religion is low indeed in college, though we are hoping for better days. The brethren appear to be in some measure at least awake. We have agreed to unite in secret concert of prayer every Sabbath morning, at sunrise, for a revival of religion in college."[74]

Benjamin Noyes participated in these special prayers. In a postscript to his December 2, 1814, letter to Mary Fish about the state of religion at Yale, Noyes recounts that two students labor under "very serious impressions," stating: "May the course of Zion prosper here and everywhere."[75] In his diary on February 18, 1815, he notes that after attending the sunrise service and the regular worship, how deeply he longs for the conversion of his classmates.

> I could not but weep when I returned to my room to think of how many of today's hearers in this institution are the companions of *Fools*—How little they apparently attended to what was delivered from the sacred desk. But I could weep for joy to think that there are some of the *dear* youths in of this Seminary, [*sic*] who are not as sheep without a shepherd exposed to the devouring beasts of prey; but that they have the Glorious Redeemer for their friend—that they are lambs whose shepherd is Jesus Christ.[76]

Noyes speaks with admiration about the seminary students. In April 1813 he befriended Elias Cornelius and on March 18, 1815, he came under the masterful influence of William Channing Woodbridge, ". . . Noyes, Lockwood, and another stranger . . . called to see me. The two former lately submitted to God; I felt, notwithstanding our ignorance of each other as if we were all of one heart—one soul, had a pleasing interview—prayer."[77] Noyes returned the following evening to walk and pray with his new friend Woodbridge. He records these meetings in his diary, his awareness of Woodbridge's awakening and subsequent experience of saving grace.

> Saturday March 18 This afternoon I went to Mr. Woodbridge's room—he was not there: I went to Mr. Cornelius'—found Mr. Woodbridge there. ——— had a very agreeable season: the dear youth seems to be absolutely reconciled—wholly given into the hands of his heavenly Father. He can't doubt of his submission—Dear youth—I fear it will not always be so. I fear he will have some severe trials yet: but I trust he will come out of them all as gold out of the fire, seven times purified: for I do believe God has changed his heart. All things appear new to him.[78]

Noyes felt envy and skepticism regarding the conversion narratives of both Woodbridge and a fellow undergraduate, Brother Nealy. After hearing Nealy explain his joy in submitting to God, Noyes writes: "I envied him almost his happiness. Now this was very wrong. I ought to have rejoiced with my whole heart. I trust I am sorry for these wicked feelings."[79] Try as he might, he could never gain that calm assurance as a child of God, although his friends assisted and encouraged his heroic, unrelenting efforts.

On March 21, Woodbridge notes, "B. Noyes called on me; he is a fervent Christian." Noyes came under Woodbridge's guidance during the revival by joining the private student group that Woodbridge visited and exhorted.

> April 1, 1815 Our hearts were animated indeed with the sight, God is indeed with us. Kibbie, Lockwood and Noyes who propose to join the church tomorrow met with me at my room that we might pray together for a

blessing on us and particularly that we may be enabled to come forward not faithless but believing and with holy boldness.[80]

The question remains as to how Noyes reached the point of suicidal despair, when by Woodbridge's account, Noyes realized the highest achievement of evangelical piety. The answer lies in his new friendship with Woodbridge, the message of New Haven theology, and a critical interview with Brother Nealy on March 28.

Woodbridge experienced a saving grace on March 15, 1815, after several years of religious concerns where he too struggled with doubt, melancholy, and suicidal inclinations. He used his recent spiritual victory as a model in exhorting Noyes and other undergraduates. Although only eighteen years old, Woodbridge had graduated from college and taught school for a year before returning for a graduate year in theology at Yale in 1814. He had not yet decided on his life's work, alternating between pursuing a career teaching chemistry under the tutelage of Benjamin Silliman or a vocation as a missionary following the charge of Timothy Dwight. He had not made a public profession of religion, waiting until May of 1815 to join the Yale church. During the momentous happenings in the spring revival, Woodbridge would find grace, receive a calling to evangelize, and choose his life's work.

His diary entries in March reveal the spiritual struggle that brought him into a selfless despair, longing for death and annihilation. After two years of alternating hope and desperation, he wrote on March 6, 1815: "I am unable to accept Christ because I am unwilling." He continues this theme of the self as an autonomous moral agent actively choosing worldliness and sin over Christ; by free choice the self chooses damnation.

> Sunday March 12, 1815 . . . the heart which rejects Christ on earth with all the restraints of a pious education, the entreaties of pious friends & parents, the confluence of the Spirit, the sense of danger & the promise of release from it must be black . . . .

> March 13, 1815 I have too a dreadful aggravation of guilt; I am breaking an express promise to dedicate myself to the service of God. The means of grace I find will not save me without God's power changing my heart. I am in perishing need of something to save me, what hope have I?[81]

Woodbridge's diary and Noyes's suicide note hinge on Taylorism. Taylor formalized this position in a sermon to pastors, "*Concio Ad Clerium*" (1828), where he defined moral depravity as "man's own act, consisting in a free choice of some object rather than God as his chief good;————or a free preference of the world and of worldly good, to the will and glory of God."[82] Taylor argued that all Christians remained duty-bound to choose God's way and righteousness over the Devil's path of sin and worldliness. Should a person experience doubt, or manifest a lack of faith or the absence of grace, these personal inadequacies, in the face of manifold divine mercy, represented a stubborn unwillingness to choose God. The abject sinner could only look inward to locate the source of guilt and unhappiness. In this manner, Taylor's doctrine of moral agency posited an omnicausal self who created the conditions of his or her own temporal and eternal misery. The believer struggled with an obstinate will and the self-made indictment of failing to fulfill the promise to devote all effort to God's service—the pledge that constituted choosing God over this world.[83] If the believer, in self-examination, found him- or herself wanting, according to Taylor, ". . . His guilt is all his own, and a just God may leave him to this choice. He is going on to a wretched eternity, the self-made victim of his woes."[84]

Woodbridge found the moral agency to choose for God, and on March 15, 1815, his sorrow turned to joy and rapture in the love of God and submission to His will: "God vouchsafed in his infinite kindness, to make me feel wholly submissive to his will. I saw I was wholly in the hands of God and knew that the judge of all the earth will do right and I rejoice that I was in his hands."[85] Armed with his own journey from despair to joy as a model for others to emulate, Woodbridge devoted himself tirelessly to the work of bringing the students, Noyes included, through this spiritual itinerary. He reminded them of his many years of doubt, of the extreme spiritual desolation and desperation that he suffered just prior to his ecstatic surrender to God. Others could expect to undergo similar religious affections as the authentic work of the Holy Spirit and preparatory to the day of grace. In this way, Noyes received encouragement to exacerbate his own spiritual desolation.

Noyes had accepted the accountability of the omnicausal self, interpreting this as weakness when confronting worldly temptations, spiritual deadness, and failure to devote himself totally to God's service. Through self-examination he uncovered convincing evidence of moral depravity punishable by eternal damnation. His suicide note admonishes his Aunt, Grace, "that God did not make mankind to damn them but that they voluntarily damn themselves."[86]

After much travail, Noyes regained several days of spiritual comfort during the last week of March. This would be his last respite before the final crisis of faith.

> Wednesday March 22nd I retired to my room and there poured out my soul in fervent prayer to almighty God. I was I think enabled to get near the mercy seat: after a time I could in prayer I thought freely give away myself into the hands of God. I did accordingly consecrate myself to God soul & body. . . .[87]

In this spirit of comfort and growing hope, he paid a visit to Nealy to set things right about his previous envy toward the youth. Nealy played the role of inquisitor in ascertaining the grounds for Noyes's hope for a renewed heart.

> I went to see Br. Nealy this evening after supper. I have been wanting to see him for some time. I sat down in his room. And we had a very intimate conversation. He asked me what were the grounds on which I build my hope in Christ. I told him that the evidence of which I most relied is what I find in the closet. I feel at times at least as though I was willing to give up my all to God, & for God. I think I feel this at times. There also I see in a measure the content and growth of my sins—hope I feel repen-

tance of them. And another ground of my hope is love for the Brethren. It seems as though I were not deceived in this particular: I know that much of my affections may be merely natural—exercised perhaps not because the Brethren are the children of God: but because they are friends and apparently have an affection for me.[88]

Next, Noyes introduces the subject of sexual sin, and with Nealy, articulates a four-part argument proving that masturbation represents a sin against God. He then confesses to Nealy, recounting the growing frequency of his sinning, and resolves again to refrain from this moral depravity.

After this subject was through I brought forward what I have had so much sorley [sic] about, for this two years. I was glad to find that he was clearly convinced in his own mind with respect to this particular. He is convinced that it is sin. And I am likewise convinced that it is actually sin against God. I can prove the point sufficiently clear to my own view. 1st. It is contrary to the purity of God's holy law—that law which contendeth to the most sineth [sic] thoughts. "He that looketh on a Woman to lust after her—he hath committed adultery with her already in his heart." It matters not the object before one's eyes—the thoughts may be on an object and then the guilt of ——— be committed. I fear I am virtually guilty of this sin. 2nd. No justifiable object is answered by this gratification. I am convinced that health does not require it: it is then a mere gratification of the flesh: and being such it is sin. "He that liveth to the flesh shall of the flesh reap corruption." 3rd. It is a duty or is it not. If it is not a duty then it is a sin for doing that which is not a duty is sin . . . . 4th It always unfits me for secret prayer & disturbs the peace of conscience. This is also a proof that it is sin: and that a very great sin—a sin that is more grievously aggravated by the light which I have had—the warnings of conscience & by the solemn resolutions which I have made against it in more than one instance. I have been looking over my diary to night [sic] and in the space of about six months I find about twenty repetitions of this sin. I look up to the date January 1814. The cases are many after this date. Here I am convicted of my guilt—Lord. I am vile what shall I answer? I prostrate myself before *Thee* O God humbly pray for the unmerited pardon through Jesus Christ. And now O Lord in thy strength *I do freely resolve never more wilfully* [sic] *to indulge this carnal desire while in an unmarried state & not unlawfully in that state should I ever be brought into it.*[89]

With this journal entry, Noyes began his final religious melancholy. During the remaining three weeks of his life, he could not eat, sleep, pray, or attend to his usual routine. God had removed his countenance and Noyes labored "under a cold, burning distress," bereft of all evidence of vital piety, possessed by a "heart of stone."[90] The reassurances and prayers of Cornelius and Safford did not assuage this torment, and at afternoon prayers on April 15, he accepted the dreadful verdict of his soul's state.

Mr Farber was there. He discussed about *hypocrites* & deceived persons— and apostates. The discourse was very solemn & exactly applicable to my case. Where the question was asked "Lord is it I." My conscience seemed to answer *"it is I."* The effect of the whole was to swell my heart with burning fear: but not to break it. I was excited some melanicolly [sic]: but little otherwise . . . .

So diary a conclusion from my present state. I must draw the conclusion that I am not a christian. Oh distressing thought for one who has a heart.[91]

The young man's suicide more profoundly shocked and threatened his friends and family than a "routine" death from natural causes. Epidemics of cholera, typhus, tuberculosis, and other infectious diseases cut down many young people. This mortality was all too common in nineteenth-century America and was interpreted as the natural order of the world and the chastening providence of God. Suicide attended with religious depression, however, challenged the fundamental ideals of evangelicals. Suicide raised the question about the possible relationship between religious experience and mental alienation, about the consequences of the relentless inner torment of the *ordo salutis*, about the responsibility of friends and the dangers the survivors faced in confronting their own godly sorrow that led them to thoughts of self-annihilation.

John Noyes, Benjamin Silliman, and Elias Cornelius each authored a memorial to Benjamin Noyes, in part, to commemorate his life and assist the family in their grieving. These tributes also addressed the disturbing questions raised by the suicide, attributing this act to a physically determined melancholy and affirming Noyes's piety and conversion. Experimental religion, in these accounts, promoted happiness and health and had no hand in the unfortunate somatic melancholy and insanity of Benjamin Noyes.

However, if we are to believe Noyes's own words, experimental religion had everything to do with this crisis. He made the *ordo salutis* the obsessive center of his existence and his recurrent spiritual crises represented Protestant psychomachy that mandated daily devotional piety—secret prayer that afforded direct communion with a personal God, and self-examination that methodically investigated the heart of experience and outward conduct for evidence of either sin or grace. Should the secret exercises of the closet reveal a cold-hearted distance from this personal God or convincing evidence of sin or the absence of a devotedness to God's service, the true believer lapsed into a spiritual crisis, sometimes a prolonged religious melancholy. This process of piety that all evangelicals embraced ineluctably produced a dilemma or contradiction because the structure of the *ordo salutis* prevented spiritual perfectionism—any final conquest over sin. Thus, evangelicals expected to find renewed evidence of sin, backsliding, and spiritual coldness. Periodically, they suffered the "dark nights of the soul." Noyes's life from his first spiritual awakening at age fifteen until his death at nineteen followed this pattern and process.

He wrote, in his journal and covenant papers, admonitions against the inevitable dark nights, scripting scenes of earthly and eternal punishment should his hand ever fall from the plough. John Noyes repeatedly wrote dire warnings to his son about these matters. Yet, both father and son understood that seasons of refreshment and warmth followed cold, despairing times. Indeed, this process of alternation was a necessary part of the pilgrim's lifelong journey and manifested maturing grace. If the son overcame previous seasons of doubting, why did he not anticipate a return of grace and hope this last time?

The evidence from the closet, the exacting logic that demonstrated repeated sexual sins recounted over several years, convinced him he had erred in ever believing himself to be a child of God. He branded himself a hypocrite, self-deluded in his erroneous profession that God had redeemed him and renewed his heart. Now the season of doubt would never pass; he had no grounds to hope as he piled the sin of hypocrisy upon the growing list of his enmity towards God. The label and status of hypocrite sealed his fate. He could never again trust his judgment and experience about the evidence of grace in his heart after discovering that he had deluded himself for the past four years. As a hypocrite, he gained absolute assurance of his eternal damnation while paradoxically relinquishing the experiential basis for acquiring an inward assurance of saving grace.

Awakenings called upon even baptized, upright, churched Christians to undergo a season of renewal and reaffirmation of the covenant of grace, to retrace the steps of the *ordo salutis*. During these times no one, the religiously indifferent or the fervent Christian, escaped the penetrating question: "Are you in Christ?"

> People who have been baptized; who bear the name of Christians; who pray to and adore Jesus Christ; who call themselves his children, his people; who partake of his sacraments; people who, for thirty or forty years call themselves, nay perhaps flatter themselves with the assurance of being true believers, and dare hope for heaven in the presumption of their faith. To ask such people whether they are in Christ, will surely offend them. But are you new creatures.[92]

For those like Noyes, who concluded that they had vainly flattered themselves with the conviction of being in Christ, the evangelical tracts and periodicals severely condemned them as hypocrites, a tool of the Devil in a saint's masquerade. "A hypocrite is a saint that goes by clock work; a machine made by the Devil's geometry, which he winds and picks to go as he pleases."[93]

Published accounts of revivals triumphantly proclaimed the discovery of hypocrites among those formerly considered pious and churched as part of the glorious work of the awakening.

> No persons were in deeper distress of soul than these; and their anxiety continued long. The hopes of many were found tottering, and of some actually abandoned. Oh, it is a tremendous time when a church member finds himself a false professor of religion. Sinners in Zion are afraid; fearfulness hath surprised the hypocrites. Who among us shall dwell with the devouring fire? Who among us shall dwell with everlasting burnings?[94]

These questions Noyes could not answer.

Finally, once Noyes had accepted his status as a hypocrite, he foundered on yet another paradox of evangelical selfhood. As an omnicausal self, he had the unrestricted moral agency to choose God and obedience to God's will or worldliness and indifference to divine things. He and he alone shouldered the responsibility for choosing hypocrisy and damnation. However, the evangelical self also needed to vanquish pride, smother the self, and surrender in ecstatic union with God. Noyes found that he could not simultaneously destroy the self and act with the moral agency as an omnicausal self. He was ever at war with himself over these two conflicting ideas of self, incapable of finding the ecstatic rapture of surrender in God, or the certitude of choosing God and rejecting the world.

His life foundered on the antipathies of evangelical character and experience, finally resting in the tormented certitude of his deceit and state of damnation. Ironically, family and friends encouraged his heroic struggle for self-knowledge, themselves assured of the healing outcome, of his unflagging piety. When Noyes reached his exacting conclusions and finally knew his authentic self as one marked, paradoxically, by deceit and hypocrisy, he remained beyond the reach of pastoral care and comfort. He chose suicide as the last volition of the omnicausal self who could no longer tolerate the burden of his existence, and who had lost the way of surrender and return into the gracious mercy of a now-distant God.

5

Sinners Who Would Fast unto Death

During the half-century preceding the Civil War, the era of grand revivals known as the Second Great Awakening coincided with the building of the modern asylum for the mentally ill. The published asylum reports and official patient census, and the unpublished patient casebooks reveal that "religious excitement" was considered an important "supposed cause" of insanity. A review of 9,433 admissions to four Eastern asylums in 1860 uncovered that 740 patients, or 7.8 percent, were diagnosed as suffering from "religious insanity." A survey of seventeen asylums operating in 1860 found that 6.1 percent of the patients manifested religious insanity.[1] Focusing upon one asylum, the Hartford Retreat in Connecticut, for its first twenty years of operation from 1824–1843, we find that 22 percent of all patients admitted, or 293 out of 1,324, were diagnosed as belonging to the category of religious insanity.[2] These patients included insane missionaries and ministers, Millerites, and believers who succumbed to mental alienation during Methodist revivals, the New Measure revivalism of Charles Grandison Finney, and others.

Whatever the percentages, asylum physicians of the early nineteenth century made the connection between revivalistic religion, religious excitement, and the perceived religious insanity of patients admitted for treatment. The belief that participation in religious revivals subjected persons to overwhelming stresses that undermined bodily health and caused insanity emerged as a widely held, official psychiatric theory.[3]

As Michel Foucault argues in his "archaeology of knowledge," the asylum movement and the elaboration of a clinical-medical discourse created a new explanatory model of religious melancholy that largely supplanted practical divinity and pastoral care for sick souls.[4] The asylum, conceived in the spirit of benevolent societal reform, also created new institutions of social control legitimated by the expertise of physicians who believed that they could cure religious melancholy using medical and moral therapies.

The asylum and the emerging secular psychiatry medicalized the perception and treatment of religious melancholy. The religious ideas, motivations, meanings, and "contents" of a patient's spiritual crisis were discounted as epiphenomenal to the underlying somatic disease process of melancholy, mania, or insanity. Physicians concerned themselves with the patient's religious experiences only to identify symptoms of irrational thought and conduct. They considered the *ordo salutis* of evangelical Pietism as a residual category of rationality, antithetical to making a Christian life through moderate, rational self-control. Clinical perception of the new alienists prevented them from "seeing" the significance of their patients' religious experience. Medical perception reduced the varieties and nuances of religious melancholia to a unitary disorder of humoral imbalance that deranged rational discourse. Religious melancholy, in all its variety and complexity, would remain sequestered behind asylum walls.

The varieties of religious melancholy in the nineteenth century were recorded by scribners in the medical diaries and patient casebooks of the new mental hospitals. For the first time, the asylum concentrated in a medical institution large numbers of the religious insane, the objects of correction, therapy, benevolence, and study. Religious melancholy was viewed increasingly as a somatic and psychiatric disease, not a spiritual illness of the sick soul immobilized in the *ordo salutis*. The disconsolate souls trapped in the slough of despond, convinced that God had forsaken them, appeared irrational and unreasonable. The many medical and moral causes of unreason illustrated the underlying disease process and affirmed the importance of early and sustained medical intervention. Religious melancholiacs were sent away, removed from civil society, sequestered in the cause of reason, rationality, and the regimen of medical therapeutics.

In this chapter, we begin with a discussion of the controversies associated with "religion and insanity," expressed in the anguished attempts of the Beecher family to come to terms with the suicide of George Beecher, and the heated debates waged by New Lights, Universalists, Unitarians, and others over the question of whether evangelical religion was a cause of mental alienation.

We will present one variety of melancholiac sequestered in the asylum—the individual suffering from evangelical anorexia nervosa. This culture-bound syndrome differed from the medieval Catholic *anorexia mirabilis* and from the secular medical syndrome, anorexia nervosa, that was identified in Europe and American in the 1870s. The asylum "captured" and concentrated those suffering from evangelical anorexia nervosa, a culture-bound syndrome midway between medieval austerities and modern anorexia. We will consider a sample from the Hartford Retreat of twenty-one patients diagnosed as religious melancholiacs. They participated in Finneyite revivals in western New York or New Measure revivalism in New England in the early 1830s. They each sought suicide through starvation, convinced that they had committed the unpardonable sin.

The nineteenth-century asylum treatment of religious melancholy foreshadowed the extensive medicalization and secularization of it that would occur in full measure in the twentieth century. Healing cults, such as those using Graham's dietary reform, hydrotherapy, Spiritualism and many others, offered alternatives to both evangelical religion and institutional psychiatry. Many Evangelicals, in the throes of religious melancholy, made spiritual migrations away from Pietism and toward the salvation promises of healing cults. In a final section, we present the strange case of how Oberlin perfectionism of New School Presbyterianism briefly allied with the promises of Grahamism to produce "starving perfectionists." We shall encounter the evangelical anorexia of Oberlin College students who adopted Sylvester Graham's therapeutic cult in search of somatic and spiritual perfection.

This discussion of several varieties of melancholy is not exhaustive, but is representative of how healing movements, conflicting explanatory models, and clinical discourse has shaped our understanding of melancholia. From the nineteenth century to the present, the mental hospital, psychiatry, and healing cults would compete with Protestant practical theology and the cure of souls for control over the domain of those forsaken by God.

Religion and Insanity

The evidence connecting religion to insanity was ubiquitous: patients seeking cure in the *materia medica* of orthodox medicine and the wild diversity of therapeutic movements that arose in the antebellum period, afflicted souls seeking the consolation of pastoral care from their local ministers, asylum admissions, accounts of the religious melancholy of notable evangelicals, and private diary records of the religious melancholy of ordinary people. Anyone living in early nineteenth-century New England could not fail to encounter common incidents of melancholy and debilitating religious crises among their acquaintances. Controversies that arose over the perceived causes, interpretations, and consequences of mental alienation and religion pitted the antirevivalist Unitarians and Universalists against evangelical denominations and secular psychiatry against the mainstream religion of the Great Awakening.

Persons brought home from revival meetings in states of despair or mental derangement were frequently referred by private-practice physicians to asylums. The casebooks and correspondence books of the Hartford Retreat contain referral letters from private physicians. The physicians' letters provide medical and treatment records and accounts of the onset of insanity. An example is a March 7, 1826, letter from Dr. Arba Blair of Rome, New York, to Dr. Eli Todd, superintendent of the Retreat. It provides background for the admission of Miss F.

> Her attack this winter was after much exposure in a Religious awakening here. She was thought to be a hopeful subject of conversion and expressed great joy on the occasion. The first time I saw her was some 3 or 4 weeks after when I found her in a state of derangement, tho in a remarkable joy and animated mood. Religion was her principle [*sic*] theme.[5]

Family and friends petitioned for the treatment of their loved ones, recounting the familiar theme of religious excitement and the onset of insanity. Samuel Stevens of Hardwick, Vermont, inquiring about how best to treat his son, sent this account of religious insanity to Dr. Todd on March 8, 1830: "About the middle of Nov. as near as we could learn from his relation one evening previous to his becoming distracted, he had been under a powerful religious excitement and a great change had taken place in his views and feelings. Appeared to have an overwhelming sense of his depravity and most exalted views of the excellency of the character of God."[6]

Members of prominent religious families who themselves championed the causes of experiential religion and the revival succumbed to religious melancholy. Lyman Beecher, whose work on moral reform and religious education became a model for the national revival, suffered periodic episodes of religious melancholy that he termed the "hypo" or hypochondria. Beginning with a crisis of conversion during his studies at Yale College under the direction of Reverend Timothy Dwight in 1797, he was visited with times of hypo throughout his early career. Writing to his fiancée, Roxana Foote, on April 16, 1798, Beecher discloses "this state of depression."

> It was the evil of a sinful, stupid heart that oppresses me—a stupidity which I could not shake off, a sinfulness that sunk me to the confines of despair. A feeling of conviction that I had never in the course of so many years been the subject of one exercise of true love to my Creator, stripped every action of my life of its seeming virtue. What, then, could I expect from any exertions, any pleadings of my own? . . . For a number of days I gave up exertion . . .[7]

Lyman Beecher imposed the most exacting standards of evangelical piety and Christian activism upon himself and his children, decreeing that they must embrace the arduous vocation of special service. "Caught in the harsh struggle for the ecstatic selflessness and the supreme usefulness that marked the elect in Beecher's theology, they worked assiduously for causes beyond themselves, won fame and suffered."[8] In addition to the insanity and suicide of his son James Beecher, the neurasthenia of his daughter Harriet Beecher, and the protracted religious melancholy of Lyman Beecher's second wife, Harriet Porter, his son George committed suicide in an episode of religious melancholy at the age of thirty-four in 1843.

Catherine Beecher took it upon herself to publish *The Biographical Remains of Reverend George Beecher,* selections from the reverend's journals, letters, and sermons. These samples presented evidence before ever-widening publics of her brother's lifelong battle with religious melancholy and recent enthusiasm regarding perfectionism. She acquainted readers with the official coroner's report of accidental death but included discrediting private evidence of mental alienation suggesting suicide. Barbara Cross concludes that "George could not endure religious apathy and died by an explosion of a gun barrel he had placed in his mouth; at the end it seemed to him as if Satan controlled him, and he lived in dread of himself and his actions."[9]

Catherine Beecher concealed her growing dissatisfaction with evangelical religion and the mix of contradictory motives that prompted her to publish many of the unsettling details of a family tragedy by invoking the genre of the spiritual biography. The hortatory tale of her brother must be retold, she tells the reader in her introduction, "to aid those, who, while compassed with infirmities, are still aiming at high attainments in Christian character."[10] Yet,

George Beecher's life story unfolds as a cautionary tale of the deleterious effects of religious motives upon the infirmities of temperament. She offers an oblique criticism of evangelical piety in an earlier work, *Letters in the Difficulties of Religion*, published in 1836. Here she notes the unbalancing propensity of evangelicals, like her brother, to consider the "excitement of the feelings" as the chief test of Christian character. However, she also states that such emphasis upon feelings promotes depression and neglect of domestic duties. In this indirect indictment of evangelical methods she says, ". . . strong and lively affections, and regular attention to the means of awakening them, is deemed the *chief* thing; so much so, that in many it receives the absorbing attention, and while a certain state of feeling is sustained, the evidence of piety is deemed satisfactory, and as these feelings diminish, Christian hopes are diminished."[11]

George Beecher was born in 1809 and spent his youth in Litchfield, Connecticut, under the care of his father and stepmother, Harriet Porter Beecher, who was particularly determined to assist her husband in rearing sons destined for the ministry and renowned for their exemplary piety. At age fourteen George Beecher prepared for college at the Hartford Grammar School. Two years later he matriculated at Yale, and experienced a saving change. However, his college years were punctuated by bouts of religious melancholy, culminating in his junior year, when he suffered a "nervous dread of all feeling and action for months."[12] Beecher never completed his divinity year, instead chosing to follow his family in their relocation westward to Cincinnati. Here he received ordination and the call to serve a congregation in Batavia, New York. He adopted a regimen of exercise, diet, and daily cold-water bathing known as "the water cure," or hydrotherapy. Writing in his journal in 1838, he notes: "With regular exercise, I am able now to study, or write, or read nine or ten hours each day, a thing I have not been able to do for years. I have lately also been adopting the cold water system, relinquishing tea and coffee, and I find the effect very beneficial to my health."[13]

Beecher married Sarah Buckingham in 1838; he enrolled in Lane Seminary, but left before completing his studies in order to accept the ministry of the Brick Church of Rochester, New York. Here he worked indefatigably in promoting revivals, attending to the pastoral needs of the congregation, conducting prayer and evening meetings, and throwing himself headlong into the continual round of public and private duties. Despite his resolution to overcome his nervous irritability and impetuosity of feeling by embracing a methodical course of "self-government and watchfulness and prayer," Beecher again suffered a season of religious despondency in 1840. Reminiscent of Catherine Beecher's indictment of experiential religion, he reflects upon the causes of his despair.

> I have so long accustomed to consider religion as consisting chiefly, in right state of *feeling*, rather than in a *calm and steady purpose of obedience*, that it is difficult to shake it off, and when I am not in a state of religious enjoyment, from bodily weakness, and feel the fear of guilt. Satan takes

advantage of it to goad me on to act beyond my strength, and then a reaction takes place.

I am in danger of being thus driven on until my nervous system is shattered, and then to feel a nervous dread and abhorrence of the course which injured me. I have been thus broken down two or three times in my past life, and suffered a nervous dread of all feeling and action for months.[14]

Three years later Beecher would take his life, prompting Catherine Beecher to expose the truth under the cover of writing a spiritual biography. Although it was a public disclosure of the tragedy of a notable evangelical family, this book was intended by Catherine Beecher to show the dangers inherent in "the religion of feeling," and that the untimely death of her brother might "shed light on the path of the common character and experience, and afford aid to all who are aiming to walk in the strait and narrow way."[15]

Not only public figures and religionists succumbed to religious melancholy—the faithful who led lives unknown beyond their families and local communities also were subject to it. Time and again the journals and private diaries of New Englanders noted in passing neighbors, friends, and congregants who lapsed into religious melancholy or mental alienation associated with religion. Ministers conducting their pastoral duties were routinely called to visit sick souls. Lyman Beecher developed a "clinical theology" of consolation and assurance and Reverend George Beecher reflected that his own propensity for melancholy made him especially sensitive and effective in treating the many congregants who suffered protracted seasons of spiritual desolation. Reverend James L. Wright of Burlington, Connecticut, himself a victim of two decades of debilitating religious melancholy, records in a journal entry a visit from one of his parishioners in the course of a revival of two months duration. He writes on March 20, 1851 that "Miss Martha Upram called me today. She had the impression that she had committed the unpardonable sin. But she said she was dreadfully nervous. Her health is very poor. She is truly an afflicted woman."[16]

Other New Englanders, such as Catherine Sedgwick, did not demur or sublimate their criticisms of experiential religion, feeling obliged to defect from the evangelical cause and launch frontal assaults upon their upbringing and tradition. Sedgwick published *A New England Tale* in 1822, which within the space of a year sold out the first two editions and became a widely read and controversial indictment of orthodox religion. Sedgwick's novel unfolds as an excoriating revelation of the venality, hypocrisy, and unbrotherliness of professed Christians in a fictitious New England village. Interjecting her opinions throughout the narrative, Sedgwick passes judgment on the piety of evangelical New Englanders: "We fear that in those times of excitement, during which many pass from indifference to holiness, and many are converted from sin to righteousness, there are also many who, . . . delude themselves and others with vain forms of words, and professions of faith."[17]

Sedgwick rejected the orthodox Calvinistic heritage of her family and embraced heterodox Unitarianism. In "Recollections of Childhood" she recounts the "cruel doctrines of Geneva" that afflicted her sister Eliza: "She was so true, so practical, that she could not evade its realities; she believed its monstrous doctrines, and they made her gloomy . . . ."[18]

Representatives of the Universalist church engaged in a prolonged public controversy during the 1820s and 1830s, condemning the national revival and the new techniques of mass conversion as contributing in part to the growing incidence of madness in the new republic.

The anti-revivalist Universalist denomination rejected any remnant of the Calvinist doctrine of predestination or the central concern for the assurance of election and the dread of eternal damnation. Universalist newspapers and periodicals repeatedly published accounts of the relationship between religious excitement and insanity. Writing in the *Universalist Magazine* in 1827, Otis Skinner relates an account of the death of three children, as follows:

> Mr. and Mrs. Stone possessed amiable dispositions, sustained good characters, and had lived together in the utmost harmony. During a late revival of religion, Mrs. S. was awakened, and supposed she had experienced a change of heart. Soon after, however, she settled down in a state of gloom and melancholy, and declared that she had committed the unpardonable sin.
>
> Under this impression, and believing that if taken off at their present tender age, the children would be happy; and believing also, that, having committed the unpardonable sin, no injury would follow to herself, while her husband was gone to a meeting on Sunday, the 14th of May, she drowned the little innocents in a spring about five feet deep.[19]

Universalist authors published continued attacks on revivals. Thomas Whittemore excoriated the pernicious effects of the Hartford revival of 1831, Otis Skinner produced long lists of the religious insane in his *Letters on Modern Revivals* (1842), and Sebastian and Russell Streeter penned vitriolic polemics against the revivals in Shirley, Massachusetts, in 1832 and Woodstock, Vermont, in 1835 as producing "these feverish excitements, these violent assaults upon the nerves and passions of the multitude (resulting in) the utter prostration of reason."[20]

Evangelicals felt a special affinity to the unorthodox forms of medical sectarianism prevalent in antebellum society. Healing sects such as Thomsonianism, Grahamism, and the group using hydrotherapy, although they explained disease and health through distinct monocausal theories, did emphasize therapeutic regimens of special diet, exercise, and self-care that encouraged individual self-reliance consistent with the religious piety of an awakening. The pathophysiologies and therapeutics of these unconventional medical sects resonated with the central ideas of the Second Great Awakening and appealed to religionists in search of a cure. The appeal to ethical moralism that advocated methodical self-control and moderation in diet, social intercourse, recreation, and religious and vocational pursuits; the sublime optimism that the world and all mankind could embrace Gospel truths, conform to both divine will and the natural laws of health and thereby eradicate sin and achieve human perfectability; these affinities made the search for cure a logical extension of the quest for *certitudo salutis*. The instrumental activism of religionists laboring to build God's kingdom in America was congruent with the instrumental activism of self-reliance in the maintenance or recovery of health. Medical sectarians provided

> . . . the physiological counterpart to the period's theological perfection-ism. Paralleling the revivalist preachers, they told their audiences that worldly happiness is intended by both divine and natural law. It followed that all we had to do to avail ourselves of God's progressive plan was to assume willful responsibility for our own physiological salvation. The medi-cal sectarians insisted that disease is by no means a deserved reprimand from a wrathful God, but was instead a natural phenomenon and thus subject to laws that human reason could discover and systematically apply.[21]

Not infrequently, evangelicals such as George Beecher, Harriet Beecher, or James Wright, who suffered bouts of religious melancholy that were inter-preted as the result of somatic imbalance and a predisposing nervous irrita-bility, initiated self-help and sought cure through hydrotherapy or Grahamism. Hydrotherapy, in particular, appealed to women who suffered "maternal depletion" associated with childbearing and nervous disorders and invalid-ism tied to the quiet rebellion against the heightened social demands of the cult of domesticity. Water-cure establishments also treated women who found themselves in religious despair. The water cure was promised to those suffer-ing from a variety of physical and nervous disorders as an alternative notion of the cause of their maladies, and a spiritually uplifting therapeutic regimen. Unlike the allopathic medical explanatory model, with its discrediting con-cepts of disease, medical sects such as hydrotherapy promised well-being through purification, self-improvement, and perfectionism.[22]

Allied with religious liberalization, medical sectarian groups, and the reform impulse of emerging feminism, Spiritualism sought to cure those suf-fering from religious anxiety and melancholy by providing direct, empirical demonstrations of the immortality of the soul. Individuals could communi-cate with the spirits of deceased friends and achieve immediate access to divine truth. Women who attended seances sought escape from the vexatious anxi-ety brought on by the belief that their departed children or relatives had died unconverted and without hope of salvation. Andrew Jackson Davis's harmonial philosophy reassured the grieving that the benevolent nature of God would not permit the damnation of unbaptized infants. Writing an editorial in his newspaper, the *Herald of Progress*, Davis maintains, "We have looked in Protestant journals in vain to discover a recommendation for penal enactments, to restrain the teachings so obviously tending to insanity."[23]

Ann Braude's study of the Spiritualist movement, *Radical Spirits*, presents numerous case histories of women who fled to Spiritualism to escape the evan-gelical religion of their youth and assuage their fears regarding evangelical doctrines of grace and election.[24] For example, Semanta Mettler described her childhood as beset by desolation at age eleven when a Congregationalist Sun-day school teacher in 1839 branded her unregenerate and thus beyond hope.

She converted the next year during a protracted meeting, but found no lasting spiritual comfort until her reconversion as a Universalist in 1842 and discovery of her clairvoyancy in 1848.[25]

Probably the most infamous example of the controversial charges of religion and insanity involved the involuntary incarceration of Mrs. Elizabeth Parsons Ware Packard in an Illinois asylum during the years preceding the Civil War. Elizabeth's husband, Theophilus, was a conservative, evangelical Presbyterian minister who held to the eighteenth-century notions of predestination and hyper-Calvinism and who himself suffered bouts of intermittent religious melancholy. When his wife publicly disavowed this orthodoxy in her Sunday school class and found comfort among Spiritualists and Universalists in a trip to western New York, Packard and two private physicians declared her to be "insane" and a "religious monomaniac," and they committed her, against her will, for three years.[26] Even after his wife's release from the asylum, Packard imprisoned her in her bedroom, nailing shut the windows to prevent escape. Ultimately, with the assistance of friends, she succeeded in winning her freedom from this domestic warfare in a public trial against her husband in 1864. Later, as an independent woman, Elizabeth Packard supported herself as an author, and through lobbying, publication, and crusading, helped reform the commitment laws in the United States.

The controversy of religion and insanity, of charge and countercharge brought by physicians against New Measure revivalists and by Universalists and Spiritualists against Calvinists proved ubiquitous in the early nineteenth century. Religious melancholy, when treated in the emerging asylum, confirmed in public opinion and asylum statistics the necessary connection between evangelical excitation and mental alienation. From the nineteenth century to the present, religious melancholiacs would flee from the spiritual discomforts of evangelical religion into the promised salvation of healing cults, moderate Protestant identity, and medical regimens. In the following section, we introduce a variant of religious melancholy—evangelical anorexia nervosa in antebellum America.

Sinners Who Would Fast unto Death

> Food she refused, and raiment; impotence
> Availed for either; neither change of place,
> Nor time, nor skill nor remedy could give her
> Senses to sleep—the power seem'd gone forever.

John Foster Reeve quoted these lines from Lord Byron in poetic lament at his inability to cure such sorrowful patients who renounced this world and embraced suicide by starvation. Reeve refers to a psychiatric patient, a married woman, under his care in a British asylum in the middle of the nineteenth century, who was thirty-eight and the mother of several children. When she was brought to the asylum, her front teeth were found to be broken as the result of failed violent attempts to feed her forcibly. She steadfastly refused to eat, "moaned incessantly, declaring she was the greatest sinner that had ever lived . . . ."[27]

The psychiatric literature in Great Britain and America noted these cases of pathological food refusal, primarily as an issue of patient management. Articles on food refusal by the insane discussed techniques and introduced patented new devices designed to assist caregivers in the coercive administration of food. Although understood as a technical challenge regarding how best to administer sufficient calories to sustain a patient determined to fast until death, asylum superintendents such as Luther Bell of McLeans Hospital in Massachusetts did note in passing the typical delusions of patients. Bell's patients in 1840 New England refused food under the conviction that God commanded them directly not to eat, it was sinful and morally wrong to eat food, and their digestive systems were disordered and they could not eat.[28] Bell's analysis applied also to religious melancholiacs treated at the Hartford Retreat.

The medicalization of fasting in the nineteenth-century asylums effectively ignored the religious meanings and motivations of evangelical anorectics. George Burrows's definitive 1828 work on moral and medical management of insanity, *Commentaries on the Causes, Forms, Symptoms, and Treatment, Moral and Medical of Insanity,* found that attempted fasting could "proceed from some fixed determination to suicide, or from some religious or fanatical resolve to emulate martyrdom by fasting . . . ."[29] Burrows, Bell, Reeve, and others described their patients as laboring under obsessive concern with sin, divine commandment, and religious themes. However, the medical categories of melancholy and mania employed to diagnose and understand these symptoms of food refusal considered this fasting one expression of somatic disease that unbalanced the bodily humors and, correspondingly, the mind. The specific content of a patient's delusions—religious obsession with sin or tortured obsession with bodily well-being—was epiphenomenal to the underlying cause and nature of the patient's disorder. Psychiatric explanatory models did not encourage nineteenth-century alienists to explore the linkage between religiously grounded personality, life-order, and suicide by starvation. This explains how asylum staff treated increasing numbers of such patients without recognizing the emergence of a new psychiatric disorder, evangelical anorexia nervosa.

A modern definition of anorexia nervosa grounds this disorder in psychological and social conditions. Hilde Bruch defines it as "self-inflicted starvation in the absence of recognizable organic disease and in the midst of ample food."[30] However, the motivation to self-starvation and the meanings associated with these behaviors prove more important than the behavioral syndrome itself. Starvation is an attempt to extricate oneself from a puppet-like manipulation and authority of others, to take control of the self and devote one's life to higher cultural values and principles. Thus, various forms of anorexia nervosa must be understood as psychological and social manifestations of the wish to be free and to forge a life and personality consistent with external cultural standards of relevance.

Evangelical anorexia represents one of a number of culture-bound syndromes of food refusal and self-starvation informed by the requirements of religiously grounded personality and life-order. The anorexia mirabilis prevalent in the late thirteenth and fourteenth centuries among European religious women is an important case in point. Caroline Walker Bynum's *Holy Fast and Holy Feast* reconstructs the lived experiences of and meanings for medieval women by placing their religious quests in the historical and cultural context of social, economic, and ecclesiastical structures, and theological and devotional traditions.[31] New opportunities for women to pursue religious virtuosity as nuns in religious orders, Beguines, and tertiaries encouraged immersion into devotional traditions of penitential asceticism, self-inflicted suffering, and mystical union with God. The development of the cult of eucharistic devotion reanimated the sacrament of communion with magical and miraculous powers. Believers fasted and mortified their bodies and approached the rite in a heightened state of anxiety and spiritual expectation. Not infrequently, the faithful experienced visions, frenzies of excitement, and miracles of food multiplication. In the eucharistic encounter the penitent affirmed the excruciating bodily pain of the crucified Christ (*imitatio crucis*) and the unspeakable pleasure of union with God. Eating God through the transubstantiation of wine and bread would sustain the faithful.

The most extreme forms of anorexia mirabilis involved years of self-starvation unto death, as in the case of Catherine of Siena (d. 1300), who maintained that the eucharistic miracle sustained her; she survived on the eucharist alone. Saints and mystics like Catherine participated in the broader cultural patterns of eucharistic devotion, the imitation of Christ and fusion with the suffering physicality of the crucified Christ. Such women rejected the limited economic and political opportunities available to them, eschewed marriage or transformed their marriages, and effectively challenged sacerdotal authority. The extremes of asceticism—maceration of the body and self-starvation—were not solely pathological and self-destructive forms of transformation of the self. Bynum argues that these women forged religiously grounded personalities devoted to the ultimate values of redemptive suffering—*imitatio Christi*, disinterested love, and caritas.

In her interpretation of anorexia mirabilis, Bynum discounts the modern clinical explanation of pathological starvation and feminist notions of the internalization of misogyny to account for the extremes of piety. Rather, she has developed a contextualized, structural phenomenology of women's religious experience. She concludes her work with this summation:

> Women saw themselves not as flesh opposed to spirit, female opposed to male, nurture opposed to authority; they saw themselves as human beings—fully spirit and fully flesh. And they saw all humanity as created in God's image, as capable of *imitatio Christi* through body as well as soul. Thus they glorified in the pain, the exudings, the somatic distortions that made their bodies parallel to the consecrated wafer on the altar and the man on the cross.[32]

The asceticism and food refusal that such medieval women pursued with virtuosity had distinct consequences. The appropriation of severe discipline motivated by higher ethical purpose and spiritual perfection conferred opportunities for self-assertion, self-control, and autonomy for women in largely patrimonial households where status, honor, property, family title, and political authority were vested in men.[33] Women forged distinctly religious personalities that transcended the trivial and mundane lives that typified the laity. The ascetic and anorectic saw their quest as self-liberating rather than self-destructive.[34] Nevertheless, as Rudolph Bell argues, the anorectic quest of self-starvation became the central organizing principle of life. Paradoxically, women who embraced the ideal of spiritual perfection and self-liberated fasting frequently destroyed themselves. Fasting unto death is an ultimate consequence and penalty suffered by those who would feast on God and sustain themselves only on the miracle of the eucharist.

Evangelical anorexia and anorexia mirabilis have much in common. Both culture-bound syndromes validated redemptive suffering in the imitation of Christ. Both traditions required ascetic discipline, penitential fasting, and purification as a preparation for the mystical union with God. Protestants, however, rejected the magical and sacramental potential of the eucharist, the extremes of self-maceration of the body, and devalued miracles, frenzy, visions, and trances. Protestants demanded that all believers heroically strive for religious virtuosity previously not required of medieval Catholic laity. Both men and women were represented among evangelical anorectics. Despite these differences, much of the spirit of anorexia mirabilis found receptive ground in the excessive regimes of fasting among men and women in the Protestant Pietist tradition.

The modern psychological disorder of anorexia nervosa that was first diagnosed in the second half of the nineteenth century differs from evangelical anorexia and anorexia mirabilis by a devaluation and secularization of the religious motives and meanings of excessive fasting. Fasting no longer represented the legitimate exercise of piety informed by devotional theology. Rather, it became a symptom of mental disease and alienation. This medicalization of fasting occurred as early as the 1820s with the admission, in New England asylums, of the religious insane who fasted excessively (evangelical anorexia). Certainly, by the late nineteenth century, as William James notes, few young women fasted according to religious motives. Those who embraced the heroic quest of saintliness appeared aberrant to modern mentalities.[35] He writes, "the general optimism and healthy-mindedness of liberal Protestant circles to-day makes mortification for mortification's sake repugnant to us. . . . In consequence of all these motives you probably are disposed, unless some special utility can be shown in some individual's discipline, to treat the general tendency to asceticism as pathological."[36]

In place of religious transcendence and mystic themes, the anorectic fasted according to secular motives and values related to ideals of feminine beauty, the rationalization of the body, and the psychosocial issues of adolescent identity formation in the emotional hothouse and intimacy of the family. Anorexia nervosa constitutes a culture-bound syndrome peculiar to the contemporary West, medicalized and defined in *Diagnostic and Statistical Manual III*. This disorder befalls young women, usually ages sixteen to twenty-three, who have an inordinate fear of becoming obese, possess a distorted body image, and fast until they lose at least 25 percent of their original body weight. Anorectics see their bodies as "fat" even when they become emaciated. Additional symptoms include hyperactivity, amenorrhea, and self-induced vomiting and the use of laxatives associated with bulimia.

Anorexia nervosa involves adolescent girls' devotion to the secular ideals of personal perfection—the slender, youthful, athletic body emblematic of individual achievement—and to a consumer culture that emphasizes beauty and erotic allure. The anorectic quietly and covertly rebels against these all-consuming images and against the emotional economy of maternal influence and overinvolvement.[37]

Physicians in the early 1870s first identified this eating disorder. Ernest-Charles Lasegue of Paris proposed the term "hysterical anorexia" and Sir William Gull in London created the diagnostic label "anorexia nervosa" for the syndrome that afflicted the young women he treated. Social historians such as Edward Shorter, Joan Jacobs Brumberg, and Nancy Theriot have argued that changes in European and American middle-class families account for the emergence of this culture-bound syndrome peculiar to adolescent girls in this historical period. Shorter explains that the sentimental family in the late nineteenth century created intensive and intimate relationships between parent and child, particularly between mother and daughter. Thus, anorexia nervosa emerged as a new "neurosis of intimacy" as daughters attempted to forge their identities in the quest for autonomy and separation from authoritarian or overprotective parents. One tactic of adolescent rebellion involved excessive fasting. As Shorter argues, "the threat of one's deliberate self-destruction is credible only in a family climate where affection and endearment cement family members one to another . . . ."[38] Brumberg's work, *Fasting Girls,* traces the intertwined meanings of love, food, and the bourgeois family after the Civil War. The thin, tightly corseted body of the young woman, who abstained from eating meat and all forms of gluttony, symbolized the moral attributes of self-control, the rejection of sexuality and carnal lust, and Thorstein Veblen's ideal of elevated social status. Slender, fragile, and pale, women embodied the ideal of a leisure class in sharp contrast to robust and ruddy farming and laboring classes.[39] Mothers took it upon themselves to nurture and shape the character, personalities, and bodies of their maturing daughters, both as an expression of maternal love and to enhance these daughters' chances in the marriage market. Families made evening meals rituals of intimacy. Mothers prepared healthy and appetizing meals as gift offerings and expressions of love. Husbands and children needed to accept these gifts of food and love by eating their meals, willingly and with gratitude.

Many daughters felt themselves to be manipulated, puppet-like creatures caught in the nexus of the excesses of the sentimental family—suffocating maternal overinvolvement. They experienced unrelenting pressures as their mothers, in the name of love, directed their education, dress, reading, leisure activities, and appearance, all with one goal in mind: to produce an attractive, marriageable daughter. Brumberg notes that in the name of love, possessiveness came to characterize mother-daughter relations, and psychopathology developed.

> Where love between parents and children was the prevailing and avowed ethic, there was always the risk of excess. Where love became suffocating or manipulative, individuation and separation from the family could become extremely painful, if not impossible. Increased intimacy with children, a concomitant to the ethic of family love, could also lead to debilitating forms of psychological interdependence, for parents as well as for children.[40]

The adolescent daughter who intentionally refused to eat created agonizing scenes of parental distress at each meal. By fasting she could seek to prevent or reverse the onset on puberty, stop her menses, and retreat from the obsession with her nubility and marriage prospects. In this private, covert rebellion, the anorectic established control and separation through starvation. Nancy Theriot argues that these early anorectics could not accept the moral education and role models of their mothers, who came of age in the 1840s in the climate of "true womanhood." Anorexia nervosa represented a generational conflict. For the mother's generation, womanhood meant the idealization of suffering as a maternal virtue, motherhood as a debilitating exercise in self-denial and a life circumscribed by the limitations of the woman's sphere of domesticity. Many of the daughters born in the 1850s questioned whether their mothers' lives were appropriate models for their aspirations.

> The "true woman" that the young girl was supposed to become was required to wait passively to be chosen in marriage, to endure patiently the physical trials of pregnancy and birth, to go quietly wherever her husband chose to live, to submit lovingly to her husband's wishes. Even in dealing with her own children, the "true woman" was not to be willful; she was to see herself as the transmitter of culture and guardian of the young, always taking direction from husbands, clergymen, physicians, and counselors.[41]

The young girl who fasted excessively was motivated by the wish to be free from the constraints of the "golden cage" of the middle-class family. The anorectic cleaved to the highest secular ideals of asceticism and personal perfection.[42]

Evangelical anorexia nervosa preceded the secular anorexia nervosa syndrome. Evangelical anorexia involved a regime of starvation driven by religious meanings and motivations. Chief among these was the conviction of having committed the unpardonable sin and the peculiar belief that eating compounded the sinner's alienation from God's love. We turn next to a consideration of unpardonable sin.

Unpardonable Sin and Religious Melancholy

Let these words of Christ stand in all their strength,
and the assurance come in that those who sin in the manner

intended against the HOLY GHOST, HAVE NEVER FORGIVENESS;
neither in this world nor in that which is to come.[43]

This admonition in the *New York Evangelist* depicted one paradox of the
Second Great Awakening. The era of grand revivalism brought the masses
under religious influence, and the theology of "evangelical Arminianism" made
conversion as much an act of the will in choosing God as the wondrous work
of the Holy Spirit in converting individual sinners and whole communities.
The promise of salvation was extended universally to all who would repent
and seek forgiveness of sin in the sudden conversions that transformed sinful
scoffers into pious children of God in the space of a four-day meeting. Yet,
paradoxically, so many Christians, even those previously converted who had
considered themselves regenerate believers, left these revivals convinced that
they had committed the unpardonable sin. How does one account for the paradox of unpardonable sin in the midst of a liberalized Calvinism that proffered a more universal vision of salvation to the masses actively promoted by
revivalistic methods?

Religious writings speak directly to the question of unpardonable sin, most
notably the sermons of Nathanael Emmons, who preaches from 1 John 5:16,
"there is a sin unto death."[44] Emmons argues that the unforgivable sin constitutes a spoken blasphemy against the Holy Spirit made in public and
motivated by a "sensible enmity against the truth and spirit of Christianity."[45]
In an era of revivalism defined as the wondrous outpourings of the Holy Spirit
in America, all Christians needed to respond to the clarion call. Unpardonable
sin consisted "in openly ascribing the peculiar operations of the Holy Ghost
to the power and agency of Satan."[46] Those who charged themselves with
opposing evangelical religion because they failed to experience conversion or
reaffirmation of a previous conversion interpreted their spiritual crisis as caused
by the commission of unpardonable sin. After all, a benevolent God offered
the promise of salvation to all who would receive it. The age of revivals created the moral machinery, acting in concert with the Holy Spirit, to effect
mass conversions. Should individuals discover themselves unable to act upon
the promises of the Gospel and the effusions of the Spirit in revivals, should
they be mired in evangelical humiliation, unable to find the inward assurance
of the remission of sin, surely their problem could be accounted for by some
larger sin. As each person recounted in self-examination a partial catalog of
past sins, his or her piety invariably would reveal sins agonizingly close to
the unpardonable sin. Sinners resolved their quandary by concluding that their
failure to receive the assurances of God's love resulted from commission of
the sin unto death. Emmons writes:

> . . . let them beware of despising religion, of trifling with the name of God,
> and of profaning his day, his house, his word, and sacred ordinances. The
> transition is easy from these sins to the sin unto death. Those who have
> habituated themselves to despise and profane divine objects in general, are
> in peculiar danger of blaspheming the Holy Ghost in particular, whenever

they have an opportunity of seeing his peculiar and powerful operations upon the hearts of men.[47]

Emmons realized that unpardonable sin was a rare occurrence, even for souls in extremis. However, in times of revivals, when the workings of the Spirit produced wonders, many believers readily accused themselves of this sin. "Those of a more tender conscience and gloomy cast of mind are extremely prone to imagine that they have actually sinned beyond the reach of pardoning mercy."[48] What Emmons does not observe is that sermons and conversion narratives implicitly encouraged believers to understand and define their experience of sinfulness in these absolute terms. The hortatory literature depicted the self-accusations of unpardonable sin as but a stage in the successful progression of each saint towards conversion. Bunyan's spiritual biography proved the truth of this experimental religion as he languished under this extreme of scrupulosity. Nineteenth-century Protestants would conduct their own exercises in this experimental religion.

Published accounts of persons in conversion crises who suffered from unpardonable sin intersperse the religious intelligence in the first wave of revivals, from 1790 to 1805. Reverend Josiah Andrews included a conversion narrative of a member of his church in Killingworth, Connecticut. A person at a critical point in conversion wrote this journal account:

> The fear of having committed the unpardonable sin, now began to arise in my mind, and I could find no rest day nor night. When my weary limbs demanded sleep, the feat of awaking in a miserable eternity preventing me from closing my eyes, and nothing gave me ease. . . . After a while, a surprising tremor seized all my limbs, and death appeared to have taken hold of me.[49]

This unnamed penitent did find forgiveness, but only after descending into the ultimate despair over the commission of the unpardonable sin. Numerous published narratives suggest the typicality of this experience. These writings warn believers to avoid blasphemy against the Holy Ghost, but paradoxically suggest that only by descending into the depths of despair could seekers entertain hope of the inevitability of salvation in their lives.

A sermon titled "Quench Not the Spirit," published in *The Christian Spectator* in 1821, depicts the consequences of the unpardonable sin. The sinner would

> exist forever and forever destined to sorrow and anguish; deprived of happiness and hope; an outcast from the favor of God. . . . Such a being has no refuge in affection, no present help in time of troubles, in sickness nothing to support him upon his bed of languishing, in death no rod and staff to comfort, or faith to give the victory————in the day of Judgment, no surety————no precious Saviour, no deliverance from the pains of Hell.[50]

Indeed, the religious intelligence published in evangelical magazines, narratives of revivals by Humphrey, Sprague, Finney, and others, promoted the

experience of unpardonable sin as a marker along the journey toward salvation. Those who would seek to ascertain the authenticity of their evangelical
humiliation and repentance would prove their willingness to be damned by
self-accusations of having committed blasphemy against the Holy Spirit. The
Awakening conversion narratives of the 1740s and Edwards's account of the
conversions in Northampton recorded the desolation of unpardonable sin,
which found ready acceptance in the modal conversions of the Second Great
Awakening.

Hannah More's *Practical Piety* (1811) was a widely read pastoral guide,
an evangelical directive that answered the perplexing concerns of anxious
Christians. More defined the religion of the heart as an internal principle that
directed the person toward an inward devotedness to God. Although detractors criticized the zealous attempts at self-abnegation, dependency, and helplessness before God as "enthusiasm," More understood that believers considered their efforts paltry and insufficient. "He is severely abasing himself before
his Maker for not carrying far enough that principle which he is accused of
carrying too far."[51]

The internal principle of selfless submission to God was a foundation for
what More terms the cultivation of a devotional spirit: frequently and
habitually retiring in prayer, and making God the center to which hearts our
tending. Paradoxically, in a moment of abject surrender, in anguish over sin,
the "supplicant filled with a sense of his own dependence, feels assured that
God is nigh, so that every burden and doubt are taken off from his mind."[52]
Evangelical pastoral care would intentionally awaken sinners, exacerbate their
spiritual crisis, and direct them to persevere in these efforts at self-annihilation. More reassures her readers that the methods of the devotional spirit will
bring success.

> The feeling of our wants, the confession of our sins, the acknowledgement
> of our dependence, the renunciation of ourselves, the supplication for mercy,
> the application to the "foundation opened for sin," the cordial entreaty
> for the aid of the Spirit, the relinquishment of our own will . . . these are
> the subjects in which the supplicant should be engaged.[53]

The therapeutic power of the awakening of sin that brought solitary
individuals to God could also awaken entire communities. Finney would define
a revival as a collective awakening of the church where "Christians are always
brought under such convictions; they see their sins in such a light, that they
often find it impossible to maintain a hope of their acceptance with God.
. . . there are always, in a genuine revival, deep convictions of sin, and often
cases of abandoning all hope."[54] Finney would champion the cause of evangelical Arminianism in the revivals of western New York from 1826 to 1831,
exhorting the assembled masses that each individual possessed a perfect ability and obligation as a sinner to end his or her rebellion against God, comply
with the requirements of the Gospel, and choose to cooperate with the Holy
Spirit in the work of conversion.[55] Delay not one instant, Finney would cry
out, as each person stands infinitely guilty for not making himself a new heart.

How ironic that such emphasis upon human ability and the freedom to will for God engendered the agonized conviction of unpardonable sin. For Finney, each sinner stood as an omnicausal agent who would bear complete responsibility for his or her individual fate. Any resistance to God would prove fatal. He writes, "People are apt to resist and grieve away the Holy Spirit without remembering where and how they did it. They were walking with God up to a certain point; then they parted from him . . . ."[56] What terror to discover on the anxious bench of the revival, in the war of psychological attrition waged against the awakened sinner during the protracted meetings, that one had indeed so casually grieved away the Holy Spirit. In a September 8, 1829, letter to Mrs. Lydia Finney, the revivalist's wife, from a Mrs. E. M. Knight of Reading, Pennsylvania, this principle of religious terror was made manifest. The Finneys maintained a voluminous correspondence with evangelical supporters whom Finney had won over in revival campaigns. Mrs. Finney's correspondents wrote of their fervent devotionalism, their self-macerating exercises of evangelical humiliation, their constant search for opportunities to nurture their holiness or bring the unconverted to Christ. Knight adopted Finney's unrelenting logic of urgent personal appeals to sinners so that they would not lose the fleeting opportunity for grace. She writes about her exhortations with one unconverted young woman named Catherine. "Catherine has been awakened, Oh that I could say converted to God. Poor child, I fear she will sin away this day of grace if she continues stifling with the blessed Spirit."[57] These very accusations of having sinned away the day of grace would be made by the religious melancholiacs at the Hartford Retreat.

Heman Humphrey devoted several pastoral sections to guidance for the unpardonable sinner. His manual instructed each pastor to inquire of the sinner whether or not he or she had resisted and blasphemed the Holy Spirit and had maliciously ascribed these acts to satanic influences. If the sinner had not blasphemed, then the conviction of having committed an unpardonable sin was in error. These self-accusations were considered to be attestations to the depth and sincerity of the sinner's humiliation and repentance. From the foundation of such repentance, the sinner could build a Christian life. Humphrey exhorted, "You are in great danger. You cannot resist the Spirit another moment without adding sin to sin, and increasing the danger; and if you hold out against God to the last, you will certainly perish as if you had committed the sin against the Holy Ghost. All sin is alike unpardonable, after death."[58]

How could anguished penitents ascertain if they had indeed committed the unpardonable sin and stood beyond the pale of divine mercy? The author of an 1820 *Christian Spectator* essay counseled the sinner to repent and experience divine forgiveness: "There is, however, a method in which the despairing sinner can ascertain that he has not sinned unpardonably. Let him repent on his sins and believe on the Lord Jesus Christ, and as surely as the Bible is the word of God, so surely shall a penitent inherit everlasting life."[59]

Religious materials published typical conversion narratives of awakened sinners languishing under despondency of unpardonable sin who ultimately triumphed as regenerate children of God. Pastoral guidance brought the anticipated results for believers who set out upon this uncertain spiritual itinerary. The self-accusation of unpardonable sin proved but a temporary sojourn into religious melancholy that prepared and quickened the heart to receive the assurance of God's love. One such case, published in 1829 by *The Religious Intelligencer*, described the conversion of a Middlebury College student during a revival. Before his final victory, his despair knew no limits as one guilty of unpardonable sin, as a youth bent upon self-starvation.

> He gave up his hope and for several months was in great agony of mind. He wasted away, and became emaciated—that he looked as if he just recovered from a severe sickness—during the time his appearance and expression were indicative of the keenest despair. "Look at me," he would say, "behold a monument of God's wrath."[60]

The optimistic resolutions to these spiritual crises depicted in religious publications represented the anticipated, desired resolution to religious melancholy and the conviction of unpardonable sinfulness. At the beginning of this spiritual journey, religionists might have been sanguine about their prospects for assurance and grace. These published accounts of the Awakening, however, revealed an undesirable outcome in the evidence of failure—insanity and suicide. The records of the Congregational church of Enfield, Connecticut, published the following entry: "Dec. 2, 1811 Susan P. Holton, age 30. Her death was occasioned from a persuasion that it was a sin to eat, and therefore starved herself until death closed the scene."[61] A letter appearing in a religious periodical dated March 9, 1822, from Manlius, New York, described the fate of a young woman, wife of a Presbyterian clergyman. She left a local revival of religion in despair. For months she languished in religious melancholy.

> She became nervous and extremely distressed in her mind; complained of the most horrid temptations of the adversary, could not eat, nor sleep much; became almost indifferent to every earthly concern . . . She continued in this state of fixed despondency—refused to receive any consolation—said her day of grace was past—that she had committed the unpardonable sin, and there was no mercy for her.[62]

She committed suicide shortly thereafter.

In these public accounts and among the patients admitted to asylums for the insane, evangelical pastoral care failed, and the melancholiacs failed to progress in the itinerary toward salvation. How to account for these failures?

In 1842 Heman Humphrey wrote another popular work, *Thirty-Four Letters to a Son in the Ministry*, directed toward ministers and the larger public. In this collection of letters to an unnamed youth entering the ministry upon completion of theological training, Humphrey relates the nature of pastoral duties and care of the congregation and the cure of souls for laity suffering spiritual perplexities. Above all, ministers needed to devote themselves to the winning of souls and to building their churches through effective preaching that taught congregants doctrine and ethics and promoted experimental religion. He argued: "Every church needs the most searching experimental sermons, that a faithful pastor can preach, not at long intervals, but frequently; that hypocrites may find no hiding place in their delusions, and that sincere Christians may be led to pray with the Psalmist, 'Search me, O God, and know my heart . . . .'"[63]

Through preaching, backsliders grown cold in religion would discover their peril, hasten to renew their conversion, and enter into a crisis of reconversion. Ministers were directed to use experimental preaching as a strategy to engender reconversion crises among those already churched. Revivals, as community-wide awakenings, as refreshing showers of the Holy Spirit, brought masses, not solitary individuals, into these conversion crises. Humphrey extolled the authenticity and benefit of revivals and devoted four letters to these topics. He deflected criticism about New Measures—anxious benches, inquiry meetings, praying aloud by females with the names of the unconverted or apostate, and protracted meetings—arguing that the moderate use of these measures was indeed legitimate for human agencies in assisting the Holy Spirit in its millennial undertakings. Religious excitement, not as mere animal feeling, but as well-grounded fear, was both necessary and desirable among the awakened. Indeed, the pastor must not provide consolation or a too-quick relief of these excitements. Excitement was prescribed and therapeutic for the soul's journey to conversion or reconversion. Religious excitement augured the work of God's spirit in each penitent marked by "agonized conviction, when the fountains of the great deep depravity in the soul are, as it were, broken up, and the sinner sees himself justly exposed to the wrath and curse of God forever."[64]

Humphrey instructed ministers to interview awakened sinners and ascertain the true cause of their distress. If the person admits to sinning against the Holy Spirit by so long resisting God, the pastor should correct this error and redirect the penitent to the correct view of terror before the law. Above all, he should render no comfort. Humphrey writes that "I can truly say, that nothing rejoices me more in the midst of a revival, than to find sinners in great distress; and to be able, by presenting the naked truth to their minds, to increase that distress instead of alleviating it; and I never knew of any one driven to despair, under judicious treatment of this sort."[65]

Evangelical ministers felt duty-bound to win souls through aggressive and relentless preaching and exhortation. They measured their self-worth and the effectiveness of their vocation by soul counts—the numbers brought to the Lord. Evangelical pastoral care emphasized preaching designed to awaken sinners, religious excitement and the terror of sinners before the law, the withholding of comfort or consolation, and the war against the carnal, worldly self directed towards the annihilation of the self. Thus, evangelical Protestants, directed by their ministers, embraced the religious excitements and religious melancholy of conversion and reconversion crises—attempts at the annihilation of the self through evangelical humiliation, mortification of the body in fasting and austerity, and the anticipated ecstasy of selfless surrender

as children of God. Should the penitent languish in prolonged religious melancholy, the logic of pastoral care could only advise the candidate to repeat
the process, to try again. As candidates did indeed try again and again, the
logic of the cure of souls encouraged the obsessive repetition of rituals of
purification, neurotic rituals of self-maceration.

Sinners in religious melancholy, self-accused of having committed the
unpardonable sin, could not receive forgiveness by church sacrament and
pastoral absolution following confession. The obsessive personal rituals of
purification and self-maceration could not coerce God through magical means
to remove the stain of sin and regenerate their hearts. Sinners could not earn
this status of election through Arminian means of good works and sanctified
conduct. Sinners required that a completely foreign, transcendental entity, the
Holy Spirit, irradiate their hearts. Through a sudden, rapturous, and transformative moment, they would experience the indisputable inward evidence
of their election and adoption as children of God. For the untold masses, the
nearly one-third of the people in antebellum America who embraced experiential religion, the structure of evangelical pastoral care established the mileposts of each spiritual pilgrimage. Spiritual success or failure, in the final
moment, remained outside of human agency and dependent upon the will of
God. The religious melancholiacs presented in the next section, who came to
the Hartford Retreat, had failed in their efforts at reconversion while attending revivals and never recovered God's love.

Melancholia Attonita

> Dr. Todd do you know what a wretched being I am—how far I am gone—
> you knew me once and was [sic] my friend—can you see the possibility
> for one so abandoned to return to the way she ought to walk I cannot live
> so—I say with Cain my punishment is greater than I can bear—will you
> think what you would advise me anything, any punishment I would sub-
> mit to feel once more that I was not cast off forever . . . . will you pray to
> God to forgive me & to take me to his fold again.

These words were written by a twenty-six-year-old, upper-class woman, a
resident of Hartford, who gave this note to her attending physician, Dr. Eli
Todd, after her readmission as a patient to the Retreat in 1827.[66] She grieved
over the recent death of a friend and had attended a series of revival meetings in 1827. She lapsed into a religious melancholy and returned to the asylum for treatment. Todd encouraged patients to send him notes, poems, and
letters, as these expressions afforded patients the opportunity to speak to the
crises in their lives. He analyzed each communication for evidence of improvement and the return of reason.

Like so many other patients admitted to the retreat during Todd's eleven-
year tenure (1823–1833), her religious melancholy involved anguish over the
commission of unpardonable sin, food refusal, suicidal inclinations, and the
certainty that God had abandoned her. Todd considered these patients to be
representatives of a special variety of melancholy and he adopted the diag-

nostic category *melancholia attonita* to interpret their symptoms. He based his clinical perception upon a 1741 medical treatise of Johann Jacob Mueller. Citing scriptural examples, Mueller identified a form of religious melancholy that struck down or assaulted patients, in the blink of an eye, with the judgment and wrath of God. Mueller writes:

> Melancholia attonita is that species of melancholia by which one so afflicted is rendered first depressed, then for a long time mute, immobile, senseless, with limbs almost rigid, emaciated, with very few movements left to him, e.g. with the result that he swallows only immediately after food has been thrust into his mouth and blinks when fingers have been moved before his eyes, and sometimes sleeps.[67]

Mueller had collected early Protestant case histories of evangelical anorexia nervosa. He cites the 1630 case of a Protestant clergyman in Lichtenberg who experienced deep-seated melancholy at age thirty due to his inability to find forgiveness of youthful sins. These sins, inconsequential from the doctor's perspective, so mortified the patient with unrelieved guilt that he "persuaded himself that he was unable to return to the grace of God and thought himself unworthy of performing his Ecclesiastical duty."[68] The experience of *melancholia attonita* presented the sufferer as one awestruck with the terrible prospect of divine judgment, responding with complete passivity and extreme social withdrawal almost to the point of catalepsy. The clergyman just cited "awaking early in the morning used to lie immobile in his bed like someone thinking deeply; lifted from his bed by his wife's efforts, he was dressed by her. After being dressed he stood like a statue . . . ."[69]

Todd applied Mueller's diagnostic category to persons who labored under the delusion that they had committed the unpardonable sin and that eating compounded their plight, causing them to attempt suicide by starvation. They required forced feeding of food and medicine administered by a stomach pump to prevent starvation and inevitable death. During the first twenty years of the retreat's operation, the medical records reveal that twenty-one persons who came for treatment suffered from *melancholia attonita* that included the extreme fasting motivated by evangelical anorexia. Because the background history and supporting letters from family and friends have not survived for over 500 patients of the 1,324 treated in this period, one cannot ascertain the typicality of these 21 cases. Thirty-two additional cases of *melancholia attonita* manifested symptoms of religious guilt and obsession with unpardonable sin but chose active, violent means of suicide, not the passivity of food refusal. For our purposes, only those individuals who manifested the syndrome of melancholia motivated by religious guilt as unpardonable sinners and who attempted to fast until death fit the category of evangelical anorexia nervosa.

Seventeen women and four men comprise this sample of case histories. All were white, native-born Americans from New England and the growing cities of upstate New York. With the exception of one charity patient, they came from middle- and upper-class families. The women ranged in age from sixteen to forty-seven, with one under the age of twenty, seven in the twenty

to twenty-nine age range, six in the thirty to thirty-nine range, and three over
the age of forty. The average age was thirty. Clearly, evangelical anorexia
nervosa was not a crisis of first conversion or youth, but one of maturity and
later middle age for women. Eleven women were unmarried, six were married. The ages of the four men were thirty-two, forty-three, forty-five, and
sixty, respectively. Again, *melancholia attonita* afflicted middle-aged and older
individuals.

With the exception of one young woman who attempted to support herself through teaching, the women defined their occupation as "engaged in
domestic pursuits" in their parental households, with their own families of
procreation, or as extended kin in a relative's family. All four men were married, and three owned farms. The fourth earned his living as a joiner and pro-
prietor of a woodworking shop in Bennington, Vermont.

Each of these patients suffered some form of adversity before the onset
of *melancholia attonita*. Sickness, death, financial reversal, or personal crisis
had touched their lives. Most importantly, each patient was reported to have
attended a religious revival before the onset of symptoms. The medical records
depict religious excitement as a "supposed cause" of the subsequent melancholia. The revivals mentioned were the New Measure awakenings in Troy,
Rome, and other communities in the "burned-over" district of New York in
1826–1827, and the revivals that punctuated the New England landscape in
1831–1832, 1836, 1839–1841.

Unfortunately, these patients did not leave spiritual biographies and other
personal documents that relate the meaning of their life crises and spiritual
predicaments. We cannot interview them from the grave. They left few documents in their own hand. The medical records, background letters, and
admission histories were written by others—ministers, local doctors, asylum
staff, and family members. An interpretation of their lives therefore must
proceed from fragmentary sources. We can never know the combination of
personal, familial, cultural, and material forces that entered into their decision, in middle age, to seek reconversion in the Awakenings. We cannot
reconstruct their childhood experiences and speak with authority that evangelical child-rearing contributed to the psychodynamics of their later depression. We cannot ascertain if the married women in this psychiatric sample
used religious transcendence as a method of rebellion against family gover-
nance, patriarchal authority, or a stifling domestic life. Nor can we state that
the preponderance of single women in this group sought religious transcendence as a culturally available modality of autonomy and self-development,
motivated by the logic of the "cult of single blessedness." Without the firsthand accounts and rationales of these patients, little direct evidence exists to
support these claims.

Recent studies of the Finneyite revivals in Utica in 1827 and Rochester
in 1831 suggest that the economic and social class dislocations from an agrarian to an urban and commercial social order displaced large numbers of young,
geographically mobile and economically unsettled women and men, sending
them to the Awakenings. The women responded to the innovations of the

New Measures that challenged established religious structure and female decorum. Indeed, women formed praying circles, prayed in public for the unredeemed in their families, and went throughout their communities exhorting others or speaking prophesy. Women championed religious and moral reform societies and worked as harbingers of the millennium.

However, by the 1840s these same iconoclastic women retreated into the separate sphere of the domestic circle, and embraced the Christian vocation of "true womanhood," replete with its explicit message of submission, and moral superiority but economic, legal, and political subordination to their husbands. With successful entrance into the middle class, economic stability, and social position, women were reintegrated into conventional religious and domestic roles.[70] These older women, committed to their domestic careers, assumed the tasks of rearing a generation of regenerate children, as "makers of the self-made men," supporting the business careers of their husbands.[71] To assuage the self-doubts engendered about Christian motherhood, they embraced an abiding devotional piety, an evangelical submission to God. These women understood that their success depended, as Sarah Seward wrote, upon "body & soul" sacrifice to God.[72] In May of 1831 Mary Mathews wrote to Finney with the confession, "I have been led to see more and more my utter weakness—and my utter dependence on Christ."[73] Nancy Hewitt interprets these statements as evidence of female submission to the demands of the post-revival middle-class normative order. This well may have been the case, but another interpretation is also possible. Evangelical women embraced both the Arminian moralism of Christian activism through benevolence and the Pietist fervor of submission to God. The trials of Christian motherhood—nurturing and forming the character and reputation of children, caring for the domestic circle in times of illness, bereavement, and other adversity—were only sustainable for a women who found strength through submission to God.

What remains unambiguously clear, though, is that these patients suffered personal adversity and sought spiritual comfort through evangelical religion. Certainly, the pastoral literature interpreted human adversity through the theodicy that God visits his saints with special providences, chastisements for sin, and a call for spiritual growth and renewal. These literate, churchly, and respectable individuals responded to the call of pastoral directives in the revival meetings. Personal salvation would heal them and answer the perplexities in their lives. If we cannot ascertain the detailed circumstances of their lives, we do know that they embraced the directives of a religiously grounded life-order and personality in an era of revitalization. They demonstrated their allegiance to the campaign of evangelical religion, accepted the millennialism of the universal salvation of mankind, and wished to serve as workers in God's kingdom. Evangelical religion transfigured the meanings of their lives as each of their converted hearts would add to the sum of the godly. They marveled about the wonders of their time and viewed their evangelical reconversion as yet another harbinger of the millennium.

Through evangelical measures, personal adversity was given ultimate meaning as each personal travail afforded an occasion for transcendence. The electrifying excitements of revivals awakened them from the stupidity of sin, and they felt that their lives, religiously grounded in God's will, had assumed transcendental importance. Their evangelical humiliation and self-accusation as unpardonable sinners demonstrated the sincerity and authenticity of the evangelical morphology of conversion, consistent with the published religious intelligence of their era. Their lives resemble the patterns of so many other evangelical Americans in this participation in the revivalism and reforms of the Second Great Awakening. The lives of these patients differed in the depth and protracted nature of their religious melancholy and their suicidal regimen of fasting.

The *melancholia attonita* patients admitted to the Hartford Retreat attended Finney's revivals in Troy and Rome in 1827 or were involved in the New Measure revivalism that spread throughout New England in the following decades. Charles Finney coordinated and systematized several revival measures: the anxious bench (special seats provided for newly awakened sinners), public prayer for lists of the unredeemed in the community, and the exhortation of sinners by spouses, family, and friends. Inquiry meetings separated sinners from the godly and situated them within a crucible of relentless pressures for conversion. Whitney Cross explains that "set apart on the one hand from the regenerate, and on the other hand from the unconverted, indifferent, and curious, the anxious ones became the subjects for unlimited and merciless exhortation."[74]

Finney conducted extended revivals that lasted from four to forty days. Known as "protracted meetings," these were attempts by evangelists to stop the mundane business and life of entire communities so that Christians could devote their undivided attention to the work of salvation. In the white-heat of religious excitement, Finney would force all to turn to God, "where worldly business of any kind, and at any time, should be made to yield and give place to a protracted meeting."[75]

Finney struck the keynote to an understanding of the measures taken to promote a general revival of religion. Excitements proved indispensable to promote religious ends. Finney states that

> the state of the Christian world is such, that to expect to promote religion
> without excitements is unphilosophical and absurd. The great political and
> other worldly excitements that agitate Christendom are all unfriendly to
> religion, and divert the mind from the interests of the soul. Now those
> excitements can only be counteracted by religious excitements.[76]

The decision to conduct this type of revival came about after a vote by the congregation. A local church generally appointed a special day to be set aside for fasting, prayer, and collective self-examination. Published accounts in the *New York Evangelist* report congregations awakened to a solemnity and anxiety over their apostasy, humbled by the renewed awareness of their sins, voting in a brotherly unity to conduct a protracted meeting. The church authorized their settled pastor to invite itinerant revival preachers to assist in this work.

These revivals provided an intensive period of religious retreat. Christians spent up to fourteen hours in a grueling round of praying, preaching, exhorting, and singing. Daily services and anxious meetings of private exhortation could extend into the early morning hours. Ranting and unrelenting preachers delivered their sermons extemporaneously, "from the heart." According to an 1833 account from North Adams, Massachusetts, this preaching was "well calculated to bring Christians into the dust before God."[77]

Finney, always the master showman, trained in the exacting evidentiary logic of the law, convicted sinners before the bar of divine judgment. He advocated extemporaneous preaching in simple, cogent sentences, using language and parables that appealed to the untutored common person. He gave a theatrical performance and spoke directly to the assembled, addressing then as "you."

Finney's sermons warned sinners of the dire consequences of their state: "you are going right to the pit. There is not a fiend in Hell, nor out of Hell, so bad as you are."[78] In the context of this fire-and-brimstone exhortation, he called upon sinners by name to repent. The zealous canvassed homes in search of unconverted, obstinate citizens who refused to heed the call. He published the names of the unconverted. Wives were instructed to exhort their husbands and children to own the Savior. Prayer groups (evening meetings in private homes) met three and four times each week to pray for the sinners and urge repentance upon them. Finney's genius lay in tapping the reserve of social pressures within families, neighborhoods, and church communities, and by the unrelenting forces of public opinion to promote a "community-wide anxiety over the inhabitant's spiritual state."[79] In Finney's ultraism, no measures appeared excessive when compared with the grand design of promoting God's will.

The crucible of the protracted meetings proved effective in bring masses of the unregenerate and the previously converted into an immediate connection with God. If sinners would but choose God as their portion, in an act of will they could repent and be washed clean in the blood of the Lamb. However painful and torturous their evangelical humiliation and repentance proved, they needed to keep in mind the unfailing promises of a benevolent God and the redeeming sacrifice of Christ. Only blasphemy as an unpardonable sin put the penitent beyond the pale of God's mercy. Paradoxically, "Finney believed that men were saved by an ever so excruciating awareness that they were lost."[80] Those whose consciousness of the odiousness of their sin brought them low in abject humility and selfless surrender accused themselves of this rare sin and were instructed that their suffering gave evidence of the authenticity of their hunger for God's love. Exhorters directed them to redouble their efforts, explaining that surely God would flood their hearts with the Spirit and remission of sin.

The published accounts of Finney's early campaigns in Rome, Troy, and Rochester in 1826–1827 and 1830 speak of thousands who flocked to the revival from all social classes and denominations—of thousands converted. A report of the 1826 Troy Awakening describes the evening prayer and inquiry meetings. "There was such a wrestling and agony in prayer as we had never before witnessed. Christians viewed their impenitent connexions and neighbors, as standing on the brink of hell, and that nothing but the mercy of God could save them. . . . In little praying circles intercessions were made for individuals by name."[81]

The sinners who undertook the journey of conversion during this revival first experienced mental anguish. Soon afterward they lapsed into an unfeeling, deadening religious melancholy, according to the accounts of Reverend John Frost, who writes, "how strange it may appear, when sinners have thus been filled with mental agony, and bodily agitation, they have complained that they had no feeling, that their hearts were hardened."[82] Frost's description of sinners in crises of conversion rivals that of Mueller's cases of the scrupulous immobilized and struck with melancholia. Those exhorted to make themselves new hearts now, without delay, lapsed into religious melancholy and lost all capacity to feel or to will.

In a sermon entitled "Rest of Saints," Finney also preached the now-familiar injunction regarding bodily appetites, self-control, and sanctified conduct. Believers were enjoined to submit to God's will and to merge with Christ. Finney, the evangelical Arminian and moralist, also intermixed a theme of fervent devotionalism founded upon his own fasting and contemplation of Christ. He writes that each Christian must emulate the saint at rest.

> We are not so much as to eat or drink for ourselves, "Whether, therefore, ye eat or drink, or whatsoever ye do, do all to the glory of God." The man who has entered into his rest, has ceased from doing it. God requires it, and he that has entered into rest has ceased to have any interest of his own. He has wholly merged his own interest in that of Christ.[83]

Finney's New Measure revivalism brought together three factors: religious melancholy where the anxious passed over from vociferous anguish to feelingless despair; the message of religious terror that a sinner could have grieved away the Holy Spirit and committed the unpardonable sin so casually, so thoughtlessly; and Finney's recommendation for fasting and prayer in search of the contemplation of the Holy Spirit. All three of these factors coalesced into the syndrome of evangelical anorexia nervosa. The stain of having committed the unpardonable sin could not be removed. They became obsessed with their sinfulness. All action, including eating, compounded their sinfulness. For reasons peculiar to each patient, they could not exercise their will and choose God over sin.

The *melancholia attonita* sufferer could not look back upon these accusations of sin from the vantage point of a believer secure in his or her faith. Unlike the evangelical heroes and heroines of the conversion narratives, they were denied successful resolution of their spiritual crises. Rather, they remained passive, inert, motionless statues—heartrending manifestations of God's wrath. The case histories that follow present these people, trapped in the terrible logic of fasting unto death to escape this world, yet in dread of eternal torment.

The medical records of case history #420, admitted to the Hartford Retreat on September 10, 1832, detail the illness of a thirty-one-year-old woman, a mother of four children and wife of a ship's master who resided in Vergennes, Vermont. The letter requesting her admission to the asylum reveals that Mrs. S visited Troy, New York, during Finney's revivals in 1827 and participated in these religious excitements. She succumbed to melancholy at that time and again in 1832 after attending a protracted meeting in Vermont. The medical diary states

> About five years since while on a visit to Troy, she was for about two months in a state of great anxiety and despondency. From that period till about fifteen months since, she enjoyed good health and a natural state of mind. The exciting causes of her present attack are supposed to be religious anxiety occasioned by an attendance on a protracted meeting. From that time till about five months had elapsed, she was in a state of great despondency and despair. This state was succeeded by one of excitement. She became very self-complacent and imagined herself set apart for a special work, became very anxious for souls and was desirous to go about from house and entreat sinners to know God. She laid aside all books, the Bible only excepted, and spent much of her time on her knees in prayer. She has continued in this state of mind up to the present time.[84]

The asylum staff noted that she spent much of her time in silent prayer. During the second month of her stay, Mrs. S refused food and medicine, would not dress, and remained in bed. The medical notes state "she thinks she sins by eating."[85] The November 6 medical log notes, "She renounces her Saviour and is adverse to eating and taking medicine believing that by doing so she commits great sin."[86]

Moral management could not cure Mrs. S. The use of forced feeding prevented starvation; opium, Spanish madeira wine, conium, and other drugs sedated the patient but could not answer her obsessive concerns with sin and salvation. The amusements of the asylum "family" might temporarily divert her mind from religious scrupulosity. After one year of hospital care, Mrs. S was deemed an incurable, chronic melancholiac. Dr. Rockwell, the retreat's assistant superintendent, agreed with the patient's husband that a long sea voyage might prove beneficial in the restoration of her reason. Like the medieval notion of the ship of fools, of lunatics cast about on the sea or pilgrimage in search of lost reason, so Rockwell concurred in a letter to the husband, "I have so frequently witnessed the beneficial effects of traveling and a change of scenery on mind disease."[87]

Miss J, a single woman from Rome, New York, twenty-three years of age, was admitted to the retreat as case history #246 on March 6, 1830. She suffered from "dread of future state," and *melancholia attonita*. The patient history indicates an evangelical childhood of exemplary and early piety. "She thought she experienced a change of heart when she was between 9 & 10 years of age—& has always been an active Christian particularly in revivals etc."[88] Described as a "naturally cheerful" person, Miss J experienced conversion during Finney's 1827 revival. For several weeks she languished in dread of her soul's fate, until the light of God illuminated her heart. The intake history reveals:

> Since that time she has enjoyed a happy state of mind until last October (1829) when on one evening the clergyman's lady came to her father's [house] and wished her and her sister to distribute tracts & left some for that purpose—after the lady was gone, [Miss J] expressed doubts of being fit for so good business. . . . [several days later] their clergyman had a conference meeting & addresed himself chiefly to the professors of religion—& strenuously insisted upon rousing them from their apathy & declared that unless they did so a calamity & judgment would soon visit them, that one of them would be cut off suddenly—She took it entirely to herself and supposed that she must of course be cut off—And from that time to this has been in a complete religious despair.[89]

Miss J attended worship services and after hearing a sermon on the election of saints, considered herself depraved beyond God's mercy. Her clergyman could not console her. She sought solitude, refused to dress herself, remained in bed, and fasted, telling her family that she felt too unworthy to take food.

Miss J was placed in the upper story of the asylum, designated for nonviolent, manageable patients. The staff noted "she groans & sobs continually thinks she is forever cut off from the mercy of God."[90] She remained in this "settled despair" for the next four months, eating only sparingly because "she thought it sinful." Miss J gradually improved, rising out of bed, attending to hygiene, dressing, and taking meals with other patients. In July, she began enjoying carriage rides outside the asylum with Dr. Todd and other patients. The staff furnished her with a Bible and permitted Miss J to attend public worship services at the Episcopal Church in Hartford. Assistant Superintendent William Rockwell wrote to her father on July 10, 1830, about the end of Miss J's melancholy and of her rapid convalescence.

> May God grant that she may continue to do so until she is perfectly restored—She says that she has, for a few days, enjoyed that peace of mind which she never expected to enjoy again. She speaks much of the kindness of her mother towards her last winter, but says that she then thought that every comfort she could receive on this world would only aggravate her misery in the next world . . . .[91]

Miss J spent her fifth and final month of convalescence reading, sewing, knitting, walking around the grounds, shopping in town, visiting the Asylum for the Deaf and Dumb, and attending public worship. As a key test of her restored faculties, the "clergyman's lady from Rome visited her on August 6 and Miss J manifested no undue excitement." At the end of the month she returned to her father's home, "Discharged—Recovered."[92]

A third case merits our attention. Mrs. H, age thirty-five, was a native of East Greenwich, Rhode Island, and resident of Monson, Massachusetts. Admitted in March 1830, she was a middle-class, literate, professing Christian. Her mental alienation was thought to be produced by "religious excitements" of a revival in Munson during the summer of 1829. "She felt she had grieved away the Spirit & thought she had committed unpardonable sin and became despondent; was unable to attend to any business, spoke of destroying herself."[93] The medical diaries note that her appetite was impaired, she refused food and medicine, and became increasingly feeble and emaciated.

Mrs. H made rapid improvement after one month of treatment. She began eating, spent time reading, riding, and walking about the grounds. Her husband visited on April 14 and they rode into town. Later in the month, Mrs. H attended public worship, visited the state prison, accompanied Todd on professional calls, attended Catherine Beecher's exhibition, and received a visit from her clergyman and his wife from Munson. The retreat discharged her as "recovered" on June 10, 1830.

Mrs. H returned to the retreat in 1836, diagnosed as a chronic and incurable religious melancholic suffering the same symptoms of *melancholia attonita*: delusions of unpardonable sin and evangelical anorexia nervosa—fasting until emaciation. She remained for three months until her removal on June 30.

The three women presented as representative cases of *melancholia attonita* and evangelical anorexia nervosa were individuals profoundly committed to evangelical religion and the cause of revivals and Christian benevolence. Each woman manifested early piety and youthful conversion followed by a later crises of reconversion when they sought to reaffirm the covenant of grace during the religious excitement of New Measure revivalism.

The exemplary conversion narratives and ubiquitous models of evangelical conversion published in religious periodicals and revival manuals, and preached as "religious intelligence" by exhorters, valorized religious melancholy. These models directed men and women in the business of making a Christian life and forging a life-order and religious grounded personality. Successful Christians needed to undergo a severe test, and for many, an episodic series of trials throughout their lives that plumbed the authenticity of their inward war against self—sin, worldliness, carnal temptations, and pride. Hopkinsonian New Divinity inquired whether a believer was willing to be damned to be saved, and Sarah Osborn, Susanna Anthony, Hannah Heaton, and many others responded by self-accusations of unpardonable sin. Yes, they were willing to be damned. These successful Christians and others who followed in their tradition had experienced, as a result of revival preaching or the direct action of God, a personal awakening of terror before the law as sinners against God. As this evangelical humiliation proceeded, they charged themselves with unpardonable sin. In a state of ultimate despair, they refused to eat, in dread that eating compounded their sins. Yet, somehow, when they reached this point of complete hopelessness and abject, passive surrender to God's sovereign judgment—in a moment of selfless ecstasy—the Spirit of God flooded their souls with God's pardoning love. The hortatory, prescriptive religious intelligence depicted religious melancholy, combined with the conviction of unpardonable sin and excessive fasting, as a publicly recognized, albeit temporary, stage in the passage to conversion. Successful children of God had found these painful spiritual exercises indispensable in their pilgrimage toward a godly life.

What religious intelligence did not mention was the fact that frequently, believers did not make the expected progression toward conversion. They remained suspended in a liminal world of dread, helplessness, hopelessness, and the absence of love. They had no evidence in their hearts of God's pardon and could not proceed in their spiritual itinerary. Unlike the champions of evangelical conversion depicted in the religious intelligence, patients admitted to the retreat found no successful resolution to their reconversion crises.

The following two cases of male patients again demonstrate the propensity for evangelicals to undergo pathological crises of reconversion in middle and later life as a consequence of pastoral direction that guided believers in times of adversity, and as a result of participation in the collective effervescence of religious excitements, revivals. These case histories need to be viewed as mirror images of the publicized "successful" conversion narratives.

Case history #514, admitted to the retreat for a six-week stay in March 1834, involved a sixty-year-old, married farmer who resided in Dalton, Massachusetts. In September 1833, "his mind became engaged on religious subjects—At first, after due time, he thought he had experienced religion & his mind was at peace—he attended many religious meetings & his health became impaired—He also became despondent—afterwards thought he had committed the unpardonable sin . . . Has thought it wrong to eat—Eats only thin gruel—does not attend to any business."[94]

Mr. H came for treatment after a prolonged period of starvation, and the medical records indicated a melancholy patient who groaned incessantly, and who was "very much emaciated."[95] During the initial weeks of his stay, Mr. H resumed eating, gained weight, and was reported on March 16 as "health improving but much emaciated. Decent in his person, at his room. He passes his time in the various exercises and amusements of the institution."[96] However, after a month of treatment, he again refused to eat and informed the medical staff that he wished to die. Despite their efforts to feed his starved body and remove what medical practitioners viewed as the delusion of religious melancholy, moral management proved unsuccessful. Mr. H returned to his family to die, consistent with medical advice that he indeed was suffering from a "quiet consumption," or wasting illness not accompanied by fever. In essence, Dr. Rockwell's diagnosis of consumption gave Mr. H permission to die of a wasting disease while removing the social stigma of suicide by starvation. Dr. Rockwell released Mr. H in the charge of an attendant and they traveled to Dalton in the Berkshires, carrying this letter, which was addressed to the patient's son:

> Soon after your father was placed at this institution he was put upon a nourishing & invigorating diet & medical treatment & for a while appeared to improve. A few days since he has had an ill turn & has been worse ever

since. He appears to be in a state of quiet consumption. He thinks himself that he shall not live long & has been very anxious to go home, so much so that we thought he ought to be gratified in this request. We were aware that his friends would be glad to have him with them in his last days.[97]

Mr. F, a married father of five, forty-three years of age, who farmed in Dover, New York, was admitted to the retreat in 1834. He suffered from religious melancholy, accusations of unpardonable sin, and evangelical anorexia nervosa. After one month of treatment, he was convalescing and taking meals with the retreat family. The medical diary notes that "he appears now to be perfectly sane—at times a little dejected. Physical health improving—goes about at large & on the premises. Neat & polite in his person & at his room."[98] However, a series of visits by his brother soon put an end to this recovery. Although we have no record of their conversations, the brother apparently introduced evangelical themes of sin and salvation. Mr. F resumed his fasting and when a lightning storm occurred on January 31, he interpreted this unusual winter weather as a portent and omen from God. He "thought lightning was flashes of hell & that he could smell brimstone."[99] During the final six weeks of his five-month stay, he was force-fed by stomach pump and would not take food or medicine except by force. Mr. F returned to his family in the same state of religious melancholy as he had arrived, determined to fast until death.

How striking that moral and medical management proved so ineffective in resolving the spiritual crises of religious melancholy. Despite the balanced moderation of Protestant self-control and character that Dr. Todd and others wished to instill through the model of the asylum family, evangelicals almost always returned to the obsessive rituals of evangelical anorexia and the extreme withdrawal of *melancholia attonita*.

The intractability of treating religious melancholias resulting from New Measure revivalism was not lost upon one physician, who mustered the courage to publish the conclusions from his 1831 clinical experience at the Hartford Retreat. In 1836 Dr. Aramiah Brigham, a distinguished physician from Hartford, Connecticut, published *Observations on the Influence of Religion Upon the Health and Physical Welfare of Mankind*, providing clinical evidence of the deleterious effects of New Measures and evangelical techniques on the physical and mental health of New Englanders. Brigham acknowledged that religious sentiments were universal, innate, and among the most powerful in human nature. Properly cultivated, religious feelings promoted health and well-being by strengthening moral and intellectual faculties, checking sensual and aggressive propensities, and orienting the faithful to a sober, rational devotionalism in the imitation of Christ.[100] True religion, uncontaminated by the doctrinal error of religious excitements, brought the faithful into worship marked by "that calm, simple, and pure manner, recommended by our Saviour, and thus prove serviceable to the cause of rational and scriptural piety."[101] However, he claimed, Methodist camp meetings and evening and protracted religious meetings overwhelmed an individual's stamina, and religionists, particularly women, became susceptible to mental disease. Brigham argues: "No one who has attended the religious meetings under consideration, or who has read accounts of them in religious periodicals, will say they are not powerfully exciting, and productive of great mental distress. Indeed this is what the conductors of these meetings seek to produce . . . ."[102]

Brigham, like Universalist authors, connected religious excitation to insanity. Citing his own clinical experience, he maintains, "I have known several cases of severe disease, which I believe originated from attending protracted meetings; and several cases of insanity, which appeared to have the same cause, have fallen under my observation."[103]

The tender nervous systems of women, children, and those predisposed to physical and mental disease fell prey to the unrelenting terrors, exertions, and anguish occasioned by attending protracted meetings and other New Measure evangelical exercises. Those in good health, and men, according to Brigham, usually escaped any untoward effects. However, he felt it imprudent to risk the health of the general populace by exposing large numbers to potential danger.

> If, therefore, a number of people be kept a long time in a state of great terror and mental anxiety, no matter whether from a vivid description of hell, and fears of "dropping immediately into it," or from any other cause, the brain and the nervous system of such a people is as liable to be injured, as the stomach and digestive organs are from frequent use . . . of very stimulating food and drink.[104]

Brigham founded his opposition to New Measures on both medical and theological grounds, stating that contemporary revivals could not claim legitimacy as emanations of the Holy Spirit. Because "mankind are not at present under any kind of miraculous dispensation," New Measures were manifestations of religious fanaticism, "and ought to be abandoned as unscriptural, and very unreasonable in this age . . . ."[105]

Not surprisingly, the publication of this medical treatise met with considerable opposition from evangelicals. *The Christian Spectator* reviewed this work and charged Brigham with infidelity and the errors of phrenology, and counted him among the enemies of Christ.[106] Local outrage in Connecticut, a center of the Second Great Awakening in New England, nearly cost him his livelihood and appointment as superintendent of the Hartford Retreat in 1840.[107]

Starving Perfectionists

Sylvester Graham's secular healing cult, founded upon vegetarianism and self-control of human appetites, exemplifies one version of self-culture (moralism) in the 1830s and 1840s in America. When Finney and the Oberlin College "perfectionists" embraced this healing cult, dietary reform assumed new proportions, turning into excessive fasting and asceticism in the quest for religious devotionalism.

Graham, an ordained Presbyterian minister and evangelical itinerant preacher in 1826, was forced into an early retirement after suffering a breakdown brought on by extreme self-mortifying asceticism, dyspepsia, exhaustion and melancholy. He spent years searching the Bible for evidence of diet and its relationship to health, seeking truths that would offer a cure for his malady. Graham worked as a lecturer on the Philadelphia Temperance Circuit in 1830, which afforded him the opportunity to exhort against the intemperate use of ardent spirits, the health perils of masturbation, prostitution, excessive marital sexuality, and gluttony.

Graham compiled the fruits of his research about human physiology and the truths gleaned from his health and temperance lectures in an 1839 work, *Lectures on the Science of Human Life*. He urged moderate ascetic self-control of all appetites and eating plain fare, such as whole-bran bread made from natural flour, as an expression of the sentimentalized love of the mother in nurturing her family. To Graham, the growing market of commercial breads adulterated by bleached flour represented the manifold evils of the market economy. Commercial bakers, motivated by profit and impersonal trade, lacked a "moral sensibility" when compared to the ideal of the warm hearth of the domestic circle.[108]

The digestive system served as the battleground between the opposing forces of civilization and the laws of the body's constitution that promoted health, emotional well-being, and longevity. Hillel Schwartz captures Graham's logic by presenting self-culture spinning perilously out of control, leading to overstimulation, gluttony, moral depravity, and disease.

> Gluttony, arch sin, was born of civilization, which seduced the natural appetite and played digestion false. The spices and ferments of hectic commerce insinuated themselves into the kitchen of the innocent wife, wreaking havoc with her sacred duties as wife and mother. Fed too often . . . children grew weak, anxious, and dyspeptic. The same children, appetites corrupted by salt and pepper, the tea and coffee of an overly rich diet, became so accustomed to sensual excitements that self-pollution was the awful but common sequel.[109]

Protection from these stimulants, excesses, and dangerous snares of an increasingly urban, market-driven civilization would come from the moralism of self-culture, which would be directed to the battleground of digestion and diet. Graham envisioned a romantic return to the values and habits of a preindustrial, agrarian village where each individual was integrated into the organicism of family, church, and community, in harmony with the natural-pastoral life and with the imperatives of human physiology. Graham advocated a simple vegetarian fare of plentiful fresh water, fruit, vegetables, and wholesome bran bread. This diet would promote sexual purity and prevent overeating and overstimulation that always produced morbid appetites and moral degradation. In this regimen of self-control he promulgated one cardinal rule of eating. "Every individual should, as a general rule, restrain himself to the smallest quantity which he finds from *careful investigation and enlightened experience and observation will fully meet the alimentary wants of the vital economy of his system, knowing that whatsoever is more than this is evil!*"[110]

Graham's vitalism was based upon the work of the French physiologists Xavier Bichat and Francois Broussais, who advocated a systematic rationalization of the body, the repression of dangerous sexual impulses, and appetite suppression and control. Graham delivered his message in public lectures before large crowds in 1830s New England. Graham's work inspired others to found the American Physiological Society in Boston. Publications such as Dr. William A. Alcott's *Moral Reformer* and David Cambell's *Graham Journal of Health and Longevity* spread the message of diet, physiology, and reform. Cambell opened Graham Boarding House on Brattle Street in Boston, where patients could immerse themselves in self-culture. Life was organized around a precise daily schedule of bathing and exercise, work and leisure. Guests took no medicine, especially patent medicines. They abstained from all stimulants: ardent spirits, cider, beer, wine, tobacco, opium, coffee, tea, pepper, and mustard. No animal flesh or animal products, including butter and milk, were eaten. Guests drank only pure water and "gruel water." They were not allowed to eat large meals and kept their bowels regular with "unbolted" wheat bread, fruit, and moderate exercise.[111]

Although Graham's system attracted controversy, critics, and detractors, these lectures, publications, and boardinghouses appealed to thousands of "Grahamites," who embraced this self-culture and found new balance in their lives. Such was the case of Reverend James Wright, a confirmed religious melancholiac, and for the hundreds of restored souls who sent Graham letters testifying to the benefits of his system. Graham published these testimonials in *The Aesculapian Tablets of the Nineteenth Century* in 1834, likening himself to an ancient physician who was honored by the creation of a healing cult in his name. Charles Lewis of New York extolled the blessing of his own cure in a letter to Graham. Before embracing self-culture, Lewis states, "I was in appearance a living skeleton."[112] He suffered dizziness, irritability, loss of appetite, involuntary twitching in his face, absence of mind, and an inability to concentrate, aversion to company, sleep disorders, and constipation. Lewis writes that he was "always subject to gloom and melancholy and despondency of spirits; and these with many other distressing difficulties, which I will mention, 'grew with my growth and strengthened with my strength' until I was about twenty-three years of age, when my health became very much impaired, and my body and mind extremely debilitated."[113]

The founders of the Oberlin Colony and later, Oberlin College, John Jay Shipherd and Phio P. Stewart, adopted a complete Graham system of physiological reform and persuaded Cambell to assume the duties of food preparation for students and faculty of the college. The college was dedicated as an instrument to promote domestic and foreign missions and revivalism, the moral reform of society, and the abolition of slavery. Physiological reform played a prominent role in the school's early years.[114] Student's were emissaries of the evangelical cause—converted by revival measures, devoted to the moralism of correct diet, sanctified conduct, and self-denying benevolence, they would reform America. Their education as minsters and missionaries made them harbingers of the millennial age. Graham's system of diet and self-culture supported a new doctrine of Oberlin perfectionism.

Charles Finney joined the Oberlin faculty as a professor of theology in 1836 and together with Asa Mahan (founder of the Oberlin Collegiate Institute) expounded a doctrine of Christian perfectionism. Finney wanted to establish the possibility of complete holiness and freedom from sin for Christians who experienced conversion and subsequent reconversion in revivals. Perfectionism involved a propensity of the will to choose sanctified conduct and reject sin, to embrace a complete moralism that freed the believer from the blemish of sin. Finney defined Christian perfection.

> It is the perfect obedience to the law of God. The law of God requires perfect, disinterested, impartial benevolence, love to God and love to our neighbor. It requires that we should be actuated by the same feeling, and to act on the same principles that God acts upon; to leave self out of the question as uniformly as he does, to be as much separated from selfishness as he is; in a word, to be in our measure as perfect as God is. Christianity required that we should do neither more nor less than the law of God prescribes. Nothing short of this is Christian perfection.[115]

Essentially, the psychiatric patients reviewed earlier in this chapter embraced these fundamental tenants of reconversion and the possibility of Christian perfectionism. How ironic that instead of reconversion and sanctification, they languished under the opposite spiritual extreme—unpardonable sin. As we have seen, these patients fasted obsessively in private rituals of purification, convinced that eating compounded their sinfulness. Questions of sin, ill-health and disability, and fasting concerned Finney. In his autobiography, as he began his new life as a regenerate Christian, he discovered the interconnection between evangelical humiliation, fasting, and the inward assurance of God's love. He writes:

> . . . whenever I fasted, and let the Spirit take his own course with me, and gave myself up to let him lead and instruct me, I universally found it in the highest degree useful. I found I could not live without enjoying the presence of God; and if at any time a cloud came over me, I could not rest, I could not study, I could not attend to anything with the least satisfaction or benefit, until the medium was again cleared between my soul and God.[116]

Finney alternated images of contemplative piety and fasting with the image of the fruits of grace—the untiring pursuit of Christian activism in benevolent and reform societies. Obedience to God's law also pertained to conformity with the laws of health and physiology. In the Oberlin community, the idea of contemplative fasting, the rigors of Graham's diet, and self-culture assumed extreme proportions. Professor John P. Cowles charged that physiological reform at the college went beyond reasonable limits. Several women students imposed great austerities on themselves, in effect fasting until near death. He charged that the trustees "have simplified simplicity, and reformed reformation, till not only the health and lives of many are in danger; but some, I fear, have been physiologically reformed into eternity."[117] Delazon Smith, a consistent critic of Grahamism, published this poem in 1837, the first stanza reproduced below:

> Sirs, Finney and Graham first—'twere shame to think
>   That you, starvation's monarchs, can be beaten;
> Who've proved that drink was never meant to drink,
>   Nor food itself intended to be eaten
> That Heaven provided for our use, instead,
>   The sand and saw-dust which compose our bread.[118]

By 1841 rumors of mass starvation enraged the Oberlin townspeople, who in April forced the resignation of Cambell and a precipitous end to physiological reform at Oberlin. It is impossible to separate the hyperbole of criticism directed against the early Oberlin perfectionists from a legitimate concern for austerities and mortifications of the flesh that they might have imposed upon themselves. Certainly, Grahamism eschewed extremes of fasting while promoting an abstemious self-culture of plain fare, the minimum required to sustain the body in health and vigor.

Finney, who had adopted Grahamism in the 1830s as a personal curative for his exhaustion and debility, publicly repudiated a strict adherence to physiological reform in 1845. If we accept Finney's use of contemplative fasting to recover God's love, and recognize that this subjective experience complemented the public activism of perfectionism, then students who immersed themselves in this spiritual hothouse might impose severe fasting regimes. The Oberlin controversy presents the possibility that when moralism—a moderate healing cult—combines with evangelical piety and fasting motivated by contemplative ends, souls that quest after Christian perfection will assume extreme forms of asceticism, including fasting unto death. Unfortunately, little historical evidence regarding this chapter of Christian perfectionism at Oberlin survives to help ascertain the precise nature of the experiment begun by "starvation's monarchs"—Finney and Graham.

Conclusion

The sinners who would fast unto death, caught in the grip of the contradictions of New School Presbyterian "perfectionism" and the Oberlin perfectionist experiment of evangelical salvation, dietary experiments, and societal reform, suggest but two examples of religious melancholy associated with food refusal in the nineteenth century. Other varieties of perfectionism produced similar regimens of starvation.

Bronson Alcott, his wife and four daughters, and a small coterie of "unpractical enthusiasts"[119] came together on a farm at Harvard, Massachusetts, in the summer and autumn of 1843, intent upon creating the "New Eden" of a "Con-Sociate Family" in an intentional community they called

Fruitlands. This short-lived utopian experiment sought to establish a new social order of personal perfectionism made possible by ascetic diet. Fruitlanders would eat fruit, vegetables, and unbolted bread as their fare. They would drink only fresh spring water. By abstaining from all animal products, milk, eggs, coffee, tea, wine, and spirits, they hoped to cleanse and purify the body so that the mind and spirit could achieve transcendental communion with "Nature," freed for higher intellectual and moral pursuits. They refused to use animal by-products such as manure, leather, and fur, or animal traction to plow their fields. Instead, these utopians wore linen clothing and canvas shoes, and plowed under their first crops to fertilize the soil.

Bronson Alcott's utopian vision of new communities, perfected of sin and evil, cleansed of impurity, and engaged in worshipful communion with nature, represents one variant of what Catherine Albanese has called Nature Religion in America.[120] By the winter of their first year, the Fruitlanders faced starvation because they had plowed under their first crops, botched the harvest of barley, and lacked reserves of fruit, fuel, and other necessaries. Only Alcott and his family remained, destitute and dependent upon the charity of friends and neighbors.

Clara Endicott Sears chronicles Alcott's despair, which bordered on insanity, at the failure of Fruitlands:

> He was tossed in mind and troubled beyond measure. All his beautiful dreams were melting away one by one. Everything seemed to be falling from his grasp. Most of the crops had failed;—the enthusiastic lovers of "The Newness" had proved themselves false and had slipped away as the cold weather approached. All his wonderful plans had come to naught. He had promised to the world the vision of a new Eden: he had believed it could exist: he had worked for it with his whole soul: he had nothing to show for it but failure.[121]

Alcott took to bed, intent upon starving himself to death. "He retired to his chamber, refused food, and was on the point of dying from grief and abstinence, when his wife prevailed upon him to continue longer in this ungrateful world."[122] Here too, religious perfectionism, allied with an ascetic dietary regimen designed to create individuals purified of sin and evil, led to extremes. In times of adversity, perfectionists, in search of transcendence, applied, the techniques of fasting with obsessional compulsivity.

John Owen King provides the concluding nineteenth-century example of Protestant obsessional pathology associated with fasting. Henry James, Sr., father of the novelist Henry James and the philosopher William James, fought a ceaseless battle against the tenets of the old religion of evangelical Calvinism and a lifelong struggle with religious melancholy. King explains that James the elder died by fasting, motivated by religious motives. "Though he attacked traditional forms of asceticism as but some secret delight famishing desire, James killed his bodily self—slowly and, if his son Henry is to be believed, cheerfully, by starving himself to death."[123] Henry James writes of his father's end:

He had no visible malady—strange as it may seem. The "softening of the brain" was simply a gradual refusal of food, because he wished to die. There was no dementia except a sort of exaltation of his belief that he had entered into "the spiritual life." Nothing could persuade him to eat, and yet he never suffered, or gave the least sign of suffering, from inanition . . . .[124]

Henry James, Sr., experienced the rigors of Calvinism as a child in the Albany, New York, household of his wealthy father, William. Henry James attended Presbyterian church and Sunday school and learned the dogma of the natural enmity between man and God, the gracious intercession of Christ, the absolute duty to submit to God's law, and the need for evangelical humiliation and self-transcendence to God. James recounts his overly scrupulous conscience, and spiritual precocity that "forced my manhood, or gave it a hot-bed development."[125] He wrestled with his adolescence "animal spirits," his idolatrous joy in nature, always susceptible to the moment when he felt forsaken by God, plunged into panic and terror. As King understands, James's soul bore the brand of the "iron of melancholy" produced by a terrible realization of the irrational hiatus between a transcendental God and a finite humanity mired in sin. In an autobiographical sketch, James writes: "The conviction of his supernatural being and attributes was burnt into me as with a red-hot iron, and I am sure no childish sinews were ever more strained than mine were in wrestling with the subtle terror of his name. This insane terror pervaded my consciousness more or less."[126]

James knew from experience the agony of the red-hot iron, as he had suffered a serious burn as a child that resulted in two amputations performed on his leg, and years of suffering, confined to bed. And the iron of melancholy would strike him down in a moment of religious terror at the beginning of his adult life. James had successfully sued and broken his father's will, thus securing financial security and freedom from the need to engage in productive labor or enter a career. He had taken a leave from Princeton Theological Seminary, married, and traveled with his wife and two young sons to Windsor, England, in the spring of 1844. Here, James pursued his study of Scriptures, intent upon recasting the Calvinist image of God. He writes, "I remember I felt especially hopeful in the prosecution of my task all the time I was at Windsor; my health was good, my spirits cheerful, and the pleasant scenery of the Great Park and its neighborhood furnished us a constant temptation to long walks and drives."[127]

One evening in May, looking into the grate at the embers of a warming fire, James remembers "thinking of nothing, and feeling only the exhilaration incident to a good digestion, when suddenly—in a lightning-flash as it were, 'fear came upon me, and trembling, which made all my bones to shake.'"[128] Suddenly and unexpectantly, as is characteristic of all terror, James was struck by religious melancholy. God had withdrawn his love and countenance. He feared having committed the unpardonable sin, thus assuring damnation.[129] James's illness resembled *melancholia attonita* in the sudden, terrific onset of the experience.

After consulting physicians, taking the water cure, and making the round of healers, James came upon the mystic theology of Emanuel Swedenborg. Here, he found the interpretive framework to understand his mental breakdown and two years of depression, as James termed the sudden onset of this affliction.

Swedenborg elaborated a three-step morphology of conversion, beginning with *vastation* (awakening) and proceeding on the *ordo salutis* through the necessary steps of *purgation* and the final illumination as rebirth into the "divine natural humanity." For James, religious terror, or vastation, had a meaning in the military sense of the word—laying to waste of the natural self, or *proprium*, rife with a creaturely, impure, selfish existence. The *proprium*, once awakened to this condition of absolute alienation from God, succumbed to religious melancholy. The spiritual remedy for melancholy involved psychomachy and the torturous inner battle to destroy the natural self so that the spiritual persona, conceived in the image of God, could live.

God the creator, conceived by Swedenborg and elaborated by James, became a "weekday divinity" who entered into the world and assisted each *proprium* in realizing his or her potential in transcending the natural, creaturely self, to find fulfillment as a spiritual creation in mystical-psychological union with God. James refers to this as a redemption where each believer enjoyed communion with the divine as a "divine-natural humanity." He writes:

> . . . what I crave with all my heart and understanding,—what my flesh and bones cry out for,—is no longer a Sunday but a weekday divinity, a working God, grimly with the dust and sweat of our most carnal appetites and passions, and bent not for an instant upon inflating our worthless pietistic righteousness, but upon the patient, toilsome, thorough cleansing of our physical and moral existence from the odious defilement it has contracted, until we each and all present at last in body and mind the deathless effigy of his own uncreated loveliness.[130]

James wished to free believers from the "insanity of conscience" of Calvinism that included scrupulosity, evangelical humiliation, obsessions with purity, blasphemous thoughts, and immobilizing guilt, and the compulsion of vocational asceticism. In place of the morbid and dictatorial conscience, he posited the contemplation of and psychological union with an immanent God. Instead of the compulsion to work and sacrifice to what William James termed the "bitch Goddess Success," he argued for work as spontaneous and free productivity. In place of the terrors and hypocrisy of the "professional religion," he spoke to a personal relationship of each believer to God.

Henry James never achieved the desired state of perfection from sin or the psychological escape from Calvinism's red-hot iron and the melancholy conscience. As King concludes,

> The elder James thus fought to describe the psychology of his moral struggle. He sought to describe the compulsive works that had broken his worldly spirit, thereby quickening his coming union with God. Eventually James did attain the detachment he had always sought; he ended his natural or

moral self by starving his body away. . . . James killed his natural self, a last eradication and final vindication of the type of conscience he had come so to loathe.[131]

The death of the elder Henry James came at the closing of an era when the iron of melancholy branded the psyches of evangelical Protestants, when psychomachy and self-annihilation augured the movement of self-transcendence and illumination as a twice-born child of God, and when sinners in search of perfection fasted unto death. In the final decades of the nineteenth century, Protestant modernism would supplant evangelical Pietism; neurasthenia, hysteria, and anorexia nervosa would emerge as new culture-bound syndromes that made "religious melancholy" an anachronistic curiosity. As William James would argue in *The Varieties of Religious Experience*, the religious heroes enjoined to transcend their morbid consciences as twice-born saints would pass out of fashion in favor of the masses committed to mind cure and the religion of healthy mindedness. The ascetics who fasted to know God gave way to fasting girls who, driven by the logic of the golden cage of the modern companionate family and the secular ideals of beauty and sexual allure, starved their bodies.

6

The Passing Away of Religious Melancholy?

By his own account, Henry Adams, the elder statesman, historian, and Boston Brahmin, haunted the Chicago Exposition of 1900, "aching to absorb knowledge, and helpless to find it."[1] Adams did indeed find the illumination that he sought in the great hall of dynamos among the behemoth generators whose motors whirled at blinding cadences, producing the enduring spiritual icon of the newborn century—the symbol of infinite power. Adams stood transfixed before the machines. "He began to feel the forty-foot dynamos as a moral force, much as the early Christians felt the cross."[2] The icon of the dynamo represented modernism—the transformation of American civilization founded upon a new faith in the secular ideas of progress, social Darwinism, and a science and technology that would master and control nature. The scientific mastery of nature extended to the rationalization of the human body and the control of sexuality and other human desires.

Adams contrasts the dynamo with another icon, that of the Virgin, which he discovered in the Louvre and at the cathedral in Chartres, France. This Christian icon, "was the highest energy ever known to man, the creator of four-fifths of his noblest art, exercising vastly more attraction over the human mind than all of the steam-engines and dynamos ever dreamed of; and yet this energy was unknown to the American mind."[3]

Adams, world-weary and a relic of a declining status group that tenaciously held to anachronistic cultural standards, felt compelled to pray to the machine, source of the infinite power and force. A scientific materialism and technology would now generate suprahuman powers that people would depend upon for both the practical systems of living and for the emotionally satisfying answers to questions about the meaning of their lives. Now those in the mainstream of American society would eschew evangelical Protestantism and center their beliefs upon progress in an anthropocentric world that operated according to Newtonian principles. The salvation need for the contemplative union with Christ and the infusion of God's love, and its accompanying religious melancholy, lost its saliency, becoming something found only in a fundamentalist minority in America.

The same year that Adams marveled at the new spirituality in the Chicago Exposition, Sigmund Freud published his masterpiece, *The Interpreta-*

tion of Dreams, with the self-conscious purpose of making a millennial contribution through his theories concerning psychoanalysis. Pioneered by a Jew
living in Catholic Vienna, psychoanalysis has achieved its greatest impact in
Protestant America.[4] As we have seen, Protestant pastoral care and the cure
of souls dispensed with Catholic sacramental grace, auricular confession, and
any magical remedies for the removal of sin and guilt. This system of pastoral care also largely failed to answer the vexing questions of religious doubt,
the scrupulous conscience, or the culture-bound syndrome of religious melancholy. Psychoanalysis provided an interpretive framework for understanding mental alienation and a practical technique for treating sufferers. Benjamin Nelson argues that the instrumental activism in American Protestantism
was committed to healing: "no cultural limits were placed upon the achievement of liberation from sin and guilt in relation to the superego. It was pre-
cisely sectarian Protestantism which encouraged the conviction that world and
self could be permanently purged of imperfection and confusion. Nowhere
else has there been so much conviction in the positive power of unashamed
love and self-expression."[5]

In 1902, William James published *The Varieties of Religious Experience*
as an investigation of believers' inner experiences. He focused upon "religious
geniuses" who heroically attempted shape their lives to be consistent with
religious values and motives. For James, every religion created a theology that
made the world and human existence meaningful, and stipulated a practical
ethic for believers to follow. The saint needed to remake the world in the
image of God, and to find rebirth (the religion of the twice-born) through a
protracted and painful conversion experience.

The religion of morbid-mindedness viewed the unconverted as vile creatures in warfare against the self, living in sinful alienation from God. James
argued that religious melancholy characterized the existential condition of
God's unregenerate people. He understood the special affinity between pietistic
Protestantism and mental alienation, "the congruity of Protestant theology
with the structure of the mind as shown in such experiences."[6]

> If the individual be of tender conscience and religiously quickened, the
> unhappiness will take the form of moral remorse and compunction, of feel-
> ing inwardly vile and wrong, and of standing in false relations to the author
> of one's being and the appointer of one's spiritual fate. This is the reli-
> gious melancholy and "conviction of sin" that have played so large a part
> in the history of Protestant Christianity.[7]

James understood religious melancholy, devoting a chapter to explorations of the "sick soul" and the melancholias of Tolstoy and Bunyan. However, the religion of morbid-mindedness that had demanded spiritual heroics
for the twice-born and directed believers into bouts of religious melancholy
became a museum-piece, an historical curiosity. At the turn of the century,
the "religion of healthy-mindedness," exemplified by the mind-cure movement
and Mary Baker Eddy's Christian Science, supplanted the religion of morbid-

mindedness. James could barely hide his disdain for the mental hygiene movement. He writes:

> The advance of liberalism, so-called, in Christianity, during the past fifty years, may fairly be called a victory of healthy-mindedness within the church over the morbidness with which the old hell-fire theology was more harmoniously related. We have now whole congregations whose preachers, far from magnifying our consciousness of sin, seem devoted rather to making little of it. They ignore, or even deny, eternal punishment, and insist on the dignity rather than the depravity of man. They look at the continual preoccupation of the old-fashioned Christian with the salvation of his soul as something sickly and reprehensible rather than admirable; and a sanguine and "muscular" attitude, which to our forefathers would have seemed purely heathen, has become in their eyes an ideal element of Christian character. I am not asking whether or not they are right, I am only pointing out the change.[8]

James correctly points out that physicians, mental healers, and liberal Protestants promoted a religion intended to foster mental hygiene, happiness, and adjustment. By the time he wrote and published his Gifford lectures as *Varieties*, the dynamic of religious melancholy had lost its saliency for most Americans.

By the late nineteenth century, psychoanalysis and new psychiatric nosologies had largely abandoned the idea of religious excitements as the "supposed cause" of insanity. Religious melancholy was no longer extensively utilized as an official psychiatric theory. As Ronald and Janet Numbers explain, "with the appearance of new classification systems for disease toward the end of the century, psychiatric authorities tended increasingly to view religious agitation as a symptom of dementia praecox (schizophrenia) or some other disease, and the term religious insanity slowly disappeared from the vocabulary of medicine."[9] A new scientific materialism and a new explanatory model achieved dominance, transforming what Foucault termed "discourse" regarding mental alienation and discounting the connection between evangelical Protestantism and religious melancholy. Religious ideation, affections, and religiously grounded "personality" were the epiphenomena of a mental disease. Religion was relegated to the status of the surface "contents," the idiom of expression of an underlying psychiatric disorder. In this manner, the culture-bound syndrome religious melancholy, first identified in 1621 by Robert Burton, was removed from medical perception, classification, and the explanatory model of mental disorders. New culture-bound syndromes would take its place; new forms of mental healing would treat these disorders.

Americans and Europeans suffered greatly in the closing decades of the nineteenth century from a variety of new culture-bound syndromes, including agoraphobia among urban women,[10] anorexia nervosa as a disease of intimacy in the middle-class family, neurasthenia or "American nervousness," and hysteria.[11] Psychoanalysis first employed hypnosis and later the talking cures of free association and dream interpretation to recover the symbolization of the archaic mind and restore to consciousness the alienating split between thought and affect. In his treatment of hysteria Freud discovered that when patients were permitted an emotional response or catharsis to a past traumatic event, when these alien, repressed memories were restored to consciousness in a milieu of empathetic support, the hysterical symptoms or somaticizations of the archaic mind ceased.[12]

When evangelical pastoral care failed to remedy religious melancholy for so many souls in nineteenth-century America, afflicted persons sought alternative healing ideas: homeopathic medicine, water cure, Grahamism, spiritualism, and later mind cure, Christian Science, and mesmerism, to name a few. Because the fusion of perfectionism and millennialism brought about by antebellum America evangelicals proved insufficient, an alternative, counter-religious movement arose to fill this need. This countermovement has continued to the present and has addressed the spiritual concerns and culture-bound syndromes of succeeding generations of Americans. Catherine Albanese has termed this "nature religion." Nature religion was never institutionalized in sect or church nor entered the public domain as a recognized religion. Nature religion was a crystallization of ideas found in a variety of culturally diverse settings. Nature religion includes Native American cosmology and reverence for nature, transcendentalism, mind cure, water cure, Grahamism and alternative healing movements, naturalists, conservationists, folk singers, the new religious consciousness of the counterculture, and today's New Age metaphysical healing. Loosely defined, "nature" provides a symbolic center or cluster of beliefs, values, and behaviors, an ultimate "Otherness" or transcendent reality that constitutes the sacred. Adherents of nature religion celebrate the harmony of nature as a model of human community and personal identity. Nature represents innocence, permanence, ethical purity, personal purification, and collective moral reform. People seek individual mastery and freedom in the context of social forces and constraints.

What religious "needs" for salvation and pastoral care that went unanswered by the Protestant covenants, secular psychiatry, and psychoanalysis were addressed by the many faces of nature religion? If the Protestant Ethic fostered the progressive disenchantment of nature objectified in the scientific, technological, and industrial dominance of urban modernity, then does not nature religion offer an enduring counterpoint of magic, enchantment, and ritual praxis?[13]

Not only had the medical vocabulary changed, but American Protestantism, allied with modernism, was transformed by the revitalization movement known as Third Great Awakening (1890–1920), which produced the Social Gospel and Liberal theology.[14] The church needed to respond to the changes in American society in the decades of industrialization, urbanization, and immigration following the Civil War. The public questions of economic and social justice for the immigrant working classes led to the articulation of a social ethic and a declining emphasis upon personal morality, evangelical piety, and the winning of souls through mass revivalism. Liberal theologians like Washington Gladden and Harry Emerson Fosdick employed the model of the historical Jesus to legitimate appeals to social justice and reform while repudiating mass revivalism.[15]

Liberalism subjected Scripture and belief to the "higher criticism," or method of historical and hermeneutic analysis that sought to reconcile the contents of faith with Darwinian evolution and the breakthroughs in natural science. The Bible was reduced to a work of sacred literature that served as the basis for an enduring cultural pattern—a chartering myth. Religious change mirrored societal development. James Luther Adams reflects upon the excesses of Liberalism in "The Liberal Christian Holds Up the Mirror":

> The conception of God became immanental; we humans were believed to be gradually becoming better and better as God unfolded himself in evolving humanity, and history was viewed as the arena of unilinear progress. Enlightenment conceptions of the human being as a rational being and the Neo-Darwinian view of human evolution progressing "onward and upward forever" were alleged to be implicit in the New Testament. These ideas, seen in succession, were taken to be evidences of "progressive revelation."[16]

Walter Rauschenbusch became a leading spokesman, theologian, and radical critic of capitalist political economy among the adherents of the Social Gospel. He lead the attack against evangelicalism, arguing in a 1904 essay, "The New Evangelism," that the "old scheme of salvation seems mechanical and remote."[17] The church enjoined believers from drunkenness, sexual misconduct, profanity, Sabbath breaking, and worldly amusements. When confronted with the most pressing social ills, however,

> the Church as a body is dumb. It has nothing to say about the justice of holding land idle in crowded cities, of appropriating the unearned increment in land values, of paying wages fixed by the hunger of laborers and taking the surplus of their output as "profits," or of cornering the market in the necessaries of life. . . . The moral guide of humanity is silent where authoritative speech today is needed.[18]

The Social Gospel formulated a new theological paradigm of Liberalism, consistent with Progressivism and pragmatism, but founded upon what was seen as the radical ethics of Jesus, and the ideas of the social dimension as crucial to human identity and society as the arena of collective sin and salvation.[19] The way to bring the present generation to God was not by the familiar evangelical appeals to moral individualism—the self in *auto-machia*, embracing a rigid moralism and finding rebirth and salvation. Rather, believers could find God and reconstitute their selves by a new form of religious experience, by self-realization and self-transcendence in "religious enthusiasm for humanity." Social Gospelers redefined the meaning of religiously grounded personality by emphasizing the social-communal aspects of self and identity. Personality here referred to the self in freedom and contingency, seeking integration and a moral center through social action, striving to implement a more just social order.[20]

George Albert Coe's *The Religion of a Mature Mind* (1902) articulated this concept of religious personality. The new century ushered in a new age characterized by the hegemony of science and the decline of the miraculous and mystery. "Modern man," like Henry Adams before the dynamos, stood in awe of the human creations of a scientifically informed technology that produced practical answers to the vexing concerns of human existence. Consistent with modernism and democracy, Christianity needed to respond by a "practical religion" that reflected this enhanced confidence in human agency, future-oriented optimism, and faith in incremental, progressive change leading individuals toward greater happiness, and societies to equilibrium.

Protestant personality no longer was forged in the crucible of Calvinist "terrors of the law," an obsessive consciousness of sin, and a paralyzing religious fear.[21] Now, sincere believers could find a more gentle conversion, an easy awareness of becoming a child of God, if they were willing to accept the abundant love of God and seek self-realization in instrumental activism—working towards a more just society. For Coe, "the end of individual life is a perfected community life."[22] Unlike the evangelical Pietist vision of Christian life as an inward pilgrimage of wayfaring and warfare against the self based upon profound emotional needs for the assurance of other-worldly salvation, Coe promoted a this-worldly salvation.

Moral, religious, and secular education proved the most effective means to awaken people and bring them to Jesus in social activism. Social Gospelers, like Coe, harshly criticized urban proselytizing to the working classes seen in the revivalism of Dwight Moody, Billy Sunday, the Salvation Army, and the Young Men's Christian Association. Using the discourse of the modern social sciences, Coe discredited revivals as collective behavior, the irrational "social contagion" of crowds. Citing the trend toward gentle, rational conversions, he argues:

> there is a marked tendency for the beginning of the new life to be less signalized by emotion. The tragic intensity, the high lights, and the deep shadows of other days are little more than memories. . . . More significant still, perhaps, is the decrease of social contagion. The strength of the old-time revival lay largely in the forces of which social psychology takes cognizance.[23]

Liberalism rejected evangelical measures and promoted a version of civil religion that championed social justice, societal reform, consideration of agonizing public issues such as the condition of the working class, child labor, peace, and civil rights, etc. Liberals have always concerned themselves with the emulation of the ethics of Jesus through social activism. Gone was the evangelical Pietist emphasis upon personality as an *ordo salutis* toward personal salvation, Bible study, and the inward struggle against sin. Whereas the evangelical Pietist knew religious melancholy in this quest for personhood, the Liberal enjoyed greater self-acceptance and was spared the lifelong battle of progressive sanctification.

Liberalism, modernism and the Social Gospel revitalized American Protestantism during the Third Great Awakening. However, a conservative countertrend, fundamentalism, emerged to dispute the claims of Liberalism.

Fundamentalists developed their theological stance as religious nationalists, critical of the Social Gospel and the evils of urban, industrial life.[24] With the evangelical application of the literal truths of the Bible, self-assured that revelation could be grounded in five "fundamentals" as developed at the Princeton Theological Seminary and adopted by the General Assembly of the Presbyterian Church in 1910, America could be saved. Fundamentalists used the *Scofield Reference Bible*, which they believed to be the inerrant word of God. They affirmed the natural depravity of mankind, justification by faith, salvation through the mediation of Jesus, and the existence of heaven and hell. They accepted the doctrine of postmillennial dispensationalism—the pessimistic view of history that anticipated a final age of tribulation for a sinful world gone mad, an apocalyptic end of the world by the forces of the Anti-Christ, and the salvation (rapture) and ascent of only those reborn into fundamentalist religion.[25]

Fundamentalism needs to be seen as a development in continuity with the tradition of American evangelical religion.[26] In *Fundamentalism and American Culture*, George Marsden argues that fundamentalism was an outgrowth and continuation of the special American affinity for revivalism. For two centuries, revivalism was largely unopposed by competing religious or cultural institutions. American evangelical religion combined the elements of biblicalism, religious individualism, and aggressive evangelical Pietism into a distinct cultural nexus that easily supported a fundamentalist worldview.

> The strong revivalist tradition in America doubtless contributed to the tendency to see things in terms of simple antitheses. The revivalist believed that the universe was divided into the realm of God and the realm of Satan, the righteous and the unrighteous. Revivalist hymns were full of simple contrasts between sorrow and joy, turmoil and rest, weakness and strength, darkness and light, defeat and victory, purity and impurity, guilt and forgiveness, the world and heaven. The whole revivalist impulse was based on the perception of an antithesis between the saved and the lost.[27]

Moody's Chicago 1857–1858 revivals and the sawdust trail of succeeding awakenings of Billy Sunday wed evangelical measures to the emerging fundamentalist movement. Moody's aphorism, adopted by the Student Volunteer movement, proclaimed that those "Ruined by Sin" could find "Redemption by Christ" and "Regeneration by the Holy Spirit."[28] Fundamentalist revivals emphasized that the most effective methods of ameliorating the condition of the urban poor or eradicating other social problems was through winning souls to Christ. The converted would demonstrate moral individualism and the character traits of Protestant personality deemed lacking in the lower classes and indispensible for a successful life.

The distinctive worldview of revivalism transformed into fundamentalism called for a radical separation from the world and other religious groups—Catholics, Jews, and other Protestant denominations—who refused to embrace the fundamentals of faith. Fundamentalism adopted an aggressively conversionist stance marked by intolerance for doctrinal difference, and a spirit of combativeness toward modernism and other Christian groups alike. By the end of World War I, a decade before the Scopes trial pitting biblical literalism against Darwinism, the majority of Protestant theologians and ministers had abandoned the conservative-fundamentalist position. From 1919 until World War II, fundamentalism was sent to the sectarian fringe of American Protestantism, winning followers in the rural South and among the dispossessed—"Bible Belt" Baptists, the Holiness movement in Methodism, and Pentecostalist churches.[29]

Fundamentalism had enjoyed the early support of Princeton, Dallas and Yale theological seminaries and the scholarship of leading theologians such as Reuben A. Torrey, Charles Hodge, Benjamin Warfield, Cyrus I. Scofield, and David Erdmann, among others. However, conservative Protestantism institutionalized its position through Bible schools such as Westminster Seminary and Moody Bible Institute, and through popular literature, "prophetic conferences," and parachurch confederations.[30] Fundamentalists largely abandoned the university-based discourse of theological seminaries and suffered both a social and intellectual marginalization. Marsden observes that "the period from about 1920 to 1950 became a sort of academic dark age for conservative evangelical scholarship."[31]

According to William McLoughlin, with the "failure of Liberalism," American society has entered a Fourth Great Awakening during the past fifty years.[32] The brutality of World Wars I and II, the totalitarian regimes on the political left and right, the unresolved and worsening social and economic problems of industrial nations, the wars of liberation arising from a dying colonialism, the threat of nuclear and ecological disaster; all of these developments question the Liberal worldview. The Fourth Awakening was multifaceted and has included the revitalization of Protestant conservatism under the broad umbrella of New or Neo-Evangelicalism. One facet of this movement evolved into a moral absolutism, using national tele-evangelist media to create political action campaigns in the 1980s to influence the political agenda over explosive issues such as school prayer, abortion and women's reproductive rights, homosexuality, and civil rights. Another face of the awakening involved the mass healing revivals of the 1950s, led by Oral Roberts and William Branham, and the charismatic and Neo-Pentecostal revivals in the 1960s to the present. Still another facet of the Awakening pertained to the counterculture, the introduction of Eastern mysticisms, healing cults, and alternative non-Western religions. The 1970s and 1980s saw many disillusioned hippies flee into self-help "cults" such as Scientology and Erhard Seminar Training. As Mark Silk remarks:

> If, at the end of World War II, a commentator on American religion had predicted that in the course of the next forty years urban mass revivalism would be rekindled . . . untold numbers of Americans would attach themselves to Oriental gurus and self-help cults . . . a fundamentalist account of the Millennium would be the best-selling book of one decade and fundamentalist ministers the best-known leaders of American Protestantism in the next, then he (or she) would likely have been dismissed as the prisoner of a bizarre, if obscure fantasy.[33]

The Fourth Great Awakening is of interest to our discussion because significant parts of this movement returned evangelical Pietist devotionalism to the center of American Protestant orthodoxy. In the crusades of Billy Graham and others, the New Evangelicalism reintroduced to mass, popular religion an intense personal relationship with God, the inward quest for the assurance of salvation, and the affinity with religious melancholy. The healing revivals, charismatics, and Neo-Pentecostals stressed the importance of sin and satanic attack that afflicted true believers with forms of mental illness, including religious melancholy. The familiar face of melancholy appears in the evangelical campaigns in the 1950s, and in those who joined the new religious groups in the 1970s and suffered conversion crises in active battles with Satan, in *auto-machia* against sin. Thus, we examine selected aspects of the Fourth Great Awakening that have reanimated religious melancholy in America.

Conservative Protestantism returned to the mainstream of American culture in the 1940s with the formation of national, parachurch, special-purpose groups such as the National Council of Christian Churches and the National Association of Evangelicals, the National Religious Broadcasting Association, National Sunday School Association, and the Evangelical Foreign Mission Association. In *The Restructuring of American Religion*, Robert Wuthnow argues that special-purpose groups facilitated a national mobilization of conservatives, bringing the message of a Neo-Evangelical movement to an increasingly middle-class, urban, college-educated laity from a diversity of denominations.[34] The founding of the Fuller Theological Seminary in 1947 and the cooperation with Chicago's Moody Bible Institute and the Dallas Theological Seminary forged evangelical doctrine that eschewed the pitfalls of previous fundamentalist sectarianism and fragmentation. The special-purpose group crusades hoped to educate and win America's youth in Youth For Christ, the Christian Evangelical Fellowship, and the various Campus Crusades for Christ. In the 1950s the New Evangelicalism fostered a united front that rejected denominational differences in order to win souls on a national scale through radio and television ministries such as those of Oral Roberts, Robert Fuller, Rex Hubbard, and Billy Graham.

New Evangelicalism encouraged church building and bringing sinners to God from across a broad denominational spectrum. Although church affiliation has declined among the more staid, mainline Protestant groups, Evangelical groups have flourished. These include more than two hundred Southern, conservative Protestant groups affiliated with the Church of God—Pentecostal and separating from the world; the Assemblies of God, Church of the Nazarene, Churches of Christ, and dozens of other varieties of Pentecostalism.[35] In addition, the broad rubric of New Evangelicalism includes many small, unaffiliated congregations and over fifty varieties of Baptist churches.[36]

Conservative Christianity restored the primary focus upon religious individualism and religiously grounded personality, calling upon Americans to experience a rebirth in Jesus, a new surge of personal piety.[37] As Wuthnow suggests, the pendulum had swung back from the Social Gospel notion of the self in transcendence through instrumental activism to the self constituted in conversion. "Against cold intellectualism, popular sermons advocated a religion capable of expressing deep inner emotions; against an outmoded social gospel, a message of personal redemption; against ineffective concern for social ills, the need to care for individual souls."[38] Writing in 1944, Ross Rolland defined this religious individualism as part of the continuity of evangelical life and thought from Paul, Augustine, Luther, and Wesley into the present age. "The personal experience of the Divine grace . . . must be considered the most important fact of human life."[39] Evangelicals stand in a line of direct succession with seventeenth-century predecessors, such as Richard Baxter, in recognizing the sinful state of mankind, the soul's need to rest everlasting in Christ, "the awful hazards of the future, and the terrible needs of perishing man" that call forth heroic efforts from each believer.[40] John Owen King is correct in asserting that the seventeenth-century texts, replete with obsessional pathology and psychomacy, continue to stamp the "iron of melancholy" upon the face of spiritual conversion in the twentieth century.[41]

The revitalization of Evangelicalism brought in a harvest of souls. From 1977 to 1991, one-third of Americans designated themselves as "born again" according to the Gallup Polls.[42] Muncie, Indiana, the site of the Middletown community studies by Helen and Robert Lynd, provides a case study of the striking resurgence of Evangelicalism in America. The studies, undertaken in the period from 1925 to 1937, predicted that secularization, modernism, and Liberalism would continue unabated. However, Neo-Pentecostal, Neo-fundamentalism, and the New Evangelicalism came to Middletown in the 1960s and 1970s. Benefiting most from this movement were the Baptist churches, with new satellite church buildings, the restoration of declining congregations, and the penetration of Baptist Evangelicalism into suburban white-collar communities.[43] In Middletown, and in America, fundamentalism now appeals to younger, college-educated, white-collar groups. This is no longer a religion of the dispossessed or one confined only to the "Bible Belt" South.

The resurgence of Protestant conservatism and the enhanced emphasis upon revivalism, the idea of religious individualism, and the concept of the spiritual itinerary of each sinner toward salvation reanimated evangelical Pietism. Following the election of Jimmy Carter, an Evangelical, as President of the United States, William McLoughlin observed,

> The old Bible-centered faith in an omniscient, omnipotent, yet personal, loving, comforting God, who forgives sins, answers prayers, and helps us solve problems by his direct spiritual presence and guidance is, of course the kind of religion many Americans want today. Its conception of God is the opposite of the current impersonal, uncaring, frustrating, bureaucratic authority that controls our lives through science, medicine, and government; this God is familiar and comfortable in a stressful world.[44]

However, the evangelical piety of the New Evangelicalism, in direct continuity with the divinity of seventeenth-century Pietists, unself-consciously restored the culture-bound syndrome known in previous times as religious melancholy. The discussions of the Billy Graham crusades, Edward J. Carnell, and Christian biography that follow provide case studies of the enduring presence of religious melancholy in the late twentieth century.

The Billy Graham Crusades: Fundamentalism as a Popular Devotional Religious Movement

The National Association of Evangelicals was begun in 1942 as a parachurch organization seeking to build a united Evangelical front that would recast fundamentalism and bring conservative Protestantism into the mainstream of American life following World War II. In the spirit of intellectual reform, Harold Ockenga, Carl Henry, Harold Lindsell, Wilbur Smith, Edward J. Carnell, and many others created New Evangelicalism. "They sought, through their own leadership and scholarly production, to cure the fundamentalist movement of its sectarian insularity and contentiousness, its disdain for learning and culture and its lack of social responsibility."[45] The New Evangelicals founded Fuller Theological Seminary in 1947 to promote an intellectually rigorous fundamentalist apologetics, and to train a new generation of ministers and missionaries.

Scholarly publications and theological seminaries do not quickly or easily reach mass audiences, however.[46] As Ockenga argues: "The goals of this movement were to experience revival of Christianity in a secular world, to recapture the denominational leadership from the inside by infiltration instead of frontal attack, to achieve respectability for orthodoxy, and to attain social reforms."[47]

Only popular religious movements and revivalists who perform on a national stage mediate theology to mass publics, through an idiom of emotional catharsis and nationalistic fervor (see Appendix B: "Revivalists As Mediatorial Elites"). The New Evangelicalism supported the post-war revivals, enlisting Billy Graham to bring Americans to Christ.

Born in 1918 near Charlotte, North Carolina, Billy Graham experienced a "saving change" in a 1934 revival lead by Mordecai Ham. He received his education at Bob Jones University and Florida Bible Institute, and was granted a license to preach through the Southern Baptist Convention. He completed his degree at Wheaton College in 1943, married, and found employment in the Youth For Christ movement.

Billy Graham conducted a protracted revival campaign in Los Angeles in 1949 that brought him national recognition and celebrity. William Randolph Hearst took a personal interest in Graham and lent his support to revivalism. Henry Luce, publisher of *Time, Life,* and *Newsweek,* also promoted this young, handsome, charismatic evangelist who deftly garnered the support of the mainline Protestant National Council of Churches as well as the more conservative fundamentalist groups. Graham later served as spiritual advisor to Presidents Dwight Eisenhower and Richard Nixon and enjoyed the endorsements of America's business elite as he articulated a civil religion of unabashed patriotism, a call for moral rearmament, and evangelical Pietism. Individual conversion opened the path to national salvation for America during the Cold

War. Graham launched his Los Angeles crusade by speaking to the pervasive anxieties of the atomic age: the arms race, the threat of godless communism, and moral decay in an America seemingly rife with divorce, crime, commercialized sex, drinking, and juvenile delinquency.[48] Graham, a modern Jeremiah, awakened America to its declension and offered the hope of collective redemption through individuals coming forward in their respective decisions for Christ: "An arms race, unprecedented in the history of the world, is driving us madly toward destruction! And I sincerely believe that it is the providence of God that He has chosen this hour for a campaign—giving this city one more chance to repent of sin and turn to a believing knowledge of the Lord Jesus Christ."[49]

Graham eschewed sectarian disputes and rejected an avowedly political or social agenda in favor of a conversionist movement to win souls and rekindle personal devotion to God. Devotionalism and religious personalism—the "direct experience of transcendence [that] seems totally authoritative within the life of the individual believer"[50]—were the cornerstones of Graham's appeal.

The New Evangelicalism found its champion in Billy Graham. Harold Lindsell recounts the triumphant New England crusade in 1950, which capped two years of small-scale revival meetings planned and sponsored by Ockenga's Park Street Church in Boston. Graham conducted an open-air mass rally at Boston Common in the raw winter; an estimated fifty thousand people attended.

> . . . Ockenga called for a peace offensive with fifty million Americans joining in. Billy spoke briefly on his own five-point peace plan, the last point of which called for a revival of real heart religion. . . . Then Harold Ockenga led the mass of people in a prayer for peace which the people repeated phrase by phrase after him. Following the outline of the peace plan and the prayer for peace, Billy preached on the subject, "Prepare to meet thy God." Hearts were touched and souls saved.[51]

The Los Angeles and Boston crusades, like the many others that would follow, were organized according to a standard formula. Local clergy from a mix of denominations agreed to invite Graham, sponsor the event, underwrite advertising and production costs, encourage participation of their congregants, and follow up those called to God. Singers such as Beverly Shea, Cliff Barrows, and Carlton Booth entertained and edified the crowds who filled the urban arenas. Part Charles Grandison Finney, part Dwight Moody and Billy Sunday, Graham refined successful revival techniques to appeal to Americans in the post-war era. He preached old-time revivalism designed to awaken sleeping sinners, to bring them to a moment of crisis that would compel them to come forward to take anxious seats as inquirers, or come forward to make a decision for Christ. As McLoughlin states:

> The end result of Graham's pulpit technique then is to exacerbate and exalt the fears and doubts, the frustrations and anxieties, both personal and world-wide, of his congregations and radio listeners. Having reduced those

who seek peace of soul to a state of panic and hopelessness, he then offers them a quick and simple way out—a mass ritual of atonement which, momentarily at least reassures them that they have done all they could, that they have been forgiven for their mistakes, and that now a higher power will take over and do what they are unable to do.[52]

Three thousand people were converted and 105,000 had attended during the eighteen days of Graham's Boston Crusade. This conservative, patriotic, New Evangelical brand of revivalism had achieved public acceptance and respectability.[53] In 1950 Graham founded the Billy Graham Evangelical Association (BGEA) to coordinate the financial and organizational needs of the expanding revival, broadcast, film, and publishing efforts. "With an increase in invitations to hold evangelistic meetings, Graham made a concerted effort to avoid traditional pitfalls and criticisms of popular revivals by maintaining rigorous financial integrity and by instituting a system to provide later contact with persons recording conversions."[54]

The "revival mechanics" by which the BGEA organized evangelical campaigns is described by William McLoughlin as a rational business enterprise. Graham received a modest salary, and his association carefully recorded and accounted for the millions of dollars in donations and contributions from followers. Detailed records were maintained of all those who attended the campaigns and made a "decision for Christ," to insure that local ministers could provide instruction and support after the crusade ended. In this manner, Graham wished to avoid charges of commercialism, financial impropriety, or claims of the temporary and "inauthentic" nature of revival conversions.

Graham conducted crusades throughout America, visiting and revisiting major urban areas, conducting thirty-two major campaigns in the United States from 1947 to 1960.[55] "The average city campaign lasted four or five weeks, had a total attendance of 300,000 to 500,000 and a total of 5,000 to 7,000 trail hitters" [persons who decided for Christ].[56] Beginning with the London campaign in 1954, Graham conducted international crusades in Europe, the former Soviet Union, Africa, and Asia. In 1950 he expanded his evangelism to radio with a weekly program, "Hour of Decision," and later added films, mass-market books, a syndicated newspaper column, the publication of *Christianity Today*, and telecasts to his ministry.

Protestant fundamentalist "personalism" can develop into an absolutist moral and political movement around issues of school prayer, pornography, abortion, and many other social questions. As A. James Reichley argues, "individuals or sects who feel they have known God . . . are likely to feel they know with certainty what God wants for the world, including the temporal society in which they happen to find themselves."[57] Graham was not prepared to follow conservative fundamentalism from religious personalism into political activism. Jerry Falwell's Moral Majority, the 1988 presidential campaign of Pat Robertson, Randall Terry's confrontational pro-life movement, Operation Rescue, to cite a few examples, have eclipsed Billy Graham's devotionalism.[58]

As one admirer wrote in 1978, "for thirty-five years, Billy Graham has moved along from glory to greater glory, growing in influence and in favor with God and man."[59] Clearly, he was a most influential shaper of the Fourth Great Awakening, a popularizer who translated the message of New Evangelicalism in terms readily understood by ordinary Americans. Graham promoted a devotional movement that emphasized individual conversion, the practice of piety, and the making of a Christian life guided by the leadings of the Holy Spirit. As we shall see, he reintroduced evangelical Pietism, including concepts of spiritual desolation and religious melancholy, to a generation of Americans who labored to make a decision for Christ.

In 1953 Graham published *Peace with God*. It sold half a million copies as a thirty-five-cent paperback edition. This work became an evangelical classic, reaching mass audiences reminiscent of those of nineteenth-century American Tract Society pamphlets. A second Graham devotional classic, *How to Be Born Again*, in 1977, introduced the ideas of *Peace with God* to the next generation of Americans who would come forward for Christ.

Like so many Pietist writers, Graham avoided intellectual-theological debate and wrote instead with a direct personal appeal to the "man on the street." He did not direct his readers to a particular sect or denomination, but towards a "clear understanding of a new way of life."[60] The untold thousands who opened their hearts as "inquirers" or who made a preparatory "decision for Christ" required instruction, edification, and spiritual direction. They had been awakened to the prospect of life as a pilgrimage, an inward spiritual journey, a "Great Quest."

Graham confronted his readers with discomforting questions. Why did Americans suffer malaise and a sense of emptiness in what W. H. Auden depicted as the Age of Anxiety? Has consumerism, science, technological progress and the material abundance of the "American Way of Life" "brought us the joy and satisfaction and reason for living that we were seeking?"[61] In *How to Be Born Again*, Graham reiterated the theme of each individual's great quest in the face of a world seemingly gone mad. "The forces building up in our world are so overwhelming that men and women everywhere are beginning to cry out in desperation. They feel like the man John Bunyan describes in the beginning of *Pilgrim's Progress* '. . . he was greatly distressed in his mind, he burst out, as he had done before, crying, "What shall I do to be saved?"'"[62]

Through the medium of mass revivalism, Graham introduced millions of Americans to questions of practical divinity that derived from the early Protestant church and the seventeenth-century English Pietists. Every believer forged a life in pilgrimage away from sin, worldliness, and Satan, and toward God. The Bible, the code book, the inerrant truth directing the quest, provided the answer. The stages of this journey, the *ordo salutis*, were divided into three well-defined steps: repentance, faith, and new birth.

Peace with God delineated a comprehensive, ordered, and meaningful worldview, anthropology and ethos that each believer could embrace. In it Graham retraced the familiar territory of evangelical Pietism, beginning with the idea of sin.

From biblical authority he presented a vision of humanity mired in the ontological sin of innate depravity, blinded by sin to Satan's machinations, alienated from God, overwhelmed with temporal afflictions and sorrow, and confronted with the certainty of death. The ubiquity of personal sin, consistent with carnal nature, brought repeated transgressions of God's law, deviation from right conduct, self-will, pride, unbelief, and commission of an unending catalog of sins of the flesh. Sin destroyed inner harmony. "It has caused man to be caught in the Devil's trap." Graham eloquently goes on to explain the wages of sin: "All mental disorders, all sicknesses, all destruction, all wars find their root in sin. It causes madness in the brain, and poison in the heart. It is described in the Bible as a dread and prostrating disease that demands a radical cure. . . . It is a deadly cancer eating its way into the souls of men."[63]

Each believer's pilgrimage began with the first step—repentance of sin. The slumbering sinner, awakened to discover the awful truth of cold-hearted disobedience to God, prostrates self and self-will before God in evangelical humiliation. Through an act of will, the sinner makes a decision for Christ and forsakes sin and Satan's plan. Graham's emphasis upon the active volition of the sinner who chooses for God over Satan is reminiscent of Finney's evangelical Arminianism.

Sinners find salvation not through acts of will or righteous conduct, but by faith alone. The second step of spiritual pilgrimage requires the seeker to discover an inward assurance of the remission of sin as evidence of the soul's redemption by God's grace. Again, Graham urges evangelical humiliation. "Self must be nailed to the Cross. The only desire you will have will be to please Him."[64] The war of annihilation against pride, selfishness, worldliness, and sin centers on the issue of surrender to God's will. *Auto-machia* prescribes that in the searing emotional experience of selfless surrender to the lordship of Christ, the seeker enjoys a moment of faith.

For Graham, the faith experience is modeled upon Luther's Christocentric theology. The substitutionary suffering of the crucified Jesus has redeemed the sins of humanity and bridged the alienation between believer and God. Imitation of Christ and meditation upon the suffering of the crucified Savior were intended to arouse powerful emotions. This is a meditation upon guilt, human frailty, and unworthiness. Each seeker embraces the idea of worm-like worthlessness to prepare for a selfless surrender to God. Graham writes:

> What brought Him to this place of horrors? Who inflicted this hideous torture upon the Man who came to teach us love? *You* did and *I* did, for it was *your* sin and *my* sin that Jesus was nailed to the cross. . . .

> Alas! and did my Savior bleed?
> And did my Sov-'reign die?
> Would He devote that sacred head
> For such a worm as I?[65]

Following the steps of repentance and the faith experience, Graham describes the final stage of new birth as a born-again Christian, a child of God.

The distinguishing marks of this new creation involve "a love that is free from all self."[66] The new creation experiences obedience, godly living, surrender to God's will, joy, and inner peace with God.

Graham ends on a cautionary note. The reborn Christian has just begun a life as a child of God and requires nurture, protection, and fellowship.[67] The practice of daily piety—Bible reading, secret prayer, reliance upon the guidance of the Holy Spirit, witness, love, and worship—will serve to encourage spiritual growth. However, the born-again Christian must remain ever vigilant to the Enemy, including Satan's temptations to new sin, unbelief, depression and discouragement, worldliness, and lusts of the flesh. The cosmic battle between God and Satan, good and evil, the forces of righteousness and those of the Enemy beset all believers. Life involves a pilgrim's progress toward progressive sanctification as preparation to enter the Celestial City.

Like Bunyan's Christian in the allegory *Pilgrim's Progress*, Graham's newborn committed their lives to a spiritual pilgrimage of wayfaring and warfaring, never immune to the troubling questions of assurance. Did they persevere as children of God or did they succumb to doubt, despair, and religious melancholy? Of regenerate believers he writes: "Every week I receive scores of letters from those who say they have doubts and uncertainties concerning the Christian life."[68] Graham urges the regenerate to engage in a spiritual warfare, enlisting the aid of the Holy Spirit to resist the satanic enemy and win a spirit-filled victory for Christ.[69]

The Billy Graham crusades have always sent the message of unbounded optimism. Individual salvation, universally open to all sinners, required only that each believer make that first decision for Christ. Founded upon the promises of Scripture, the inerrant word of God, Graham assures his audiences that rebirth will answer all their questions, heal their wounds, satisfy their predicaments, and bring them a lasting inner peace. The more hagiographic accounts of the Billy Graham crusades, Curtis Mitchell's *Those Who Came Forward* and Lewis Gillenson's *Billy Graham and Seven Who Were Saved*, recount the lives of socialites, sports stars, artists, entertainers, businessmen, and ordinary Americans from all walks of life.[70] These stories reveal a common pattern of troubled, unfulfilled, perplexed men and women who found a new birth through the good offices of Billy Graham as God's servant. The idiom of those once lost and now found implies a future of spiritual assurance and peace as children of God. This naïveté masked the complex, self-torturous process of making a godly life.

Reinhold Niebuhr clearly understood Graham as an Evangelical determined to restore the primacy of pietistic moralism in place of Protestant Liberal (modernist) concern for the Social Gospel. In 1956, writing in *The Christian Century*, he explains Graham's central concern with individualism and personal salvation:

> The ultimate religious commitment is a personal and individual one, and
> it can therefore be most effectively made by a pietist who narrows the vision

of religious awareness to highly personal dilemmas and needs. Hence the pietistic evangelist is probably most effective among individuals who have pressing personal, moral and religious perplexities.[71]

Not surprisingly, Graham never resolved the questions of assurance and enduring peace with God for the regenerate. Although the manifest promises of Scripture justified the motif, "Life as Therapeutic Renewal," these same authorities also introduced the counterpoint of "Life as Pilgrimage." The Christian life required ceaseless warfare against the remnants of indwelling sin of the "natural man" and the ever-present power of Satan to thwart each child of God. Evangelical Pietists everywhere forged a religiously grounded personality founded upon *auto-machia*. Not infrequently, Pietists succumbed to times of desolation—religious melancholy. The inner lives of God's chosen oscillated between point and counterpoint, between the warmhearted assurance of being God's child, and the dreaded times of feeling forsaken by God.

Graham acknowledged the propensity of born-again pietistic Christians to suffer spiritual trials and depressive episodes. *The Holy Spirit* (1978) depicts the Christian's inner struggle between two natures, the "Spirit" and the "Flesh." The highest good in life is to become a vessel for the Holy Spirit, made possible through surrender to God's will. Sin, yielding to the Devil's temptations of the flesh, constitutes the bane of existence. Graham writes of his own life spiritual warfare between Spirit and Flesh:

> Many times in my life the thing I have never meant to do in my mind I did in the flesh. I have wept many a bitter tear of confession and asked God the Spirit to give me the strength at that point. But this lets me know that I am engaged in a spiritual warfare every day. I must never let down my guard—I must keep armed.[72]

He then recounts how born-again Christians frequently experience times when they lack the fullness of the Spirit; dispirited times when through sin they have "grieved the Spirit" or charged themselves with blasphemy against the Spirit—the unpardonable sin. In this manner, Graham restores a multi-dimensionality to the born-again's spiritual itinerary. Times of joyous possession of the Spirit punctuate episodes of religious melancholy when the godly stand self-accused of the unpardonable sin or of grieving the Spirit.

The Holy Spirit resounds with themes that harken back to the seventeenth-century practical divinity of William Perkins, Richard Baxter, and John Goodwin, or the evangelical Pietism of Cotton Mather. The letters that Graham received from many troubled converts resemble the asylum accounts of persons self-accused of grieving the Spirit or of unpardonable sin.

Unselfconsciously, Graham mediated to his mass audiences the credal and emotional cultural directives common to early modern Pietists. Concerning his followers, he writes that:

> Many of the young people I meet are living defeated, disillusioned, and disappointed lives even after coming to Christ. They are walking after the flesh because they have not had proper teaching at this precise point. The

old man, the old self, the old principle, the old force, is not yet dead or wholly renewed . . . . Only when we yield and obey the new principle in Christ do we win victory.[73]

The spirit-filled victories for Christ proved evanescent. Periods of spiritual desolation complemented life's continual struggle between the two warring principles. Joyful submission to God counterbalanced painful depressive episodes. Graham tells his readers to expect this inner warfare, the alternation of joy and desolation. The experiences of Christians authenticated this. Graham himself suffered depression as he prepared for the 1954 crusade in London.

> We sailed for England in 1954 for a crusade that was to last for three months. While on the ship, I experienced a definite sense of oppression. Satan seemed to have assembled a formidable array of his artillery against me. Not only was I oppressed, I was overtaken by a sense of depression, accompanied by a frightening feeling of inadequacy for the task that lay ahead. Almost night and day I prayed. I knew in a new way what Paul was telling us when he spoke about "praying without ceasing." Then one day in a prayer meeting with my wife and colleagues, a break came. As I wept before the Lord, I was filled with deep assurance that power belonged to God and He was faithful.[74]

In the style of Richard Baxter, *The Holy Spirit* concludes with an appeal to the practice of daily, devotional piety. Continued repentance for sin, evangelical humiliation, and surrender to God would bring the "fruits of the Spirit": love, joy, peace, patience, kindness, goodness, faithfulness, and self-control. Despite this promise, Graham told his audiences, directly and by implication, to expect seasons of trial and desolation. As one of the most influential evangelists of his time, as a national religious leader, he promoted the primacy of evangelical Pietist conversion and religious personhood, directing believers into spiritual warfare, telling them to expect what we have termed religious melancholy as a mark of an authentic inner journey to God.

Graham served as the premier salesman for a new Protestant fundamentalism, a Neo-Evangelicalism that hoped to avoid sectarianism, schism, and denominational intolerance and to promote the winning of souls en masse to Christ in the Fourth Great Awakening. Neo-Evangelicalism returned pietistic conversion to the mainstream of American Protestantism. Ironically, New Evangelicalism brought a heightened pastoral awareness of the re-emergence of depressive illness and religious melancholy among the born-again. We shall next examine the propensity of New Evangelicals to suffer from religious melancholy, as exemplified in the life and work of Edward J. Carnell, a major force and exponent of the Fourth Great Awakening.

The Melancholy Apologetics of Edward J. Carnell

Edward J. Carnell (1919–1967) died in the spring of 1967 from an apparent overdose of sleeping pills, a self-inflicted death, whether suicide or accident. This untimely end followed years of addiction to barbiturates to alleviate chronic anxiety and palliate lifelong insomnia. Carnell suffered an emotional collapse in 1961, and underwent a brief psychiatric hospitalization, electric shock treatments, and continued outpatient therapy for unrelieved depression in the decade preceding his death.[75] What distinguishes this story from other cases of mid-life crisis and depressive illness is his stature as a national religious leader.

Edward J. Carnell was a theologian with degrees from Wheaton College and Westminster Seminary, including doctorates from Harvard Divinity School and Boston University. A self-styled "conservative," he championed the New Evangelicalism as a professor at, and later as President of, Fuller Theological Seminary. Carnell devoted his life to Christian apology, or the rationalist defense of faith, seeking to bring intellectual rigor to Evangelical thought and bridge the hiatus between fundamentalism and liberal, mainstream Protestantism.[76] He would doubtless have agreed with James Luther Adams that an unexamined, undefended faith is not worth having, that the cold logic of theology masks an inner, personal struggle with existential issues—"faith seeking understanding—understanding of yourself and understanding of reality."[77] What was Carnell's struggle with faith, his inward journey of self-revelation that motivated the apologetics and resulted, finally, in a spirit broken by melancholy and an intellect short-circuited by repeated shock therapy? Carnell's biographer, Rudolph Nelson, suggests that concern with undoing the childhood stigma of fundamentalism became an enduring theme in Carnell's public theology and private struggles. Although we cannot offer a comprehensive exegesis of Carnell's work, certain themes prove suggestive of the pathogenic nature of Protestant theology and the association of evangelical child-rearing and religious melancholia. Carnell offers a glimpse of the trials of one who came to a mid-life realization that the recovery of God's love and spiritual consolation proved impossible for one reared in the "tyrannical legalism" of fundamentalism.[78]

By 1948 Carnell had completed his doctorate at Harvard, published an award-winning first book, *Introduction to Christian Apologetics*, and accepted a faculty position at Fuller Theological Seminary, where he would teach until he assumed the presidency in 1954. "Still a year short of his thirtieth birthday, he had not veered one degree off course since that time ten years earlier when he had caught the vision of how the life of the mind could serve the cause of Christ."[79]

Carnell joined a faculty and institution committed to the realization of the seemingly impossible goals of achieving preeminence in their fields, contributing to Christian missions, and revitalizing American Protestantism. As George Marsden argues in *Reforming Fundamentalism,*

> The Fuller professors were renowned for their hard work. They were trying to do everything at once. They were going to rise to the top of their professions, fill the Christian world with outstanding books and popular literature, be great teachers, be active in their churches, Sunday schools, and on the Bible conference trail, be models in their mostly young households, and maintain contacts with their admiring students. The norms they

set for themselves combined all the usual expectations for faculty of graduate schools, liberal arts colleges, and Bible institutes and no doubt *contributed to the striking number of psychological breakdowns, mostly temporary, among Fuller faculty during its history.*[80] (emphasis added)

As we shall see, it was neither overwork nor unrealizable goals alone that accounted for Carnell's nervous breakdown.

Fuller theologians John Ockenga, Carl Henry, Wilbur Smith, Clarence Roddy, Charles Woodbridge, and George Ladd, among others, articulated the New School or New Evangelicalism, embracing an inclusive parachurch and eschewing denominational disputes. The New School abandoned the anti-intellectualism of J. Gresham Machen's defense of fundamentalism and rejected the doctrines of separatism, inerrancy, and the demand for confessional unity.[81]

Carnell's system of apologetics proved essential for the defense of a reformulated fundamentalism. With rigorous logical precision, striving toward systematic consistency, Carnell built his defense of faith in philosophical theism. He would later expand the rational grounds of apologetics with arguments derived from biblical hermeneutics and church history.[82] This inclusive methodology allowed the widest debates with theologians well beyond the pale of orthodoxy, including Kierkegaard, Karl Barth, Paul Tillich, and Niebuhr. Thus, the New School could consider questions raised by existentialism, the problem of unbelief, the call for social justice promulgated during the 1950s, and the Fourth Great Awakening.[83] However, Carnell moved from a rationalist "apologetics of the mind" to a "perspective of inwardness," or "apologetics of the heart,"[84] in the period from 1957 to 1960, with the publication of *Christian Commitment* (1957), *The Case for Orthodox Theology* (1959), and *The Kingdom of Love and the Pride of Life* (1960). How does one explain this uncharacteristic alteration in perspective?

Carnell experienced a personal breakthrough of heightened awareness in this period, and confronted the long-repressed memories of his fundamentalist childhood. He began a public attack upon fundamentalism, contending "Fundamentalism is orthodoxy gone cultic."[85] In the March 30, 1960, issue of *Christian Century*, Carnell published a vitriolic polemic, arguing that fundamentalism had earned a negative status by its separatism from other denominations and by its intolerance of even small doctrinal differences. If the church universal is an inclusive institution founded upon love, then cultic fundamentalism exalts in particularism, disunity, and separation from fellow Christians.[86] Carnell writes, "I know that much of this will sound elementary to outsiders. But to one reared in the tyrannical legalism of fundamentalism, the recovery of a genuine theology of grace is no insignificant feat. The feat calls for a generous outlay of intellectual honesty and personal integrity."[87] Carnell's principle of inwardness would recover and address the central contradiction of his own childhood: how could a doctrine ostensibly founded upon love effect such cruelty upon children?

Born into a fundamentalist Baptist family, Edward's father, Herbert Carnell, trained at the Moody Bible Institute and imposed a rigorous evangelical moralism upon his family. In a 1959 *Christian Century* essay, Edward Carnell charged his father with imposing "the tyrannical legalism of fundamentalism."[88] This tyranny included sexual repression, and prohibitions against masturbation, dancing, and worldly entertainments. The harsh, authoritarian father judged, punished, and annihilated the sinful self of young Edward, recasting the boy in the image of godliness. Edward Carnell recovered these childhood memories of evangelical child-rearing when, during the period from 1959 until his breakdown in 1961, he wrote about the apologetics of the heart. He remarked to a friend "'I have never been able to put my Saturday father together with my Sunday father,' a reference to his childhood perceptions of a father who he felt tyrannized the family on Saturday when he was preparing his sermon and then was all sweetness and light in the pulpit on Sunday."[89]

Carnell helped edit his father's unpublished memoirs, producing a kinder and more gentle remembrance of his life with a fundamentalist Baptist father. The details and narratives of his family life were excised. However, the effects of his childhood continued to haunt his dreams and trouble him with obsessions and unrelieved guilt. Sexual themes and guilt about masturbation intersperse his writings and lectures. In his final years as a professor of ethics, he made these obsessions the basis for lectures, as one student remembers.

> He startled the Ethics class (me anyway) at the start of the course by commenting on the therapeutic effects of masturbation in relieving life's tensions (not only sexual tensions), and by advocating it as a release when pressures—academic and otherwise—built up. This may be something that every one knew—but it wasn't something one expected an evangelical professor of theology in an ethics course to come out and advocate.[90]

Dr. Philip Wells, the psychiatrist who treated him, underscores the persistence of this childhood trauma.

> He was troubled during the years with severe and persistent obsessive thoughts and dreams which he could not prevent. They made him feel very guilty, because of his strict upbringing, and often very depressed. He was often angry at the rigidity of creedal and moral codes in which he was trapped by his connection with Fuller Theological Seminary, which was his life work. He got some satisfaction in working some of this out with his students, especially in his ethics class.[91]

Carnell's last work on apologetics would address the question of healing the trauma of an Evangelical childhood, of discovering the way to self-acceptance and the way to surrender in God's love. *The Kingdom of Love and the Pride of Life* begins with the idea that Christianity is founded upon the law of love—the unconditional acceptance and nurture of each child of God. The essay adopts the image of the happy and loved child, secure in the bosom of Jesus, and by analogy, indicates that adult believers may also find spiritual assurance and consolation through adoption as God's children. The happy, well-loved child serves as a metaphor for the relationship of each believer to divine love.

> A happy child bears witness to the release that love brings: release from
> anxiety, fear and dread of not counting. A child completes his life through
> the wisdom and power of those who watch over him. He is not sufficient
> unto himself, nor does he pretend to be. Jesus says we should go and do
> likewise. We must learn to rest in the sovereignty of God.[92]

Carnell explains that happy children enjoy the blessings of the Kingdom
of Love, convinced, through the mediation of Jesus, that God's love abides,
and each person "counts" as a worthy person in spite of sinfulness and imper-
fections. God's children do, however, feel the angst of constructive anxiety
in seeking to live by God's laws and surrender into his will as a tool of transcendental purpose. What happens, then, to Christians who cannot "rest in
the sovereignty of God".[93] They forfeit citizenship in the Kingdom of Love.

Without the assurance of love, believers succumb to destructive anxiety
that leaves them with undefined goals, full of pride, and self-centered. Carnell
found that encounters with constructive anxiety in his own self-examination
of sin frequently induced protracted episodes of destructive anxiety when he
could not recover the inner peace of God's love. Again, he stumbled over the
intense feelings of pollution engendered by masturbation.

> Since Christians are confronted by the law of God, they may invite psy-
> chic distress out of their very effort to live up to the terms of this law. The
> more they see imperfection in themselves, the more vulnerable they become
> to guilty feelings. . . . For example, a Christian may be distressed because
> he cannot overcome the habit of masturbation. He struggles and struggles,
> only to end defeated and guilty. If he does not learn to rest in the imputed
> righteousness of Christ, he may lose himself by trying to save himself. In
> this case he illustrates the paradoxical way in which constructive anxiety—
> anxiety suffered because the soul loves God—can open the sluice gate for
> destructive anxiety.[94]

He placed blame on fundamentalist doctrine and practice for engendering
destructive anxiety in believers. This religious ethos and world view was pathogenic. Carnell states that the church

> can serve as a *neurosis-producing agency* by substituting legalistic attitudes
> for the freedom of grace in Christ Jesus. In this case the church becomes a
> cult which tries to play the role of the Holy Spirit by monitoring lives.
> The ethic of honesty is impaired, and believers are forced to repress their
> true feelings. Prolonged repression can damage both the emotions and the
> nervous system.[95] (emphasis added)

Carnell was not alone in the charge that fundamentalism was pathogenic.
His colleague at Fuller, Clarence Roddy, also languished in depression, and
the two men saw the same therapist.[96] Roddy's son, Sherman, published a
scathing denunciation of fundamentalists and ecumenicity in *Christian Century*
in 1958. He called the New Evangelicals victims of fear, "compelled to defend
tenaciously a cultural pattern which seems to make life unendurable. . . ."[97]
Sherman Roddy argues that their God is a supreme sadist compelling self-

torture as they whip themselves with accusations of depravity. "This false God of holiness can only produce despairing neurotics and pharisaical prigs."[98]

In Freud's theory of psychosexual development and psychoanalysis Carnell found a new perspective on love—the foundational love experienced in a happy childhood, and the healing love between psychotherapist and analysand in the transference relationship, which re-enacts previous familial relationships and seeks to mend childhood trauma. He observes that "Freud taught his patients the art of seeing themselves through their own childhood. He believed that people become anxious and thus lessen their chances of leading happy, normal lives, because somewhere along the line they have lost the natural zest and unconditional faith of childhood."[99] Carnell was forced to conclude that the destructive anxieties, obsessions, and mental anguish of adult Christians were evidence of the neurosis-producing and cultic doctrines of fundamentalism, of what we have termed evangelical nurture. His own psychotherapy allowed him to recover childhood memories of his father's authoritarian cruelty and neglect, which made these conclusions unavoidable.[100]

Carnell reassured his readers that psychotherapy could assist the believer troubled by destructive anxiety to achieve greater self-acceptance and release from guilt and obsessive thoughts and acts. Concomitantly, he noted that the compassion of Jesus brought spiritual hope to the downtrodden who listen to the promises of the Gospel. "When the conscience is pierced with the stings of guilt, and the soul writhes under a wound which no human medicine can heal, the promises of the gospel are like a balm of Gilead, a sovereign cure for this intolerable and deep-seated malady. Under its cheering influence, the broken spirit is healed and the burden of despair is removed far away."[101] But Carnell never achieved either the psychoanalytic ideal of a reintegrated and self-accepting personality, or the spiritual peace of assurance as God's child.

Many events probably contributed to Carnell's collapse in 1961. At the age of forty, his stellar success was behind him, and he failed to gain acceptance and preeminence among both fundamentalists and liberals. The attack upon fundamentalism had produced endless controversy and wearying contention. Carnell held the presidency of Fuller Theological Seminary from 1954 until his resignation in 1959. He was ill-suited for this administrative post and his term ended in a chaotic and failed presidency. Confiding to Ockenga his deep guilt at leaving the school in such disorder, and anxiety that swept over him "with the force of a tidal wave," he had "never realized that it was possible to suffer such intense inwardness, while all the time giving the outward impression that all is well."[102]

He plumbed the depths of inwardness and foundered on the contradiction of childhood cruelty imposed in the name of Christian love. Jonathan Lear's *Love and Its Place in Nature, A Philosophical Interpretation of Freudian Psychoanalysis*, offers an interpretation of Freud that accords with Carnell's perspective of inwardness. Lear holds that Freud's theory of mind was devised to interpret and explain the "intraspychic transference" between the somaticizations and unconscious processes of the archaic mind, and the conceptual thinking or secondary processes of consciousness. Dreams provide the key to the archeology of the mind and the recovery of meanings in the archaic mind. Freud's stage theory of human psychological development or topological self—id, ego, and superego—could be better understood if we substitute the concept "I" for ego, "It" for id, "super-I" for superego, and "love" for sex or libido. Each infant begins life psychologically fused with parent and world, and gradually forges a sense of "I" as opposed to other by investing I and world with love. At the most fundamental level, each individual must identify and introject, through love, representations of self, other, and world. "Love is not just a feeling or a discharge of energy, but an emotional orientation toward the world. That orientation demands that the world present itself to us as worthy of our love."[103]

Love is the developmental force that impels each infant to break from the primordial unity with parent and identify and attach with objects in the world. Thus, love constitutes a force of differentiation and complexity in seeking new unities with object relations, and the basis for individuation and autonomy for each person. Lear states that

> In a good-enough world, the outcome of this process will be a certain harmony in the soul. That the world which is internalized is a loving world will allow, on the one hand, the development of a super-I that is loving and tolerant of the drives and, on the other, the development of an I that is sufficiently attractive as to allow ever greater levels of sublimation, whether in psychic structure or in creative activity. . . . But this harmony is of its essence derivative: it is the outcome and re-creation within the soul of the loving relationships in a good-enough world. In that sense, the harmony is a manifestation of and response to love.[104]

Lear's brilliant rendering of Freud locates the source of love within the human psyche or soul in an anthropocentric universe of interpersonal and cultural object relations. As Freud knew, the memory of love or first unity with the nurturing mother endures, and for many otherwise healthy and individuated psyches, there exists the ever present potentiality for regression to early states of love and gratification. Where the Evangelical longed to please a paternal God and find love's union through contemplation, only to experience religious melancholy, the modern soul needed no reference to a transcendental God or religious values. The life-order and personality of the secular modern knew nothing of sin, religious guilt, sanctification, or God's glorification.

The individual as constituted in psychoanalytic thought was free to select from among a complex array of competing cultural standards. Economic, political, scientific, vocational, familial, and aesthetic life-orders confronted each modern person. Through active choice each autonomous individual appropriated and internalized these ideal-I commitments. But the modern individual soul accepted no predetermined script and would not lapse into bad faith or unthinking, reflexive conformity to collective demands. The soul in individuated harmony makes constant inner appeals to conscience and this proves dangerous and subversive to the logic of mass society—conformity and de-individuation.[105]

For Evangelicals, selfhood and identity proved the very antithesis of the Freudian developmental ideal of love's psychic economy. In place of inner harmony the Evangelical knew *auto-machia*. Instead of a loving and tolerant super-I, the Evangelical internalized the demanding, rigid parent who always found fault, sin, and error. The Evangelical was not reared by "good-enough" parents who fostered a sense of I tolerant of drives, but rather of internalized guilt and shame for being all-too human. The evangelical I resulted from the systematic assault upon the will, upon autonomy, by parents who demanded unquestioning obedience. The evangelical I waged incessant warfare against the drives and the body, against the autonomy of the self which was denounced as worldly, prideful, and venal. Ever haunted by the loss of primordial parental love, never able to prove themselves worthy of parental or divine love, Evangelicals struggled in adult life, searching for contemplative union with God and assurance of God's love, but visited by religious melancholy. Life's pilgrimage entailed intermittent episodes of self-torture by an internalized repressive super-I.

Nearly a quarter century after his untimely death, Edward J. Carnell needs to be reconsidered and his works reread, not because he was a theologian of the stature of a Tillich or Barth. We "follow in his train,"[106] because he has left a legacy, in his final apologetics, of his courageous and honest personal discovery that "cultic" fundamentalism transforms the law of love in Christianity into tyrannical legalism that is responsible for childhood cruelty and adult melancholia. He identifies the "neurosis-producing," pathogenic doctrines and practices of a major Protestant denomination. His life and death illustrate that even one who possessed a powerful intellect and the benefits of psychoanalytic treatment and insight could not achieve personal reintegration, healing, and self-acceptance. He suffered the unrelieved terrors of memory, dreams, and compulsions that electro-convulsive shock, tranquilizers, and sedation could barely palliate. Although he was a loving and gently tolerant father to his own children, and was forgiving of the shortcomings of his students and colleagues, he never could forgive himself. Carnell's self-inflicted ending to his sojourn as a twentieth-century "Christian" demonstrates that he was an individual who languished as one forsaken by God.

Religious Melancholy and
Contemporary Christian Biography

Religious melancholy, whether as a diagnostic category in psychiatry or as a malaise of the sick soul within pastoral theology, was absent from medical and religious explanations of depressive illness in the early twentieth century. The new development psychologies of G. Stanley Hall and Edwin Starbuck relegated conversion crises to one idiom of the life transitions of adolescence. Freud and psychoanalysis provided a humanistic and psychosexual explanation of religion as an individual, obsessive disorder, and as a universal obsessional neurosis and collective illusion. The activism and moralism of the Social Gospel produced a cure of souls that directed the perplexed to seek "adjustment" to social environments, and later, "insight" into the intrapsychic wellsprings of spiritual malaise. Gone was the piety and inner pilgrimage of evangelical religion. Psychiatrists, psychologists, and pastoral healers thus did not need to concern themselves with the questions of religious melancholy. Yet, in the midst of this change in perspective, believers from both liberal and fundamentalist groups continued to suffer bouts of religious melancholy. Many struggled to come to terms with their experiences and published biographical accounts of a spiritual sickness known to believers in past times as religious melancholy. Twentieth-century Americans would rediscover this culture-bound syndrome, harkening back to seventeenth-century sources.

In 1942, Georgia Harkness published "If I Make My Bed in Hell" in the *Christian Century* as an autobiographical account of a "sense of spiritual desolation, loneliness, frustration, and despair which grips the soul of one who, having seen the vision of God and been lifted by it, finds the vision fade and the presence of God recede."[107] She received ten times the volume of the usual reader mail in reply and in 1945, to come to terms with religious depression, wrote *The Dark Night of the Soul*.

Georgia Harkness (1881–1971) studied at Cornell University and received a doctorate from Boston University in 1923. During her youth, she became a Methodist and joined the Student Christian Association and the Student Volunteer movement. "The Social Gospel's vision of human progress combined with the deep personal piety of her childhood to shape her underlying faith."[108] Trained in the Boston Personalist tradition of philosophical theology, she devoted her life to teaching, scholarship, and consideration of important social questions—war and pacifism, immigration and social justice for the poor, racism and civil rights.[109]

Harkness integrated her liberal social concerns with a theology of mysticism—communion with the Holy Spirit, an abiding inward sense of God's love, and a Christ-centered devotional life.[110] The foundation of a Christian life involved the contemplative "vision" of God. She writes that communion with God in this vision compels the Christian to ethical action. "The God who is Lord of all life takes the initiative in love. He discloses himself, in a vision unsurpassed, to those who are formally free but spiritually bound. By this vision, blind eyes are opened and dull hearts quickened to new life."[111]

What happened to the Christian when God withdrew this vision, when the believer felt bereft of God's love? Harkness recounts an early experience of unbelief, of feeling forsaken by God. "I felt alone, bereft, queer. I knew of nobody else who did not believe in God, and was too appalled at myself to talk to anybody about it. I clearly remember lying awake alone at night, sobbing because I could not pray and could have no certainty that God existed."[112]

In 1939 she accepted a teaching position at Garrett Biblical Institute, and contracted brucellosis—a protracted and wasting disease. A fall and severe spinal injury followed. Harkness became emaciated and afflicted with chronic, intractable pain exacerbated by insomnia and depression. She wrote *The Dark Night of the Soul*, taking the title from the classic by John of the Cross, to demonstrate that her nervous breakdown (as she describes this experience) was an opportunity for spiritual renewal and reaffirmation similar to the spiritual exercises of Job, Jeremiah, Guyon, Bunyan, and Fox.

Harkness admits that "when one examines the modern literature of religious therapy and psychology of religion, one finds a surprising vacuum in regard to this experience."[113] Spiritual "dryness," the inner torment of the "sensitive soul who is caught by the unresolved conflict of his insight and his impotence,"[114] needed to be understood on its own terms. How could she conceptualize her season in hell? Did God afflict her as chastisement for sin? Was her nervous breakdown a somatic illness? Robert Burton posed these very questions in *The Anatomy of Melancholy*, and like Harkness, came to view melancholy as both a somatic illness and a condition of the sick soul.

Harkness, like Burton, created an anatomy of religious melancholy, identifying four characteristics of this malady: a frustrated quest for divine presence; self-distrust and self-condemnation; loneliness as isolation from God and other believers; and spiritual impotence—the experience of being trapped and immobilized.[115] She drew upon her particular suffering to define a universal condition that afflicts believers who seek a devotional, inner-worldly, mystical contemplation of the vision of God. Harkness re-presented the anatomy of religious melancholy to mid-twentieth-century Christians.

"The New York tradition" associated with Union Theological Seminary, a center of Liberalism, never abandoned the theological significance of the sick soul in spiritual pilgrimage.[116] The overpowering evidence of religious melancholy that came to light in spiritual biographies forced a reconsideration of these issues. As Freud plumbed the archeology of his own inner life to provide a universal framework for understanding mind, identity, and culture, so Christian autobiographers needed to confront the enduring themes of spiritual pilgrimage and the propensity for religious melancholia.

The study of the relationship of religion to depressive illness owes a debt to Anton Boisen. During his youth, Boisen suffered a difficult and prolonged religious crisis that required two hospitalizations, the first at the Bloomingdale Asylum in 1921. He shared his story and sought to universalize his experience in *Out of the Depths, An Autobiographical Study of Mental Disorder and Religious Experience*. Christian biography and the emphasis upon "religious experience" as transformative crisis made Boisen aware of the centrality of what we have termed the culture-bound syndrome of religious melancholy.

Boisen recounts his pilgrimage from a career in forestry to an awakening and call to a religious vocation in the ministry, service as a chaplain in France and Germany in World War I, and subsequent collapse. Boisen writes of an abiding sense of personal failure, inadequacy and sinfulness, and sexual obsessions during this crisis. He explains: "every crisis period is a period of opportunity and also of danger. It may result in religious quickening, or it may eventuate in mental illness."[117] What psychiatry views as symptom, practical divinity perceives as an exercise of spiritual maturation. Boisen wishes to reclaim the inner world and dynamics of the soul's progress as an alternative to the secular explanatory model of psyche and mental dysfunction.

Boisen was a graduate of Union Theological Seminary, studied psychology at Harvard and Boston Psychopathic Hospital, and worked in a clinical program at Worcester State Hospital. Through his extensive training and autobiographical analysis of his own spiritual crises, he came to the realization that the structure of conversion will induce such crises. He welcomed the time when each believer experiences the discomforting conviction of sin. Speaking of the necessity of the crisis of sin, he writes of his first breakdown, "The church has long taught that conviction of sin is the first step on the road to salvation. It seeks to make a man face the facts of his own life in light of the teachings of Christ and to square his accounts, even though it may make him very uncomfortable."[118]

After his recovery, Boisen worked as an asylum chaplain, theologian, and psychological investigator. He identified the significance of his own illness pattern, and in 1936, published *The Exploration of the Inner World, A Study of Mental Disorder and Religious Experience.* Modeled after James's pragmatic study of religious experience, Boisen's exploration maintained that souls in spiritual pilgrimage journeying toward conversion undertook a wrenching "transformation of character" as they attempted to remake their selves. Boisen argued that types of functional mental disorder also involved individuals attempting radical reorganization of character and identity. What distinguishes the religious pilgrimage from the mental disorder is the outcome, not the process: "The difference lies in the outcome. Where the attempt is successful and some degree of victory is won, it is commonly recognized as religious experience. Where it is unsuccessful or indeterminate, it is commonly spoken of as 'insanity.'"[119]

Religious "heroes" of the seventeenth-century Radical Reformation in England—George Fox, a Quaker, and John Bunyan—exemplify the extreme crisis of the inner world and provide exemplars of creative solutions in the making of a Christian life. Drawing upon the historical precedent of early spiritual biography, Boisen argues that "successful madmen" have emerged from the terrors of the inner world with reintegrations of personality. At these times a wayfaring and inner warfare ". . . seem to be attempts to solve problems, and those problems have to do with the personal destiny and ultimate loyalties and values as seen through the eyes of the individual. Who am I? Why am I in this world?. . . How can I make atonement for my mistakes and sins?"[120] Both Boisen and James understood that a religious system that begins with a divided self and demands a twice-born restructuring of character—the vanquishing of the vile and carnal self requisite to the conversion or turning toward the will of God—entails great risk and psychic costs. These costs include religious melancholy, as James's diagnosis of the existential condition of the believer at war with the self in sinful alienation from the creator, and for Boisen, mental alienation for the unsuccessful pilgrims who find themselves trapped along the way to conversion and character reorganization.

O. Hobart Mowrer's polemic, *The Crisis in Psychiatry and Religion* (1961), argues that mental illness has a religious cause, significance, and treatment. Mowrer brands Freudian psychoanalysis as demonic; he excoriates pastoral theology for denying its birthright by treating the sick soul through psychoanalytic referral, and accuses the Protestant church of encouraging personal irresponsibility and sociopathy.

> ... Calvinist Protestantism took the first major step toward that brand of personal irresponsibility which is sociopathy, by making us supposedly powerless to do anything constructive about our guilt and sin; and then psychoanalysis came along and took us the rest of the way by insisting that not only can we not help ourselves move toward recovery; we are wrong to blame and punish ourselves in the first place.[121]

If we ignore the over-simplifications and purple prose, we can see that Mowrer is calling attention to the need for a reformulated practical divinity and system of pastoral care to answer the secular, anthropocentric discourse in psychiatry that had "overwritten" the religious significance of spiritual crisis and mental alienation with a medicalized explanation of mental illness. He follows in the tradition of fundamentalist attacks upon modern psychology best exemplified by Gresham Machen.

Religious melancholy created by unresolved guilt and accusations of sin was not, according to Mowrer, a quaint epiphenomenon that could be safely ignored. One example of this epiphenomenalism is found in N.J.C. Andreasen's "The Role of Religion in Depression." Andreasen, like so many alienists, conceives of depressive illness as a underlying disease and religion as merely the idiom or vocabulary in which patients express their symptoms. "People suffering from depression often express their illness in terms of religion."[122] Yet Andreasen had to depart from psychiatric terminology and speak to the issues identified by patients: feelings of guilt, sin, and worthlessness, alienation from God, and commission of the unpardonable sin.

This "crisis" in psychiatry and religion was a contest over which explanatory model, theocentric or anthropocentric, would gain ascendancy in determining the diagnostic categories, meaning of illness, and form of therapeutics devised to treat sufferers. Most important, Mowrer identified this crisis not as theoretical disputation, but as one driven by practical exigencies. American Protestantism had embarked upon the Fourth Great Awakening with the resurgence of piety, a heightened emphasis upon mass conversion in the New Evangelicalism of the parachurch. The cases of religious melancholy, of conversion crisis, and those beset by sinful obsessions demanded a new treatment founded upon the dialogue between psychiatry and theology.

Mowrer's attempt to restore primacy to the concept of sin achieved national recognition as the topic of a symposium sponsored by the American Psychological Association in 1959. Albert Ellis presented a paper, "There Is

No Place for the Concept of Sin in Psychotherapy," in which he argued that sin, as Mowrer defined it, produced mental illness. When confronted as a sinner, a believer succumbed to: "(1) a deepseated feeling of personal worthlessness; (2) an obsessive-compulsive occupation with and possible performance of the wrong act for which he is blaming himself; (3) denial or repression of the fact that his immoral act was actually committed by him. . . ."[123] Both Mowrer and Ellis overstate their positions; yet both could agree, based upon Mowrer's own nervous breakdowns and Ellis's clinical experience with patients, that sin produced a spiritual sickness that often led to depressive illness.

Many other psychotherapists and pastoral ministers recognized the significance of religion in depressive disorders. Jesse Cavenar and Jean Spaulding, two psychiatrists who practice in the "Bible Belt," have treated numerous cases of religious melancholy associated with conversion crises. They cite evidence of the evangelical revival in the 1970s reported in the Gallup survey—50 million Americans said they had experienced a rebirth. In an apologetic vein they suggest that many of their patients have been cured of depression through conversion. They do, however, present case studies of suicides and unresolved spiritual crises, and admit that "there is not a scientific explanation of the meaning of religious conversion in the medical literature since Freud's description. . . . This is puzzling, since psychiatrists must treat many patients who have had religious conversions if in fact one in three persons have such an experience."[124]

Pastoral counselors such as Dwight Cumbee have perceived the structure of church doctrine and spiritual direction as inextricably connected to "ecclesiogenic neurosis." Cumbee defines this depression as having its ". . . primary etiology for the rearing, teaching, preaching, and value-setting that has been propagated by churches and church representatives called 'Christian.' "[125]

Cumbee carefully avoids identifying any particular denomination of Christianity, but clearly ecclesiogenic neurosis pertains to New Evangelicalism or fundamentalism, whose teachings and child-rearing produce: "(1) morbid, false or neurotic guilt; (2) despair resulting from the failure of a works/righteousness life style; (3) a 'worm' theology. . . ."[126]

Eric J. Cohen identifies an "induced Christian neurosis," caused by the theological traps and psychological double-binds that confront the faithful in their attempts to find assurance and conversion:

> Christians often become paralyzed and immobilized by their pragmatic struggle to "die so that Christ might live." Each real-life decision thrusts them into an endless discernment as to whether they are truly allowing God to act "through" them or whether they are merely implementing their own human desires and drives. The anxiety which accompanies each decision can escalate to clinical proportions.[127]

Clinical manifestations include obsessive thoughts about committing the unpardonable sin and morbid sinfulness, compulsive indecision, personal rituals to avoid or remit sin, despair over failure to achieve spiritual perfection or consistency in the realization of a religious ethos, and feelings of worthlessness and hopelessness engendered by meditation upon a theology of human depravity.[128]

Terms such as induced Christian neurosis and ecclesiogenic neurosis, like the insights of Boisen, Mowrer, and Harkness that spiritual crises of conversion, sin, and guilt figure prominently in depressive illness, represent recent attempts to conceptualize the culture-bound syndrome of religious melancholy identified by Burton in the seventeenth century. Since twentieth-century religionists and mental healers have long forgotten this concept, they are forced to reinvent it, to rediscover the dialogue between religion and melancholy with considerably less erudition and humor than Burton had shown in *The Anatomy of Melancholy*.

From the 1950s to the present, the proliferation of Christian spiritual guides, inspirational literature, self-help and personal development manuals attests to concerns about, and heightened awareness of, the psychological dimensions of conversion and spirituality. Some individuals have referred to this as the "psychological captivity" of Evangelicalism, wherein the measure of spiritual authenticity revolves around psychological standards of balance and emotional maturity or the alleviation of guilt, anxiety, depression, and stress. The pastoral literature is held captive to the standards of popular psychology, particularly Rogerian concepts of self-realization and Erik Erickson's model of psychosocial development.[129]

E. Brooks Holifield describes what Philip Rieff has termed "the triumph of the therapeutic," where religionists accepted psychoanalytic discourse and recast religious experience as "God's psychiatry," heralding the benefits of faith for emotional health and maturity.[130]

> The introspective piety in the American Protestant heritage—the preoccupation with inwardness, rebirth, conversion, revival—was easily translated into a secular psychological piety. And the new vocabulary of the psychologists and psychotherapists then reshaped the older Protestant vision.[131]

James Hunter terms this Protestant vision an evangelical "psychological Christocentrism—a view of authentic mental and emotional health as rooted in the 'establishment of a harmonious relationship with God through Jesus Christ, for only God really transforms.'"[132]

Hunter examines a score of evangelical "classics" of the Fourth Great Awakening, including Matilda Nordtvedt's *Defeating Despair and Depression*, Maria Nelson's *Why Christians Crack Up*, and Tim LaHaye's *How to Win Over Depression*. In each of these, sin causes emotional suffering, unhappiness, guilt, and mental anguish. The sinner must find his or her way back to God through faith—the means of grace—prayer, Bible reading and study, worship, and pastoral guidance. "If you are a child of God, you have the capacity to live a depressed-free life. That does not guarantee you will, but you possess the external power that will enable you to do so."[133] Psychological Christocentrism proclaims what I term a theme of "life as therapeutic renewal"—the promise of a future-oriented, power of positive thinking optimism where the abundant love of God and mercy of Christ will solve all personal trials.[134]

Psychological Christocentric books on depression adopted a standard formula in delineating the theme of therapeutic renewal. Each manual devoted chapters to the definition, causes, and cure of depressive illness. Roy W. Fairchild's *Finding Hope Again, A Pastor's Guide to Counseling Depressed Persons,* Michael Lawson's *Facing Depression, Toward Healing the Mind, Body & Spirit,* Dorothy Rowe's *Depression, The Way Out of Your Prison,* Richard Winter's *The Roots of Sorrow* and many others use this format. These authors explain depressive illness as an affective disorder caused by many factors: heredity; biochemical imbalances; cognitive proclivities; reactive illness to life events of change, loss, and grief; existential despair: and satanic attack.

From an evangelical perspective, the cure for depression depends upon salvation through faith and godly living. However, some pastoral writers, such as Winter, introduce a theme of "life as pilgrimage" and caution that each believer must engage in warfare against the sinful, fallen world, human depravity, and the temptations of the Devil.

Christian spiritual manuals equivocated over the two divergent themes. Did making a life unavoidably entail inner warfare and times of religious melancholy as suggested by life as pilgrimage? Or could the Christian expect peace, joy, and other abundant fruits of the Spirit as suggested by life as therapeutic renewal? Holifield and David Watt both argue that the theme of life as therapeutic renewal overshadows the sobering life as pilgrimage motif. Holifield points out the contrast between the contemporary emphasis upon the sufficiency of God's love to assist each believer in self-realization and the seventeenth-century obsession with sin and *auto-machia*.

> In the late twentieth century, the people who drew most frequently on the vocabulary of development, growth, actualization, and self-realization often seemed impatient with too much dreary talk about sin; for some, the language of actualization appeared to provide an alternative. In the seventeenth century, in contrast, it was the acute awareness of sin that made it seem necessary to talk about development. Inner development—defined as an increasing "sanctification"—was construed precisely as a struggle against sin.[135]

The awareness of sin at times achieved ascendancy; at other times, however, the sanguine prospect of self-actualization eclipsed the fear and trembling of seventeenth-century themes.

David Harrington Watt has argued that the integration of popular psychology with evangelical religion signals a decline in the efficacy of traditional religion. Psychological Christocentrism reversed the trend for Evangelicals to battle the secular, humanistic worldview of modern psychology that characterized the debates of early fundamentalists in the 1920s and 1930s. Tim LaHaye of the Moral Majority wrote self-help books designed to assist Christians in improving their sex lives, win over depression, find self-acceptance, and overcome anxiety. James Dobson's *Dare to Discipline* incorporates behavior modification into his idea of evangelical child-rearing. In his advice on Christian family life, Bill Gothard's approach resembles transactional analysis. David Watt writes that "By the 1960s, popular evangelicalism had been profoundly influenced by its encounter with modern psychology. A stress on the here and now, a lack of concern for the afterlife, and a constant emphasis on the importance of self-esteem—these were some of the hallmarks of popular evangelicalism in the 1960 and 1970s."[136]

Possibly Watt is correct that the appropriation of popular psychology portends a declining fundamentalist worldview. However, religious authors adopted the motif of life as therapeutic renewal because this satisfied the psychological concerns of the laity. Clearly, the message of popular psychology was critical in addressing the unmet needs of evangelicals with respect to self-esteem, anxiety, and depression. As we have seen, Protestant practical theology has never resolved these questions of psychological assurance, especially for God's chosen and reborn. The messages of popular psychology counterbalanced the dour theme of life as pilgrimage, reassuring children of God that they might find moments of peace, grounds for self-esteem, and the right to personal happiness.

Yet, modern adjustment psychology only palliated the harshness of evangelical Pietist practical divinity, with its haunting seventeenth-century themes of life's pilgrimage as *auto-machia* against sin and the ever present snares of Satan. Writers such as Vernon Grounds made this motif the foundation of their pastoral advice, diminishing the importance of therapeutic renewal.

In *Emotional Problems and the Gospel*, Vernon Grounds rejected the optimism of psychological Christocentrism. Arguing that the Gospel offers *the* answer to the problems and fears that confront people in an age of anxiety, he urges readers to deepen their faith in Jesus. A life of faith does bring an inward peace with God and psychological assurance. However, even the most devout believer is, at times, attacked with fear and doubts. Did not Jesus himself suffer immobilizing anxiety at Gethsemane? The pattern of forging a Christian life involves ceaseless struggle against Satan, sin, temptations of the flesh, doubt, and unbelief.

In his concluding chapter, "A Christian Perspective on Mental Health," Grounds rejects Marie Jahoda's criteria for the "mentally healthy individual," which include self reliance and self-acceptance, self-actualization, an integrated personality with coping skills, and adaptation to the social environment with capacities for love, work, and play. Grounds asks whether or not outstanding spiritual persons such as Paul, Peter, Jan Hus, Calvin, Fox, Bunyan, and David Brainerd "could qualify as models of mental health. . . . Were they well-integrated, well-balanced, well-adjusted individuals, tranquil and relaxed, the kind of people who would be pleasant companions at a beach-party on a summer afternoon?"[137] Spiritual excellence frequently precludes psychological health; thus many evangelical Christians today suffer from scrupulosity, depression, anxiety, and fear.

Grounds maintains that Christianity is primarily concerned with the individual's relationship to God, not with producing healthy mindedness. He shares William James's contempt for the reduction of religion to the pursuit of mental hygiene. Grounds writes a God-centered perspective on mental health:

> 1. An individual, quite completely free from tension, anxiety, and conflict, may be only a well-adjusted sinner who is dangerously maladjusted to God. . . .
> 2. Healthy mindedness may be a spiritual hazard which keeps an individual from turning to God precisely because he has no acute sense of need.
> 3. Emotional illness springing ultimately—*ultimately!*—from the rift which sin has driven between the Creator and creature may prove a disguised blessing, a crisis which compels an individual to face the issues of his divine relationship and eternal destiny.
> 4. Thus in a choice between spiritual renewal and psychic recovery, Christianity unhesitatingly assigns priority to the spiritual dimension of personality.
> 5. Mental illness may be an experience which drives a believer into a deeper faith-commitment; hence mental illness may sometimes be a gain rather than a loss.[138]

Grounds restores life as pilgrimage to the center of Christian living, welcoming religious melancholy as an opportunity for spiritual quickening and maturation. Other writers emphasize another aspect of pilgrimage—the ubiquity of religious melancholy occasioned by satanic attack.

Matilda Nordtvedt recounts her collapse and institutionalization, attributing her "dark tunnel" at age forty-two to Satan, who brought doubt, tempting her to disappointment, depression, and discouragement.[139] Maria Nelson ascribes depression to satanic attack and urges her readers to gird themselves for warfare: "Satan's aim with Christians is to get them to do that which is contrary to God's Word and to prevent them from obeying God. In order to promote his plan he tries to deceive the Christian as to what is the truth."[140]

D. Martyn Lloyd-Jones's *Spiritual Depression, Its Causes and Cure* places much of the blame for spiritual depression upon the work of the devil. "From the moment we become Christians we become the special objects of the attention of the devil. As he besieged and attacked our Lord, so does he besiege and attack the Lord's people."[141]

C. S. Lewis reiterates this message in *The Screwtape Letters*, written as a serial for *The Guardian* during World War II. Lewis embarks upon a sardonic adventure in the form of letters of advice and supervision between devils as they attempt to turn one man away from God and win his soul for Satan. The entire correspondence reveals the many dimensions of satanic attack upon believers, and is a scathing criticism of human folly. Letters 7 and 9 focus upon how to exploit periods of spiritual dryness when Christians descend into the "Slough of Despond," when they "undulate" between peace and despair.[142] Lewis's series remains in print fifty years after first publication as an enduring spiritual manual.

Nancy Tatum Ammerman's study of a fundamentalist sect finds that believers struggle daily with Satan. As one member states: '. . . Satan is going to try and discourage you right away. You have to warn new Christians right away so they will be prepared.'[143]

Steven Tipton's *Getting Saved from the Sixties* presents a case study of a charismatic Pentecostal sect, the pseudonymous Living World Fellowship (LWF), a "born-again, spirit-filled fellowship numbering 300 members."[144] LWF members come from lower-middle-class and countercultural backgrounds. Located in a San Francisco suburb, the church attracts "Jesus freaks" who have abandoned this-worldly Gnosticism, a drug-induced quest for ecstasy, community founded upon individual freedom, spontaneity, and cosmic love of the counterculture. They have renounced the worldview of collectivities of like-minded individuals who had dropped out of conventional middle-class families and careers, tuned in to the cosmic harmonies of love's vibrations, and turned on to new communities of open sexuality and expanded consciousness supported by the ethos of "do-your-own-thing." The fabled "death of hippie" in the 1967 "summer of love" in Haight-Asbury—the bad trips, hard drug abuse, violence, commercialization of the flower children, and other disillusionments, left counterculturalists disoriented and bitter about the failure of their early lives. "Tales of injury, betrayal, and cruel indifference among fellow hippies are commonplace in LWF testimony."[145] The LWF founded by "Pastor Bobbi" provided an opportunity to reconstruct their lives in psychologically satisfying ways by adopting the worldview and ethos of an "authoritative Christian" sect.

> In the atmosphere of disappointment and depression that followed the conflicts and failures of the sixties, many youths sought out alternative religious movements. Disoriented by drugs, embittered by politics, disillusioned by the apparent worthlessness of work and the transiency of love, they found a way back through these movements, a way to get along with conventional American society and to cope with the demands of their own maturing lives.[146]

The LWF based its church community upon Pastor Bobbi's special prophetic rendering of Pentecostal teachings and Matthew 22:37-40: "Do God's will and Love Him!" The LWF offers membership only to the religiously qualified who have experienced a rebirth and have devoted their lives to obedience to God's will. The LWF supports an ethos of inner-worldly asceticism prohibiting premarital and extramarital sexuality and de-emphasizing marital eroticism. The church prohibits any form of drug use, and requires that believers fight constantly against the flesh, sin, and the ever present powers of Satan. Conversion entails the recitation and rejection of one's previous hippie biography, the living testimony of what Jesus has done for the believer, the ecstatic surrender of the reborn self—the "circumcision of the heart"— that creates the seal of the covenant with God. Clearly, the new member joins a Christian fellowship of strict moral authority based upon biblical literalism, codes of love that regulate *agape*, *philos*, and *eros*, and a church community committed to separation from the fallen world in these times of tribulation, in preparation as Christian survivalists for the postmillennial Advent. Within this millenarian worldview and religious rejection of secular society, human relationships are imbued with ethical meaning by God-willed codes of conduct because only worthy, true Christians will ascend in the rapture at the apocalyptic end of time. Personality is forged upon this powerful idea of salvation, which emphasizes purity of the heart and ceaseless *auto-machia*. LWF members enjoy many of the pentecostal gifts of the spirit in worship including "speaking in tongues," testifying, and ecstatic-cathartic moments of self-transcendence as the Holy Spirit enters their hearts. Like others who seek the possession of God's *pneuma*, they encounter times of spiritual desolation. Thus, members are not immune to religious melancholy or threats of demonic attack, as one recent convert recounts during a pastoral conversation with Pastor Bobbi:

> She began to pray for me right there, and I actually doubled over—this is without ever having seen a deliverance or knowing anything about screaming demons, none of that. I began feeling something coming up through my body from my stomach through my mouth. It was like water all stopped up with a cork, and every time the cork moves, you can feel a tug. It was a horrible thing. After a while the demon actually used my voice. It came all the way from the bottom of my gut, this terrible voice. . . . My body went berserk. It was fighting and trying to knock off the ministers who were holding me down. It was the demon fighting back, because it was being threatened.[147]

The elements necessary to form the Christian personality required by adherents of the LWF include the heroic inward struggle against sin and the outward battles against sin, worldliness, and Satan. Although, as Tipton argues, the church has rescued marginalized individuals who were cast adrift in a drugged itinerancy, and offers powerful institutional and psychological supports, believers do suffer times of spiritual desolation—religious melancholy.

Olive Wyon's *On The Way* is a handbook for making a Christian life as a pilgrimage leading to wholeness, union with God and dark nights of the soul, Christian warfare against sin, and never-ending battles against the idolatry of the self through "purgation."

> This process of "purgation" or purification comes about in different ways: sometimes mainly through a deepened awareness of God, given in prayer; sometimes through the more painful experiences of life. . . . But when we know what God is doing with us, and that He is using all these different experiences to cleanse us from pride and self-will, we are at peace.[148]

The issues of religious melancholy that were first identified by pastoral theology in the seventeenth century and codified into a culture-bound syndrome by Robert Burton did not disappear in the twentieth century. The New Evangelicals, and fundamentalists and Pentecostals viewed Christian life as a constant inner battle against the inroads of sin, against the active demonic personality of Satan as a real force in the world and in the lives of each believer. Although a psychological Christocentrism might seek to reassure the perplexed and remit the guilt of those beset by convictions of sin, the marrow of this practical divinity and pastoral theology resonated with seventeenth-century themes of religious melancholy. Contemporary Evangelicals, like their seventeenth-century predecessors, found themselves trapped in a slough of despond, in warfare against Satan's fiery darts, in anguish over unpardonable sins, and disconsolate at being forsaken by God.

Ammerman's study of the "Southside" fundamentalist congregation reveals a "theodicy of dualism," with believers engaged in a lifelong battle with Satan that leads them through severe tests of faith and a pilgrimage of spiritual growth. Through painful surrender of self and will to God, believers find assurance of divine love. Step outside of God's plan through sin, and Southside members knew that God would forsake them.[149] Despite the ebullient optimism that members express, they do suffer times of religious melancholy.

Elaine Lawless's study of the Oneness Pentecostal Church, *God's Peculiar People,* reveals an ecstatic religion of speaking in tongues, trances, possession by the Holy Spirit, praying, singing, shouting, and testifying. When these Pentecostalists "get happy," "get a blessing," and the church is like a "house on fire for God," religious experience offers an opportunity for emotional catharsis, and a anticlimatic peace that passeth all natural understanding is common for believers after testifying. The other side of ecstasy requires a wrestling with God, a battle with the Devil, and inner struggle against sin. Are not these the very elements from which religious melancholy emerges as a culture-bound syndrome?[150]

Susan F. Harding investigates fundamentalist Baptist conversion and the obligation to bear witness and induce in others a spiritual crisis through an awareness of being lost in sin, of coming under conviction.

> When you come under conviction, you cross through a membrane into belief; when you get saved, you cross another membrane out of disbelief. This passage is more problematic for some lost souls, for what outsiders would say were reasons of education, class, intellect, and insiders would say was hardness of the heart, ego or pride, the work of the devil.[151]

Do not these trials of conversion and spiritual maturation pertain to the key question of the persistence of religious melancholy? The case studies of fundamentalist and Pentecostal sects all point to the continuity of religious melancholy in contemporary America.

A second major mass revivalism, the healing and charismatic movements of the Neo-Pentecostals, have changed the American religious landscape since World War II, creating parachurch institutions and national evangelical leaders who circumvented denominational control or local church influence. David Edwin Harrell's *All Things Are Possible, The Healing and Charismatic Revivals in Modern America*, analyzes the rise of national tele-evangelists such as Oral Roberts, Kathryn Kuhlman, Rex Humbard, Jimmy Swaggert, Gordon

Lindsay, and many others. By the 1970s an estimated five million Americans, many from the business elite and the college-educated middle classes, had participated in this Neo-Pentecostalism.[152]

The early healing revivals and the subsequent charismatic parachurch Evangelism differed from the New Evangelicalism of Billy Graham and the National Association of Evangelists (NAE). Unlike mainstream Evangelicals, "theirs was a signs-gifts-healing, a salvation-deliverance, a Holy Ghost-miracle revival. Salvation from sin was preached, but, whatever the intention of the evangelist, it was never the central theme of their meetings. . . . The common heartbeat of every service was the miracle—the hypnotic moment when the Spirit moved to heal the sick and raise the dead."[153]

Neo-Pentecostalism proclaimed a theocentric life as therapeutic renewal founded not upon popular psychology but upon the gifts of the Holy Spirit to heal sickness. However, the counterpoint of life as pilgrimage achieved a competing prominence as revivalists emphasized demonic attack in the lives of believers. The battles with Satan produced temptations to sin, the withdrawal of the Holy Spirit, and the onset of disease and mental illness. During the 1960s Oral Roberts preached the message that demon possession caused illness as he claimed to cast out evil spirits from the afflicted.

A. A. Allen wrote two books on the perils of satanic attack and became the Pentecostal specialist in this subject. In the 1963 book, *Curse of Madness*, Allen reported "clinical" evidence of eighteen pictures of demons that possessed one mental patient. "These Satanic beings have the power to torment you mentally and physically until you are driven into the insane asylum, and the Lord permits it when disobedience is continued."[154]

Let us consider a final example of contemporary Christian biography, *New Life in the Church* (1961), by Robert A. Raines. In this autobiography we see the motifs of therapeutic renewal and pilgrimage in dynamic tension. A voice in the Fourth Great Awakening, Raines endeavored to reanimate the Liberal Protestant tradition that had lost a sense of mission. Small, charismatic prayer groups would encourage devotional piety and a renewed concern for aggressively evangelical conversion. He found "new life in the church" and, in his own life, profound spiritual growth through fellowship in Aldersgate Church in Cleveland, Ohio, in the late 1950s. Both spiritual biography and pastoral guide, his book proclaims the *koinonia* group as a proven experiment of experiential religion. James Luther Adams defines *koinonia pneumatos* as those who receive, following the teachings of Paul, the rushing wind of God, "which in immediacy gathers the ecstatic band of believers into the unity of the eschatological community of the Spirit. . . . These *charismata* have a common source in the Holy Spirit, and they are subordinate to the love of the brethren and the upbuilding of the church."[155] The ecstatic freedom of the spirit breaks through the deadening bureaucratization and moralism of the church, encouraging an appeal to the "inner light," and the religion of the transmoral conscience as a grounding for individual action and freedom.

Raines's pastoral guide to questions of conversion heralds the efficacy of *koinonia* groups in promoting a fellowship of the Holy Spirit—the privatization of piety and religious fervor. These groups fulfill the requirements of evangelical Pietism: the reliance upon scriptural guidance, the immediacy of a personal relationship to God, and the continued need for pneumatics, or the illumination of divine love and spirit in the soul of each believer. It will come as no surprise that religious melancholy is a common feature in Raines's discussion of spirituality. He writes of the prideful, selfish heart, captive to sin, and the neverending battle against the will for those called as disciples. "We all go through these times of depression and dryness in our spiritual life when the romantic glow of our early turning to God is fading, and we have to face the realistic business of making this commitment work and grow to maturity. We are now entering the severest struggle of life, the struggle to overcome ourselves."[156]

Raines suggests that each believer who perseveres as a disciple of Christ will enjoy increasing spiritual maturity, especially when assisted by daily devotions in the "means of grace." In *koinonia* groups of Christian fellowship, the wayfarer could read and study the Bible, bear witness, serve others, and offer charitable acts. Speaking for himself and many in his congregation, he universalizes the contribution of this fellowship to forging *authentic* Christian personhood.

> The new life *has* come for many. There is again a stirring in our souls, a warming of our hearts, a stretching of the mind, a new power for our wills. There is rising among us a sense of urgent mission. . . . It is life in the Spirit. It brings forth the desire to serve and witness. Although we are only in the infancy of this new creation, we know that we are being driven on mission into the world.[157]

Raines's pronouncement of a new age for individuals and the church, founded upon the work of charismatic communities during the Fourth Great Awakening, reaffirms the stance taken during the Radical Reformation in seventeenth-century England. James Luther Adams terms this the "Age of the Spirit," which "brings in its train the demand for freedom of Spirit and of conscience, a radical laicism and new forms of ecclesiastical and social organization that disperse power and responsibility. Indeed, a new conception of an autonomous Christian personality supported by 'inner light'. . . ."[158]

What Raines fails to understand is the propensity for evangelical Pietists to suffer religious melancholia. Wed to the pneumatics of receiving the continued infusion of the Holy Spirit, members of *koinonia* will encounter many dark nights of the soul. Like Edward J. Carnell, Raines came to an even more startling inward awareness as he approached middle age.

A decade later, in 1970, this spiritual center of conversion and authenticity could no longer hold for Raines. Things fell apart. He tells this part of his biography in *Going Home,* resuming the narrative as a forty-year-old minister, married to a devoted wife, and about to assume the duties of a new parish in Columbus, Ohio. Raines decides to spend twelve days at the National Training Laboratory in Bethel, Maine, before assuming his new duties. In this intensive round of counterculture-style encounters, he experiences a transformative break, the beginnings of a middle-life crisis and a confrontation with the long repressed anger toward his father engendered in childhood.

> It was as though I'd been damming up my tears for forty years and they wouldn't be contained any longer. The shaking, sobbing, and heaving were totally strange and appalling. . . . [A man asked,] "What do you resent?" I heard myself saying, "I resent God for loading on me this burden of obligation. I resent my parents for laying this trip on me and the church for binding me into my role, and I resent myself for buying it all."[159]

The catharsis at Bethel produced a litany of complaints and charges: of living in a repressive shell, of unreflecting obedience to the will of God and the discipline and expectations of an authoritarian father, a retired bishop of the United Methodist church. Raines also felt the stultifying effects of extreme sexual repression, trapped within a façade marriage built upon the foundations of mutual weaknesses. His personal, professional, and spiritual life appeared counterfeit, hollow, and lacking in authenticity. He writes of self-alienation:

> I had emphasized in my experience and practice of Christianity a piety that was desiccated, prudish, desexed, moralistic, and legalistic. I put a smooth patina over what was rough, abrasive, ugly, and raw in me. I exalted order and tried to excommunicate chaos from myself and the systems in which I operated.[160]

True to the cultural logic of the 1960s, he eventually dropped out of his parish and career, his marriage, and even his life. He tuned into new messages—a vocabulary of Jungian and life-span developmental psychology, in pointing the way home to the authentic self. He began a new marriage and new pastoral duties as director of a retreat and a psychoanalytic foundation for spirituality. The previous charismatic basis for making a Christian life through evangelical Pietism no longer "worked" for Raines. He did not come to the realization that this system of belief, ethos, and religiously grounded personality might in fact be pathogenic, personally, for him, and institutionally, for many others. He did not renounce his previous advocacy of evangelical Pietism, or see the connection with religious melancholy. He only had to refashion his former self and recast his protean identity in the terms of a psychologically informed American individualism.[161]

In summary, the evidence found in spiritual biographies from liberal, fundamentalist, and Pentecostal believers reveals the persistence of religious melancholy. When people embrace a worldview of a cosmic battle between God and Satan, and a religiously grounded personality forged in *auto-machia*, selfless surrender to Christ, and the continual devotional need for the infusion of God's Holy Spirit, then religious melancholy is unavoidable. When sufferers attempted to understand the times when they felt forsaken by God, they looked to seventeenth-century models of piety as exemplars of the successful life as pilgrimage. Paradoxically, they also found solace in the Christocentric psychology that promised life as therapeutic renewal. So many troubled souls remain trapped in the alternation between these two motifs that recast William James's dialectic between the religion of healthy mindedness, and the religion of the twice-born.

James offered no ready solution to the paradoxes of asceticism or the urge to flee from its discomforts into the popular psychology of mental hygiene. To those who seek the spiritual heroics of the twice-born, he advises:

> Let us be saints, then, if we can, whether or not we succeed visibly and temporally. But in our Father's House are many mansions, and each of us must discover for himself the kind of religion and the amount of saintship which best comports with what he believes to be his powers and feels to be his truest mission and vocation. There are no successes to be guaranteed and no set orders to be given to individuals, so long as we follow the methods of empirical philosophy.[162]

The Future of Religious Melancholy

In his 1987 Warfield Lecture, Roy W. Fairchild identified an upsurge of spirituality in America evidenced by the vitality of new religious movements and by the masses of Americans who reported to researchers of their hunger for an experience of transcendence. The term "spirituality" has displaced the older Protestant vocabulary that included concepts of piety, devotion, godliness, holiness, and the devout life.[163] Fairchild explains: "The spiritual person is one who is indwelt by the Holy Spirit of God. You are spiritual when you have God's life in you—in, with, and under all you are."[164]

With so many Americans looking inward in spiritual pilgrimage, Fairchild hungers for contemporary "theological diagnosticians" to guide the perplexed, as Jonathan Edwards and William James did in past times. He asks, "What will it take for us to be spiritual guides in the midst of the spiritual explosion of our day? How do we deal with our dispirited selves?"[165]

In his congregation at Ross Christian Church in Ross, Ohio, George Mark Fisher researched congregants who felt forsaken by God. Fisher himself succumbed to religious melancholy before accepting his ministerial duties at Ross and wished to explore the more universal dimensions of this spiritual sickness. He began his project by preaching special sermons to educate his congregants about the biblical context of being forsaken by God and to create a milieu where people felt encouraged to speak freely about this sensitive matter. He then conducted surveys, focus groups, and individual interviews.

The crisis engendered by feeling forsaken of God involved the perception of abandonment by Him, usually caused by personal adversity. This feeling can lead to depression, despair, and the imitation of the crucified Christ, who exclaimed, "My God, my God, why have you forsaken me?" (Matt. 27:46)[166]

Fisher discovered that this feeling of forsakenness was very prevalent among members of his church. He concludes:

I had thought that many people in the church had probably felt forsaken
by God, yet were not willing to say so. The issue of forsakenness, I thought,
was one of those taboo topics among Christians. Yet, given the right context, people would reveal that it was fairly common to feel abandoned by
God. My findings showed that this was indeed the case.[167]

Fairchild and Fisher concur that a religious life founded upon the immediacy of the indwelling spirit (spirituality or God's presence in one's heart)
also produced problems of "dispirited souls," and those who feel bereft of
God in their hearts. In the light of these findings, the future of religious melancholy unfortunately looks bright.

Ideas never die out completely, they just pass in and out of currency, at
times championed by factions removed from the mainstream, only later to
return to preeminence in subsequent revitalizations. Even during the half-
century of liberalism in American political and religious thought, religious
melancholy persisted. Varieties of religious melancholy (*anfechtungen*) have
always been associated with Anabaptist conventicles and intentional communities in America such as those of the Hutterites and the Bruderhof.[168]

This study has been largely confined to evangelical Pietism in New
England during a century of revivalism. Other times, places, and denominations were not included. Examination of religious melancholy in Baptist and
Methodist groups, whether on the frontiers or in long-settled parts of America,
and in the context of the holiness and fundamentalist movements, would
broaden and enrich our understanding. Religious melancholy pertaining to
adherents and apostates of contemporary "New Religious movements," of
cults, healing sects, and the charismatic revival within Catholicism and Protestant groups merit future study.

Consideration of these questions shall remain for another time and another
telling. We shall conclude by remembering that evangelical Pietism drew upon
the structure of religious experience and selfhood of Augustinian piety. Religious personality, self, and identity were forged in the crucible of redemptive
suffering. Many believers freely chose to live inside this prison of ideas—to
constitute their identity in the self-torture of *auto-machia*. Others who suffered evangelical nurture and languished in spiritual desolation were trapped,
not by their own choice, but by the persistent memory of childhood cruelty.
By desire or accident of birth, wherever Protestants committed themselves to
the heroic pilgrimage of forging a life consistent with the ultimate values of
devotional piety, of achieving a religiously grounded personality that demands
the rationalization of the self and the body, and accepts as the seal of grace
the inward assurance of God's love, religious melancholy afflicted them. With
life cast as a continual inner warfare and a rejection of the "natural man,"
melancholy reigned.

The motifs of *psychomacy* and the "iron of melancholy" have endured
and continue to leave their imprint upon American religious identity, according to John Owen King. This cultural text continues to shape the spirituality
of late-twentieth-century Protestants and presents a cruel irony. Believers who

strive to cultivate a lifelong, personal relationship with God, often find themselves bereft of the Spirit—forsaken by God. Those devoted to making a Christian life by ceaselessly nurturing their souls embrace a regimen of obsessional pathology that puts their psyches in jeopardy.

Who can say that this culture-bound syndrome, which passed out of fashion by the year 1900 only to re-emerge at mid-century with the Fourth Great Awakening, will not reappear in the future in revitalized forms? As the millennial year 2000 nears, Americans flee in disillusionment from the icon of the dynamo or the psychoanalytic ideal of the harmonious soul, self-accepting, and residing in a "good-enough" world. For who among us can state with conviction that they live in a good-enough world?

Appendix A: Pastoral Care

Pastoral care pertains to a system of practical theology and directives provided to the laity and ministers who would advise, guide, sustain, and heal persons suffering from religious melancholy or other maladies. In its many forms and long history, Protestant pastoral care never resolved the central question of remission of sin or nagging doubts about assurance of election as a child of God.[1] Without recourse to sacramental, magical, and confessional means of resolving spiritual agony, individual Protestants confronted doubt versus assurance, and sin versus sanctification. The table and discussion that follow investigate how evangelical and moderate forms of pastoral care in the early nineteenth century attempted to guide, sustain, assure, and heal religious melancholias.

Modes of Pastoral Care

	Sentiment	Volition	Rationality	Personality
Evangelical Pastoral Care	Benevolence	Evangelical Arminianism	Identification with transcendental Other	Evangelical self
Moderate Pastoral Care	Domestic religion	Sin as choice not ontology	Consciousness concept	Self-culture

The categories of sentiment, volition, rationality, and personality prove useful in the analysis of the differing mentalities of early nineteenth-century Protestants. Sentiment refers to the experience and expression of emotions, including the cultural directives that provided templates for the affective life. Volition pertains to the perceived powers and limitations of action, agency, and the free exercise of the will. Rationality refers to the capacity of the knowing subject to enjoy the use of reason, the intellect, and most important, the theological grounds for discovering truth about one's own life and religious status. Personality is a religiously grounded life-order devoted to the realization of ultimate values, or other forms of personhood.

241

Evangelical pastoral care gushed forth with extremes of sentimentality symbolized by the emotionally effusive vision of a perfect, loving deity whose moral government and plan for all humankind and for America, in particular, was organized around the principle of benevolence. In the refreshing showers of the Holy Spirit, assisted by human means through the use of revival techniques, all people could be brought under divine influence. Through the emotional crucible of self-abnegation and ecstasy, regenerate Christians, in cooperation with God's benevolent moral government, would dedicate their lives to some form of Christian activism and reform. Sentiment fused with perfectionism in the idea of the masses renouncing sin, turning toward God, and eradicating evil from society, thereby hastening the millennial day.

Evangelicals acknowledged an Arminian idea—humans' ability to choose God as their portion—as we have seen in the discussion of Edwards, Hopkins, and New Divinity thought. However, the question of the status of sin and its ontology remained ambiguous. The concept of innate depravity—a vestige of earlier Calvinism—continued to be part of evangelical thought. All were born into sin, yet people enjoyed the power of the will to reject their nature, choose godliness, and seek self-transformation and perfection from sin. However, the power of the will alone could not effect this transformation.

Evangelicals emphasized that through reason sinners might learn the dry truths of God's word. However, only when the religious affections had been excited by human or divine agency, in the throes of emotional catharsis, could the sinner proceed toward grace. The wholly external, transcendent seal of grace from God, transmitted by the irradiation of God's love and spirit ravishing the hearts of the penitent, proved satisfactory as evidence of conversion. In his work *Consciousness in New England*, James Hoopes argues "Out of abject surrender emerged a triumphant identification with the Other. There *was* a contradiction in the attempt of the self to escape the self, but the contradiction, far from showing conversion to have been a delusion, was the hinge on which conversion swung."[2]

Finally, Evangelical pastoral care portrayed adult personality as one forged in the sudden, terrifying awakening of the slumbering sinner and the annihilation of the carnal self, and, through the ecstatic moment of selflessness, reconstituted into a new identity as a contemplative self—the humble child of God. As we have seen, the evangelical Pietist devoted a life to religious humiliation in search for the episodic recovery of the contemplative experience of God's love and the warmhearted assurance of grace. The mentality as represented by evangelical pastoral care legitimated "ultraism"—the resource to extreme measures to realize religiously valued ends.[3] Religious excitement was necessary and indispensable to bring sinners to God. Excesses of self-abnegation and evangelical humiliation were legitimated as measures proven to effect conversion and to cause the converted person to remain on his or her pilgrimage toward sanctification and the ultimate glorification of God. For example, Finney testified to the proven experimental principle of fasting in assisting him in recovering the Spirit of God—the identification with the Other, the external evidence that certified each believer's state of grace.

Moderate pastoral care articulated a controlled, temperate, and balanced emotional economy represented by images of domestic religion, domestic affection, practiced within the sentimentalized family circle. The profusion of tracts published in the nineteenth century defined domestic religion and "depicted a family scene with mother and children gathered around as father read from pious literature. . . ."[4] Jesus, symbolizing the qualities of patience and gentleness, was upheld as a meek and loving model for all to imitate in their lives.

Philip Greven refers to "moderate" forms of religiously grounded personality and Protestant character in America as one alternative to evangelical selfhood:

> Moderates shared the conviction that legitimate authority, parental as well as other kinds, was limited, that human nature was sinful but not altogether corrupted, that reason ought to govern the passions, that a well-governed self was temperate and balanced, and that religious piety ought to be infused with a concern for good and virtuous behavior as well as for grace. . . . The dominate theme that recurs in the lives and writings of these moderate and authoritative families over the centuries is one of "love and duty" rather than "love and fear" which marked so many evangelical families.[5]

Those who followed the moderate modes of Protestant personality and life-order perceived that the love of the child for the parent, and of each person for God, served as the motivation for a voluntary, affectionate obedience. Parents could use this abiding affection for their children to mold the child's character and bend the will. A child's character and personality were understood to develop in a gradual process from infancy until adolescence. Parents planted the seeds of virtue and nurtured their charges with love by setting limits and boundaries for action and the expression of emotion. Each adult personality needed to adopt a form of self-government and rigorous self-control that internalized these limits. Moderate personality was devoted to engendering habits of sober, temperate, and balanced inner regulation of human appetites and emotions. Through temperate self-denial in diet, dress, and consumption styles, through systematic industriousness and self-discipline, each person forged a life of moralism and duty.

The moderate eschewed evangelical ideals of will-breaking, the conquest of the child, and the total submission of each personality to the parents' will and later, the will of God. They rejected the extreme inner conflict of *automachia*, attempts at self-annihilation, and the self-mortifying asceticism of the Evangelical. In place of piety and the sudden conversion experience, the moderate embraced a life of unremitting moralism—of ethically correct conduct. The moderate needed to find a balance in life and eschew unbridled ambition, avarice, conspicuous consumption, and the outward expression of anger. Each indicated a loss of self-control and the failure of the inner goal of moderation and temperance in all things. Moderates recognized that the free exercise of political and economic rights in the new republic had a parallel effect upon the idea of human volition and will in spiritual matters. As E. Brooks Holifield argues in *A History of Pastoral Care in America*, "The combined forces of revivalism, the Wesleyan theology, the New Haven Doctrines, and the Unitarian movement were sufficient to move popular American Protestantism gradually towards an understanding of sin as an act rather than a status—as a volitional decision rather than a common condition."[6] Sin was a willful disobedience of an ethical code, a failure of duty, an act and not an ontological status of innate depravity.

Moderate pastoral care depicted rationality through the concept of "consciousness." This refers to the importance of John Locke's empiricism, and to Scottish moralists such as Thomas Reid and Dugal Stewart and their epistemology that granted to each person the capacity for self-reflective knowledge. Consciousness was defined "as the mind's cognizance of its own phenomenon."[7] Each knowing subject had immediate access to, and certain knowledge about, the faculties and operation of his or her mind: perceptions, sensations, emotions, volitions, and desires. Armed with this new "way of ideas," moderates could refuse to undergo a conversion process that involved humiliation, selflessness, and submersion into the Other. For example, Catherine Beecher proclaimed her own self-sufficiency in her relationship with God.[8] Evangelicals like Finney employed the consciousness concept to ascertain a self-righteous certainty of their actions. In this manner the empirical mental science notion of consciousness might coexist or conflict with the evangelical concept of a conscience dependent upon God for truth claims. Affinity for the consciousness concept influenced the New Divinity thought of Edwards, Hopkins, and their followers, nineteenth-century New Haven theology, and other evangelical schools.[9] For the religious melancholiac, the mix and balance of conscience versus consciousness weighed heavily on the scale of the scrupulous mind. Moderate pastoral care attempted to replace the tortured conscience that awaited God's external evidence of love with the self-assured, self-reflective, and knowing consciousness that eschewed humiliation and found inner harmony in the habits of moralism.

Moderate pastoral care de-emphasized the vital or experiential piety of Evangelicals and, in its place, promoted self-culture. Self-culture entailed "unremitting self-control: the control of appetites, passions, pride, envy, and covetousness."[10] The moderate self needed to shape a life in conformity with the ethical issues of religious moralism and the will of God. But this self, unlike that of the evangelical, did not seek to discover God's will through devotional piety and exercises of contemplative flight. God's will was knowable when the self was brought into conformity with higher ideals codified in moderation, industry, self-control, and benevolence towards others. Self-culture envisioned an balance of reason, the affections, and volition.

Appendix B:
Revivalists as Mediatorial Elites

During the four periods of religious revitalization in America, national evangelical leaders redefined the nature of the morphology of conversion in response to a perceived crisis in religion and society. As William McLoughlin has argued, awakenings are revitalizations of culture, responses to

> critical disjunctions in our self-understanding. They are not brief outbursts of mass emotionalism by one group or another but profound cultural transformations affecting all Americans and extending over a generation or more. Awakenings begin in periods of cultural distortion and grave personal stress, when we lose faith in the legitimacy of our norms, the viability of our institutions, and the authority of our leaders in church and state. They eventuate in basic restructurings of our institutions and redefinitions of our social goals.[1]

In these times of cultural revitalization, revivalists help forge new meanings about the covenants that constitute our American identity. The covenant of grace that directs the meaning of conversion and making of a Christian life, the church covenants that define instrumental activism and the Social Gospel in local communities, and the federal covenant of America as a nation under God's mandate; all of these undergo revision and renewal in times of awakening. And revivalists bring these new cultural meanings to the masses, instructing them how to make a godly life and find salvation, how to reform their local communities, and how to participate in building the Kingdom of God in America. In this manner, evangelical leaders act as mediatorial elites, transmitting the new cultural forms to Americans. Benjamin Nelson's cultural sociology helps explain the function of mediatorial elites.

Nelson developed the foundation for a theory of cultural sociology in a 1964 essay, "Cultural Cues and Directive Systems."[2] Cultures may be interpreted through a series of interrelated metaphors:

> a. Culture as a *Dramatic Design*, serving to redeem time from the sense of flux by investing passage and process with the appearance of aim, purpose, and historical form.

b. Culture as *Defensive System*, comprising an array of beliefs and attitudes that help to defend us against vexing doubts, anxieties, and aggressions.

c. Culture as a *Directive System*, that is, a complex of instructions charging us to perceive, feel, think and perform in desired ways.

d. Culture as a *Symbol Economy* . . . Society is here perceived to constitute an inevitably scarce supply of coveted symbols.[3]

The conceptualization of culture as a directive system demonstrated how the shared meanings that oriented persons to act according to prescribed norms were communicated by special "mediatorial elites," or "influential others." In the most general sense these elites included yogis, philosophers, psychiatrists, commissars, cultural paragons, and cynosures who shouldered the responsibility of defending the interests of governing powers, and of recruiting, interpreting, and directing others. Key functionaries in the institutional domains of religion, polity, philosophy, science, and medicine served in this role. They invented, dispensed, or consumed the coveted rewards obtained from a symbolic economy. Nelson maintained that members of a mediatorial elite "achieve, maintain, and reinforce their position by appearing to offer convincing evidence that they control access to (or supremely embody) central values which are highly prized by significant numbers of people whatever they may be seeking: self-definition, social significance, meaning, influence, deference, income, salvation, health, or whatever."[4]

Nelson argued that directive culture operated as *streams of cues* "which are mediated to individuals with a view to charging and aiding them to define and respond to any possible point of reference—sign, symbol, object, event, person, situation—they might chance to encounter or fancy."[5] Nelson identified six distinct classes of cues, which include:

(1) Percipienda cues—this first and most embracing class of cues comprises directives which charge us to perceive any possible object, person, or occasion in one way or another way.

(2) Sentienda cues—this second class of cues directs us to have one or another feeling in relation to any possible person, object, event, or situation. . . .

(3) Agenda cues—this third set of cues charges us to perform or not to perform one or another act on sanction of penalty or promise of reward.

(4) Credenda cues—are those signals or symbols which tell us what or how we ought to believe or not to believe.

(5) Miranda cues—are those directives which define what or whom or how we ought to hold in awe, what or whom we ought to marvel at.

(6) Emulanda cues—this sixth set of cues influences us to emulate persons or imitate behaviors of those presented to us as role models, social paradigms, cynosures.[6]

McLoughlin views religious revitalization as a form of cultural therapeutic that restores individual and national self-confidence. In Nelson's terms, the formulation of new systems of spiritual direction and collective identity are mediated to diverse publics by elites, who direct people to see, feel, believe, marvel, emulate, and understand the order of things in their lives. The streams of cultural cues transcend the preceding period of anomic crisis and achieve greater consistency, stability, and congruity with the actual experience of social "reality."

The idea of revitalization as cultural catharsis and therapy, or culture as an orienting map, however, neglects the important insight of John Owen King. He suggests that religious leaders ("mediatorial elites," in Nelson's parlance) introduced and elaborated a morphology of spiritual conversion founded upon seventeenth-century English Puritanism. Bunyan's *Pilgrim's Progress*, Timothy Bright's and Robert Burton's discussions of religious melancholy, among others, formed a core of devotional texts, a genre that Americans would follow as guides to orient the faithful in the arduous journey of godly living. In every era, from colonial settlement until the present, Americans would return to these texts as exemplars of piety.

King argues that the conceptualization of an American self and Protestant religious identity rests upon a foundation replete with obsessional pathology, stamped by the "iron of melancholy."[7] Religious and cultural elites, from Cotton Mather to Billy Graham, embraced the evangelical Pietism of seventeenth-century English Puritanism, interpreting it in light of the predicaments of their times, building upon the motifs of spiritual pilgrimage, the inward battle against the self (*psychomacy*), and inevitability of religious melancholy. These elites published and promulgated the stories of their individual journeys of conversion, seeking to universalize their experiences for others to emulate. King recounts the "stories of diseased souls wandering within the desert of Christ's temptations in hope of achieving through virtuous labor, what Max Weber termed a this-worldly ascetic ideal, what wholeness may be said to exist."[8] The hortatory appeal for people to benefit by another's spiritual passage created an unbroken chain of religious intelligence—a genre of spiritual biography—that was passed down through the generations and that structured the *ordo salutis* of authentic conversion. These spiritual pilgrimage stories were rife with themes of Christians obsessed with sin, with religious melancholy as the imprimatur of spiritual heroics.

King acknowledges that the genre of spiritual biography—the texts that *express* each soul's pilgrimage—organizes the religious *experiences* of ever widening publics who adopt these texts as models for living. As we have seen, through published "evangelical classics," tele-evangelism broadcast, the revival encampments of the sawdust trail, major urban crusades, Finneyite protracted meetings, fire-and-brimstone sermons preached before small congregations, and many other modalities, revivalists mediated cultural meanings that were simultaneously therapeutic and melancholiac. Indeed, the message rang out that the path to salvation (the therapeutic) required the faithful to descend into the slough of despond, to gaze in horror into the iron cage of despair, to suffer spiritual desolation (the melancholiac) as one forsaken by God's love. Only the Christian who forged his soul in the smithy of religious melancholy could hope to find repose in God in the Celestial City.

Notes

1. Doris Lessing, *Prisons We Choose to Live Inside*, 6.
2. Stanley W. Jackson, *Melancholia and Depression, From Hippocratic Times to Modern Times*, 3; Arthur Kleinman and Byron Good, eds., *Culture and Depression, Studies in the Anthropology and Cross-Cultural Psychiatry of Affect and Disorder*, 492–493.
3. Jackson, *Melancholia and Depression*, 7, 383.
4. Juliana Schiesari, *The Gendering of Melancholia, Feminism, Psychoanalysis, and the Symbolics of Loss in Renaissance Literature*, 233. See Lawrence Babb, *The Elizabethan Malady: A Study of Melancholia in English Literature from 1580–1642*.
5. Schiesari, *Gendering of Melancholia*, 7. See also Wolf Lepenies, *Melancholy and Society*, 19.
6. Jackson, *Melancholia and Depression*, 71.
7. Ibid., 334.
8. Philip Greven, *The Protestant Temperament, Patterns of Child-Rearing, Religious Experience, and the Self in Early America*, 12–17.
9. James Robe, *Narrative of the Extraordinary Work of the Spirit of God at Cambusland, Kilsyth*, 255.
10. Robert Blakeway, *An Essay Towards the Cure of Religious Melancholy in a Letter to a Gentlewoman Afflicted with It*, 8–9.
11. Ibid., 40.
12. Ibid., 49, 69, 85, 111.
13. Ibid., 19.
14. Ibid., 39.
15. Benjamin Fawcett, *Observations on the Nature, Causes and Cure of Melancholy: Especially of That Which Is Commonly Called Religious Melancholy*, 28.
16. Ibid., 40.
17. Jackson, *Melancholia and Depression*, 133–134.
18. Roy Porter, *A Social History of Madness, The World Through the Eyes of the Insane*, 100, 82–101.
19. George Burrows, *Communication on the Causes, Forms, Symptoms and Treatment of Insanity*, 29.
20. John Cheyne, *Essays on the Partial Derangement of the Mind in Supposed Connection with Religion*, 133.
21. Jackson, *Melancholia and Depression*, 341.

22. Kleinman and Good, *Culture and Depression*; 491–492. See also Anthony
J. Marsella and Geoffrey M. White, eds., *Cultural Concepts of Mental Health and
Therapy*; Anthony J. Marsella, George Devos, and Francis L. K. Hsu, *Culture and
Self, Asian and Western Perpspectives*; Richard A. Shweder, *Thinking Through Cul-
tures, Expeditions in Cultural Psychology*, 99ff.

23. A. Irving Hallowell, *Culture and Experience*, 87.

24. Kleinman and Good, *Culture and Depression*, 496.

25. Gananath Obeyesekere, "Depression, Buddhism and the Work of Culture
in Sri Lanka," 139–141. See also Gananath Obeyesekere, *The Work of Culture, Symbolic Transformations in Psychoanalysis and Anthropology*.

26. See Arthur Kleinman, *The Illness Narratives, Suffering, Healing Healing and
the Human Condition*, 23–24. Examples of culture-bound syndromes include life-
threatening semen loss in South Asia, "fright" that causes "soul loss" in Mexican
and Asian cultures, "nerves" in the Americas, anxiety that the penis is shrinking
among Southeast Asians, and *latah* or echoing behavior, among Malays.

27. John Owen King, *The Iron of Melancholy, Structures of Spiritual Conversion in America from the Puritan Conscience to Victorian Neurosis*, 10.

28. Benjamin Nelson, "Conscience and the Making of Early Modern Cultures:
The Protestant Ethic Beyond Max Weber," 11. For a general introduction to the
sociology of Max Weber, see Wolfgang Schluchter, "The Paradox of Rationaliza-
tion: On the Relation of Ethics and World," 41. Max Weber, *From Max Weber:
Essays in Sociology*, 292ff. See also Max Weber, *Economy and Society, An Outline
of Interpretive Sociology. From Max Weber* includes "The Social Psychology of the
World Religions," and "Religious Rejections of the World and Their Directions";
Jeffrey C. Alexander, *The Classical Attempt at Theoretical Synthesis: Max Weber*,
22–29; Stephen Kalberg, "Max Weber's Types of Rationality: Cornerstones for the
Analysis of Rationalization Processes in History," 1146; Wolfgang Schluchter, *The
Rise of Western Rationalism, Max Weber's Developmental History*, 141–148; Wolfgang Schluchter, *Rationalism, Religion and Domination, A Weberian Perspective*,
41–52, and part 2, "Toward a Comparative Sociology of Religious Rationalism,"
83–278; Sam Whimster and Scott Lasch, eds., *Max Weber, Rationality and Modernity*, 8; Alan Sica, *Weber, Irrationality and Social Order*, 192–199. The term rationalization eludes precise definition. Whimster and Lasch view rationalization as "a
process that is common to all religious belief systems—the drive to consistency,
coherence, and greater applicability." Weber, in "Confucianism and Puritanism," the
concluding chapter of *The Religion of China*, defines the process of rationalization:
"To judge the level of rationalization a religion represents we may use two primary
yardsticks which are in many ways interrelated. One is the degree to which the religion
has divested itself of magic; the other is the degree to which it has systematically
unified the relation between God and the world and therewith its own ethical relationship to the world." Max Weber, *The Religion of China*, 226.

29. Harvey Goldman, *Max Weber and Thomas Mann, Calling and the Shaping
of the Self*, 153. For other commentaries on Weber's concept of personality see
Wolfgang Mommsen, "Personal Conduct and Societal Change"; Wilhelm Hennis,
"Personality and Life Orders: Max Weber's Theme"; and E. B. Portis, "Max Weber's
Theory of Personality," 113–114.

30. Goldman, *Max Weber and Thomas Mann*, 153. However, Weber did not
believe that all social actors would necessarily or invariably develop "personality"
or succeed in this heroic ethic quest. As Kalberg notes in his discussion of substan-

tive-rational action, a concept related to personality: "Many persons, for example, do not possess, according to Weber, the "religious qualifications" to pattern their actions consistently in behalf of a value constellation. Thus, they believe in these values not as absolute ethical principles but as mere guidelines for action that can be upheld or discarded according to momentary demands. . . . This possibility is illustrated by the means-end rational motives of the businessmen who joined Calvinist sects in order to acquire reputations for impeccable honesty and thereby secure the trade of sect and other community members." Kalberg, "Max Weber's Types," 1162.

31. Portis, "Max Weber's Theory," 118.

32. Ibid., 116.

33. Max Weber, "Freudianism," 385–386.

34. Max Weber, *The Protestant Ethic and the Spirit of Capitalism*, 97.

35. Max Weber, "Anticritical Last Word on the Spirit of Capitalism," 1113.

36. Weber, *From Max Weber*, 321.

37. Weber, *Protestant Ethic*, 104.

38. Ibid., 117.

39. Arnold Eisen, "Called To Order: The Role of the Puritan *Berufsmench* in Weberian Sociology." Eisen argues that Weber's ideal type of the Protestant inner-worldly ascetic relied upon an analysis of the early pastoral writings of the seventeenth century but neglected the other dimensions of the theology of assurance that developed after Cromwell's Revolution. Eisen concurs with Weber's rendering of the importance of success in a calling for psychological assurance in early Puritan theology. "Weber, we find, exaggerated neither the importance of calling in Puritan writings, nor the psychological sanctions brought to bear on the anxious believer, nor the attempt to mould total personalities who might then alter the world according to a prescribed plan . . ." (p. 208). However, Eisen finds that for later Puritans, most notably William Perkins, there was a relaxation of asceticism.

40. Max Weber, "Max Weber On Church, Sect and Mysticism," 147–148.

41. Weber, *Protestant Ethic*, 118–119.

42. Weber, *Religion of China*, 244.

43. Schluchter, *Rise of Western Rationalism*, 4.

44. This modern economic enterprise required the formal separation of household economy from firm and business enterprise, and the continual investment and reinvestment of capital in production activities oriented toward earning rationally calculable and limited profits in an impersonal market economy. Although Weber identified many other structural developments in law, banking and finance, and political organization that accounted for modern capitalism, the Protestant Ethic essays emphasized the crucial role that Protestant vocational asceticism played in providing the rationales that motivated the bourgeoisie to reject economic traditionalism—or unbridled avarice and speculative greed—and champion this new economic form. As Benjamin Nelson has noted, "Weber always intended the notion of the 'Protestant Ethic' to refer to the existential and cultural foundations of any society committed to the mastery of this world through intensive discipline and consensual organization of the personal and social orders." Benjamin Nelson, "Weber's Protestant Ethic: Its Origins, Wanderings and Foreseeable Futures," 83.

45. Schluchter, *Rise of Western Rationalism*, 156–166.

46. Max Weber, *The Methodology of the Social Sciences*, 97–104.

47. Weber, *Protestant Ethic*, 98.

48. Weber, *Religion of China*, 244.

49. Weber, *Protestant Ethic*, 130.

50. William James, *The Varieties of Religious Experience, A Study in Human Nature*, 200.

51. Ibid., 146.

52. Richard Rabinowitz, *The Spiritual Self in Everyday Life, The Transformation of Personal Religious Experience in Nineteenth-Century New England*, xv–xvi.

53. King, *Iron of Melancholy*, 192.

54. Ibid., 196.

55. Ibid., 196.

56. Ibid., 11.

57. Lawrence A. Schaff, *Fleeing the Iron Cage, Culture, Politics, and Modernity in the Thought of Max Weber*, 73ff.

58. Benjamin Nelson, "Max Weber's 'Author's Introduction' (1920): A Master Clue to His Main Aims," 271.

59. Weber, *Protestant Ethic*, 182.

60. Weber never pursued the research program that he set before himself at the conclusion of *Protestant Ethic*—showing its relationship to science and technology, and to secular rationalism. Indeed, the Protestant Ethic had direct connections to the emergence of political democracy, as Weber's contemporary, Georg Jellineck, demonstrated in *The Declaration of the Rights of Man and of Citizen, A Contribution to Constitutional History*. But Weber would never pursue these issues, as he found himself at the center of great controversy that did not cease with the publication of "Anti-Critical Last Word" some five years later. He set about the task of a comparative and developmental history of Western rationalism and put aside the Protestant Ethic questions. Weber was no stranger to what John Owen King has termed the stamp of the "iron of melancholy," given Weber's own mental breakdown at the death of his father in 1898. Due to a combination of scholarly and personal issues, Weber did not explore the relationship of the Protestant Ethic to religious melancholy.

61. Roger A. Johnson, ed., "Introduction," *Psychohistory and Religion: The Case of Young Man Luther*; Rudolf M. Dekker and Herman W. Rodenburg, "A Suitable Case for Treatment? A Reappraisal of Erikson's *Young Man Luther*," 775–800.

62. Erik H. Erickson, *Young Man Luther, A Study in Psychoanalysis and History*, 12.

63. Alister E. McGrath, *Luther's Theology of the Cross, Martin Luther's Theological Breakthrough*, 96.

64. Roland H. Bainton, *Here I Stand, A Life of Martin Luther*, 28ff.

65. Ibid., 28.

66. Stanley W. Jackson, "Acedia The Sin and its Relationship to Sorrow and Melancholia," 43–62. See Jean Leclercq, "Modern Psychology and the Interpretation of Medieval Texts, 476–490.

67. Benjamin Nelson, "Conscience," 14–17.

68. McGrath, *Luther's Theology*, 100.

69. Bainton, *Here I Stand*, 66. See Roland H. Bainton, *The Reformation of the Sixteenth Century*.

70. McGrath, *Luther's Theology*, 118ff.

71. Bainton, *Here I Stand*, 65.

72. McGrath, *Luther's Theology*, 52.

73. Paul Tillich, *The Protestant Era*, 143.

74. Ibid., 145.

75. Ibid., 146.

76. Bainton, *Here I Stand*, 361.

77. Paul Hacker, *The Ego in Faith, Martin Luther and the Origins of Anthropocentric Religion*, 126.

78. McGrath, *Luther's Theology*, 171.

79. Gerhard Ritter, "Luther," 632–633.

80. William J. Bouwsma, *John Calvin, A Sixteenth-Century Portrait*, 32.

81. Ibid., 30.

82. Ibid., 9.

83. Walter E. Stuerman, *A Critical Study of Calvin's Concept of Faith*, 26.

84. John Calvin, *On the Christian Faith, Selections from the Institutes, Commentaries, and Tracts*, 43–44.

85. John Calvin, *Institutes of the Christian Religion*, bk. 3, chap. 12, vol. 1, p. 479.

86. Stuerman, *Critical Study*, 106.

87. Calvin, *Institutes*, bk. 3, on nature of prayer.

88. Stuerman, *Critical Study*, 185.

89. Calvin, *Institutes*, bk. 3, vol. 2, pp. 60–67.

90. Calvin, *Institutes*, bk. 3, vol. 1, p. 469.

91. Stuerman, *Critical Study*, 96, 102.

92. Calvin, *Institutes*, bk. 3, vol 2, p. 16.

93. Ronald J. Wallace, *Calvin's Doctrine of the Christian Life*, 191.

94. Bouwsma, *John Calvin*, 30.

95. Calvin, *Institutes*, bk. 3, chap. 17, vol. 2, pp. 103–118.

96. Calvin, *Institutes*, bk. 3, chap. 24, 5, vol. 2, p. 245.

97. Calvin, *Institutes*, bk. 3, chap. 13, vol. 2, p. 483.

98. Calvin, *Christian Faith*, 72.

99. Wallace, *Calvin's Doctrine*, 30.

100. Calvin, *Institutes*, bk. 3, chap. 2, vol. 1, p. 484.

101. Bouwsma, *John Calvin*, 11.

102. Ibid., 45.

103. Ibid., 41.

104. Ibid., 141.

105. Ibid., 180.

106. Ibid., 47.

107. Ibid., 41.

108. Ibid., 45.

109. Ibid., 140–141.

110. Ernest F. Stoeffler, *The Rise of Evangelical Pietism*, 15.

111. C. C. Goen, "Introduction," in *Jonathan Edwards, The Great Awakening*, 1.

112. Benjamin Nelson, "Self-Images and Systems of Spiritual Direction in the History of European Civilization," 72.

113. Geoffrey F. Nuttall, *The Holy Spirit in Puritan Faith and Experience*, 22–23.

114. Benjamin Nelson, "Self-Images," 72.

115. Stoeffler, *Rise of Evangelical Pietism*, 74.

116. Norman Pettit, *The Heart Prepared: Grace and Conversion in Puritan Spiritual Life*, 49.

117. John von Rohr, *The Covenant of Grace in Puritan Thought*, 9; Pettit, *Heart Prepared*, 56.

118. Pettit, *Heart Prepared*, 17.

119. Ibid., 19.

120. Rohr, *Covenant of Grace*, 13.

121. Ibid., 13.

122. Pettit, *Heart Prepared*, 50–51.

123. Rohr, *Covenant of Grace*, 83ff.

124. Richard Baxter, *The Saints Everlasting Rest*, 21.

125. Richard Baxter, *A Treatise of Conversion, Practical Works of Rev. Richard Baxter*, 51–52.

126. Ibid., 55.

127. Ibid., 75.

128. Ibid., 93.

129. Baxter, *Saints Everlasting Rest*, 203.

130. Stoeffler, *Rise of Evangelical Pietism*, 58, 78.

131. Owen C. Watkins, *The Puritan Experience: Studies in Spiritual Autobiography*, 28.

132. Ibid., 2.

133. Ibid., 1.

134. Ibid., 13–14.

135. John Bunyan, *Grace Abounding to the Chief of Sinners*, 54. See also the account of the life of Thomas Goodwin in Alan Simpson, *Puritanism in Old and New England*, 2–4.

136. Bunyan, *Grace Abounding*, 81.

137. Rohr, *Covenant of Grace*, 122.

138. Ibid., 164.

139. Ibid., 160.

140. Richard Baxter, *The Right Method for a Settled Peace of Conscience and Spiritual Comfort, Practical Works of Rev. Richard Baxter*, vol. 9, 121.

141. Ibid., 130

142. Ibid., 286.

143. Rohr, *Covenant of Grace*, 175.

144. Baxter, *Right Method*, vol. 9, 282.

145. Ibid., 278.

146. Ibid., 191–192.

147. Thomas F. Merrill, ed., *"A Discourse of Conscience," William Perkins*, 39–40. See also Gordon Stevens Wakefield, *Puritan Devotion: Its Place in the Development of Christian Piety*, 124–125.

148. Merrill, *"Discourse of Conscience,"* 118.

149. Robert Burton, *The Anatomy of Melancholy*, 102.

150. Ruth A. Fox, *The Tangled Chain, The Structure of Disorder in the Anatomy of Melancholy*, 15. See also Stanley W. Jackson's chapter, "Religion, the Supernatural and Melancholia," 326ff.

151. Burton, *Anatomy*, 118.

152. Ibid., 118–119.

153. Ibid., 886–887.

154. Fox, *Tangled Chain*, 196.

155. Burton, *Anatomy*, 939.

156. Ibid., 946.

157. Ibid., 948.

158. Ibid., 963–964.

159. Ibid., 970

160. Fox, *Tangled Chain*, 120.

161. Burton, *Anatomy*, 970.

162. Evans Bergen, *The Psychiatry of Robert Burton*, 11.

163. Michael MacDonald and Terence R. Murphy, *Sleepless Souls: Suicide in Early Modern England*, 64.

164. H. C. Porter, *Reformation and Reaction in Tudor Cambridge*, 207ff.

165. Michael MacDonald, *Mystical Bedlam, Madness, Anxiety and Healing in Seventeenth Century England*, 31, 220–221; Stanley W. Jackson, *Melancholia & Depression*, 330–341.

166. MacDonald and Murphy, *Sleepless Souls*, 39.

167. Ibid., 65.

Chapter 2

1. Derek Hirst, *Authority and Conflict England, 1603–1658*, 167; Perry Miller, *Errand Into the Wilderness*, 1–15.

2. King, *The Iron of Melancholy*, 40–49.

3. Edmund S. Morgan, *Visible Saints, The History of a Puritan Idea*. See also John Demos, *Past, Present and Personal, The Family and the Life-Course in American History*; Philip J. Greven, *Four Generations: Population, Land, and Family in Colonial Andover, Massachusetts*; Roger Thompson, *Sex in Middlesex, Popular Mores in a Massachusetts County, 1649–1699*.

4. Andrew Delbanco, *The Puritan Ordeal*; William G. McLoughlin, *Revivals, Awakenings, and Reform, An Essay on Religion and Social Change in America, 1607–1977*, 34–35.

5. Delbanco, *Puritan Ordeal*, 57ff.

6. Ibid., 43.

7. Charles Lloyd Cohen, *God's Caress, The Psychology of Religious Experience*, 109.

8. Ibid, 109ff. Cohen provides a telling critique of Weber's Protestant Ethic by placing Weber's exaggeration of activist, vocational asceticism against the backdrop of the competing irrational quest for the reception of God's love.

9. Charles E. Hambrick-Stowe, *The Practice of Piety, Puritan Devotional Disciplines in Seventeenth-Century New England*, 20.

10. Ibid., 285.

11. Ibid., 287.

12. Sacvan Bercovitch, *The Puritan Origins of the American Self*, 23.

13. Patricia Caldwell, *The Puritan Conversion Narrative: The Beginnings of American Experience*, 50.

14. See Alden T. Vaughan and Edward W. Clark, eds., *Puritans Among the Indians, Accounts of Captivity and Redemption, 1676–1724*. Also, narratives of Puritans captured by Indians during King Philip's War in 1675 combined spiritual autobiography and pilgrimage depicting the warfare of the Christian with the Indian as Satan's agent. Returned captives, most notably Mary Rowlandson (1684), published accounts of their adversity and spiritual trials. These narratives included a sermon that admonished believers that captivity and adversity resulted from sin and refusal to acknowledge divine sovereignty—a jeremiad warning of spiritual deadness. And what did Rowlandson learn from her sojourn with "savages" in a time of warfare, brutality, and wholesale death?

She spoke to her contemporaries, "The Lord hath showed me the vanity of these outward things. That they are the vanity of vanities and vexation of spirit, that they are but a shadow, a blast, a bubble, and things of no continuance. That we must rely on God himself and our whole dependence must be upon Him. If trouble from smaller matters begin to arise in me, I have something at hand to check myself and say, why am I troubled? It was but the other day that if I had the world I would have given it for my freedom or to have been a servant to a Christian. I have learned to look beyond present and smaller troubles and to be quieted under them, as Moses said, Exod. 14:13. 'Stand still and see the salvation of the Lord'" (p. 75).

15. Daniel B. Shea, Jr., *Spiritual Autobiography in America*; Eugene H. White, *Puritan Rhetoric, The Issue of Emotion in Religion*, 10–12.

16. Caldwell, *Puritan Conversion*, 120.

17. Ibid., 121–122, 136.

18. Ibid., 150.

19. Pettit, *Heart Prepared*, 84.

20. Delbanco, *Puritan Ordeal*, 143.

21. Ibid., 142.

22. Ibid., 211.

23. John Owen King, *Iron of Melancholy*, 35.

24. Philip Greven, *The Protestant Temperament, Patterns of Child-Rearing, Religious Experience, and the Self in Early America*, 12–17. Greven's typology also includes "moderate" and "genteel" modalities of Protestant temperament and personality. These alternate types will receive extended treatment in Chapter 5 in the discussion of moral treatment of the insane in the nineteenth-century asylum.

25. Ibid., 50. See also William G. McLoughlin, "Evangelical Childrearing in the Age of Jackson: Francis Wayland's Views on When and How to Subdue the Willfulness of Children," 21–39.

26. Greven, *Protestant Temperament*, 55.

27. Ibid., 61.

28. Ibid., 109.

29. Ibid., 73.

30. Ibid., 85.

31. Ibid., 143–144.

32. Michael G. Kenny, *The Passion of Ansel Bourne, Multiple Personality in American Culture*, 6–7.

33. Ibid., 32.

34. Ibid., 35.

35. Richard F. Lovelace, *The American Piety of Cotton Mather, Origins of American Evangelicalism*, 35. See also Bercovitch, *Puritan Origins*, 3–33 and chap. 3.

36. Lovelace, *American Piety*, 35.

37. Ibid., 96.

38. Cotton Mather, *Magnalia Christi Americana*, vol. 1, 376; Mary Ann Jimenez, *Changing Faces of Madness, Early American Attitudes and Treatment of the Insane*, 12–30.

39. Mather, *Magnalia Christi*, 396.

40. David H. Hall, *Worlds of Wonder, Days of Judgment, Popular Religious Belief in Early New England*, 131.

41. Cotton Mather, "The Case of a Troubled Mind," 11–28.

42. Cotton Mather, *Angel of Bethesda*, 134.

43. Ibid., 135.

44. Mather, *Magnalia Christi*, vol. 1, 396.

45. Benjamin Colman, *The Case of Satan's Fiery Darts in Blasphemous Suggestions and Hellish Annoyances*, 21.

46. Ibid., 74.

47. Hall, *Worlds of Wonder*, 134–135. Lovelace, *American Piety*, 104. See also Morgan, *Visible Saints*.

48. Lovelace, *American Piety*, 87, 104.

49. See William K. B. Stoever, *A Faire and Easie Way to Heaven, Covenant Theology and Antinomianism in Early Massachusetts*; Lovelace, *American Piety*, 87.

50. Lovelace, *American Piety*, 97.

51. Ibid., 104.

52. Peter Gay, *The Freud Reader*, 433–435.

53. Kenneth Silverman, *The Life and Times of Cotton Mather*, 221; David Levin, *Cotton Mather, The Young Life of the Lord's Remembrancer, 1663–1703*, 47.

54. See Baird Tipson, "How Can the Religious Experiences of the Past Be Recovered? The Examples of Puritanism and Pietism," 695–709; Murray G. Murphey, "The Psychodynamics of Puritan Conversion," 135–147; Howard M. Feinstein, "The Prepared Heart: A Comparative Study of Puritan Theology and Psychoanalysis," 166–176. James Hoopes, *Consciousness in New England, From Puritanism and Ideas to Psychoanalysis and Semeiotic*, 19–26.

55. Lovelace, *American Piety*, 143–144.

56. Cohen, *God's Caress*, 22.

57. Cotton Mather, *The Diary of Cotton Mather, Volume 1, 1681–1709*, 28.

58. Lovelace, *American Piety*, 80. For a discussion of the "work of culture" with respect to depressive illness, see Obeyesekere, "Depression, Buddhism," 139–141. Paul Ricoeur, *Freud and Philosophy: An Essay on Interpretation*, bk. 2, part 2, "The Interpretation of Culture," 159–260.

59. Hall, *Worlds of Wonder*, 130.

60. Evangelical nurture is a semantically neutral term used to designate the system of child-rearing, and its consequences, devised by evangelical Pietists from the seventeenth century to the present. Many writers in the nineteenth century, and several contemporary social scientists employ the concept of "soul murder." Soul murder is an evocative term with a long and complex history. I acknowledge the important psychoanalytic work of L. Shengold in *Soul Murder, The Effects of Childhood Abuse and Deprivation*. Shengold explores the early use of the term in the nineteenth-century literature of Ibsen, and the remarkable spiritual biography of Daniel Paul Schreber, *Memoirs of My Nervous Illness*. See also Morton Schatzman; Lucy Bregman, "Religion and Madness: Schreber's *Memoirs* as Personal Myth"; Nathan Church, "Schreber's *Memoirs*: Myth or Personal Lamentation." However, Freud, in his early writings on the relationship between religion and melancholy or obsessive-compulsive actions, forever changed the way that social science and secular psychiatry would view the relationship between religion and mental alienation. Freud made the cultural and theological contents of a patient's life and symptomatology largely epiphenomenal to the underlying structure of the mind and the intrapsychic dynamics of psychosexual development. Freud prided himself on achieving a new interpretation of culture founded upon the secular, anthropocentric dynamics of identification, cathexis, sublimation, projection, transference, and the defense mechanisms. Freud employed these concepts to reconstruct the origins and workings of Judeo-Christian thought and myth, and to understand the conflicts and sufferings of patients troubled by obsessive actions infused with religious guilt. He largely recast the meanings of

the conversion crises of believers struggling to forge a relationship with God. Psychoanalysis depicted religious guilt and melancholy as a displacement of affect from one's temporal father to a projection of God the Father. The intrapsychic dynamics of the Oedipus complex and the family romance explained the symptoms of these believers. Each sufferer created a private, personal system of rituals and beliefs directed toward resolving the central questions of existence. In its collective and institutional form, religion served as the universal obsessional neurosis. (See Sigmund Freud, *Collected Papers*, vol. 5, 94ff; Peter Gay, ed., *The Freud Reader*, 435.) When Freud applied this explanatory model to his secondary analysis of the paranoid psychosis of Schreber, he ignored key cultural and familial considerations in Schreber's life crisis, including the draconian forms of evangelical Protestant discipline, will-breaking, and physical cruelty inflicted upon the young Schreber by his father. Freud chose to dismiss the existence of soul murder. My purpose is to recover the evangelical practices of child-rearing, the experiences of the brutalized children, and to link this trauma, legitimated by a religious heritage, to religious melancholia in adults.

61. Seymour Byman, "Child Raising and Melancholia in Tudor England," 81.

62. Ibid., 69.

63. Philip Greven, *Spare the Child, The Religious Roots of Punishment and the Psychological Impact of Physical Abuse*, 132.

64. Shengold, *Soul Murder*, 2.

65. Alice Miller, *Banished Knowledge, Facing Childhood Injuries*, 37ff.

66. Alice Miller, *The Untouched Key, Tracing Childhood Trauma in Creativity and Destructiveness*, 27.

67. Greven, *Spare the Child*, 48.

68. Ibid., 65ff, 87.

69. Philip Greven, "'Some Root of Bitterness': Corporal Punishment, Child Abuse, and the Apocalyptic Impulse in Michael Wigglesworth," 94.

70. Ibid., 101

71. Michael Wigglesworth, *The Day of Doom*, quoted in Greven, "'Some Root of Bitterness,'" 96.

72. Ibid., 103–104.

73. Ronald A. Bosco, *The Poems of Michael Wigglesworth*, 131.

74. Ibid., 131.

75. Ibid., 132.

76. Edmund S. Morgan, ed., *The Diary of Michael Wigglesworth 1653–1657, The Conscience of a Puritan*, 8, 14, 53.

77. Ibid., 53.

78. Ibid., 13.

79. Ibid, 33.

80. Ibid., 91.

81. James Axtell, *The Invasion Within, The Contest of Cultures in Colonial North America*. See also Francis Jennings, *The Ambiguous Iroquois Empire, The Covenant Chain Confederacy of Indian Tribes with English Colonies from its Beginnings to the Lancaster Treaty of 1744*; Stephen Cornell, *The Return of the Native, American Indian Political Resurgence*.

82. Axtell, *Invasion Within*, 220.

83. Francis Jennings, *The Invasion of America, Indians, Colonials, and the Cant of Conquest*, 228–253.

84. Neal Salisbury, "Red Puritans: The Praying Indians of Massachusetts Bay and John Eliot," 86.

85. Ibid., 76; Axtell, *Invasion Within*, 131ff. See also Alden T. Vaughan, *New England Frontier Puritans and Indians, 1620–1675.*

86. James Axtell, *After Columbus, Essays in the Ethnohistory of Colonial North America*, 50–51.

87. Ibid., 51.

88. See Henry W. Bowden and James P. Ronda, eds., *John Eliot's Indian Dialogue: A Study in Cultural Interaction*; Axtell, *After Columbus*, 100–121.

89. John Eliot and Thomas Mayhew, *Tears of Repentance: Or, A Further Narrative of the Progress of the Gospel Amongst the Indians In New England*, 7.

90. Ibid., 145.

91. Ibid., 9.

92. Axtell, *Invasion Within*, 232.

93. Axtell, *After Columbus*, 56–57, 120–121.

94. Experience Mayhew, *Indian Converts: Or Some Accounts of the Lives and Dying Speeches of a Considerable Number of the Christianized Indians of Martha's Vineyard in New England*, 206.

95. Ibid., 195–196.

96. See Pettit, *Heart Prepared*, 150ff. Morgan, *Visible Saints*, 130–138.

97. Paul R. Lucas, *Valley of Discord, Church and Society Along the Connecticut River, 1636–1725*, 134.

98. Thompson, Sex in Middlesex, 34–70, 169–190. See also McLoughlin, *Revivals; Awakenings*, 54–58; Kenneth A. Lockridge, *A New England Town, The First Hundred Years*, 57–58, 162–163.

99. Richard L. Bushman, *From Puritan to Yankee, Character and the Social Order in Connecticut, 1690–1765*, 147–182.

100. Ibid., 190.

101. Ibid., 190. See also Sacvan Bercovitch, *The American Jeremiad.*

102. Bushman, *Puritan to Yankee*, 187.

103. McLoughlin, *Revivals, Awakenings*, 48–50.

104. Ibid., 52.

105. J. M. Bumsted, ed., *The Great Awakening, The Beginnings of Evangelical Pietism in America*; Edwin S. Gaustad, *The Great Awakening in New England.*

106. McLoughlin, *Revivals, Awakenings*, 75. See also Alan Heimert, *Religion and the American Mind.*

107. McLoughlin, *Revivals, Awakenings*, 7.

108. Gail Thain Parker, "Jonathan Edwards and Melancholy," 199.

109. C. C. Goen, *Revivalism and Separatism in New England, 1740–1800, Strict Congregationalists and Separate Baptists in the Great Awakening*, 8–31.

110. Jonathan Edwards, *Representative Selections, With Introduction, Bibliography, and Notes*, 164.

111. McLoughlin, *Revivals, Awakenings*, 58.

112. Joseph Conforti, *Samuel Hopkins and the New Divinity Movement: Calvinism, the Congregational Ministry, and Reform in New England Between the Great Awakenings.*

113. Benjamin Trumbull, *Complete History of Connecticut*, vol. 2, 155–156, quoted from Goen, *Revivalism and Separatism*, 18. See also David S. Lovejoy, *Religious Enthusiasm in the New World, Heresy To Revolution*, 189–193.

114. Jonathan Edwards, *A Faithful Narrative, in The Great Awakening*, 205–207, quoted in Patricia J. Tracy, *Jonathan Edwards, Pastor: Religion and Society in Eighteenth Century Northampton*, 116.

115. Tracy, *Jonathan Edwards,* 136; letter from Jonathan Edwards to Prince, 12 December, 1743, in Goen, *Jonathan Edwards,* 545–548.

116. Jonathan Edwards, *The Great Awakening,* 161, 47.

117. Parker, "Jonathan Edwards," 201–203.

118. Jonathan Edwards, *Great Awakening,* 162.

119. Ibid., 332.

120. Ibid.

121. Ibid., 335.

122. Ibid., 334–335.

123. Ibid., 341.

124. Goen, *Revivalism and Separatism,* 17.

125. Barbara E. Lacey, "Gender, Piety, and Secularization in Connecticut Religion, 1720–1775," 807.

126. Joy D. Buel and Richard Buel, Jr., *The Way of Duty, A Woman And Her Family in Revolutionary America,* 8.

127. Journal of Mary Fish, 4–5 (hereafter referred to as Mary Fish Journal).

128. Buel and Buel, *Way of Duty,* 18–26.

129. Ibid., 62.

130. Cotton Mather, "Insanabilia: An Essay Upon Incurables," 3.

131. Ibid., 8–9.

132. Mary Fish Journal, 30–31.

133. John Flavel, *Divine Conduct, Or The Mystery of Providence,* 100–107.

134. Ibid., 144.

135. Ibid., 145.

136. Mary Fish Journal, January 16, 1771, 44.

137. Ibid., January 21, 1771, 45.

138. Ibid., January 22, 1771, 45.

139. Ibid., April 15, 1771, 50.

140. Ibid., April 27, 1771.

141. Ibid., July 1, 1771.

142. Ibid., February 11, 1772.

Chapter 3

1. Anne Fremantle, *The Protestant Mystic,* viii.

2. William James, *Varieties,* 239.

3. Raymond Prince, "The Concept of Culture-Bound Syndrome: Anorexia Nervosa and Brain-Fag," 198.

4. Wolfgang G. Jilek and Louis Jilek-Aall, "The Metamorphosis of 'Culture-Bound' Syndrome," 205.

5. Bryan S. Turner, *The Body and Society, Explorations in Social Theory,* 165–166. See also Bryan S. Turner, *Medical Power and Social Knowledge,* 19–38; Abram De Swaan, *The Management of Normality, Critical Essays in Health and Welfare.*

6. Joseph Tamney, "Fasting and Dieting: A Research Note," 255.

7. Joseph G. Jorgensen, *The Sun Dance Religion, Power to the Powerless,* 231–244; Benjamin Nelson, *On The Roads To Modernity: Conscience, Science and Civilization; Selected Essays,* 91; see in particular the discussion of "Consciousness–Type 1 and Type 2."

8. Tamney, "Fasting and Dieting," 255–256. The development of salvation religions founded upon exemplary and ethical prophecy, as Weber notes, produced

an intellectualization of the meaning of human existence in this world, particularly regarding the questions of the problem of theodicy and human suffering. Ethical prophecy produced rationalized theology that enunciated promises of salvation available to believers who acted consistent with the ethical requirements of God's commandments. Disobedience was sin that alienated the believer from God. Fasting expressed an ethically required mental attitude of piety, humility, and penitence towards the deity.

9. Turner, *Body and Society*, 166.

10. William James, *Varieties*, 301–302, quoted in Turner, *Body and Society*, 166.

11. Keith Thomas, *Religion and the Decline of Magic*, 75–76.

12. Ibid., 75–76.

13. Hall, *Worlds of Wonder*, 71–117.

14. Ibid., 168.

15. Ibid., 196.

16. Ibid., 203–211.

17. Ibid., 233–234.

18. K. Thomas, *Religion*, 114.

19. Ibid., 117.

20. Elspeth Graham et al., eds., *Her Own Life, Autobiographical Writings by Seventeenth-Century English Women*, 197.

21. Ibid., 203.

22. Ibid., 207.

23. John Moore, "On Religious Melancholy: A Sermon Preached Before the Queen at White-Hall, March 6, 1691," 3.

24. Ibid., 4–11.

25. Ibid., 16.

26. John Langhorne, *Letters on Religious Retirement, Melancholy and Enthusiasm*, 20–21.

27. Ibid., 42.

28. Ibid., 42.

29. Elias Boudinot, "Memoirs of Rev. William Tennent, Late Pastor of the Presbyterian Church at Freehold in New Jersey."

30. Milton Coalter, Jr., *Son of Thunder, A Case Study of the Impact of Continental Pietism's Upon the First Great Awakening in the Middle Colonies*, 17ff.

31. Hughes Oliphant Old, "Gilbert Tennent and the Preaching of Piety in Colonial America: Newly Discovered Tennent Manuscripts in Speer Library," 137.

32. Ibid., 137.

33. Gilbert Tennent, "*De Impotentia Hominis*," Sermon # 29, *Gilbert Tennent Sermons 1742–1763*.

34. Ibid.

35. Archibald Alexander, *Biographical Sketches of the Founder, and Principal Alumni of the Log College: together with an account of the revivals of religion under their ministry*, 166.

36. The Compact Edition of the *Oxford English Dictionary* provides this definition of the early modern usage for the term hectic.

37. A. Alexander, *Biographical Sketches*, 167.

38. Ibid., 168.

39. Ibid., 171.

40. Boudinot, "Memoirs," 56–57.

41. Ibid., 9.

42. Ibid., 3.

43. Joseph Conforti, "Jonathan Edwards's Most Popular Work, 'The Life of David Brainerd' and Nineteenth-Century Evangelical Culture."

44. Edwards, *Life of Brainerd*, 500.

45. Ibid., 147.

46. Conforti, "Jonathan Edwards's," 195.

47. Edwards, *Life of Brainerd*, 506.

48. Ibid., 186, quoted in Weddle, 307.

49. Edwards, *Life of Brainerd*, 186.

50. Ibid., 233.

51. Ibid., 233.

52. Ibid., 233.

53. Ibid., 1985, 241.

54. Ibid., 283.

55. Ibid., 190, 205.

56. Weddle, 306.

57. Ibid., 306.

58. Edwards, *Life of Brainerd*, 531.

59. Ibid.

60. Conforti, "Jonathan Edwards's," 192.

61. Ibid., 190.

62. Journal of Isaac Bird, entry for November 29, 1813 (hereafter referred to as Isaac Bird Journal).

63. Isaac Bird Journal; letter from Isaac Bird to James Winchell, December 13, 1813.

64. Ibid., January 1, 1814,

65. Ibid., January 12, 1814.

66. Ibid., February 1, 1814.

67. Ibid., February 6, 1814.

68. Ibid., February 12, 1814.

69. Ibid., February 26, 1814.

70. Ibid., March 1, 1814.

71. Ibid., March 10, 1814.

72. Ibid., June 25, 1814.

73. Ibid., August 14, 1814.

74. Ibid., May, 1815.

75. Isaac Bird Diary and Correspondence, "Sermons 1816–1823," "The Importance of Sincerity."

76. Isaac Bird Diary and Correspondence, "Lecture Notes for Class with Dr. Leonard Woods" January 1818, "Rules for Students."

77. Ibid.

78. David O. Morton, *Memoir of Reverend Levi Parsons*, 84.

79. Ibid., 131.

80. Ibid., 215.

81. Ibid., 159.

82. Leonard Woods, *History of Andover Theological Seminary*, 40ff.

83. Conforti, *Samuel Hopkins;* William Breitenbach, "The Consistent Calvinism of the New Divinity Movement"; William Breitenbach, "Unregenerate Doings: Selflessness and Selfishness in New Divinity Theology."

84. Conforti, *Samuel Hopkins*, 24.

85. Ibid., 26.

86. Samuel Hopkins, *Works*, vol. 1, 18.

87. Ibid.

88. Ibid., vol. 1, 19.

89. Ibid.

90. Ibid., vol. 1, 26.

91. Ibid.

92. Frank Hugh Foster, *Genetic History of the New England Theology*, 139.

93. Breitenbach, "Unregenerate Doings," 489.

94. Samuel Hopkins, "A Dialogue Between a Calvinist and Semi-Calvinist," *Works*, vol. 1, 148.

95. Breitenbach, "Unregenerate Doings," 491.

96. Joseph Bellamy, *Works*, vol. 1, 336–337.

97. Nathanael Emmons, *Works*, vol. 3, 480.

98. Ibid., vol. 3, 487.

99. Stephen G. Post, *Christian Love and Self-Denial, An Historical and Normative Study of Jonathan Edwards, Samuel Hopkins, and American Theological Ethics*, 2.

100. Ibid., 2–3.

101. Hopkins, *Works*, vol. 1, 190–191.

102. Ibid., vol 3, 30. See also Breitenbach, "Unregenerate Doings," 497–501.

103. Nathan Bangs, *The Errors of Hopkinsonianism Detected and Refuted in Six Letters to the Reverend S. Tillison*, 272.

104. Samuel Hopkins, *The Life and Character of Miss Susanna Anthony*, 18.

105. Ibid., 23–24.

106. Ibid., 30.

107. Ibid., 150.

108. Sarah Osborn and Susanna Anthony, *Familiar Letters Written by Mrs. Sarah Osborn and Miss Susanna Anthony*, 31.

109. Ibid., 58.

110. Ibid., 138.

111. Sarah Osborn Letters, American Antiquarian Society, Worcester, Massachusetts, Correspondence, December 26, 1760 (hereafter referred to as Osborn Correspondence).

112. Osborn Correspondence, May 10, 1761.

113. Ibid.

114. B. B. Edwards, ed., *Memoirs of the Reverend Elias Cornelius*, 19.

115. Ibid., 22.

116. Ibid., 230.

117. Samuel Hopkins, *Memoirs of the Life of Mrs. Sarah Osborn who died at Newport Rhode Island*, 22.

118. Ibid., 24.

119. Ibid., 31.

120. Osborn Correspondence, letter sent from Sarah Osborn to Reverend Joseph Fish, Stonington, Connecticut, ca. 1743.

121. Sarah Osborn, *The Nature, Certainty, and Evidence of True Christianity, in a Letter from a Gentlewoman in New England to another dear friend in great distress, doubt, and concern of a religious nature*, 3.

122. Osborn and Anthony, *Familiar Letters*, 161.

123. Osborn Collection, letter sent from Sarah Osborn to Reverend Joseph Fish, Stonington, Connecticut, April 7, 1762.

124. Hopkins, *Memoirs of the Life,* 364.

125. Ibid., 364.

126. Osborn Collection, letter from Sarah Osborn to Reverend Joseph Fish, Stonington, Connecticut, ca. 1743.

127. Mary Beth Norton, "'My Resting Reaping Times': Sarah Osborn's Defense of Her 'Unfeminine' Activities, 1767," 520.

128. Osborn Collection, letter from Sarah Osborn to Reverend Joseph Fish, Stonington, Connecticut, ca. 1743.

129. Osborn Correspondence, August 9, 1766.

130. Osborn and Anthony, *Familiar Letters,* 10.

131. Quoted in Norton, "'My Resting Reaping Times,'" 527.

132. Hopkins, *Works,* vol. 1, 99–105; Congregational Church Records. Records of the First Congregational Church state that later in the nineteenth century the Osborn House served as a refuge for poorer members and aged women. Unfortunately, the records of this society, such as membership and subscription lists, the charter, by-laws, names of officers, and personal documents of members, cannot be located. Without these public and private sources, the identities and devotional piety of these women remain unknown.

133. Ralph Waldo Emerson, *Lectures and Biographical Sketches,* volume 10 of *Collected Works,* 399.

134. Phyllis Cole, "The Advantage of Loneliness: Mary Moody Emerson's Almanacks, 1802–1855," 7. See also George Tolman, *Mary Moody Emerson.*

135. Lee Virginia Chambers-Schiller, *Liberty a Better Husband, Single Women in America: The Generation of 1780–1840,* 21.

136. Almanack of Mary Moody Emerson, quoted in Chambers-Schiller, *Liberty a Better Husband,* 58.

137. Mary Moody Emerson. Almanacks and Correspondence. Almanack, Folder 1, November 7, 1804 (hereafter referred to as Mary Moody Emerson Almanack).

138. Mary Moody Emerson Almanack, Folder 1, November 11, 1804.

139. Ibid., November 21, 1805.

140. Ibid., Folder 3, December 21, 1805.

141. David R. Williams, "The Wilderness Rapture of Mary Moody Emerson: One Calvinist Link to Transcendentalism," 5.

142. Mary Moody Emerson Almanack, Folder 1, November 7, 1804.

143. Ibid., November 17, 1804.

144. Cole, "Advantage of Loneliness," 12.

145. Ibid., 13.

146. Mary Moody Emerson Almanack, Folder 3, December 24, 1806.

147. Ibid., February 12, 1807.

148. Ibid., April 11, 1807.

149. Ibid., December 24, 1806.

150. Ibid.

151. Ibid., December 30, 1806.

152. Ibid., December 20, 1806.

153. Cole, "Advantage of Loneliness," 21.

154. Mary Moody Emerson Almanack, Folder 3, May 1807.

155. Ralph Waldo Emerson, *Lectures,* 428–429.

156. Ibid., 429–430.

157. Ibid., 399. See also Barbara E. Lacey, "The World of Hannah Heaton: The Autobiography of an Eighteenth-Century Connecticut Farm Woman"; Experiences Or Spiritual Exercises of Hannah Cook Heaton, 1734–1793, 4.

158. *Testimonies of the Life, Character, Revelations and Doctrines of Mother Ann Lee*, 4–5, 37, 269–273.

Chapter 4

1. Joan Jacobs Brumberg, *Mission for Life, The Story of the Family of Adoniram Judson*, x–xi.

2. Richard Rabinowitz, *Spiritual Self*, 217.

3. Ibid., 49.

4. Ibid., 50.

5. Ibid., 94.

6. Ibid., 184.

7. Jonathan Edwards, *Representative Selections*, 220.

8. William B. Sprague, *Lectures on Revivals of Religion, with an Introduction by Leonard Woods*, 98. See also Heman Humphrey, *Revival Sketches and Manual*; E. Porter, *Letters on Revivals of Religion Which Prevailed About the Beginning of the Present Century*; Heman Humphrey, *Christian Memoirs, Or the Nature of Conviction of Sin and Regeneration Illustrated in Narratives of Conversion of Eminent Christians*; John Woodbridge, "Revivals: The Appropriate Means of Promoting True Religion"; Bennet Tyler, *New England Revivals, As They Existed at the Close of the Eighteenth Century and the Beginning of the Nineteenth Century.*

9. Asahel Nettleton, *Remains of the Late Reverend Asahel Nettleton, D.D.*, 336.

10. Ibid.

11. E. Porter, *Letters on Revivals*, 75, 53–54.

12. Susan Juster, "In a Different Voice: Male and Female Narratives of Religious Conversion in Post-Revolutionary America," 34.

13. Bennet Tyler, *New England Revivals*, 176–177.

14. Richard D. Birdsall, "The Second Great Awakening and the New England Social Order," 387. See also Barbara Leslie Epstein, *The Politics of Domesticity, Women, Evangelism and Temperance in Nineteenth-Century America*, 56–61.

15. Juster, "Different Voice," 37–38.

16. McLoughlin, *Revivals, Awakenings*, 114.

17. Nathaniel Taylor, *Moral Government*, vol. 1, 307.

18. Nathaniel Taylor, *Mental Philosophy*, 279–281.

19. Taylor, 1843, 289–290.

20. I have applied the analysis of covert rebellion of the adolescent Victorian daughter against maternal overinvolvement developed by Joan Jacobs Brumberg, *Fasting Girls, The Emergence of Anorexia Nervosa as a Modern Disease*, to the question of covert rebellion among religious melancholiacs.

21. Buel and Buel, *Way of Duty*, 271–272.

22. William Channing Woodbridge, Diary, April 24, 1815, MS# 1078 (hereafter referred to as Woodbridge Diary).

23. Woodbridge Diary, May 6, 1815.

24. Silliman Family Correspondence, May 15, 1815, Benjamin Noyes's Suicide Note (hereafter referred to as Silliman Family Correspondence).

25. Letter from Mary Fish to Benjamin Silliman, May 7, 1815, Silliman Family Correspondence.

26. Letter from John Noyes to Mary Fish, May 7, 1815, Silliman Family Correspondence.

27. Henry E. Noyes and Harriet E. Noyes, *Genealogical Record of Some of the Noyes Descendants of James, Nichols, and Peter Noyes*, vol. 2, 105.

28. Buel and Buel, *Way of Duty*, 195; John Noyes, *Letters, Chiefly of a Moral and Religious Nature to Friends of Various Conditions*, 8.

29. Buel and Buel, *Way of Duty*, 256–257.

30. John Noyes, *Letters*, 5.

31. Buel and Buel, *Way of Duty*, 142ff.

32. John Noyes, *Letters*, 132.

33. Ibid., 140.

34. Ibid., 144.

35. Buel and Buel, *Way of Duty*, 62, 250ff.

36. Ibid., 242.

37. Benjamin Silliman, "Memoir of Benjamin Noyes," Noyes Family Papers (hereafter referred to as Memoir).

38. Joseph F. Kett, *Rites of Passage, Adolescence in America 1790 to the Present*, 14–37.

39. Memoir, 1815 (n.p.).

40. Ibid.

41. Ibid.

42. Ibid.

43. Diary of Benjamin Noyes, August 18, 1811, Noyes Family Papers (hereafter referred to as Benjamin Noyes Diary).

44. Benjamin Noyes Diary, August 16, 1812. See also John Todd, *The Student's Manual*; G. J. Barker-Benfield, *The Horrors of the Half-Known Life, Male Attitudes Toward Women and Sexuality in Nineteenth-Century America*, 135–174.

45. Benjamin Noyes Diary, August 16, 1812.

46. Letter from John Noyes to Benjamin Noyes, November 4, 1812, Noyes Family Papers.

47. Ibid.

48. Letter from Benjamin Noyes to John Noyes, November 17, 1812, Noyes Family Papers.

49. Edwards, *Representative Selections*, 214.

50. Letter from Benjamin Noyes to John Noyes, December 26, 1812, Noyes Family Papers.

51. "Benjamin Noyes Covenant," Silliman Family Correspondence, 1814.

52. Ibid.

53. John Noyes, *Letters*, 105–106.

54. Benjamin Noyes Diary, April 4, 1813.

55. Ibid.

56. Ibid., July 19, 1813.

57. Ibid., August 20, 1813.

58. Ibid., "Course of the Day."

59. Ibid., August 7, 1814.

60. Letter from Benjamin Noyes to Mary Fish, December 2, 1814, Silliman Family Correspondence.

61. Benjamin Noyes Diary, January 1, 1815.

62. Ibid.

63. Ibid.

64. Ibid., February 21, 1815.

65. Ibid., February 25, 1815.

66. Ibid., March 4, 1815.

67. Chauncey Goodrich, "Narrative of the Revivals of Religion in Yale College, From Its Commencement to the Present Time," 301.

68. Ibid., 301.

69. B. B. Edwards, *Memoir*, 34–55.

70. Diary of William Channing Woodbridge, May 9, 1815.

71. Goodrich, "Narrative," 302.

72. Charles Roy Keller, *The Second Great Awakening in Connecticut*, 42.

73. Hugh S. Fraser, *Pedagogue For God's Kingdom, Lyman Beecher and the Second Great Awakening*, 11–12.

74. B. B. Edwards, *Memoir*, 32.

75. Letter from Benjamin Noyes to Mary Fish, December 12, 1814, Silliman Family Correspondence.

76. Benjamin Noyes Diary, February 18, 1815.

77. William Channing Woodbridge Diary, March 18, 1815.

78. Benjamin Noyes Diary, March 18, 1815.

79. Ibid., March 19, 1815.

80. William Channing Woodbridge Diary, April 1, 1815.

81. Ibid., March 12 and 13, 1815.

82. Nathaniel Taylor, "*Concio Ad Clerium*," 8.

83. Foster, *Genetic History*, 249. I borrow the term "omnicausal self" from the work of Steven M. Tipton, *Getting Saved From the Sixties, Moral Meaning in Conversion and Cultural Change*, 210–231.

84. Taylor, "*Concio Ad Clerium*," 40.

85. William Channing Woodbridge Diary, March 15, 1815.

86. Benjamin Noyes Suicide Note.

87. Benjamin Noyes Diary, March 22, 1815.

88. Ibid., March 28, 1815.

89. Ibid., March 28, 1815.

90. Ibid., April 12, 14, 1815.

91. Ibid., April 15, 1815.

92. Anon., *Religious Intelligencer*, 9, no. 14, 432.

93. Anon., *Religious Intelligencer*, 9, no. 41, 656.

94. Anon., *Religious Intelligencer*, "An Account of the Revival of Religion in Newington, the Second Parish in Wethersfield, Connecticut," 794–795.

Chapter 5

1. William Sims Bainbridge, "Religious Insanity in America: The Official Nineteenth Century Theory," 226–227; Ronald L. Numbers and Janet S. Numbers, "Religious Insanity, History of a Diagnosis," 57–64; Ronald L. Numbers and Janet S. Numbers, "Millerism and Madness: A Study of 'Religious Insanity' in Nineteenth-Century America," 94–97.

2. Julius H. Rubin, *Mental Illness in Early Nineteenth Century New England and the Beginnings of Institutional Psychiatry as Revealed in a Sociological Study of the Hartford Retreat, 1824–1843*, 59.

3. See Ruth B. Caplan, *Psychiatry and Community in Nineteenth Century America, the Recurring Concern with the Environment and the Prevention of*

Mental Illness; Eric Carlson and Norman Dain, "The Psychotherapy that Was Moral Treatment," 519–524; Norman Dain and Eric Carlson, "Milieu Therapy in the Nineteenth Century: Patient Care at the Friends' Asylum, Frankford, Pennsylvania, 1817–1861," 227–290; Sanborn J. Bockhoven, *Moral Treatment in American Psychiatry.*

4. Michel Foucault, *Madness and Civilization, A History of Insanity in the Age of Reason,* 221 ff; Michel Foucault, *The Birth of the Clinic, An Archaeology of Medical Perception,* 18–19.

5. Medical Diaries and Patient Correspondence, Hartford Retreat, Patient 1826 A-7.

6. Letter from Samuel Stevens to Dr. Eli Todd, March 8, 1830, Medical Archives, Hartford, Retreat.

7. Lyman Beecher, *The Autobiography of Lyman Beecher,* vol. 1, 51.

8. Ibid., xiii. See also Milton Rugoff, *The Beechers, An American Family in the Nineteenth Century,* 203–206; Lyman Beecher Stowe, *Saints, Sinners and Beechers,* 111; Marie Caskey, *Chariots of Fire, Religion and the Beecher Family,* 98–99.

9. Lyman Beecher, *Autobiography,* xiii.

10. Catherine Beecher, *Biographical Remains of the Reverend George Beecher,* 6–7.

11. Catherine Beecher, *Letters on the Difficulties of Religion,* 159.

12. Rugoff, *Beechers,* 203.

13. Catherine Beecher, *Biographical Remains,* 38.

14. Ibid., 56, 83.

15. Ibid., 6.

16. James Lockwood Wright, Student Diaries and Correspondence, March 20, 1851, MS #1078.

17. Catherine M. Sedgwick, *A New England Tale and Miscellanies,* 39.

18. Mary E. Dewey, ed., *Life and Letters of Catherine M. Sedgwick,* 68.

19. Otis Skinner, "Account of the Death of Phileman, William and Cyrus, the only Children of Mr. Zaphua and Mrs. Lois Stone," 167–168. See also Russell E. Miller, *The Larger Hope, The First Century of the Universalist Church in America, 1770–1870,* 267, 269–271.

20. Sebastian and Russell Streeter, *Universalist Quarterly,* November, 1840, 394, 396, quoted from Miller, *Larger Hope,* 270.

21. Robert C. Fuller, *Alternative Medicine and American Religious Life,* 20, 34–36. See also Susan E. Cayleff, *Wash and Be Healed, The Water-Cure Movement and Women's Health,* 173–175.

22. Jane B. Donegan, *Hydropathic Highway to Health, Women and Water Cure in Antebellum America,* xi-xii.

23. Ann Braude, *Radical Spirits, Spiritualism and Women's Rights in Nineteenth Century America,* 37.

24. Ibid., 37–38.

25. Barbara Sapinsley, *The Private War of Mrs. Packard,* 23, 32.

26. Ibid., 121ff.

27. John Foster Reeve, "On A Method of Administration, By Means of a New Contrivance, Nourishment to Insane Persons Who Refuse Food," 313. *See also* S. Williams, "Remarks on the Refusal of Food in the Insane." 366–370. I am particularly indebted to the work of Joan Jacobs Brumberg, *Fasting Girls,* 75–78.

28. Luther Bell, "On the Coercive Adminstration of Food to the Insane," 224–226.

29. George Man Burrows, *Commentaries on the Causes, Forms, Symptoms, and Treatment, Moral and Medical of Insanity,* 295, 665.

30. Hilde Bruch, "Differential Diagnosis" as quoted in Caroline Walker Bynum, *Holy Feast and Holy Fast: The Religious Significance of Food to Medieval Women,* 201. See also Hilde Bruch, *Eating Disorders: Obesity, Anorexia Nervosa and the Person Within.*

31. Bynum, *Holy Feast,* 5, 26–67ff.

32. Ibid., 296.

33. Rudolph Bell, *Holy Anorexia,* 14. See also Gail Corrington, "Anorexia, Asceticism, and Autonomy: Self-Control as Liberation and Transcendence," 60.

34. Corrington, "Anorexia," 61.

35. Brumberg makes this insightful use of William James in *Fasting Girls,* 184–185.

36. William James, *Varieties,* 239, 286–287.

37. Representative works on contemporary eating disorders among women include Kim Cherlin, *The Hungry Self, Women, Eating and Identity;* Susan Orbach, *Hunger Strike, The Anorectic's Struggle as a Metaphor for Our Age;* Angelyn Spignesi, *Starving Women, A Psychology of Anorexia Nervosa.*

38. Edward Shorter, "The First Great Increase in Anorexia Nervosa," 84.

39. Brumberg, *Fasting Girls,* 87, 230ff.

40. Ibid., 137.

41. Nancy M. Theriot, "Psychosomatic Illness in History: The 'Green Sickness' Among Nineteenth-Century Adolescent Girls," 472.

42. Turner, *Body and Society,* 185. See also Hilde Bruch, *The Golden Cage: The Enigma of Anorexia Nervosa.*

43. Anon., *New York Evangelist.*

44. Nathanael Emmons, *Works,* 720.

45. Ibid., 724.

46. Ibid., 732.

47. Ibid.

48. Ibid., 721.

49. Bennet Tyler, *New England Revivals,* 292–293.

50. Anon., "Quench Not the Spirit," 515–516.

51. Hannah More, *Practical Piety, Or the Influence of the Religion of the Heart Upon the Conduct of Life,* 16.

52. Ibid., 73.

53. Ibid., 81–82.

54. Charles G. Finney, *Lectures on Revivals of Religion,* 14–15.

55. Benjamin B. Wisner, "Review of 'The New Divinity Tried,' Being an Examination of a Sermon Delivered by the Rev. C. G. Finney in Making a New Heart," 34.

56. Charles G. Finney, *Principles of Devotion,* 55.

57. Letter from E. M. Knight to Mrs. Lydia Finney, September 8, 1829, Charles Grandison Finney Papers.

58. Heman Humphrey, *Revival Sketches and Manual,* 442–443.

59. Anon., "On Despair of Mercy," 624.

60. Anon., *The Religious Intelligencer,* 765.

61. Francis Olcott Allen, *The History of Enfield, Connecticut,* vol. 2, 1411.

62. Anon., *The Religious Intelligencer,* 130.

63. Heman Humphrey, *Thirty-Four Letters to A Son in the Ministry,* 90.

64. Ibid., 266.

65. Ibid., 325.

66. Medical Diaries and Patient Correspondence, Medical Archives, Hartford Retreat, Case History #121.

67. Johann Jacob Mueller, *De Melancholia Attonita Raro Litteratorum Affectu*, 5. I wish to express my appreciation for the translation rendered by Professor Barbara Patla, Albertus Magnus College, New Haven, Connecticut, and Professor Judith Perkins, Saint Joseph College, West Hartford, Connecticut.

68. Ibid., 8.

69. Ibid., 9.

70. Nancy A. Hewitt, "The Perimeters of Women's Power in American Religion"; Carroll Smith Rosenberg, "Women and Religious Revivals: Anti-Ritualism, Liminality, and the Emergence of the American Bourgeoisie"; Mary Ryan, *Cradle of the Middle Class: The Family in Oneida County, New York, 1790–1865*; Paul E. Johnson, *A Shopkeeper's Millennium, Society and Revivals in Rochester, New York, 1815–1837*.

71. See Ryan, *Cradle*, 146–155.

72. Hewitt, "Perimeters of Women's Power," 247.

73. Ibid., 248.

74. Whitney R. Cross, *The Burned-Over District, The Social and Intellectual History of Enthusiastic Religion in Western New York, 1800–1850*, 181.

75. Finney, *Lectures on Revivals*, 243.

76. Ibid., 11. See also Perry Miller, *The Life of the Mind in America from the Revolution to the Civil War*; Alice Felt Tyler, *Freedom's Ferment, Phases of American Social History from the Colonial Period to the Outbreak of the Civil War*; Bernard A. Weisberger, *They Gathered at the River, The Story of the Great Revivalists and Their Impact Upon Religion in America*; George M. Marsden, *The Evangelical Mind and the New School Presbyterian Experience, A Case Study of Thought and Theology in Nineteenth Century America*.

77. Anon., *The New York Evangelist*, January 1834, 7.

78. Finney, *Lectures on Revivals*, 133.

79. Cross, *Burned-Over District*, 181.

80. Leonard I. Sweet, "The View of Man Inherent in New Measure Revivalism," 211.

81. John Frost, Moses Gillet, and Noah Coe, *Narrative of the Revival of Religion in the County of Oneida Particularly in the Bounds of the Presbytery of Oneida, in the Year 1826*, 12.

82. Ibid., 12.

83. Charles G. Finney, *Lectures to Professing Christians*, 278.

84. Medical Diaries and Patient Correspondence, Medical Archives, Hartford Retreat, Case History #420.

85. Ibid.

86. Ibid.

87. Ibid.

88. Medical Diaries and Patient Correspondence, Medical Archives, Hartford Retreat, Case History # 246.

89. Ibid.

90. Ibid.

91. Ibid.

92. Ibid.

93. Medical Diaries and Patient Correspondence, Medical Archives, Hartford Retreat, Case History #247.

94. Medical Diaries and Patient Correspondence, Medical Archives, Hartford Retreat, Case History #514.

95. Ibid.

96. Ibid.

97. Ibid.

98. Medical Diaries and Patient Correspondence, Medical Archives, Hartford Retreat, Case History #563.

99. Ibid.

100. Aramiah Brigham, *Observations on the Influence of Religion Upon the Health and Physical Welfare of Mankind*, xiv-xxiv, 320. Brigham draws upon the work of Burrows, *Commentaries.*

101. Brigham, *Observations*, 43.

102. Ibid., 170.

103. Ibid., 171–172.

104. Ibid., 296.

105. Ibid., 330–332.

106. Anon., *Christian Spectator*, March 1832, 61–62.

107. Francis J. Braceland, *The Institute of Living, The Hartford Retreat, 1822–1972*, 64.

108. Stephen Nissenbaum, *Sex, Diet and Debility in Jacksonian America, Sylvester Graham and Health Reform*, 18–20; see also Jayne A. Sokolow, *Eros and Modernization, Sylvester Graham, Health Reform, and the Origins of Victorian Sexuality in America.*

109. Hillel Schwartz, *Never Satisfied, A Cultural History of Diets, Fantasies and Fat*, 25.

110. Sylvester Graham, *Lectures on the Science of Human Life*, 583.

111. Sylvester Graham, *The Aesculapian Tales of the Nineteenth Century*, 103.

112. Ibid., 64.

113. Ibid., 62.

114. Robert Samuel Fletcher, *A History of Oberlin College From the Foundation Through the Civil War*, vol. 1, 316–341.

115. Keith J. Hardman, *Charles Grandison Finney, 1792–1875, Revivalist and Reformer*, 333.

116. Charles G. Finney, *Memoirs of Rev. Charles G. Finney, Written By Himself*, 35–36.

117. Robert Samuel Fletcher, "Bread and Doctrine at Oberlin," 65.

118. Delazon Smith, " A History of Oberlin; Or New Lights of the West," quoted in Fletcher, "Bread and Doctrine," 65.

119. Clara Endicott Sears, *Bronson Alcott's Fruitlands*, xvii.

120. Catherine L. Albanese, *Nature Religion in America, From the Algonkian Indians to the New Age.*

121. Sears, *Bronson Alcott's Fruitlands*, 126.

122. Ibid., 127. See also F. B. Sanborn and William T. Harris, *A. Bronson Alcott, His Life and Philosophy*, vol. 2, 380–381 for a discussion of the distinguished English psychiatrist Dr. Tuke, who answers the question, "Was Alcott Insane?" "That such a man should induce others to imitate him and for a community, would astonish us, were it not an oft-repeated fact in history . . . I find no evidence whatever of mental disease, and regard such things as illustrations of peculiar psychical constitutions,

which under remarkable upheavals of religious thought fell into eccentric courses, but did not become insane."

123. John Owen King, *Iron of Melancholy*, 138.

124. Austin Warren, *The Elder Henry James*, 187.

125. Henry James, Sr., *The Literary Remains of the Late Henry James*, 184.

126. Ibid., 185.

127. Henry James, Sr., *Henry James, Senior, A Selection of His Writings*, 55.

128. Ibid., 55–56.

129. John Owen King, *Iron of Melancholy*, 91.

130. Henry James, 1885, 39–40. Henry James argued that the work of the Creator God in completing the spiritual conversion of each believer eradicated the "natural" *proprium* and allowed the new spiritual persons, the "Divine-Natural Humanity" to emerge. However, James insisted that the movement of redemption necessitated the social, the collective. Society would serve as the arena of spiritual perfection and collective morality. See Katherine Weissbourd, *Growing Up in the James Family, Henry James, Sr., as Son and Father*, 53ff; Dwight W. Hoover, *Henry James, Sr. and the Religion of Community*, 63. Hoover states, "Leading men back into union with God, redemption supplemented the original separative work of creation. It was the inward or spiritual being of creation designed to invest man with divine good. In this sense redemption, as conceived by both James and Swedenborg, was more glorious than creation, for redemption completed the positive phase of creation. . . . for God and man unified to produce the final God, divine-natural humanity."

131. John Owen King, *Iron of Melancholy*, 90.

Chapter 6

1. Henry Adams, *The Education of Henry Adams, An Autobiography*, 378.

2. Ibid., 380.

3. Ibid., 385.

4. Benjamin Nelson, *On the Roads to Modernity*, 54.

5. Ibid., 54.

6. William James, *Varieties*, 200.

7. Ibid., 146.

8. Ibid., 87–88.

9. Numbers and Numbers, "Religious Insanity," 74; Ronald L. Numbers and Janet S. Numbers, "Millerism and Madness: A Study of 'Religious Insanity' in Nineteenth-Century America," in *The Disappointed*, 94–95.

10. De Swaan, *Management of Normality*, 139–142.

11. George M. Beard, *American Nervousness, Its Causes and Consequences*; Tom Lutz, *American Nervousness, 1903: An Anecdotal History*.

12. Lear, *Love and Its Place in Nature*, 29–68; Edward Shorter, *From Paralysis to Fatigue, A History of Psychosomatic Illness in the Modern Era*, 233ff.

13. Albanese, *Nature Religion*. See also Donald B. Meyer, *The Positive Thinkers, Popular Religious Psychology from Mary Baker Eddy to Norman Vincent Peale and Ronald Reagan*, 60–72.

14. McLoughlin, *Revivals, Awakenings, and Reform, An Essay on Religion and Social Change in America, 1607–1977*, 141ff.

15. Ibid., 173.

16. James Luther Adams, *An Examined Faith, Social Context and Religious Commitment*, 314.

17. Walter Rauschenbusch, "The New Evangelism," 111–112.

18. Ibid., 113.

19. William McGuire King, "An Enthusiasm for Humanity: The Social Emphasis in Religion and Its Accommodation in Protestant Theology," 52.

20. Ibid., 54.

21. George Albert Coe, *The Religion of a Mature Mind*, 374.

22. Ibid., 172.

23. Ibid., 264.

24. C. Allyn Russell, *Voices of American Fundamentalism, Seven Biographical Studies*, 16.

25. Nancy Tatum Ammerman, *Bible Believers, Fundamentalists in the Modern World*; James Davison Hunter, *American Evangelicalism, Conservative Religion and the Quandary of Modernity*; A. G. Mojtabai, *Blessed Assurance, At Home with the Bomb in Amarillo, Texas*.

26. George M. Marsden, *Fundamentalism and American Culture, The Shaping of Twentieth-Century Evangelicalism: 1870–1925*, 224.

27. Ibid.

28. Ibid., 25.

29. Hunter, *American Evangelicalism*, 38,

30. Russell, *Voices*, 17.

31. George M. Marsden, "Evangelicals and the Scientific Culture: An Overview," 44.

32. McLoughlin, *Revivals, Awakenings*, 179ff.

33. Mark Silk, *Spiritual Politics, Religion and America Since World War II*, 15.

34. Robert Wuthnow, *The Restructuring of American Religion, Society and Faith Since World War II*, 71ff.

35. Frank J. Mead, *Handbook of Denominations in the United States*, 81–94.

36. Randall Balmer, *Mine Eyes Have Seen the Glory, A Journey into the Evangelical Subculture in America*, 229.

37. Wuthnow, *Restructuring*, 316.

38. Ibid., 57.

39. Ross W. Rolland, "The Continuity of Evangelical Life and Thought," 249.

40. Ibid., 250, quotation from W. R. Nicoll, *The Evangelical Succession*, vol 3, 69.

41. John Owen King, *Iron of Melancholy*, 7–9.

42. American Institute of Public Opinion, *Religion in America, 1990*, 41.

43. Theodore Caplow et al., *All Faithful People, Change and Continuity in Middletown's Religion*, 66–67.

44. McLoughlin, *Revivals, Awakenings*, 213.

45. Joel A. Carpenter, ed., *Two Reformers of Fundamentalism, Harold John Ockenga and Carl F. H. Henry*, 1.

46. Betty A. DeBerg, *Ungodly Women, Gender and the First Wave of American Fundamentalism*, 99; Charles H. Lippy, ed., *Twentieth-Century Shapers of American Popular Religion*, xix.

47. Harold J. Ockenga, "From Fundamentalism, Through New Evangelicalism, to Evangelicalism," 44. See also Mark Silk, "The Rise of the 'New Evangelicalism': Shock and Adjustment," 278ff.

48. Silk, *Spiritual Politics*, 65.

49. Ibid., 65.

50. A. James Reichley, "Pietist Politics," in Norman J. Cohen (ed), *The Fundamentalist Phenomenon, A View from Within; A Response from Without*, 82. See Samuel S. Hill, Jr.,"The Shape and Shapes of Popular Southern Piety," 97. "A high degree of personal intensity prevails among EPs (evangelical Protestants). The Lord's business is indeed serious business. It is made so by God's grace, Christ's saving death, and the desperate condition of sinful humanity. These being matters of utmost significance, the Christian is rightly a dedicated, devout, disciplined person."

51. Carpenter, *Two Reformers*, 195.

52. William G. McLoughlin, Jr., *Billy Graham, Revivalist in a Secular Age*, 146. See also Lippy, *Twentieth-Century Shapers*, 184.

53. McLoughlin, *Billy Graham*, 53–54.

54. Lippy, *Twentieth-Century Shapers*, 180.

55. McLoughlin, *Billy Graham*, 148–149.

56. Ibid., 146.

57. Reichley, "Pietist Politics," 82.

58. Lippy, *Twentieth-Century Shapers*, 182. Frank J. Lechner, "Fundamentalism Revisited," 88–89.

59. William Martin, "Billy Graham," 73.

60. Billy Graham, *Peace with God*, 7.

61. Ibid., 15.

62. Billy Graham, *How to Be Born Again*, 143.

63. Billy Graham, *Peace with God*, 85.

64. Ibid., 108.

65. Ibid., 54. The second part of this quotation is taken from the Lutheran hymn composed by Isaac Watts (1674–1748), "Alas! And Did My Savior Bleed." Watts composed this work for the 1707 edition of *Hymns and Spiritual Songs*.

66. Ibid., 117.

67. Ibid., 154.

68. Ibid., 143.

69. Ibid., 158.

70. Curtis Mitchell, *Those Who Came Forward, Men and Women Who Responded to the Ministry of Billy Graham*; Lewis W. Gillenson, *Billy Graham and Seven Who Were Saved*.

71. Reinhold Niebuhr, "Liberalism, Individualism and Billy Graham," 642.

72. Billy Graham, *The Holy Spirit, Activating God's Power in Your Life*, 89.

73. Ibid.

74. Ibid., 102.

75. Rudolph Nelson, *The Making and Unmaking of an Evangelical Mind, The Case of Edward Carnell*, 11, 120–121.

76. John G. Stackhouse, Jr. "'Who Follows in His Train', Edward J. Carnell As a Model of Evangelical Theology," 20.

77. James Luther Adams, *Examined Faith*, 1, 20.

78. Rudolph Nelson, *Making and Unmaking*, 117.

79. Ibid., 73.

80. George M. Marsden, *Reforming Fundamentalism*, 128–129.

81. John R. Muether, "Contemporary Evangelicalism, A Triumph of the New School," 346–347.

82. Rudolph Nelson, *Making and Unmaking*, 127.

83. Ibid., 10–11.

84. Ibid., chap. 7, 8.

85. Edward J. Carnell, *The Case for Christian Orthodoxy*, 113.

86. Edward J. Carnell, *The Case for Biblical Christianity*, 44–47.

87. Ibid., 46, cited in Rudolph Nelson, *Making and Unmaking*, 108.

88. Carnell, *Biblical Christianity*, 44–47, quoted in Rudolph Nelson, *Making and Unmaking*, 124.

89. Rudolph Nelson, *Making and Unmaking*, 172.

90. Ibid., 115.

91. Ibid., 117.

92. Edward J. Carnell, *The Kingdom of Love and the Pride of Life*, 7.

93. Ibid., 92.

94. Ibid., 92–93.

95. Ibid., 93.

96. Marsden, *Reforming Fundamentalism*, 193.

97. Sherman Roddy, "Fundamentalists and Ecumenicity," 1109, quoted in Marsden, *Reforming Fundamentalism*, 187.

98. Ibid., 1110.

99. Carnell, 1960, 6–7.

100. Rudolph Nelson, *Making and Unmaking*, 116.

101. Carnell, *Kingdom of Love*, 153.

102. Marsden, *Reforming Fundamentalism*, 194.

103. Lear, *Love and Its Place*, 153.

104. Ibid., 187.

105. Ibid., 212.

106. Stackhouse, "Who Follows," 20. Carnell was a theologian working out insights from his biography and universalizing them for all believers.

107. Georgia Harkness, *The Dark Night of the Soul*, 9.

108. Diane Carpenter and Rolaine Franz, "Georgia Harkness as a Personalist Theologian," 161.

109. Hilah F. Thomas and Rosemary Skinner Keller, *Women in New Worlds, Historical Perspectives on the Wesleyan Tradition*, 121–131.

110. Ibid., 136.

111. Ibid., 119.

112. Ibid., 135.

113. Harkness, *Dark Night*, 9.

114. Ibid., 15.

115. Ibid., 27.

116. E. Brooks Holifield, *A History of Pastoral Care in America, From Salvation to Self-Realization*, 244.

117. Anton T. Boisen, "The Therapeutic Significance of Anxiety," 9.

118. Anton T. Boisen, *Out of the Depths, An Autobiographical Study of Mental Disorder and Religious Experience*, 135–136.

119. Anton T. Boisen, *The Exploration of the Inner World, A Study of Mental Disorder and Religious Experience*, ix. Anton T. Boisen, "Religious Experience and Psychological Conflict," 568.

120. Boisen, *Exploration*, 80.

121. O. Hobart Mowrer, *The Crisis in Psychiatry and Religion*, 162–163. See also LeRoy Aden and David G. Berimer, eds., *Counseling and the Human Predicament, A Study of Sin, Guilt and Forgiveness*, 77ff.

122. N.J.C. Andreasen, "The Role of Religion in Depression," 153.

123. Albert Ellis, "There Is No Place for the Concept of Sin in Psychotherapy," 191.

124. Jesse O. Cavenar, Jr., and Jean G. Spaulding, "Depressive Disorders and Religious Conversion," 210.

125. Dwight W. Cumbee, "Depression as an Ecclesiogenic Neurosis," 255.

126. Ibid., 255.

127. Eric J. Cohen, "Induced Christian Neurosis: An Examination of Pragmatic Paradoxes and the Christian Faith," 5.

128. See Gary W. Hartz and Henry C. Everett, "Fundamentalist Religion and Its Effect on Mental Health," 207ff, for a discussion of Fundamentalists Anonymous, a group that alleges there is a propensity for adherents of fundamentalism to suffer from depressive illness. See also Dennis L. Gibson, "The Obsessive Personality and the Evangelical," 31–33.

129. Jack O. Balswich, "The Psychological Captivity of Evangelicalism," 144ff; Peter Homans, "Protestant Theology and Dynamic Psychology: New Thoughts on An Old Problem," 125–137.

130. Philip Rieff, *The Triumph of the Therapeutic, Uses of Faith After Freud*, 266.

131. Holifield, *History of Pastoral Care*, 365.

132. Hunter, *American Evangelicalism*, 95.

133. Tim LaHaye, *How to Win Over Depression*, 87, quoted in Hunter, *American Evangelicalism*, 96.

134. In *Ungodly Women*, DeBerg argues that both women's conversion narratives and fundamentalist teaching rejected modern feminist thought. Rather than support the issues of women's autonomy, divorce, sexual freedom, equal rights, reproductive rights, and other social questions, fundamentalism urged women to reappropriate the doctrine of "separate spheres"—more traditional, nineteenth-century gender roles that promoted the "Cult of True Womanhood" with its call for submission and surrender to God and husbandly authority. See also Virginia Lieson Brereton, *From Sin to Salvation, Stories of Women's Conversions, 1800 to the Present*, 90ff. "In the typical version of later twentieth-century narratives, a converted woman learns to love 'her man' better, including sexually, because she has learned surrender and submission to God. She no longer needs to doubt or prove her lovableness; she *feels* she is lovable. She better tolerates any failings and weaknesses of her husband. She submits with a lighter heart and more patience to the demands of her children. . . . Her release from anxiety may give her energy to be better at things that women are supposed to do well: to be more loving, and giving and nurturing and uncomplaining."

Yet, the need for submission was always a burden when women lapsed and attempted to act with self-assurance, independence, and agency. Thus, the evangelical woman always fought inner battles against this dimension of the self, seeking renewed submission to God's will and the leadings of her husband. The theme of submission versus autonomy provides an ideal point of departure for studies of contemporary depression among women. This is a gender-related variation upon the theme of life as pilgrimage. See Ann Kiemel Anderson, *I Gave God Time*, 147ff, for an account of the dialectic of submission and autonomy.

135. Holifield, *History of Pastoral Care*, 352.

136. David Harrington Watt, *Transforming Faith, Explorations of Twentieth-Century American Evangelicalism*, 154.

137. Vernon Grounds, *Emotional Problems and the Gospel*, 108.

138. Ibid., 110.

139. Matilda Nordtvedt, *Defeating Depression and Despair*, 92.

140. Maria Nelson, *Why Christians Crack Up*, 139–140.

141. D. Martyn Lloyd-Jones, *Spiritual Depression: Its Cause and Cure*, 66.

142. C. S. Lewis, *The Screwtape Letters*, 36ff.

143. Ammerman, *Bible Believers*, 65.

144. Steven M. Tipton, *Getting Saved from the Sixties, Moral Meaning in Conversion and Cultural Change*, 31. See also Meredith B. McGuire, *Ritual Healing in Suburban America*, 38–78. R. Stephen Warner has produced an interesting study of how a hippie commune was transformed from a countercultural Gnostic group devoted to atomistic individualism, drug-induced experiences of communion, and sexual freedom, into a Pentecostalist sect. This occurs as a subplot seen against the wider conservative revitalization of a liberal congregation. See R. Stephen Warner, *New Wine in Old Wineskins, Evangelicals and Liberals in a Small-Town Church*.

145. Tipton, *Getting Saved*, 41.

146. Ibid., 30.

147. Ibid., 61.

148. Olive Wyon, *On the Way, Some Reflections on the Christian Life*, 36–37.

149. Ammerman, *Bible Believers*, 64–67.

150. Elaine J. Lawless, *God's Peculiar People, Women's Voices and Folk Tradition in a Pentecostal Church*.

151. Susan F. Harding, "Convicted by the Holy Spirit: The Rhetoric of Fundamental Baptist Conversion," 179.

152. David Edwin Harrell, *All Things Are Possible, The Healing and Charismatic Revivals in Modern America*, 5.

153. Ibid., 6.

154. A. A. Allen, *The Curse of Madness*, 99.

155. James Luther Adams, *Examined Faith*, 340.

156. Robert A. Raines, *New Life in the Church*, 39.

157. Ibid., 6–7.

158. James Luther Adams, *Examined Faith*, 343.

159. Robert A. Raines, *Going Home*, 5–6.

160. Ibid., 10.

161. Robert N. Bellah et al., *Habits of the Heart, Individualism and Community in American Life*.

162. William James, *Varieties*, 297.

163. Roy W. Fairchild, "Issues in Contemporary Spirituality: The Upsurge of Spiritual Movements," 5.

164. Ibid., 5.

165. Ibid., 14.

166. George Mark Fisher, "A Ministry of Encouragement to Those Who Feel Forsaken By God at Ross Christian Church, Ross, Ohio," 94.

167. Ibid., 96.

168. Joseph W. Eaton and Robert J. Weil, *Culture and Mental Disorders, A Comparative Study of Hutterites and Other Populations*; Benjamin Zablocki, *The Joyful Community, An Account of the Bruderhof, A Communal Movement Now in Its Third Generation*; John McKelvie Whitworth, *God's Blueprints, A Sociological Study of Three Utopian Sects*, 167ff. Many allegations have been made about what we have termed evangelical nurture and religious melancholy among a contemporary Anabaptist community—the Bruderhof. The KIT Information Service, founded in 1989 by Ramon Sender, publishes a monthly newsletter distributed to 300 previ-

ous members of the Bruderhof. Remembrances and personal accounts published in KIT speak of mind control, and emotional and physical abuse of children and adults. A KIT brochure states, "For example, the high incidence of mental breakdowns and even suicide among both members and graduates (ex-members) is a troubling matter that KIT seeks to explore and ameliorate." KIT Information Service, P.O. Box 460141, San Francisco, CA 94146.

Appendix A

1. William A. Clebsch and Charles R. Jaekle, *Pastoral Care in Historical Perspective*; Benjamin Nelson, "Self-Images," 349ff.

2. James Hoopes, *Consciousness in New England*, 21.

3. Cross, *Burned-Over District*.

4. Holifield, *History of Pastoral Care*, 139.

5. Greven, *The Protestant Temperament*, 151.

6. Holifield, *History of Pastoral Care*, 143–144.

7. Ibid., 149.

8. Hoopes, *Consciousness*, 32ff.

9. Ibid., 123.

10. Holifield, *History of Pastoral Care*, 157.

Appendix B

1. McLoughlin, *Revivals, Awakenings*, 2.

2. Benjamin Nelson, *On the Roads to Modernity*, 17–33.

3. Ibid., 23.

4. Benjamin Nelson, "Faces of Twentieth Century Analysis," 18. See Shorter, *From Paralysis to Fatigue*. Shorter has written a social history of psychosomatic illnesses, demonstrating that physicians, psychiatrists, and other alienists have developed generally accepted, paradigmatic clinical "perceptions" of psychosomatic symptomatology. These perceptions are mediated to patients as texts that shape the experience, expression, and understanding of illness. Paradigms help shape and legitimate the pathotherapeutics of a patient's malaise and presenting symptoms; and paradigms "recruit" patients by publicizing a new illness. Shorter examines the peculiar social histories of motor hysteria, spinal irritation, dissociation, and hysteria in the nineteenth century that doctors explained through the idea of mind-body interaction, reflex-arch, and the pelvic organs as the source of illness. These illnesses included hysterical blindness and paralysis, and hysteria. By the close of the nineteenth century, doctors changed their paradigms, citing the central nervous system as the cause of neurasthenia. Later, the psychoanalytic understanding of somatization as a process of using bodily distress as a modality of expression of intrapsychic and interpersonal conflicts attempted to supplant the central nervous system explanatory model. Late–twentieth-century patients no longer fall ill to motor hysteria and psychosomatic paralysis. Today, chronic fatigue syndrome, psychogenic chronic pain, and fixed illness belief represent the most common types of somatization.

5. Benjamin Nelson, *On the Road to Modernity*, p. 24.

6. Ibid., 25–26.

7. John Owen King, *Iron of Melancholy*, 2

8. Ibid., 7.

Bibliography

Unpublished Manuscripts

Bird, Isaac. Diary and Correspondence. Isaac Bird Papers, Manuscripts and Archives, Sterling Memorial Library, Yale University, New Haven, Connecticut.

Congregational Church Records. Osborn House, MS Book #1999. Newport Historical Society Library, Newport, Rhode Island.

Emerson, Mary Moody. Almanacks and Correspondence. Ralph Waldo Emerson Papers, Ralph Waldo Emerson Memorial Association, Houghton Library Manuscripts, Harvard University, Boston, Massachusetts.

Experiences Or Spiritual Exercises of Hannah Cook Heaton, 1734–1793. Whitney Library of the New Haven Colony Historical Society (typescript version of manuscript owned by Winifred N. Lincoln and Maryanne Lincoln, Bethany, Connecticut).

Finney, Charles G. Correspondence. Charles Grandison Finney Papers, Oberlin College Library, Oberlin, Ohio.

Fish, Mary. Journal and Correspondence. Silliman Family Papers, Manuscripts and Archives, Sterling Memorial Library, Yale University, New Haven, Connecticut.

Medical Diaries and Patient Correspondence. Medical Archives, Hartford Retreat, Ruth B. P. Burlingame Library, The Institute of Living, Hartford, Connecticut.

Moore, John. "On Religious Melancholy: A Sermon Preached Before the Queen at White-Hall, March 6, 1691." London, 1691. Archives of the Watkinson Library, Trinity College, Hartford, Connecticut.

Noyes, Benjamin. Diaries and Correspondence. Silliman Family Papers, Manuscripts and Archives, Sterling Memorial Library, Yale University, New Haven, Connecticut, and Noyes Family Papers, New Canaan Historical Society, New Canaan, Connecticut.

Osborn, Sarah. Correspondence. Sarah Osborn Collection, American Antiquarian Society, Worcester, Massachusetts, and Sarah Osborn Papers, Newport Historical Society, Newport, Rhode Island.

Silliman Family Correspondence. Silliman Family Papers. Manuscripts and Archives, Sterling Memorial Library, Yale University, New Haven Connecticut.

Taylor, Nathaniel. Mental Philosophy, 1843. Manuscripts and Special Collections, Yale University Divinity School Library, New Haven, Connecticut.

Tennent, Gilbert. Gilbert Tennent Sermons, 1742–1763. Heritage Patron Micropublications No. 225, Princeton Theological Seminary Library, Princeton, New Jersey.

Woodbridge, William Channing. Diaries and Correspondence. William Manning Woodbridge Papers. Manuscripts and Archives, Sterling Memorial Library, Yale University, New Haven, Connecticut.

Wright, James Lockwood. Student Diaries and Correspondence. James Lockwood Wright Papers, Manuscripts and Archives, Sterling Memorial Library, Yale University, New Haven, Connecticut.

Secondary Sources

Adams, Henry. *The Education of Henry Adams.* Boston: Houghton Mifflin, 1961.

Adams, James Luther. *An Examined Faith, Social Context and Religious Commitment.* Edited by George K. Beech. Boston: Beacon Press, 1991.

Aden, LeRoy, and Berimer, David G., eds. *Counseling and the Human Predicament, A Study of Sin, Guilt and Forgiveness.* Grand Rapids, Mich.: Baker Book House, 1989.

Albanese, Catherine L. *Nature Religion in America, From the Algonkian Indians to the New Age.* Chicago: University of Chicago Press, 1990.

Alexander, Archibald. *Biographical Sketches of the Founder, and Principal Alumni of the Log College: Together with an Account of the Revivals of Religion under Their Ministry.* Princeton, N.J.: J. T. Robinson, 1845.

Alexander, Jeffrey C. *The Classical Attempt at Theoretical Synthesis: Max Weber.* Theoretical Logics in Sociology, vol. 3. Berkeley: University of California Press, 1983.

Allen, Francis Olcott. *The History of Enfield Connecticut.* Lancaster, Pa.: Wickersham Printing Company, 1900.

Allen, Hannah. *Satan his Methods and Malice Baffled. A narrative of God's gracious dealings with that choice Christian, Mrs. Hannah Allen (afterwards married to Mr. Hatt) reciting the great advantages the Devil made of her deep melancholy, and the triumphant victories, rich and sovereign graces, God gave her over all his stratagems and devices.* London: Printed by John Wallis, 1683.

Ammerman, Nancy Tatum. *Bible Believers, Fundamentalists in the Modern World.* New Brunswick, N.J.: Rutgers University Press, 1988.

Anderson, Ann Kiemel. *I Gave God Time.* Wheaton, Ill.: Tyndale House Publishers, 1983.

Andreasen, N.J.C. "The Role of Religion in Depression." *Journal of Religion and Health* 11, no. 2 (1972): 153–166.

Anon. "On Despair of Mercy." *The Christian Spectator* 2, no. 12 (December 1820): 514–516.

Anon. "Quench Not the Spirit." *The Christian Spectator* 3, no. 10 (October 1821): 515–521.

Anon. *Religious Intelligencer* 2, no. 16 (March 9, 1822): 130.

Anon. "An Account of the Revival of Religion in Newington, the Second Parish in Wethersfield, Connecticut." *Religious Intelligencer* 6, no. 50 (May 1822): 793–796.

Anon. *Religious Intelligencer* 9, no. 14 (December 1824): 432–433.

Anon. *Religious Intelligencer* 9, no. 41 (March 1825): 655–656.

Anon. *Religious Intelligencer.* "Active Piety a Remedy for Despondency." 13, no. 8 (May 1829): 765–766.

Anon. *Christian Spectator* 3, 3rd ser. (March 1832): 61–62.

Anon. *New York Evangelist* 4, no. 2 (January 1834): 50–80.

Anon. *New York Evangelist* 11, no. 32 (August 29, 1840): 5–9.

Axtell, James. *The Invasion Within, The Contest of Cultures in Colonial North America*. New York: Oxford University Press, 1985.

———. *After Columbus, Essays in the Ethnohistory of Colonial North America*. New York: Oxford University Press, 1988.

Babb, Lawrence. *The Elizabethan Malady: A Study of Melancholia in English Literature from 1580–1642*. East Lansing: Michigan State College Press, 1951.

Bainbridge, William Sims. "Religious Insanity in America: The Official Nineteenth Century Theory." *Sociological Analysis* 45, no. 3 (Fall 1984): 223–240.

Bainton, Roland H. *Here I Stand, A Life of Martin Luther*. New York: Abington Press, 1950.

———. *The Reformation of the Sixteenth Century*. Boston: Beacon Press, 1952.

Balmer, Randall. *Mine Eyes Have Seen the Glory, A Journey into Evangelical Subculture in America*. New York: Oxford University Press, 1989.

Balswich, Jack O. "The Psychological Captivity of Evangelicalism." In *Religious Sociology, Interfaces and Boundaries*. Edited by William H. Swatos, Jr. New York: Greenwood Press, 1988.

Bangs, Nathan. *The Errors of Hopkinsonianism Detected and Refuted in Six Letters to the Reverend S. Tillison*. New York: John C. Totten, 1815.

Barker-Benfield, G. J. *The Horrors of the Half-Known Life, Male Attitudes Toward Women and Sexuality in Nineteenth-Century America*. New York: Harper Colophon, 1976.

Baxter, Richard. *The Right Method for a Settled Peace of Conscience and Spiritual Comfort, Practical Works of Rev. Richard Baxter*. London: James Duncan, 1830.

———. *A Treatise of Conversion, Practical Works of Rev. Richard Baxter*. London: James Duncan, 1830.

———. *Practical Works of the Rev. Richard Baxter*. London: James Duncan, 1830.

———. *The Saints Everlasting Rest*. New York: American Tract Society, 1850.

Bayley, Lewis. *Practice of Pietie directing a Christian how to walke that he may please God*. Amsterdam: J. Stafford, 1649.

Beard, George M. *American Nervousness, Its Causes and Consequences*. New York: Arno Press, 1972.

Beecher, Catherine. *Letters on the Difficulties of Religion*. Hartford, Conn.: Belknap & Hemersley, 1836.

———. *Biographical Remains of the Reverend George Beecher*. New York: Leavitt, Trow & Co., 1844.

Beecher, Lyman. *The Autobiography of Lyman Beecher*. Edited by Barbara M. Cross. Cambridge: Belknap Press of Harvard University, 1961.

Bell, Luther. "On the Coercive Administration of Food to the Insane." *American Journal of Insanity* 6 (1850): 224–226.

Bell, Rudolph. *Holy Anorexia*. Chicago: University of Chicago Press, 1985.

Bellah, Robert N.; Marsden, Richard; Sullivan, William M.; Swidler, Ann; and Tipton, Steven M. *Habits of the Heart, Individualism and Community in American Life*. Berkeley: University of California Press, 1985.

Bellamy, Joseph. *Works*. Boston: Doctrinal Tract and Book Society, 1853.

Bercovitch, Sacvan. *The Puritan Origins of the American Self*. New Haven: Yale University Press, 1975.

————. *The American Jeremiad*. Madison: University of Wisconsin Press, 1978.

Bergen, Evans. *The Psychiatry of Robert Burton*. New York: Columbia University Press, 1944.

Birdsall, Richard D. "The Second Great Awakening and the New England Social Order." *Church History* 39 (September 1970): 345–364.

Blakeway, Robert. *An Essay Towards the Cure of Religious Melancholy in a Letter to a Gentlewoman Afflicted with It*. London: Bezaleel Creake, 1717.

Bockhoven, Sanborn J. *Moral Treatment in American Psychiatry*. New York: Springer Publishing Company, 1963.

Boisen, Anton T. *Explorations of the Inner World, A Study of Mental Disorder and Religious Experience*. Chicago: Willet, Clark and Company, 1936.

————. "The Therapeutic Significance of Anxiety." *The Journal of Pastoral Care* 5, no. 2 (1951): 1–11.

————. "Religious Experience and Psychological Conflict." *American Psychologist* 13, no. 10 (October 1958): 568–570.

————. *Out of the Depths, An Autobiographical Study of Mental Disorder and Religious Experience*. New York: Harper and Brothers, 1960.

Bosco, Ronald A. *The Poems of Michael Wigglesworth*. New York: University Press of America, 1989.

Boudinot, Elias. "Memoirs of Rev. William Tennent, Late Pastor of the Presbyterian Church at Freehold in New Jersey." Morristown, N.J.: H. P. Russell, 1807.

Bouwsma, William J. *John Calvin, A Sixteenth-Century Portrait*. New York: Oxford University Press, 1985.

Bowden, Henry W., and Ronda, James, P., eds. *John Eliot's Indian Dialogue: A Study in Cultural Interaction*. Westport, Conn.: Greenwood Press, 1980.

Braceland, Francis J. *The Institute of Living, The Hartford Retreat, 1822–1972*. Hartford (Published by The Institute of Living), 1972.

Braude, Ann. *Radical Spirits, Spiritualism and Women's Rights in Nineteenth-Century America*. Boston: Beacon Press, 1989.

Bregman, Lucy. "Religion and Madness: Schreber's *Memoirs* as Personal Myth." *Journal of Religion and Health* 16, no. 2 (1977): 119–135.

Breitenbach, William. "Unregenerate Doings: Selflessness and Selfishness in New Divinity Theology." *American Quarterly* 34, no. 5 (1982): 479–502.

————. "The Consistent Calvinism of the New Divinity Movement." *William and Mary Quarterly* 41, no. 2 (April 1984): 241–261.

Brereton, Virginia Lieson. *From Sin to Salvation, Stories of Women's Conversion, 1800 to the Present*. Bloomington: Indiana University Press, 1991.

Brigham, Aramiah. *Observations on the Influence of Religion Upon the Health and Physical Welfare of Mankind*. Boston: Marsh, Capen & Lyon, 1835. Reprint. New York: Arno Press, 1973.

Bruch, Hilde. *The Golden Cage: The Enigma of Anorexia Nervosa*. Cambridge: Harvard University Press, 1978.

————. *Eating Disorders: Obesity, Anorexia Nervosa and the Person Within*. New York: Basic Books, 1988.

Brumberg, Joan Jacobs. *Mission for Life, The Story of the Family of Adoniram Judson, the Dramatic Events of the First American Foreign Mission, and the Course of Evangelical Religion in the Nineteenth Century*. New York: Free Press, 1980.

————. *Fasting Girls, The Emergence of Anorexia Nervosa as a Modern Disease*. Cambridge: Harvard University Press, 1988.

Buel, Joy D., and Buel, Richard, Jr. *The Way of Duty, A Woman and Her Family in Revolutionary America.* New York: W. W. Norton, 1984.

Bumsted, J. M., ed. *The Great Awakening, The Beginnings of Evangelical Pietism in America.* Waltham, Mass.: Blaisdell Publishing Company, 1970.

Bunyan, John. *Grace Abounding to the Chief of Sinners.* Chicago: Moody Press, 1959. Originally published 1666.

Burrows, George. *Commentaries on the Causes, Forms, Symptoms and Treatment, Moral and Medical of Insanity.* London, 1828.

Burton, Robert. *The Anatomy of Melancholy.* Edited by Floyd Dell and Paul Jordan-Smith. New York: Farrar and Rinehart, 1927.

Bushman, Richard L. *From Puritan to Yankee, Character and the Social Order in Connecticut, 1690–1765.* New York: W. W. Norton, 1976.

Byman, Seymour. "Child Raising and Melancholia in Tudor England." *Journal of Psychohistory* 5 (Spring 1978): 67–92.

Bynum, Caroline Walker. *Holy Feast and Holy Fast: The Religious Significance of Food to Medieval Women.* Berkeley: University of California Press, 1987.

Caldwell, Patricia. *The Puritan Conversion Narrative: The Beginnings of American Experience.* Cambridge: Cambridge University Press, 1983.

Calvin, John. *On the Christian Faith, Selections from the Institutes, Commentaries, and Tracts.* Edited by John T. McNeill. New York: Bobbs, Merrill Company, 1957.

———. *Institutes of the Christian Religion.* Grand Rapids, Mich.: William B. Eerdmans Publishing Company, 1957.

Caplan, Ruth B. *Psychiatry and Community in Nineteenth-Century America, the Recurring Concern With the Environment and the Prevention of Mental Illness.* New York: Basic Books, 1963.

Caplow, Theodore; Bahr, Howard M.; Chadwick, Bruce A.; Hoover, Dwight W.; Martin, Laurence A.; Tamney, Joseph B.; and Williamson, Margaret Holmes. *All Faithful People, Change and Continuity in Middletown's Religion.* Minneapolis: University of Minnesota Press, 1983.

Carlson, Eric, and Dain, Norman. "The Psychotherapy That Was Moral Treatment." *American Journal of Psychiatry* 117 (1960): 519–524.

Carnell, Edward J. *Introduction to Christian Apologetics.* Grand Rapids, Mich.: Eerdmans, 1948.

———. *Christian Commitment.* New York: Macmillan, 1957.

———. *The Case for Orthodoxy Theology.* Philadelphia: Westminster Press, 1959.

———. "Post-Fundamentalist Faith." *Christian Century* 76 (August 26, 1959): 971.

———. *The Kingdom of Love and the Pride of Life.* Grand Rapids, Mich.: Eerdmans, 1960.

———. *The Case for Biblical Christianity.* Edited by Ronald N. Nash. Grand Rapids, Mich.: Eerdmans, 1969.

Carpenter, Diane, and Rolaine Franz. "Georgia Harkness as a Personalist Theologian." In *The Boston Personalist Tradition in Philosophy, Social Ethics, and Theology.* Edited by Paul Deats and Carol Robb. Macon, Ga.: Mercer University Press, 1986.

Carpenter, Joel A., ed. *Two Reformers of Fundamentalism, Harold John Ockenga and Carl F. H. Henry.* New York: Garland Press, 1988.

Caskey, Marie. *Chariots of Fire, Religion and the Beecher Family.* New Haven: Yale University Press, 1978.

Cavenar, Jesse O., and Spaulding, Jean G. "Depressive Disorders and Religious Conversion." *The Journal of Nervous and Mental Disease* 165, no. 3 (1977): 209–212.

Cayleff, Susan E. *Wash and Be Healed, The Water-Cure Movement and Women's Health*. Philadelphia: Temple University Press, 1987.

Chambers-Schiller, Lee Virginia. *Liberty a Better Husband, Single Women in America: The Generation of 1780–1840*. New Haven: Yale University Press, 1984.

Cherlin, Kim. *The Hungry Self, Women, Eating and Identity*. New York: Harper & Row, 1985.

Cheyne, John. *Essays on the Partial Derangement of the Mind in Supposed Connection with Religion*. Dublin: William Curry & Company, 1843.

Church, Nathan. "Schreber's *Memoirs*: Myth or Personal Lamentation." *Journal of Religion and Health*, 18, no. 4 (1979): 313–326.

Clebsch, William A., and Jaekle, Charles R. *Pastoral Care in Historical Perspective*. New York: J. Aronson, 1983.

Coalter, Milton, Jr. *Son of Thunder, A Case Study of the Impact of Continental Pietism upon the First Great Awakening in the Middle Colonies*. New York: Greenwood Press, 1986.

Coe, George Albert. *The Religion of a Mature Mind*. Chicago: Fleming H. Revell Company, 1902.

Cohen, Charles Lloyd. *God's Caress, The Psychology of Religious Experience*. New York: Oxford University Press, 1986.

Cohen, Eric J. "Induced Christian Neurosis: An Examination of Pragmatic Paradoxes and the Christian Faith." *Journal of Psychology and Theology* 10 (Spring 1982): 5–12.

Cohen, Norman J., ed. *The Fundamentalist Phenomenon, A View from Within; A Response from Without*. Grand Rapids, Mich.: Eerdmans, 1990.

Cole, Phyllis. "The Advantage of Loneliness: Mary Moody Emerson's Almanacks, 1802–1855." In *Emerson: Prospect and Retrospect*. Edited by Joel Porte. Cambridge: Harvard University Press, 1982.

Colman, Benjamin. *The Case of Satan's Fiery Darts in Blasphemous Suggestions and Hellish Annoyances*. Boston: Rogers and Fowle, 1744.

Conforti, Joseph A. *Samuel Hopkins and the New Divinity Movement, Calvinism, the Congregational Ministry, and Reform in New England Between the Great Awakenings*. Grand Rapids, Mich.: Christian College Consortium, 1981.

———. "Jonathan Edwards's Most Popular Work, 'The Life of David Brainerd' and Nineteenth-Century Evangelical Culture." *Church History* 54 (1985): 188–198.

Cornell, Stephen. *The Return of the Native, American Indian Political Resurgence*. New York: Oxford University Press, 1988.

Corrington, Gail. "Anorexia, Asceticism and Autonomy: Self-Control as Liberation and Transcendence." *Journal of Feminist Studies in Religion* 2, no. 2 (Fall 1986): 51–61.

Cowper, William. *Memoir of the Early Life of William Cowper, Esq.*, 2nd ed. London: R. Edwards, 1816.

Cross, Whitney R. *The Burned-Over District, The Social and Intellectual History of Enthusiastic Religion in Western New York, 1800–1850*. New York: Harper & Row, 1950.

Cumbee, Dwight W. "Depression as an Ecclesiogenic Neurosis." *Journal of Pastoral Care* 34, no. 4 (December 1980): 254–267.

Dain, Norman, and Carlson, Eric. "Milieu Therapy in the Nineteenth Century: Patient

Care at the Friends' Asylum, Frankford, Pennsylvania, 1817–1861." *Journal of Nervous and Mental Disease* 31 (October 1960): 227–290.

Deats, Paul, and Robb, Carol, eds. *The Boston Personalist Tradition in Philosophy, Social Ethics and Theology*. Macon, Ga: Mercer University Press, 1986.

DeBerg, Betty A. *Ungodly Women, Gender and the First Wave of American Fundamentalism*. Minneapolis: Fortress Press, 1990.

Dekker, Rudolph M., and Rodenburg, Herman W. "A Suitable Case For Treatment? Reappraisal of Erickson's *Young Man Luther*." *Theory and Society* 12, no. 6 (1983): 775–800.

Delbanco, Andrew. *The Puritan Ordeal*. Cambridge: Harvard University Press, 1989.

Demos, John. *Past, Present and Personal, The Family and the Life-Course in American History*. New York: Oxford University Press, 1986.

De Swaan, Abram. *The Management of Normality, Critical Essays in Health and Welfare*. London: Routledge, 1990.

Dewey, Mary E., ed. *Life and Letters of Catherine M. Sedgewick*. New York: Harper Brothers, 1871.

Dobson, James. *Dare to Discipline*. Wheaton: Ill.: Tyndale House, 1970.

Donegan, Jane B. *Hydropathic Highway to Health, Women and Water Cure in Antebellum America*. Westport, Conn.: Greenwood Press, 1986.

Eaton, Joseph W., and Weil, Robert J. *Culture and Mental Disorders, A Comparative Study of Hutterites and Other Populations*. Glencoe, Ill.: Free Press, 1955.

Edwards, B. B., ed. *Memoir of the Rev. Elias Cornelius*. Boston: Perkins, Marvin & Company, 1834.

Edwards, Jonathan. *A Treatise Concerning Religious Affections*. Edited by John E. Smith. New Haven, Conn.: Yale University Press, 1959.

———. *Representative Selections*. Edited by Clarence H. Faust and Thomas H. Johnson. New York: Hill and Wang, 1962.

———. *A Faithful Narrative, in The Great Awakening*. Edited by C. C. Goen. New Haven: Yale University Press, 1972.

———. *The Life of David Brainerd*. Edited by Norman Pettit. New Haven, Conn.: Yale University Press, 1985.

Eisen, Arnold. "Called to Order: The Role of the Puritan *Berufmensch* in Weberian Sociology." *Sociology* 13 (1979): 203–218.

Eliot, John, and Mayhew, Thomas. *Tears of Repentance: Or, A Further Narrative of the Progress of the Gospel Amongst the Indians in New England*. London: P. Cole, 1653.

Ellis, Albert. "There Is No Place for the Concept of Sin in Psychotherapy." *Journal of Counseling Psychology*. 7, no. 3 (1960): 188–197.

Emerson, Ralph Waldo. *Collected Works*. Boston: Houghton Mifflin, 1904.

Emmons, Nathanael. *Works*. Boston: Congregational Board of Publication, 1862.

Epstein, Barbara Leslie. *The Politics of Domesticity, Women, Evangelism and Temperance in Nineteenth-Century America*. Middletown, Conn.: Wesleyan University Press, 1981.

Erickson, Erik H. *Young Man Luther, A Study in Psychoanalysis and History*. New York: W. W. Norton, 1958.

Fairchild, Roy W. *Finding Hope Again, A Pastor's Guide to Counseling Depressed Persons*. New York: Harper & Row, 1980.

———. "Issues in Contemporary Spirituality: The Upsurge of Spiritual Movements." *Princeton Seminary Bulletin* 8, no. 5 (1987): 4–16.

Fawcett, Benjamin. *Observations on the Nature, Causes and Cure of Melancholy:*

Especially of that Which Is Commonly Called Religious Melancholy. Shrewsbury, England: J. Eddowes, 1780.

Feinstein, Howard M. "The Prepared Heart: A Comparative Study of Puritan Theology and Psychoanalysis." *American Quarterly* 22 (1970): 166–176.

Finney, Charles G. *Lectures to Professing Christians.* London: Milner and Company, 1837.

————. *Memoirs of the Rev. Charles G. Finney, Written By Himself.* New York: A. S. Barnes & Company, 1876.

————. *Lectures on Revivals of Religion.* Edited by William G. McLoughlin. Cambridge: Harvard University Press, 1960.

————. *Principles of Devotion.* Edited by Louis Gifford Parkhurst, Jr. Minneapolis: Bethany House Publications, 1987.

Fisher, George Mark. "A Ministry of Encouragement to Those Who Feel Forsaken by God at Ross Christian Church, Ross, Ohio." Nashville, Tennessee: The Historical Commission of the Southern Baptist Convention, Publication No. 6540, 1990.

Flavel, John. *Divine Conduct, Or the Mystery of Providence.* London: S. Bridge, 1786.

Fletcher, Robert Samuel. "Bread and Doctrine at Oberlin." *Ohio State Archeological and Historical Quarterly* 65 (1940): 58–67.

————. *A History of Oberlin College from the Foundation Through the Civil War.* Chicago: Donnelly and Sons, 1943.

Foster, Frank Hugh. *Genetic History of the New England Theology.* Chicago: University of Chicago Press, 1907.

Foucault, Michel. *Madness and Civilization, A History of Insanity in the Age of Reason.* New York: New American Library, 1965.

————. *The Birth of the Clinic, An Archaeology of Medical Perception.* New York: Pantheon Books, 1973.

Fox, Ruth A. *The Tangled Chain, The Structure of Disorder in the Anatomy of Melancholy.* Berkeley: University of California Press, 1976.

Fraser, Hugh S. *Pedagogue for God's Kingdom, Lyman Beecher and the Second Great Awakening.* Lanham, N.H.: University Press of America, 1985.

Fremantle, Ann. *The Protestant Mystic.* Boston: Little, Brown, 1964.

Freud, Sigmund. *Collected Papers.* Edited by James Strachey. New York: Basic Books, 1959.

Frost, John; Gillet, Moses; and Coe, Noah. *Narrative of the Revival of Religion in the County of Oneida Particularly in the Bounds of the Presbytery of Oneida in the Year 1826.* Utica: Hastings and Troy, 1826.

Fuller, Robert C. *Alternative Medicine and American Religious Life.* New York: Oxford University Press, 1989.

Gaustad, Edwin S. *The Great Awakening in New England.* New York: Harper & Row, 1957.

Gay, Peter, ed. *The Freud Reader.* New York: W. W. Norton, 1989.

Gibson, Dennis L. "The Obsessive Personality and the Evangelical." *Journal of Pastoral Counseling* 2, no. 3 (Fall 1983): 30–35.

Gillenson, Lewis W. *Billy Graham and Seven Who Were Saved.* New York: Trident Press, 1967.

Glock, Charles Y., and Hammond, Philip E., eds. *Beyond the Classics? Essays in the Scientific Study of Religion.* New York: Harper & Row, 1972.

Goen, C. C. *Revivalism and Separatism in New England, 1740–1800, Strict Congregationalists and Separate Baptists in the Great Awakening.* Middletown, Conn.: Wesleyan University Press, 1987.

Goldman, Harvey. *Max Weber and Thomas Mann, Calling and the Shaping of the Self*. Berkeley: University of California Press, 1988.

Goodrich, Chauncey. "Narrative of the Revivals of Religion in Yale College, From Its Commencement to the Present Time." *Journal of the American Education Society* 10 (February 1838): 298–310.

Goodwin, Thomas, and Simpson, Alan. *Puritanism in Old and New England*. Chicago: University of Chicago Press, 1955.

Graham, Billy. *Peace with God*. New York: Doubleday & Company, 1953.

———. *How to Be Born Again*. Waco, Texas: Word Publishing Books, 1972.

———. *The Holy Spirit, Activating God's Power in Your Life*. London: William Collins and Sons, 1978.

Graham, Elspeth; Hinde, Hilary; Hobby, Elaine; and Wilcox, Helen, eds. *Her Own Life, Autobiographical Writings by Seventeenth-Century English Women*. London: Routledge, 1989.

Graham, Sylvester. *The Aesculapian Tales of the Nineteenth Century*. Providence, R.I.: Weeden and Cory, 1834.

———. *Lectures on the Science of Human Life*. Boston: Marsh, Capen, Lyon & Swebb, 1839.

Greven, Philip. *Four Generations: Population, Land, and Family in Colonial Andover Massachusetts*. Ithaca, N.Y.: Cornell University Press, 1970.

———. *The Protestant Temperament, Patterns of Child-Rearing, Religious Experience, and the Self in Early America*. New York: New American Library, 1979.

———. *Spare the Child, The Religious Roots of Punishment and the Psychological Impact of Physical Abuse*. New York: Knopf, 1991.

———. "'Some Root of Bitterness': Corporal Punishment, Child Abuse, and the Apocalyptic Impulse in Michael Wigglesworth." In *The Transformation of Early American History, Society, Authority and Ideology*. Edited by James A. Henretta, Michael Kammen, and Stanley N. Katz. New York: Knopf, 1991.

Grounds, Vernon. *Emotional Problems and the Gospel*. Grand Rapids, Mich.: Zondervan, 1976.

Hacker, Paul. *The Ego in Faith, Martin Luther and the Origins of Anthropocentric Religion*. Chicago: Franciscan Herald Press, 1970.

Hall, David H. *Worlds of Wonder, Days of Judgment, Popular Religious Belief in Early New England*. New York: Knopf, 1989.

Hallowell, A. Irving. *Culture and Experience*. New York: Shocken Books, 1967.

Hambrick-Stowe, Charles E. *The Practice of Piety, Puritan Devotional Disciplines in Seventeenth-Century New England*. Chapel Hill: University of North Carolina Press, 1982.

Harding, Susan F. "Convicted by the Holy Spirit: The Rhetoric of Fundamental Baptist Conversion." *American Ethnologist* 14 (Fall 1987): 167–181.

Hardman, Keith J. *Charles Grandison Finney, 1792–1875, Revivalist and Reformer*. New York: Syracuse University Press, 1987.

Harkness, Georgia. *The Dark Night of the Soul*. New York: Abingdon-Cokesbury Press, 1945.

Harrell, David Edwin. *All Things Are Possible, The Healing and Charismatic Revivals in Modern America*. Bloomington: Indiana University Press, 1975.

———, ed. *Varieties of Southern Evangelicalism*. Macon, Ga.: Mercer University Press, 1981.

Hartz, Gary W., and Everett, Henry C. "Fundamentalist Religion and Its Effect on

Mental Health." *Journal of Religion and Health* 28, no. 3 (Fall 1989): 207–217.

Heimert, Alan. *Religion and the American Mind.* Cambridge: Harvard University Press, 1966.

Hennis, Wilhelm. "Personality and Life Orders: Max Weber's Theme." In *Max Weber, Rationality and Modernity.* Edited by Sam Whimster and Scott Lasch. London: Allen and Unwin, 1987.

Hewitt, Nancy A. "The Perimeters of Women's Power in American Religion." In *The Evangelical Tradition in America.* Edited by Leonard I. Sweet. Macon, Ga.: Mercer University Press, 1984.

Hill, Samuel S. "The Shape and Shapes of Popular Southern Piety." In *Varieties of Southern Evangelicalism.* Edited by David Edwin Harrell. Macon, Ga.: Mercer University Press, 1981.

Hirst, Derek. *Authority and Conflict, England 1603–1658. The New History of England.* Edited by A. G. Dickens and Norman Cash. Cambridge, Mass.: Harvard University Press.

Holifield, E. Brooks. *A History of Pastoral Care in America, From Salvation to Self-Realization.* Nashville, Tenn.: Abingdon Press, 1983.

Homans, Peter. "Protestant Theology and Dynamic Psychology: New Thoughts on An Old Problem." Theology and Culture, Essays in Honor of Albert J. Mullegin and Clifford L. Stanley. Edited by W. Taylor Stevenson. *Anglican Theological Review* 11 (1976): 125–137.

Hoopes, James. *Consciousness in New England, From Puritanism and Ideas to Psychoanalysis and Semeiotic.* Baltimore: Johns Hopkins University Press, 1989.

Hoover, Dwight W. *Henry James, Sr. and the Religion of Community.* Grand Rapids, Mich.: Eerdmans, 1969.

Hopkins, Samuel. *The Life and Character of Miss Susanna Anthony.* Boston, 1799.

———. *Memoirs of the Life of Mrs. Sarah Osborn Who Died at Newport, Rhode Island.* Worcester, Mass.: Leonard Worcester, 1799.

———. *Works.* Boston: Doctrinal Tract and Book Society, 1852.

Humphrey, Heman. *Christian Memoirs, Or the Nature of Conviction of Sin and Regeneration Illustrated in Narratives of Conversion of Eminent Christians.* Boston: William Pierce, 1836.

———. *Thirty-Four Letters to A Son in the Ministry.* Amherst: J. S. & C. Adams, 1842.

———. *Revival Sketches and Manual.* New York: American Tract Society, 1859.

Hunter, James Davison. *American Evangelicalism, Conservative Religion and the Quandary of Modernity.* New Brunswick, N.J.: Rutgers University Press, 1983.

Hutcheson, William, ed. *American Protestant Thought: The Liberal Era.* New York: Harper & Row, 1968.

———. *Between the Times, The Travail of the Protestant Establishment in America, 1900–1960.* Cambridge: Cambridge University Press, 1989.

Jackson, Stanley W. "Acedia The Sin and Its Relationship to Sorrow and Melancholia." In *Culture and Depression, Studies in the Anthropology and Cross-Cultural Psychiatry of Affect and Disorder,* edited by Arthur Kleinman and Byron Good. Berkeley: University of California Press, 1985.

———. *Melancholia and Depression, From Hippocratic Times to Modern Times.* New Haven: Yale University Press, 1986.

James, Henry, Sr. *The Literary Remains of the Late Henry James.* Edited by William James. Boston: James R. Osgood and Company, 1885.

———. *Henry James, Senior, A Selection of His Writings.* Edited by Giles Gunn. Chicago: American Library Association, 1974.

James, William. *The Varieties of Religious Experience, A Study in Human Nature.* New York: Collier Books, 1961.

Jellineck, Georg. *The Declaration of the Rights of Man and of Citizen, A Contribution to Constitutional History.* New York: Henry Holt, 1901.

Jennings, Francis. *The Invasion of America, Indians, Colonials, and the Cant of Conquest.* New York: W. W. Norton, 1976.

———. *The Ambiguous Iroquois Empire, The Covenant Chain Confederacy of Indian Tribes with English Colonies from its Beginnings to the Lancaster Treaty of 1744.* New York: W. W. Norton, 1984.

Jilek, Wolfgang G., and Jilek-Aall, Louis. "The Metamorphosis of 'Culture-Bound' Syndrome." *Social Science and Medicine* 21, no. 2 (1985): 205–210.

Jimenez, Mary Ann. *Changing Faces of Madness, Early American Attitudes and Treatment of the Insane.* Hanover, N.H.: University Press of New England, 1987.

Johnson, Paul E. *A Shopkeeper's Millennium, Society and Revivals in Rochester, New York, 1815–1837.* New York: Harper & Row, 1978.

Johnson, Roger A., ed. *Psychohistory and Religion: The Case of Young Man Luther.* Philadelphia: Fortress Press, 1982.

Jorgenson, Joseph G. *The Sun Dance Religion, Power to the Powerless.* Chicago: University of Chicago Press, 1972.

Juster, Susan. "In a Different Voice: Male and Female Narratives of Religious Conversion in Post-Revolutionary America." *American Quarterly* 41 (March 1989): 34–62.

Kalberg, Stephen. "Max Weber's Types of Rationality: Cornerstones for the Analysis of Rationalization Processes in History." *American Journal of Sociology* 85, no. 5 (1980): 1145–1179.

Kantzer, Kenneth S. *Evangelical Roots, A Tribute to Wilbur Smith.* Nashville, Tenn.: Thomas Nelson, 1978.

Keller, Charles Roy. *The Second Great Awakening in Connecticut.* New Haven: Yale University Press, 1942.

Kenny, Michael G. *The Passion of Ansel Bourne, Multiple Personality in American Culture.* Washington, D.C.: Smithsonian Institution Press, 1986.

Kett, Joseph F. *Rites of Passage, Adolescence in America 1790 to the Present.* New York: Basic Books, 1977.

King, John Owen. *The Iron of Melancholy, Structures of Spiritual Conversion in America from the Puritan Conscience to Victorian Neurosis.* Middletown, Conn.: Wesleyan University Press, 1983.

King, William McGuire. "An Enthusiasm for Humanity: The Social Emphasis in Religion and Its Accommodation in Protestant Theology." In *Religion and Twentieth-Century American Intellectual Life,* edited by Michael J. Lacey. Cambridge: Cambridge University Press, 1989.

Kleinman, Arthur. *The Illness Narratives, Suffering, Healing and the Human Condition.* New York: Basic Books, 1988.

Kleinman, Arthur, and Good, Byron, eds. *Culture and Depression, Studies in the Anthropology and Cross-Cultural Psychiatry of Affect and Disorder.* Berkeley: University of California Press, 1985.

Lacey, Barbara E. "The World of Hannah Heaton: The Autobiography of an Eighteenth-Century Connecticut Farm Woman." *William and Mary Quarterly* 45 (April 1988): 280–304.

———. "Gender, Piety, and Secularization in Connecticut Religion, 1720–1775." *Journal of Social History* 24, no. 4 (1991): 799–821.

Lacey, Michael J., ed. *Religion and Twentieth-Century American Intellectual Life.* Cambridge: Cambridge University Press, 1989.

LaHaye, Tim. *How to Win Over Depression.* Grand Rapids, Mich.: Zondervan Publishing House, 1974.

Langhorne, John. *Letters on Religious Retirement, Melancholy and Enthusiasm.* London: H. Payne and W. Cropley, 1762.

Lawless, Elaine J. *God's Peculiar People, Women's Voices and Folk Tradition in a Pentecostal Church.* Lexington: University Press of Kentucky, 1988.

Lawson, Michael. *Facing Depression, Toward Healing the Mind, Body, & Spirit.* Mystic, Conn.: Twenty-Third Publications, 1990.

Lear, Jonathan. *Love and Its Place in Nature, A Philosophical Interpretation of Freudian Analysis.* New York: Farrar, Straus and Giroux, 1990.

Lechner, Frank J. "Fundamentalism Revisited." In *In Gods We Trust, New Patterns of Religious Pluralism in America,* 2d ed. Edited by Thomas Robbins and Dick Anthony. New Brunswick, N.J.: Transaction Books, 1991.

Leclercq, Jean. "Modern Psychology and the Interpretation of Medieval Texts." *Speculum* 47, no. 3 (1973): 476–490.

Lepenies, Wolf. *Melancholy and Society.* Translated by Jeremy Gaines and Doris Jones. Cambridge: Harvard University Press, 1992.

Lessing, Doris. *Prisons We Choose to Live Inside.* New York: Harper & Row, 1987.

Levin, David. *Cotton Mather, The Young Life of the Lord's Remembrancer, 1663–1703.* Cambridge: Harvard University Press, 1978.

Lewis, C. S. *The Screwtape Letters.* rev. ed. New York: Collier Books, 1982.

Lippy, Charles H., ed. *Twentieth-Century Shapers of American Popular Religion.* New York: Greenwood Press, 1989.

Lloyd-Jones, D. Martyn. *Spiritual Depression, Its Cause and Cure.* Grand Rapids, Mich.: Eerdmans, 1965.

Lockridge, Kenneth A. *A New England Town, The First Hundred Years.* New York: W. W. Norton, 1970.

Lovejoy, David S. *Religious Enthusiasm in the New World, Heresy to Revolution.* Cambridge: Harvard University Press, 1985.

Lovelace, Richard F. *The American Piety of Cotton Mather, Origins of American Evangelicalism.* Grand Rapids, Mich.: Christian University Press, 1979.

Lucas, Paul R. *Valley of Discord, Church and Society Along the Connecticut River, 1636–1725.* Hanover, N.H.: University Press of New England, 1976.

Lutz, Tom. *American Nervousness, 1903: An Anecdotal History.* Ithaca, N.Y.: Cornell University Press, 1991.

MacDonald, Michael. *Mystical Bedlam, Madness, Anxiety and Healing in Seventeenth Century England.* Cambridge: Cambridge University Press, 1981.

MacDonald, Michael, and Murphey, Terence R. *Sleepless Souls, Suicide in Early Modern England.* Oxford: Oxford University Press, 1990.

Marsella, Anthony J.; Devos, George; and Hsu, Francis L. K. *Culture and Self, Asian and Western Perspectives.* New York: Tavistock Publications, 1985.

Marsella, Anthony J., and White, Geoffrey M. *Cultural Concepts of Mental Health and Therapy.* London: D. Reidel, 1982.

Marsden, George M. *The Evangelical Mind and the New School Presbyterian Experience, A Case Study of Thought and Theology in Nineteenth-Century America.* New Haven: Yale University Press, 1970.

———. *Fundamentalism and American Culture, The Shaping of Twentieth-Century Evangelicalism: 1870–1925.* New York: Oxford University Press, 1980.

———. "Evangelicals and the Scientific Culture." In *Religion and Twentieth-Century American Intellectual Life.* Edited by Michael J. Lacey. Cambridge: Cambridge University Press, 1989.

———. *Reforming Fundamentalism.* Grand Rapids, Mich.: Eerdmans, 1987.

Martin, William. "Billy Graham." In *Varieties of Southern Evangelicalism.* Edited by David Edwin Harrell. Macon, Ga.: Mercer University Press, 1981.

Mather, Cotton. Insanabilia: An Essay Upon Incurables." Boston: T. Fleet for Samuel Gerrish, 1714.

——— "The Case of a Troubled Mind." Boston, 1717.

———. *Magnalia Christi Americana.* Hartford, Conn.: Silas Andrus, 1820.

———. *The Diary of Cotton Mather Volume 1, 1681–1709.* New York: Frederick Langer, 1957.

———. *The Angel of Bethesda.* Edited by Gordon W. Jones. Barre, Mass.: American Antiquarian Society, 1972.

Mayhew, Experience. *Indian Converts; Or Some Accounts of the Lives and Dying Speeches of a Considerable Number of the Christianized Indians of Martha's Vineyard in New England.* London: S. Gerrish, 1727.

McGrath, Alister E. *Luther's Theology of the Cross, Martin Luther's Theological Breakthrough.* London: Basil Blackwell, 1985.

McGuire, Meredith. *Ritual Healing in Suburban America.* New Brunswick, N.J.: Rutgers University Press, 1988.

McLoughlin, William G. *Billy Graham, Revivalist in a Secular Age.* New York: Ronald Press Company, 1960.

———. "Evangelical Childrearing in the Age of Jackson: Francis Wayland's Views on When and How to Subdue the Willfulness of Children." *Journal of Social History* 9, no. 1 (1975): 21–39.

———. *Revivals, Awakenings, and Reform, An Essay on Religion and Social Change in America, 1607–1977.* Chicago: University of Chicago Press, 1978.

Mead, Frank J. *Handbook of Denomination in the United States*, 9th ed. Nashville, Tenn.: Abingdon Press, 1990.

Merrill, Thomas F., ed. *"A Discourse of Conscience," William Perkins.* Netherlands: Nieuwkoop de Graaf, 1966.

Meyer, Donald B. *The Positive Thinkers, Popular Religious Psychology from Mary Baker Eddy to Norman Vincent Peale and Ronald Reagan.* Middletown, Conn.: Wesleyan University Press, 1988.

Miller, Alice. *Banished Knowledge, Facing Childhood Injuries.* Translated by Leila Vennewitz. New York: Anchor Books, 1990.

———. *The Untouched Key, Tracing Childhood Trauma in Creativity and Destructiveness.* Translated by Hildegarde Hannum and Hunter Hannum. New York: Anchor Books, 1990.

Miller, Perry. *Errand into the Wilderness.* New York: Harper Torchbooks, 1964.

———. *The Life of the Mind in America from the Revolution to the Civil War.* New York: Harcourt, Brace and World, 1965.

Miller, Russell E. *The Larger Hope, The First Century of the Universalist Church in America, 1770–1870.* Boston: Unitarian Universalist Association, 1977.

Mitchell, Curtis. *Those Who Came Forward, Men and Women Who Responded to the Ministry of Billy Graham.* New York: Chilton Books, 1966.

Mojtabai, A. G. *Blessed Assurance, At Home with the Bomb in Amarillo, Texas.* Boston: Houghton Mifflin Company, 1986.

Mommsen, Wolfgang. "Personal Conduct and Societal Change." In *Max Weber, Rationality and Modernity,* edited by Sam Whimster and Scott Lasch. London: Allen and Unwin, 1987.

More, Hannah. *Practical Piety, Or the Influence of the Heart Religion on the Conduct of Life.* Boston, 1811.

Morgan, Edmund S. *Visible Saints, The History of a Puritan Idea.* Ithaca, N.Y.: Cornell University Press, 1965.

Morgan, Edmund S., ed. *The Diary of Michael Wigglesworth 1653–1657, The Conscience of a Puritan.* Glouster, Mass.: Peter Smith, 1970.

Morton, David O. *Memoir of Reverend Levi Parsons.* Burlington, Vt.: C. Goodrich, 1830.

Mowrer, O. Hobart. *The Crisis in Psychiatry and Religion.* New York: D. Van Nostrand, 1961.

Mueller, Johann Jacob. *De Melancholia Attonita Raro Litteratorum Affectu.* Jena, Frederici Ritteri, 1741.

Muether, John R. "Contemporary Evangelicalism, A Triumph of the New School." *Westminster Theological Review* 50 (1988): 339–347.

Murphey, Murray G. "The Psychodynamics of Puritan Conversion." *American Quarterly* 31 (1979): 135–147.

Myerson, Joel, ed. *Studies in the American Renaissance.* New Haven: Yale University Press, 1986.

Nelson, Benjamin. "Faces of Twentieth Century Analysis." *The American Behavioral Scientist* (February 1962): 16–18.

———. "Self-Images and Systems of Systems of Spiritual Direction in the History of European Civilization." In *The Quest for Self-Control, Classical Philosophies and Scientific Research,* edited by Samuel Z. Klausner. New York: Free Press, 1965.

———. "Conscience and the Making of Early Modern Cultures: The Protestant Ethic Beyond Max Weber." *Social Research* 36, no. 4 (1969): 4–21.

———. "Weber's Protestant Ethic: Its Origins, Wanderings and Forseeable Futures." In *Beyond the Classics? Essays in the Scientific Study of Religion.* Edited by Charles Y. Glock and Philip E. Hammond. New York: Harper & Row, 1973.

———. "Max Weber's 'Author's Introduction' (1920): A Master Clue to His Main Aims." *Sociological Inquiry* 44, no. 4 (1974): 269–278.

———. *On the Roads to Modernity, Conscience, Science and Civilizations; Selected Essays.* Edited by Toby E. Huff. Totowa, N.J.: Rowman and Littlefield, 1981.

Nelson, Maria. *Why Christians Crack Up.* Chicago: Moody Bible Institute, 1974.

Nelson, Rudolph. *The Making and Unmaking of an Evangelical Mind, The Case of Edward Carnell.* New York: Cambridge University Press, 1987.

Nettleton, Asahel. *Remains of the Late Reverend Asahel Nettleton, D.D.* Edited by Bennet Tyler. Hartford, Conn.: Robbins and Smith, 1845.

Nicoll, William R. *The Evangelical Succession,* vol. 3 (1944): 69.

Niebuhr, Reinhold. "Liberalism, Individualism and Billy Graham." *The Christian Century* (May 23, 1956): 641–643.

Nissenbaum, Stephen. *Sex, Diet and Debility in Jacksonian America, Sylvester Graham and Health Reform.* Westport, Conn.: Greenwood Press, 1980.

Nordtvedt, Matilda. *Defeating Depression and Despair*. Chicago: Moody Bible Institute, 1976.

Norton, Mary Beth. "'My Resting Reaping Times': Sarah Osborn's Defense of Her 'Unfeminine Activities,' 1767." *Signs* 2, no. 2 (1976): 515–529.

Noyes, Henry E., and Noyes, Harriet E. *Genealogical Record of Some of the Noyes Descendants of James, Nichols, and Peter Noyes*. Boston, Mass. [S. N.] 1904.

Noyes, John. *Letters, Chiefly of a Moral and Religious Nature to Friends of Various Conditions*. New Haven, Conn., 1844.

Numbers, Ronald L., and Numbers, Janet S. "Millerism and Madness: A Study of 'Religious Insanity' in Nineteenth-Century America." In *The Disappointed, Millerism and Millenarianism in the Nineteenth Century*, edited by Ronald L. Numbers and Jonathan M. Butler. Bloomington: Indiana University Press, 1987.

———. "Religious Insanity, History of a Diagnosis." *Second Opinion, Health, Faith and Ethics* 3 (1986): 52–77.

Nuttall, Geoffrey F. *The Holy Spirit in Puritan Faith and Experience*. Oxford: Basil Blackwell, 1946.

Obeyesekere, Gananath. "Depression, Buddhism and the Work of Culture in Sri Lanka." In *Culture and Depression, Studies in the Anthropology and Cross-Cultural Psychiatry of Affect and Disorder*. Edited by Arthur Kleinman and Byron Good. Berkeley: University of California Press, 1985.

———. *The Work of Culture, Symbolic Transformations in Psychoanalysis and Anthropology*. Chicago: University of Chicago Press, 1990.

Okenga, Harold J. "From Fundamentalism, Through New Evangelicalism, to Evangelicalism." In *Evangelical Roots, A Tribute to Wilbur Smith*. Edited by Kenneth S. Kantzer. Nashville, Tenn.: Thomas Nelson, Inc., 1978.

Old, Hughes Oliphant. "Gilbert Tennent and the Preaching of Piety in Colonial America: Newly Discovered Tennent Manuscripts in Speer Library." *Princeton Seminary Bulletin* 2 (1989): 132–137.

Orbach, Susan. *Hunger Strike, The Anorectic's Struggle as a Metaphor for Our Age*. New York: W. W. Norton, 1986.

Osborn, Sarah. *The Nature, Certainty, and Evidence of True Christianity, in a Letter from a Gentlewoman in New England to Another Dear Friend in Great Distress, Doubt, and Concern of a Religious Nature*. Boston: S. Kneeland, 1755.

Osborn, Sarah, and Anthony, Susanna. *Familiar Letters Written by Mrs. Sarah Osborn and Miss Susanna Anthony*. Newport, R.I.: *Newport Mercury*, 1807.

Parker, Gail Thain. "Jonathan Edwards and Melancholy." *The New England Quarterly* 41 (1968): 193–212.

Perkins, William. *A Discourse of Conscience*, 2d ed. Cambridge, U.K.: John Ligate, 1608.

Pettit, Norman. *The Heart Prepared: Grace and Conversion in Puritan Spiritual Life*. New Haven: Yale University Press, 1966.

Porte, Joel, ed. *Emerson: Prospect and Retrospect*. Cambridge: Harvard University Press, 1982.

Porter, E. *Letters on Revivals of Religion Which Prevailed About the Beginning of the Present Century*. Boston: Congregational Board of Publishing, 1858.

Porter, H. C. *Reformation and Reaction in Tudor Cambridge*. Cambridge: Cambridge University Press, 1950.

Porter, Roy. *A Social History of Madness, The World Through The Eyes of the Insane*. New York: E. P. Dutton, 1989.

Portis, E. B. "Max Weber's Theory of Personality." *Sociological Inquiry* 48, no. 2 (1980): 113–119.

Post, Stephen G. *Christian Love and Self-Denial, An Historical and Normative Study of Jonathan Edwards, Samuel Hopkins, and American Theological Ethics.* New York: University Press of America, 1987.

Prince, Raymond. "The Concept of Culture-Bound Syndrome: Anorexia Nervosa and Brain-Fag." *Social Science and Medicine* 21, no. 2 (1985): 197–203.

Rabinowitz, Richard. *The Spiritual Self in Everyday Life, The Transformation of Personal Religious Experience in Nineteenth-Century New England.* Boston: Northeastern University Press, 1989.

Raines, Robert A. *Going Home.* San Francisco: Harper & Row, 1979.

———. *New Life in the Church.* San Francisco: Harper & Row, 1980.

Rauschenbusch, Walter. "The New Evangelicalism." In *American Protestant Thought: The Liberal Era*, edited by William R. Hutcheson. New York: Harper & Row, 1968.

Reeve, John Foster. "On a Method of Administration, By Means of a New Contrivance, Nourishment to Insane Persons Who Refuse Food." *Journal of Psychological Medicine* 6 (1856): 311–314.

Reichley, A. James. "Pietist Politics." In *The Fundamentalist Phenomenon, A View from Within; A Response from Without.* Edited by Norman J. Cohen. Grand Rapids, Mich.: Eerdmans, 1990.

Religion in America, 1990. Princeton, N.J.: The Princeton Religion Research Center, 1990.

Ricoeur, Paul. *Freud and Philosophy: An Essay on Interpretation.* New Haven: Yale University Press, 1970.

Rieff, Philip. *The Triumph of the Therapeutic, Uses of Faith After Freud.* New York: Harper & Row, 1968.

Ritter, Gerhard. "Luther." *Encyclopedia of the Social Sciences.* Vol. 9. New York: Macmillan and Company.

Robbins, Thomas, and Anthony, Dick, ed. *In Gods We Trust, New Patterns of Religious Pluralism in America.* New Brunswick, N.J.: Transaction Books, 1991.

Robe, James. *Narrative of the Extraordinary Work of the Spirit of God at Cambusland, Kilsyth.* Glasgow: David Niven, 1790.

Rogers, Timothy. *A Discourse Concerning Trouble of Mind, and the Disease of Melancholy.* London: Thomas Parkhurst and Thomas Cockerill, 1691.

Rohr, John von. *The Covenant of Grace in Puritan Thought.* Atlanta: Scholars Press, 1986.

Rolland, Ross W. "The Continuity of Evangelical Life and Thought." *Religion in Life* 13, no. 2 (Spring 1944): 245–253.

Rosenberg, Carroll Smith. "Women and Religion Revivals Anti-Ritualism, Liminality, and the Emergence of the American Bourgeoisie." In *The Evangelical Tradition in America.* Edited by Leonard I. Sweet. Macon, Ga.: Mercer University Press, 1984.

Roth, Guenther, and Schluchter, Wolfgang. *Max Weber's Vision of History: Ethics and Methods.* Berkeley: University of California Press, 1979.

Rowe, Dorothy. *Depression, The Way Out of Your Prison.* Boston: Routledge & Kegan Paul, 1983.

Rubin, Julius H. *Mental Illness in Early Nineteenth Century New England and the Beginnings of Institutional Psychiatry as Revealed in a Sociological Study of the Hartford Retreat, 1824 to 1843.* Ann Arbor: University Microprint, 1979.

Rugoff, Milton. *The Beechers, An American Family in the Nineteenth Century.* New York: Harper & Row, 1981.

Russell, C. Allyn. *Voices of American Fundamentalism, Seven Biographical Studies.* Philadelphia: Westminster Press, 1976.

Ryan, Mary. *The Cradle of the Middle Class: The Family in Oneida County, New York, 1790–1865.* Cambridge: Cambridge University Press, 1981.

Salisbury, Neal. "Red Puritans: The Praying Indians of Massachusetts Bay and John Elliot." *The American Indian Past and Present.* 3d ed. Edited by Roger L. Nichols. New York: Alfred A. Knopf, 1986.

Sanborn, F. B., and Harris, William T. *A. Bronson Alcott, His Life and Philosophy.* Boston: Roberts Brothers, 1893.

Sapinsley, Barbara. *The Private War of Mrs. Packard.* New York: Paragon House, 1991.

Schaff, Lawrence A. *Fleeing the Iron Cage, Culture, Politics, and Modernity in the Thought of Max Weber.* Berkeley: University of California Press, 1989.

Schiesari, Juliana. *The Gendering of Melancholia, Feminism, Psychoanalysis, and the Symbolics of Loss in Renaissance Literature.* Ithaca, N.Y.: Cornell University Press, 1992.

Schluchter, Wolfgang. "The Paradox of Rationalization: On the Relation of Ethics and World." In *Max Weber's Vision of History: Ethics and Methods.* Edited by Guenther Roth and Wolfgang Schluchter. Berkeley: University of California Press, 1979.

———. *The Rise of Western Rationalism, Max Weber's Developmental History.* Translated by Guenther Roth. Berkeley: University of California Press, 1985.

———. *Rationalism, Religion and Domination, A Weberian Perspective.* Translated by Neil Solomon. Berkeley: University of California Press, 1989.

Schreber, Daniel Paul. *Memoirs of My Nervous Illness.* Edited and translated by Ida Macalpine and Richard A. Hunter. London: Taylor and Francis, 1955.

Schwartz, Hillel. *Never Satisfied, A Cultural History of Diets, Fantasies and Fat.* New York: Anchor Books, 1986.

Sears, Clara Endicott. *Bronson Alcott's Fruitlands.* Boston: Houghton Mifflin, 1915.

Sedgwick, Catherine M. *A New England Tale and Miscellanies.* New York: George P. Putnam & Co., 1853.

Shea, Daniel B., Jr. *Spiritual Autobiography in America.* Princeton, N.J.: Princeton University Press, 1968.

Shengold, Leonard. *Soul Murder, The Effects of Childhood Abuse and Deprivation.* New York: Fawcett Columbine, 1989.

Sherman, Roddy. "Fundamentalism and Ecumenicity." *Christian Century* 75 (1958): 1109–1111.

Shorter, Edward. "The First Great Increase in Anorexia Nervosa." *Journal of Social History* 21 (Fall 1987): 69–96.

———. *From Paralysis to Fatigue, A History of Psychosomatic Illness in the Modern Era.* New York: Free Press, 1992.

Shweder, Richard A. *Thinking Through Cultures, Expeditions in Cultural Psychology.* Cambridge: Harvard University Press, 1991.

Sibbes, Richard. *A Consolatory Letter to an afflicted conscience full of pious admonitions and divine instructions.* London: Francis Cowles, 1641.

Sica, Alan. *Weber, Irrationality and Social Order.* Berkeley: University of California Press, 1988.

Silk, Mark. *Spiritual Politics, Religion and America Since World War II.* New York: Simon and Schuster, 1988.

———. "The Rise of the 'New Evangelicalism': Shock and Adjustments." In *Between the Times, The Travail of the Protestant Establishment in America, 1900–1960.* Edited by William R. Hutchinson. Cambridge: Cambridge University Press, 1989.

Silverman, Kenneth. *The Life and Times of Cotton Mather.* New York: Columbia University Press, 1984.

Simpson, Alan. *Puritanism in Old and New England.* Chicago: University of Chicago Press, 1955.

Skinner, Otis. "Account of Death of Phileman, William and Cyrus, the only Children of Mr. Zaphua and Mrs. Lois Stone. *Universalist Magazine* 8, no. 42 (April 7, 1827), exerpted from *Western Reserve Chronicle* (May 1, 1827).

Sokolow, Jayne A. *Eros and Modernization, Sylvester Graham, Health Reform, and the Origins of Victorian Sexuality in America.* Teaneck, N.J.: Fairleigh Dickinson University Press, 1983.

Sprague, William B. *Lectures on Revivals of Religion, with an Introduction by Leonard Woods.* Albany, N.Y.: Webster & Skinners, 1832.

Spignesi, Angelyn. *Starving Women, A Psychology of Anorexia Nervosa.* Dallas: Spring Publications, 1983.

Stackhouse, John G., Jr. "'Who Follows in His Train,' Edward J. Carnell as a Model of Evangelical Theology." *Crux* 21, no. 2 (June 1985): 19–27.

Stoeffler, Ernest F. *The Rise of Evangelical Pietism.* Leiden: E.J. Brill, 1965.

Stoever, William K. B. *A Faire and Easie Way to Heaven, Covenant Theology and Antinomianism in Early Massachusetts.* Middletown, Conn.: Wesleyan University Press, 1978.

Stowe, Lyman Beecher. *Saints, Sinners and Beechers.* New York: Bobbs Merrill, 1943.

Stuerman, Walter E. *A Critical Study of Calvin's Concept of Faith.* Ann Arbor, Mich.: W. Edwards Brothers, 1952.

Swatos, William H., ed. *Religious Sociology, Interfaces and Boundaries.* New York: Greenwood Press, 1987.

Sweet, Leonard I. "The View of Man Inherent in New Measure Revivalism." *Church History* 45 (1976): 206–221.

Sweet, Leonard I., ed. *The Evangelical Tradition in America.* Macon, Ga.: Mercer University Press, 1984.

Tamney, Joseph. "Fasting and Dieting: A Research Note." *Review of Religion Research* 27, no. 3 (March 1986): 255–263.

Taylor, Nathaniel. "*Concio Ad Clerium.*" New Haven, Conn.: A. H. Maltby and Homan Hallock, 1828.

———. *Moral Government.* Boston, 1851.

Testimonies of the Life, Character, Revelations and Doctrines of Mother Ann Lee. 2d ed. Albany, N.Y.: Weed, Parsons and Company, 1888.

Theriot, Nancy. "Psychosomatic Illness in History: The 'Green Sickness' Among Nineteenth-Century Adolescent Girls." *The Journal of Psychohistory* 15, no. 4 (Spring 1988): 461–480.

Thomas, Hilah F., and Keller, Rosemary Skinner. *Women in New Worlds, Historical Perspectives on the Wesleyan Tradition.* Nashville, Tenn.: Abingdon, 1981.

Thomas, Keith. *Religion and the Decline of Magic.* New York: Charles Scribner's Sons, 1971.

Thompson, Roger. *Sex in Middlesex, Popular Mores in a Massachusetts County, 1649–1699.* Amherst: University of Massachusetts Press, 1986.

Tillich, Paul. *The Protestant Era.* Translated by James Luther Adams. Chicago: University of Chicago Press, 1948.

Tipson, Baird. "How Can the Religious Experiences of the Past Be Recovered? The Examples of Puritanism and Pietism." *Journal of the American Academy of Religion* 43, no. 4 (December 1975): 695–709.

Tipton, Stephen J. *Getting Saved From the Sixties, Moral Meaning in Conversion and Cultural Change.* Berkeley: University of California Press, 1982.

Todd, John. *The Student's Manual.* Northampton, Mass.: J. H. Butler, 1835.

Tolman, George. *Mary Moody Emerson.* Cambridge, Mass. [S.N.] 1929.

Tracy, Patricia J. *Jonathan Edwards, Pastor: Religion and Society in Eighteenth-Century Northampton.* New York: Hill and Wang, 1979.

Trumbull, Benjamin. *A Complete History of Connecticut, Civil and Ecclesiastical, from the Emigration of the First Planters, from England in the Year 1630, to the year 1764; and the Close of the Indian Wars.* New London, Conn.: H. D. Utley, 1898.

Turner, Bryan S. *The Body and Society, Explorations in Social Theory.* Oxford: Basil Blackwell, 1984.

———. *Medical Power and Social Knowledge.* Berkeley: Sage Publications, 1987.

Tyler, Alice Felt. *Freedom's Ferment, Phases of American Social History from the Colonial Period to the Outbreak of the Civil War.* New York: Harper & Row, 1962.

Tyler, Bennet. *New England Revivals, As They Existed at the Close of the Eighteenth Century and the Beginning of the Nineteenth Century.* Boston: Massachusetts Sabbath School Society, 1846.

Vaughan, Alden T. *New England Frontier Puritans and Indians 1620–1675.* Boston: Little, Brown, 1965.

Vaughan, Alden T., and Clark, Edward W., eds. *Puritans Among the Indians, Accounts of Captivity and Redemption, 1676–1724.* Cambridge: Belknap Press of Harvard University, 1981.

Wakefield, Gordon Stevens. *Puritan Devotion: Its Place in the Development of Christian Piety.* London: Epworth Press, 1957.

Wallace, Ronald J. *Calvin's Doctrine of the Christian Life.* Grand Rapids, Mich.: Eerdmans, 1959.

Warner, R. Stephen. *New Wine in Old Wineskins, Evangelicals and Liberals in a Small-Town Church.* Berkeley: University of California Press, 1989.

Warren, Austin. *The Elder Henry James.* New York: Macmillan Company, 1934.

Watkins, Owen C. *The Puritan Experience: Studies in Spiritual Autobiography.* New York: Schocken Books, 1972.

Watt, David Harrington. *Transforming Faith, Explorations of Twentieth-Century American Evangelicalism.* New Brunswick, N.J.: Rutgers University Press, 1991.

Watts, Isaac. *Hymns and Spiritual Songs.* Exeter, N.H.: C. Norris, 1815 (1707).

Weber, Max. *From Max Weber: Essays in Sociology.* Edited by Hans H. Gerth and C. Wright Mills. New York: Oxford University Press, 1946.

———. *The Methodology of the Social Sciences.* Edited and translated by Edward A. Shills and Henry A. Finch. New York: Free Press, 1949.

———. *The Religion of China.* Edited and translated by Hans H. Gerth. New York: Free Press, 1951.

———. *The Protestant Ethic and the Spirit of Capitalism.* Translated by Talcott Parsons. New York: Charles Scribner's Sons, 1958.

———. *Economy and Society, An Outline of Interpretive Sociology.* Edited by Guenther Roth and Claus Wittlich. New York: Bedminster Press, 1968.

———. "Max Weber on Church, Sect and Mysticism." [Edited by Benjamin Nelson and translated by Jerome L. Gittleman] *Sociological Analysis* 34, no. 2 (1973): 140–152.

———. "Anticritical Last Word on the Spirit of Capitalism." *American Journal of Sociology* 83, no. 5 (1978): 1105–1131.

———. "Freudianism." In *Weber, Selections in Translation.* Edited by W. G. Runciman. Translated by Eric Matthew. Cambridge: Cambridge University Press, 1929.

———. *Weber, Selections in Translation.* Edited by W. G. Runciman. Translated by Eric Matthews. Cambridge: Cambridge University Press, 1979.

Weddle, David L. "The Melancholy Saint: Jonathan Edwards's Interpretation of David Brainerd as a Model of Evangelical Spirituality." *Harvard Theological Review* 81 (3 1988): 297–318.

Weisberger, Bernard A. *They Gathered at the River, The Story of the Great Revivalists and Their Impact Upon Religion in America.* New York: Quadrangle Books, 1958.

Weissbourd, Katherine. *Growing Up in the James Family, Henry James, Sr, as Son and Father.* Ann Arbor, Mich.: UMI Research Press, 1985.

Whimster, Sam, and Lasch, Scott, eds. *Max Weber, Rationality and Modernity.* London: Allen and Unwin, 1987.

White, Eugene H. *Puritan Rhetoric, The Issue of Emotion in Religion.* Carbondale: Southern Illinois University Press, 1972.

Whitworth, John McKelvie. *God's Blueprints, A Sociological Study of Three Utopian Sects.* London: Routledge & Kegan Paul, 1975.

Wigglesworth, Michael. *The Day of Doom; Or, A Pastoral Description of the Great and Last Judgement, with Other Poems.* Edited by Kenneth B. Murdock. New York: Spiral Press, 1929.

Williams, David R. "The Wilderness Rapture of Mary Moody Emerson: One Calvinist Link to Transcendentalism." In *Studies in the American Renaissance.* Edited by Joel Myerson. New Haven: Yale University Press, 1986.

Williams, S. "Remarks on the Refusal of Food in the Insane." *Journal of Mental Science* 10 (1855): 366–380.

Winter, Richard. *The Roots of Sorrow, Reflections on Depression and Hope.* Hants, United Kingdom: Marshal Morgan and Scott, 1985.

Wisner, Benjamin B. "Review of 'The New Divinity Tried,' Being an Examination of a Sermon Delivered by Rev. C. G. Finney in Making a New Heart." Boston: Peirce & Parker, 1832.

Woodbridge, John. "Revivals: The Appropriate Means of Promoting True Religion." Bridgeport, Conn., 1841.

Woods, Leonard. *History of Andover Theological Seminary.* Boston: James R. Osgood and Company, 1885.

Wuthnow, Robert. *The Restructuring of American Religion, Society and Faith Since World War II.* Princeton, N.J.: Princeton University Press, 1988.

Wyon, Olive. *On the Way, Some Reflections on the Christian Life.* London: SCM Press, 1985.

Zablocki, Benjamin. *The Joyful Community, An Account of the Bruderhof, A Communal Movement Now in Its Third Generation.* Baltimore: Penguin Books, 1971.

Index